God Between Their Lips

God Between Their Lips

*Desire Between Women in
Irigaray, Brontë, and Eliot*

Kathryn Bond Stockton

Stanford University Press
Stanford, California
1994

Stanford University Press
Stanford, California
© 1994 by the Board of Trustees of the
Leland Stanford Junior University
Printed in the United States of America

CIP data are at the end of the book

Stanford University Press publications
are distributed exclusively by
Stanford University Press within
the United States, Canada, and Mexico;
they are distributed exclusively by
Cambridge University Press
throughout the rest of the world

For Marilyn, Ed, and Thalie

Acknowledgments

For a book that addresses material concealments and unpaid labor, acknowledgments seem both particularly crucial and particularly inadequate. I am quite sure, nonetheless, that Priscilla Mason, Cindy Harger, Andrea Davis, Scotty Davis, Ray Lagan, Rich Ainsworth, Linda Moore, Cheryl Moore, Scott Davis, Julie Ciucias, Sally Logvin, Joanie Lavigne, Wenda Lagan, Anita Coco, Martha Dewey, Chuck Pilling, Kathryn Johnson, Claudia Wright, and especially Deb Sorterup have shaped my thinking in ways I cannot easily convey. I am just as sure that Peter Hawkins, by virtue of his mind and his devotions, is to "blame" for my turn from systematic theology to literary studies. Ellen Rooney, Jock Reeder, and Roger Henkle most of all, whose death opened new windows onto loss, gave generous time and good humor during this book's dissertation phase. Informal talks with Karen Bock, Diana Fuss, Carole-Anne Tyler, and my "soul-mate" over oceans, Claudia Benassi (of the infamous "charts"), were some of the most formative engagements I have known. At Utah, many colleagues, at many stages, have paid me the respect of their intelligent criticisms: Srinivas Aravamudan, Meg Brady, Bruce Haley, Colleen McDannell, Jacqueline Osherow, Peggy Pascoe, Henry Staten, and Tom Stillinger. In particular, Robert Caserio, Karen Lawrence, and Barry Weller, whose editorial support has been tireless, have read more drafts than I care to remember; without their intellects, wisdom, and support, I would not have brought this book to completion. Stephanie Pace, Debra Burrington, and Melanee Cherry have taught me my most important lessons in feminist exchange, offering me the pleasure of collectivities and the kind of partnership I most seek. Constance Merritt, on another front, has prepared me for books I have yet to write. Additional thanks go to Margaret Ferguson, Jennifer Wicke, and Meg Sachse for editorial assistance on Chapter 1, and to my editors, Helen Tartar, Tom Ireland, Julia Johnson Zafferano, and Amy Klatzkin, at Stanford University Press. To Henry Abelove I owe warmest thanks for wise guidance and kind support offered at this book's most crucial stage.

Closer to home, my brother, David, as one who has always gone before me, has set me the example of a brilliant scholar. My grandmother, Ruth, whose tendency at Thanksgiving dinner is to take only whatever turkey meat no one else wants, has taught me about domestic sainthood; she has also schooled me, with finer shades of wisdom, in the arts of joy and sorrow. Possessing the long view, my parents, Ed and Marilyn, my single greatest and sustaining influence, see the continuities with my earlier thoughts that I at times forget; they will remain committed to me and I to them long after I have moved on from these reflections to some new space. Finally, I am grateful to Shelley White, who with keen percussive sense has performed for me the one thing needful: she has kept me close to the rhythms of life.

K. B. S.

Contents

Part II

Abbreviations

CT	Weed, *Coming to Terms*
E	Lacan, *Ecrits*
EC	Feuerbach, *The Essence of Christianity*
FS	Lacan, *Feminine Sexuality*
PE	Weber, *The Protestant Ethic and the Spirit of Capitalism*
PP	Carlyle, *Past and Present*
QG	Ruskin, "Of Queens' Gardens"
S	Irigaray, *Speculum of the Other Woman*
SC	Jameson, *Sisters of Charity*
SK	Haraway, "Situated Knowledges"
TS	Irigaray, *This Sex Which Is Not One*
TTB	Gallop, *Thinking Through the Body*
WW	Bodichon, *Women and Work*
WWC	Butler, *Women's Work and Women's Culture*

All quotations from the Bible are from the King James Version, unless otherwise specified.

Prelude

~✺

Inside you there are sobs you can't explain. They linger on
the brink of you as if they were outside, they can't reach you
and be wept.

—Marguerite Duras, *The Malady of Death*

This book traces something I have learned. I have learned it from Irigaray, Brontë, and Eliot—three women (I will call them women) that you
may know from the skin of their texts. I have learned it from women (I
will call them women) that you do not know. I have learned it, also,
strangely, from religion; from countless hours of reading theology and
theologizing everything from sex to sobs.

This book trains on sex and sobs—on ecstasy's attachment to grief, a
Victorian shadow now made bold in the age of AIDS.

This book touches on women's sex—not necessarily on lesbian sex,
although you may read my remarks in this vein.

This book teases out women's sobs—sobs over lack, but also sobs *for*
a lack that we cannot reach on our own or by ourselves, sobs that remain
unknown and unwept.

This book teeters with pleasure on "the brink"—on what takes place
at the brink of one's body, where a lover, or someone we desire, stands
positioned, receiving sobs formed from the outside in.

To put it precisely, this book tears on desire between bodies positioned
as women—the erotics, I will say, of a feminine fracture.

Finally, at the threshold, to drop a last puzzle into your laps: this book
trades on the opaque labor of desire between women that might take place
when women exchange and accumulate loss.

Introduction

_～ঽ_

I have been trying for years to understand the relations I have lived—
relations between spirituality and desire, between sex and sorrow, between gendered lack and escape through wounds. This book, as part of
such an effort, explores desire between women as a form of "spiritual materialism" in writings by Luce Irigaray, Charlotte Brontë, and George
Eliot. To begin with my study's underlying paradox, "spiritual materialism": I wish to understand why the act of grasping materialities—a sob
in the body or the body itself—has so often required a spiritual discourse;
why materialism, as a way of naming matter-on-its-own-terms, and material relations that still lie submerged, hidden from view, evoke the shad-
owy forms we call "spiritual."* Reaching toward these relations, I am

*My definition of "spiritual" and its relation to the term "religious" is given on pp.
7–9; the distinction I draw between these terms is one largely based on religion's ties
to institutional forms and to the established theological doctrines anchored in these institutions, making "religious" a narrower term than "spiritual" for my purposes. This
particular distinction has been stressed by contemporary feminists who wish to explore
and affirm women's nonpatriarchal attachments to whatever they deem to be "divine."
(For examples of this trend, see Spretnak, ed., *The Politics of Women's Spirituality* [1982]
and Umansky and Ashton, eds., *Four Centuries of Jewish Women's Spirituality* [1992]).
Though I could have used "mystical" throughout this study to convey my sense of escape, shadow, and inarticulate utterance—and, indeed, I often do—I take the term
"spiritual," again, to be broader: inclusive of what is mystical, yet more malleable in
the sense that it can more easily encompass Brontë's biblical focus and Eliot's Feuerbachian sympathies. Both of these spiritual investments touch upon the mystical, to be
sure, as will become evident, but both are bound up as well with the kinds of Victorian
religious thought and devotion that are not recognizably mystical in form. (I should
say explicitly at the start that my book will not address Victorian and contemporary
"spiritualism," which lies beyond the scope of this study.) Finally, Victorianists will no

anxious to know if spiritual language can "body forth" materialities that seem so covered over by constructions.

I am not alone. Glassed in shadowed chambers of their own, anxious to reach beyond the brink of conventional "outsides" that have formed the only pathways "in" to women's bodies, post-structuralist feminists are getting spiritual over materialism, spiritualizing material relations in order to touch upon them. In fact, these feminists—post-structuralists as diverse as Donna Haraway, Jane Gallop, and especially Luce Irigaray—seem to know this: even to gesture toward material bodies apart from their constructions (or toward secret sobs, never spoken, that convulse them) requires the same move mystics know well. It requires one to discourse upon escapes from discourse; to borrow discursive categories that, *within discourse*, are meant to signal a beyond-the-brink that we can never get to through language.

No wonder connections, though umbrageous, cloaked, come to light between post-structuralists and Victorians. Post-structuralist feminists are caught on the horns of a Victorian obsession: how to chart channels between realms commonly considered approachable and those considered finally inaccessible. If, for Victorians, 'God' seems the realm that is finally inaccessible, for post-structuralist feminists, as we shall see, it has become the body-apart-from-its-constructions that eludes conceptual, linguistic grasps. In Chapter 1, I will sketch this homology that makes materialism a hidden God.

Beginning in that chapter, I will also set in motion the terms *opacity*, *lack*, and *labor*, which have everything to do with women's desire and desire between women—as conceived by my writers. I will trace the unexpected logic that links them in writings by Irigaray, Brontë, and Eliot, for this is a logic that traps a dilemma: what remains opaque about women, from the standpoint of dominant constructions, has been taken for lack; *lack*, on a grand scale, has been etched into women's bodies and relations in ways that wound them, even though *lacking*, in the form of desire, has largely been denied to them. The trick thus becomes how to acquire desire (lacking) without being bound to the lack that denies the pleasures of longing.

The strategy shared by Irigaray, Brontë, and Eliot, I believe, is to bend lack back toward "material opacity" and to cast lacking as a form of labor,

---

doubt recognize that I begin my book on a note of inversion (or at least what might seem like one), turning inside out Carlyle's famous phrase "natural supernaturalism" in the paradox I offer. Thinking I had coined the phrase *spiritual materialism*, I was intrigued to learn that the phrase has also been used by Chögyam Trungpa in his book *Cutting Through Spiritual Materialism*.

productive of pleasure.* In this way, these writers take back the lack on behalf of women by rendering women's bodies and relations opaque— but *visibly* opaque so that what is revealed, writ large for all eyes, is women's material resistance to conventional labors and loves. These writers, in fact, cherishing lack, conceive sex as fracture, erotic exchange as productive loss. For the most part, they portray the exchanges that charge them as erotic commerce between women's bodies (or bodies positioned toward each other as women). Defying the dictates of domestic ideologies, they oppose the prescriptions of women's labor as "self-regulation," women's work as sublime self-denial. Particularly, they depict desire between women as opaque forms of labor, often linking these labors to forms of women's work that remain culturally invisible *as* work (i.e., domestic labor and unpaid sexual labor for men). What these labors of desire yield for women is something I will call "anticapital": *accumulations of loss* used for pleasure.†

One important twist remains with respect to Irigaray, Brontë, and Eliot: spiritual discourse, and the figuration of 'God' most explicitly, relays relations these women fashion among opacity, lack, and labor. 'God'

---

*"Material opacity" is Irigaray's phrase, as we shall see (*TS*, 179). For Irigaray, commodified forms and values are "transparent" (too available), whereas bodies apart from these forms and values prove "opaque" (elusive, inaccessible). The sense I render here of "bend[ing] lack back" toward material opacity will be linked (in Chapter 1) to my sense of a post-structuralist "return" to materialism and (in Chapters 1 and 2) to Lacan's developmental scheme of the child's separation from the body when he/she enters language.

†Nancy Armstrong, in her path-breaking book, *Desire and Domestic Fiction: A Political History of the Novel*, delineates domestic expectations for middle-class women. Beginning in the early eighteenth century, Armstrong argues, conduct books and women's fiction gave rise to the domestic woman, to whom was given authority over the household, courtship procedures, and kinship relations. The novel's rise thus hinged upon attempts to say what made this new woman desirable. With regard to women's work, Armstrong stresses that conduct books did not exalt labor, but, rather, represented women who worked as morally bankrupt. They predictably split male (middle-class) duties from female and thus reinforced the division between political and domestic spheres. His duty was to "accumulate," hers to "regulate." Or, as Armstrong puts it, "The domestic woman executes her role in the household by *regulating her own desire.* . . . So conceived, *self-regulation became a form of labor* that was superior to labor" (81; my emphasis). (For a multifaceted discussion of women's work as "a vision of perfect regulation" in the context of nineteenth-century American literature, see Gillian Brown's *Domestic Individualism: Imagining Self in Nineteenth-Century America*, 66.) Unlike this self-regulation as labor that Armstrong finds in conduct book advice, Brontë and Eliot (at least in *Villette* and *Middlemarch*, respectively) imagine an alternate form of labor and productivity in household spheres: desire between women, spiritually conceived as work for God, that produces pleasure by making loss amount to something other than denial.

even knits these conceptions together by figuring *all* of them, standing successively, and sometimes simultaneously, as the material opacity of women's bodies, as the lack that forms the fracture of desire, as the labor that "bod[ies] forth the form of Things Unseen" (Carlyle's phrase [*PP*, 205]).* 'God', for Irigaray and Brontë, even figures the body of a lover who wears 'his' lack—his wounds unveiled—for all to see. It remains to be explained why this extraordinary collapse of conceptions into 'God' is shared by a post-structuralist feminist and two Victorian novelists who offer us scenes of desire between women. Why should 'God', we will want to ask, appear between their lips? In lieu of a reply at the start, I will say why Irigaray, Brontë, and Eliot hold my focus.

Irigaray uniquely forms a hinge between post-structuralist feminists and Victorian women novelists. To begin, she makes overt the tendencies we find obliquely arising in her contemporaries. That is to say, the spiritual materialism I discover subtly informing the likes of Gallop and Haraway explodes in Irigaray, expanding into a drama that explains so much about the materialist crux post-structuralists face and how they "spiritualize" now when addressing it. My first chapter can only begin to gesture at what I think is a very large conundrum, spreading out to snare gay studies, black studies, gender studies, and even conceptions of science as a whole, especially physics.† But Irigaray, if she sharpens this postmodern perplexity, also speaks well to Victorian fixations, even as she finds herself spoken, quite elaborately, by an earlier century.‡

*Carlyle models this phrase on a line from Shakespeare's *A Midsummer Night's Dream*, V.i.14–15.

†The problem, of course, is how to account for bodies and relations in terms other than the dominant terms available, which prescribe a set logic. For a discussion of this dilemma in the realm of lesbian and gay studies, see Judith Butler, "Imitation and Gender Insubordination," in which Butler, too, starts to use the word "opacity" in reference to *coming out* of "the closet" (15–16); see my first note in the Interlude below. For black theorists' use of "the black hole" as a trope for "an invisible, attractive force" and "unimaginable" dimensions, see Houston A. Baker, Jr., *Blues, Ideology, and Afro-American Literature: A Vernacular Theory*, 144–47; and Michele Wallace, *Invisibility Blues: From Pop to Theory*, 218; see my note on page 9. On the landscape of physics, theoretical speculations about "dark matter," "shadow matter," "cosmic strings," and "superstrings" have led commentators—especially those writing for the burgeoning ranks of "lay" readers of science—to compare investigations at the frontiers of science to medieval theology (see, for example, Morris, *Edges of Science*). For another "lay" index to this issue, see *Time*'s cover story, "Science, God, and Man" (Robert Wright), in which we learn that the Nobel prize–winning physicist Leon Lederman plans to publish a book called *The God Particle*.

‡I choose Irigaray over Kristeva—another overtly spiritualizing feminist—not only for how Irigaray's mysticism opens onto materialism but also for how her mysticism

In her earlier writings on desire between women, Irigaray powerfully unlocks the Victorian fixation on women's mirrored relations. Her theories make lucid how these mirrored relations turn autoerotic for women, when women exchange lack and loss between them. By means of Irigaray, we can even explore why "lesbianism" and "female friendship" prove inadequate to name what Brontë and Eliot, coupled with Irigaray, represent: the erotics of a feminine fracture that puts 'God' between women's lips. For many reasons, only one of which is the arguable anachronism of applying the identity "lesbian" to same-sex relations in the nineteenth century, "lesbian" seems to lay too much stress on object-choice in the erotics I explore (especially since in the writers I discuss this erotics may include a man). I insist, above all, upon the self-pleasure of the woman who desires. By the same token, the discourse on female friendship, so crucially rendered in Carroll Smith-Rosenberg's "The Female World of Love and Ritual," seems, like the term "lesbian," too suggestive of dyadic structures that imagine discrete, bounded individuals. Though "autoeroticism" may sound like the height of individualism and autonomy, I argue otherwise, working out a theory of how self-pleasure in all of my writers must arise through forms of self-parting.*

----

crosscuts Victorian fascinations, such as I discuss below. Obviously, I take issue with Rita Felski's assertion that French feminism could not speak to realist novels, based upon her primary assumption that French feminism only concerns itself with "the celebration of an anonymous and amorphous textuality as the location of the feminine" (*Beyond Feminist Aesthetics: Feminist Literature and Social Change*, 44).

*This slant on self-parting takes me down a slightly different path, as well, from Eve Kosofsky Sedgwick, in her piece "Jane Austen and the Masturbating Girl," though I strongly agree with Sedgwick's conviction that "in our reimaginings of the history of sexuality 'as' (we vainly imagine) 'we know it,' through readings of classic texts, the dropping out of sight of the autoerotic term is also part of what falsely naturalizes the heterosexist imposition of these books, disguising both the rich, conflictual erotic complication of a homoerotic matrix not yet crystallized in terms of 'sexual identity,' and the violence of heterosexist definition finally carved out of these plots" (826). Having worked on this book for the past seven years in a vacuum of feminist address to concepts of autoeroticism, I feel encouraged to see another theorist claim that "thinking about autoeroticism is beginning to seem a productive and necessary switchpoint in thinking about the relations—historical as well as intrapsychic—between homo- and heteroeroticism" (821).

I should also say, as a kind of side note, that the move in lesbian/gay studies to term the "thing" that changes over centuries (and that takes different forms in different cultures) "same-sex relations" or "same-sex sex" (as opposed to "homosexuality," for example) repeats a problematic that I will discuss throughout this book: It almost seems to lend a material, matter-on-its-own-terms status to the "same-sex sex" that changes over centuries, constructed and experienced differently over time. "Same-sex sex" begins to function as a fundamental substratum—the thing that is always taking place in

Yet Brontë and Eliot part us from Irigaray, turning the tables on this relation, by displaying what Irigarayan scholars have not examined: how women's mirrored relations fracture (often for pleasure) according to class position and work. To say it plainly: Brontë and Eliot write the most revealing *class* limitations to Irigaray's visions of 'God' between the lips. Through a shared cultural heritage—Evangelicalism—they write the versions of 'God' that Irigaray's theories imply but to which these theories do not yet give extended expression. In particular, by depicting women's desire as opaque forms of labor, Brontë and Eliot scout the *privilege* of material opacity—who gets to claim it, perform it, or fund it.

The first three chapters prepare for these turns, which are then followed out in the chapters on the novels (4 through 7). Chapters 1 through 3, as a complex, explore the slide between opacity, lack, and labor, fastening onto each of these terms in succession and contextualizing Irigaray's theories in diverse ways: post-structuralist feminism (Chapter 1), Lacanian psychoanalysis (Chapter 2), and (largely Victorian) essays on work (Chapter 3). I intend in this book to scrutinize contemporary theory as much as, and also by means of, Victorian fiction. Tempted as I am to generalize beyond Irigaray, Brontë, and Eliot, I need to argue within these limits, even though I experiment with larger speculations along the way. My address to three writers, and my attention to only two novels, comes from my decision to perform close readings that allow me to show, not just to claim, the dynamics of colliding terms over the course of these novels' complications, and suggest how thoroughly these texts are imbued with these collisions.

In the book's second part, I turn to the novels, *Villette* and *Middlemarch*, but I also contextualize my readings by providing a set of backlights by which to view them. In each case—that is, in "Recollecting Charlotte Brontë" (Chapter 4) and "Recognizing George Eliot" (Chapter 6)—by returning to the author's "life," I explain, but do not presume, how to read the author's signature; how to understand the composition of (what we take to be) the voice behind the text, in its double sense of author and narrator. Each writer's tangled relation to religion—especially Evangelicalism—supplies a crucial piece to this puzzle of voice, since it shapes for each writer a spiritual discourse that holds onto bodies and their sexual relations. For all of their differences, and for what is no doubt a marked secularization in the progression from Brontë's scriptural discourse to

---

every century, but always to the tune of new constructions. In this respect, "same-sex sex" never appears in a naked form, but functions as the fiction that makes its manifestations all "family."

Eliot's Feuerbachian discourse on sympathy, these women share a spiritual heritage. Brontë, raised in Yorkshire where the Evangelicals began their movement, persisted in a conscious adherence to many Evangelical doctrines. George Eliot, despite her early intense involvement with Evangelicalism, represented herself as having thrown it over for free-thinking and, later, Feuerbachian sensibilities. Nonetheless, her choice of protagonist in *Middlemarch*, with all of her aspirations to sainthood, suggests that Eliot's debate with her early beliefs continued long into adulthood.

Together, of course, *Villette* and *Middlemarch* have been dominant books in the feminist canon—though in different ways. *Villette* is the prime example of a novel largely ignored and considered problematic at its time of publication, but one which, through feminist recuperation, has blossomed in critics' estimation. *Middlemarch* offers an opposite scenario. It secured George Eliot's reputation in her lifetime and fixed her canonical status as a classic English writer in the mainstream curriculum; and yet this novel (along with its author) has consistently proven a thorn in the side of feminist expositors. Feminists want to approve of *Middlemarch* but many end up finding they cannot. The domestication of Eliot's St. Theresa, Dorothea, is precisely the sticking-point for those readers who find such feminist hope in Lucy's bereaved independence at the end of *Villette*. Additionally, these novels offer diverse challenges to my focus on women's desire-as-labor, since they have split psychoanalytic and materialist (or at least sociohistorical) interests between them. I am anxious, therefore, in Chapter 5, to interrogate materialist concerns in *Villette* (a novel so consistently read as "psychological") and, in Chapter 7, to explore the convolutions of desire in *Middlemarch* (a novel that has largely resisted the scrutiny of psychoanalysis). Two such different novels may help us to understand a confluence, which leads these narratives into the channels of autoeroticism negotiated by Irigaray as well. Specifically, we find that, in *Villette*, the heroine's parting from her lover (an obvious figure for Christ) gives rise to the autoerotic labors with which she is left as a single school-owner, while Eliot's novel centers on "a saint" who is left with desire, with her own self-partings for pleasure, vocationally fixed amidst the permeable boundaries of domestic space, between bourgeois women and the servants who attend them.

Obviously, my greatest speculative risk is to do—or attempt—what Victorians often did: to bring together (as another pair of lips, separated by time) "past and present" (the title of a well-known book by Thomas Carlyle). I wish, in this way, to chance a study that unfolds an elaborate convergence of minds, working through a shared circuit of concerns.

This eye on convergence is risky business given "theory's" current love of difference, because of which to historicize, these days, seems to mean proving historical divergence. Understandable though it is in this climate of difference, which to my mind has immeasurably benefited criticism (as has historicism), we need not be shy about exploring remarkable points of contact between viewpoints and categories so often held apart. The distinctions that academic culture acknowledges between the domains I discuss in this book—post-structuralist and Victorian discourse, spirituality and materialism, work and pleasure—are familiar and well rehearsed. What may seem more arresting are the correspondences I display. The obvious and important historical differences between Victorian and postmodern periods only seem to dramatize how surprising these lines of connection prove to be. Clearly, we need to imagine new ways of conceiving what might carry over between centuries or, intriguingly, return.

I imagine, for example, that one effect of contemporary feminisms and other politically engaged forms of criticism has been to return some academic critics to expressive forms long dismissed as "Victorian": sentiment and sobs. Currently, AIDS as a widening devastation is one of those developments in response to which academic cultural critics (I include myself) might deem emotional extravagance fitting, joining "us" to the surrounding culture at the precise point where we often seek to keep our distance: public sentiment. In fact, the specter of a material opacity—in the case of AIDS, the trace of a body so alive in our loss of it—creates the occasion, almost always ambivalently charged for academics, whether we are the producers or the "listeners," for teasing out sobs. One might envision that AIDS could teach us how to visit loss, and how to understand our conflicts over our visitations of it, in other places where loss and sorrows of material oppression so dramatically shape us.

If we would do so, we will have to entertain a form of writing that certain academics (many feminists, in particular) have embraced: the form of the personal. Though I employ it only briefly in this book, its implications, as a form, for the intellectual projects of Irigaray, Brontë, and Eliot should at all times be remembered. At its best, what it offers are the otherwise unacknowledged points of saturation in a life, where something can be seen and felt as forming an extraordinarily subtle, and often unimagined, convergence: those accretions of moments endowed with meaning by a writer's backward glance. The risk of this form, it seems to me now, lies not in its revelations or transgressions—the ability to shock has long since diminished to a glimmer of surprise—but precisely in its sentiment. The personal can easily fail when it succeeds. It can deliver its ardor all too readily, hand over its sense without enough shadow. Of personal confession, academics, in particular, demand the most opacity: the revelation that keeps to itself.

My writers scout this principle on the many levels of their spiritual and material investments in opacity. Irigaray, then, might be seen not so much as a conscious heir to Victorian traditions but as a relevant (if unconscious) consummation of them. There can be no formulas for working out these crossings—only readings I hope may strike other readers as convincing, or at least as worthwhile for the sake of what they make us see, no matter how opaque.

Part I

Chapter 1

Bodies and God: Post-structuralist Feminists Return to the Fold of Spiritual Materialism

~⁊

> In contemporary feminist theory, no issue is more vexed than that of determining the relations between the feminine body as a figure in discourse and as material presence or biological entity. The debates surrounding this question in recent years have been the most highly charged, but also perhaps the most fruitful.
>
> —Mary Jacobus, Evelyn Fox Keller, Sally Shuttleworth, in their introduction to *Body/Politics: Women and the Discourses of Science*

> What if matter had always, already, had a part but was yet invisible, beyond the senses, moving in ways alien to any fixed reflection.
>
> —Luce Irigaray, *Speculum of the Other Woman*

Irigaray's Matrix: Post-structuralists and Victorians

Post-structuralist feminists are the new Victorians. What 'God' was to Victorian thinkers, 'the body' is to post-structuralist feminists: an object of doubt and speculation but a necessary fiction and an object of faith.* Cultivating belief in 'real bodies' as 'material presence', post-structuralist

---

*When I refer to *post-structuralist* feminists or to *post-structuralists*, I will be referring to those theorists who live in the postmodern age (post–World War II) and who consciously borrow heavily from deconstruction. Although I considered using the term *postmodern* in this way—as signaling both a period designation and a theoretical orientation—I decided to choose (what might be regarded as) a narrower term. I wish, in this way, to mark my awareness that some theorists (mostly European) still distinguish between the terms *postmodern* and *post-structuralist* as a way to distinguish philosophically oriented forms of deconstruction (which they call *post-structuralist*) from the postmodern playfulness of Lyotard and Baudrillard.

3

feminists seek now to compensate for deconstruction, along with extreme forms of social constructionism, both of which so heavily stress how language constructs human beings and their world.* That is to say, post-structuralist feminists are becoming believers as they return to the fold of materialism.†

Yet what can *materialism* mean to post-structuralists? Materialism is now difficult to think; it is the opaque impasse post-structuralists have reached. Here I do not mean materialism in the sense of those ideologies by which we live out our relations to the world (ideology as "a material practice," Althusser would say).‡ Few would deny that materialism in this sense is laced with constructions. I mean materialism in its strongest sense: *the material onto which we map our constructions*, 'matter on its own terms' that might resist or pressure our constructions, or prove independent of them altogether. This materialism is the nondiscursive something post-

---

*Let me call attention to a typographical dilemma that relates to my argument. In accordance with the *Chicago Manual of Style*, I am required to enclose philosophical terms in single quotation marks. (The style book furnishes the examples of 'being', 'nonbeing', 'the divine'.) Words emphasized as words are italicized; words used ironically are enclosed in double quotation marks, along with material quoted from texts. My dilemma is this: I wish to mark several terms in this essay as terms post-structuralists now interrogate—terms such as 'God', but also terms such as 'body', 'reality', 'man', 'woman', 'objectivity', and 'biology', which have not traditionally been deemed philosophical but which have been deemed so over the course of post-structuralist discussions. Even so, the reader will notice that in the case of 'body', 'real', and 'reality' I will at times let quotation marks drop. By this move I wish to emphasize that the body outside quotation marks (real bodies that exist apart from cultural markings) forms the object of post-structuralist belief.

†I use the word *return* to describe these feminists' reconsideration of what may look like positivist materialist claims, even though they return *as* post-structuralists. I use this term because *going back* and reexamining prior theories and assumptions is how these feminists seem to view what they are doing. Haraway's repeated worry over having gone too far "with the lovely and nasty tools of semiology and deconstruction" surfaces in "Situated Knowledges," as I will discuss. See SK, 185.

‡Althusser explains: "Where only a single subject (such and such an individual) is concerned, the existence of the ideas of his [ideological] belief is material in that *his ideas are his material actions inserted into material practices governed by material rituals which are themselves defined by the material ideological apparatus from which derive the ideas of that subject*" (Althusser, *Lenin and Philosophy*, 169). Alex Callinicos provides this gloss: "Despite the repetition of the word 'material' like an incantation, we can see that the materiality of a set of ideological beliefs derives from the fact that they are, firstly, embodied in particular social practices, and, secondly, the products of what Althusser calls an Ideological State Apparatus (ISA)" (Callinicos, *Althusser's Marxism*, 63–64). Althusser would countenance the distinction I am making, since he himself notes: "At the risk of being taken for a Neo-Aristotelian (NB Marx had a very high regard for Aristotle), I shall say that 'matter is discussed in many senses', or rather that it exists in different modalities, all rooted in the last instance in 'physical' matter" (166).

structuralist feminists now want to embrace, the extradiscursive something they confess necessarily eludes them. This materialism stands as a 'God' that might be approached through fictions and faith but never glimpsed naked. 'Real bodies' are what never appear.

I want to speculate on this strange eclipse, as if to keep vigil with this newly emerging feminist tendency to spiritualize bodies, to endow bodies with sacred enigmas and mystical escapes—all in order to gesture toward bodies that stand apart from the constructions that render them. Poststructuralist feminists like Jane Gallop, for example, admit that bodies elaborately present themselves as objects for construction. Yet, Gallop argues, bodies resist domination by the mind. The body is "a bodily enigma," "an inscrutable given," and "points to an outside—beyond/before language" (*TTB*, 13, 16). "The body is enigmatic," moreover, "because it is not a creation of the mind" and "will never be totally dominated by man-made meaning" (*TTB*, 18, 19).

Gallop exemplifies the post-structuralist feminist who—*in the act* of making problematic what (we think) Victorians often took for granted: the body's presence—ends up sounding like a Victorian believer. Stranger yet, post-structuralist feminists write their own versions of a *spiritual* materialism that remarkably echo Victorian discussions of bodies and God. For instance, we find the Victorian Thomas Carlyle bent around conundrums that do not die out in the nineteenth century but that surface, resurgent, to plague post-structuralists. This bend is particularly true of Carlyle's discussion of bodies as "mystic unfathomable Visibilities." I seek to illuminate this unexpected join between post-structuralist feminists and Victorians such as Carlyle. By doing so, I believe, we better locate the conceptual dilemmas these feminists face in their returns to materialism and can better understand why spiritualizing gestures suggest themselves to feminists as ways to produce escapes *back* to bodies.

Three exemplars of this feminist curve have emerged in Donna Haraway, Jane Gallop, and Luce Irigaray. Admittedly, Haraway and Gallop, along with Irigaray, are among those feminists I seek when I look to be shaken into feminist disturbance. Gallop and Haraway present, moreover, an intriguing pair, since they would not be, to my mind, likely candidates for spiritual gestures. Yet, both of these feminists, succored by poststructuralist theory and its largely constructionist slant, now worry about where the body might stand apart from, or at times against, the representations that encode it at every turn. Unfolding their worry, we will find that Gallop and Haraway evince a more oblique form of spiritual materialism. They, unlike Irigaray, do not overtly use Christian discourse in order to accomplish their returns upon the body. We could distinguish, in this way, between greater and lesser spiritual materialisms, or, as I prefer to regard them, materialisms that are oblique or overt in their spiritualizing character. Nonetheless, however we may cut between Gallop and Haraway on the one hand, and Irigaray (and Carlyle) on the other, I suggest that the antitranscendental stance of post-structuralist feminists only masks their deep dependence upon the kinds of gestures commonly deemed spiritual by Victorian thinkers.

Haraway, a biologist and philosopher of science, is clearly seeking new ways to conceptualize 'objectivity' and 'biology'; she thinks we lose too much if we see "the body itself" as only "a blank page for social inscriptions" without seeing how our bodies, by being agents themselves, resist linguistic capture.* Gallop, a psychoanalytic theorist and literary critic of French and American texts (quite removed from Haraway, in this respect), continues to explore the linguistic and materialist issues she has pondered for over a decade: the frictions and rubs between bodies and language and between political and psychoanalytic categories.† Hence her attempt in *Thinking Through the Body* to make "bedfellows" of Adrienne Rich and Roland Barthes, and to explore "the impossibility in our cultural tradition of separating an earnest attempt to listen to the material from an agenda for better control" (*TTB*, 4). For both Haraway and Gallop, political responsibility to real bodies and political rage against "agenda[s] for better control" spur their different "attempt[s] to listen to the material."‡ This responsibility and rage is shared by Irigaray, the widely read deconstructive feminist philosopher and psychoanalyst, steeped in French intellectual traditions. Irigaray is almost always read as an essentialist, sometimes dismissed but only superficially understood as a mystic, rarely se-

---

*Haraway captured feminists' attention with her now-legendary essay, "A Manifesto for Cyborgs: Science, Technology, and Socialist Feminism in the 1980's." The publication of her work on primatology, *Primate Visions: Gender, Race, and Nature in the World of Modern Science*, has only strengthened her position as a leading theoretical voice.

†Gallop's influential career began with her book on Sade, *Intersections: A Reading of Sade with Bataille, Blanchot, and Klossowski*. Her next two books focused squarely on psychoanalytic theory: *The Daughter's Seduction: Feminism and Psychoanalysis* and *Reading Lacan*. *Thinking Through the Body* follows as an extended meditation on, and challenge to, the mind-body split, containing a collection of Gallop's essays written over a ten-year span.

‡On the issue of control, Haraway confesses her "nervousness about the sex/gender distinction in the recent history of feminist theory," by means of which "sex is 'resourced' for its re-presentation as gender, which 'we' can control" (SK, 198).

riously deemed a materialist, and never read as a spiritual materialist, as I primarily wish to read her. It strikes me as curious that her materialism always gets reduced to essentialism, since her early works so clearly contain Gallop and Haraway's same concerns for (female) bodies that resist constructions and agendas for control.

At first glance, of course, the subversive possibilities of resubmitting to anything spiritual would not appear promising. In the discussions of many post-structuralists, "god-talk," as Haraway tags it, serves as the most convenient foil to subversive theorizing. Clearly, I am kicking against the goads when I argue that some materialist theories may be read as forms of spiritual discourse. Understand, however, my remarks are not meant to criticize these feminists, as if I were upbraiding them for writing spiritualities. Nor is my goal to argue for a more pristine post-structuralist stance. My aim is to dramatize a difficulty, daunting even for post-structuralists: how to depart from forms of faith or mysticisms when we are anxious to move beyond oppression. Desire for escape, even at this historical juncture, often finds its way, and quite unknowingly, into recaptures of spiritual schemas.*

Unbind *spiritual*. The connotations of *religious doctrine* and *religious practices* would seem to be implied, and, indeed, *spiritual* can include such meanings. Yet, *spiritual discourse* is not merely language-use bound to religious institutions or to the representations of traditionally religious behaviors. Spiritual discourse is discourse on what exceeds human sign systems; discourse on where human meanings fail; discourse on escapes from discourse; and, most importantly, culturally constructed discourse on es-

---

*For example, I would argue that Derrida, at the end of "Choreographies," repeats a spiritual schema: He writes a teleology. Though he tries to avoid "determined location," he nonetheless envisions what we might be reaching toward: "What if we were to reach, what if we were to approach here (for one does not arrive at this as one would at a determined location) the area of a relationship to the other where the code of sexual marks would no longer be discriminating? . . . As I dream of saving the chance that this question offers I would like to believe in the multiplicity of sexually marked voices. . . . Does the dream itself not prove that what is dreamt of must be there in order for it to provide the dream?" (Derrida and MacDonald, "Choreographies," 76). Derrida's last line could be seen to trace a logic also presented by the orthodox Christian writer C. S. Lewis in his book *The Weight of Glory*: "A man's physical hunger does not prove that that man will get any bread; he may die of starvation on a raft in the Atlantic. But surely a man's hunger does prove that he comes of a race which repairs its body by eating and inhabits a world where eatable substances exist. In the same way, though I do not believe (I wish I did) that my desire for Paradise proves that I shall enjoy it, I think it is a pretty good indication that such a thing exists and that some men will" (6).

capes from culture, though from the present standpoint these escapes are always incomplete and deferred.* *Spiritual* can illumine both Victorians' and post-structuralists' reliance on general categories of inscrutabilities.

One might wonder whether these features of spiritual discourse prove *unique* to spiritual discourse. Some post-structuralists might argue that my definition of spiritual discourse could also be cited for literary discourse. I am not convinced that the difference matters. It may not matter because I simply want to show that the post-structuralist stance on language (with its stress on the failure of language fully to capture materiality) makes post-structuralist gestures toward real bodies correspond to gestures Victorians called spiritual. When they bend back to bodies, post-structuralists almost inevitably repeat a Judeo-Christian problematic, since they must invest in beliefs in something real that escapes and exceeds human sign systems. At the very least, the post-structuralist distinction between a hidden material 'reality' and a hidden spiritual 'reality' must fall into question.†

A second clarification concerns what could seem a too-neat correspondence. I mean this: The correspondence I note between Victorian and post-structuralist thinkers does not make their gestures identical. True, for many Victorian intellectuals, among them Carlyle (a major contributor to

---

*Readers may wonder how Judeo-Christian people of the Book can be linked to the failure of human meaning and to discourse on what exceeds human sign systems. Let me underscore, then, how much the sense of both Old and New Testament revelations carries the sense of inscrutable communications—whether it be the opaque revelation of Yahweh ("I AM THAT I AM" [Exodus 3:14]) or the puzzling statements by and about Jesus Christ that make the opacity of his Person the Word that escapes full human comprehension. By their enigmatic qualities, these revelations purposely, and divinely, cause human meanings to fail their familiar transparencies—all in order to open onto meaning that can appear only as discourse in excess of established discourse.

Let me say, in addition, that lest it seem I slip imprecisely between the terms *exceeds*, *fails*, and *escapes* (and I could easily add *eludes*), these are terms that are used synonymously both by the post-structuralist feminists I discuss in this chapter and by those who write on mysticism generally. For evidence with regard to mysticism, see Evelyn Underhill, *Mysticism*, 3–37. See also the full texts of Gallop's "Thinking Through the Body" (*TTB*, 1–9) and "The Bodily Enigma" (*TTB*, 11–20) and Haraway's "Situated Knowledges." For example, Gallop uses *failure*, *exceeds*, and *impossibility* in fairly close succession (*TTB*, 4) in opposition to the term *transparent* on her previous page. Both Gallop and Haraway, to be sure, distance themselves from the term *transcendence* even while they continue to use the terms I list above; in the mystical literature a term like *escape* is consistently used in apposition to the term *transcend* (Underhill, *Mysticism*, 33).

†Another answer to the question I pose—could my definition of spiritual discourse also be cited for literary discourse?—might follow the lines of M. H. Abrams in *Natural Supernaturalism* by arguing that so much of the canonical tradition in Euro-American literature is itself rooted in the Judeo-Christian problematic.

Victorian religious thought), spirituality lies equally close, if not closer, to conceptions of enigma, inscrutability, and escape as it lies close to the religious doctrines of their day. Unlike post-structuralist thinkers, however, many Victorian intellectuals hold their spiritual discourse in obvious tension with the traditional religious contexts out of which they write. Post-structuralists, by contrast, are generally so dismissive of religion in terms of institutions and practice that their spiritualizing seems idiosyncratic, cut free from the dominant strands of Judeo-Christian traditions—even when it is not.

We need to unbend the post-structuralist investment in writing possible escapes back to bodies. This particular impetus for escapes emerges from a sense that the dominant culture's allowed relations to 'one's own body' (especially if one lives under a 'woman' sign) are not desirable.* Desire for escape from the constructions and commodifications of the body accompanies, furthermore, a desire to produce those bodies elsewhere, in some other cultural space, where bodies might be returned upon, and so touched upon, on different terms and in different ways.† This is where humanist concepts of alienation join hands with post-structuralist concepts of indeterminacy. Before post-structuralism, *alienation* conveyed the sense that the dominant culture's allowed relations to one's own body fundamentally conflicted with one's real self—from which one was alienated.‡

---

*Feminist classics along these lines are Kate Millett's *Sexual Politics* and Susan Brownmiller's *Against Our Will*, among others. Rosalind Coward's *Female Desires* is a more recent study in this vein.

†Cultural feminisms, in their variety, have based themselves upon this desire for an alternate space, either existing or at least imaginable. Sonia Johnson's call to women to get up and leave their marriage to patriarchy (and to find separate spaces) expresses this urge. The work of Charlotte Perkins Gilman—for example, *Herland*—exemplifies the utopian end of this spectrum. We see this impetus for escape-as-return in other significant (and overlapping) quarters of theorizing. Michele Wallace, for example, revisits Houston Baker's trope of the black hole as a way of conceiving how black feminist creativity escapes prevailing classifications and interpretations (even those that prevail among white feminists and African-American men): "An object or energy," she writes, "enters the black hole, is infinitely compressed to zero volume, as Baker reported, then it passes through to another dimension, whereupon the object or energy reassumes volume, mass, form, direction, velocity, all the properties of visibility and concreteness, but in another, perhaps unimaginable, dimension" (Wallace, *Invisibility Blues*, 218).

‡Marx, of course, is the famous example here. For a discussion of "the alienation of labor," which demonstrates that "labor is *external* to the worker, i.e., it does not belong to his essential being," see *The Economic and Philosophic Manuscripts of 1844*, 106–119. For a feminist version of alienation, see MacKinnon, "Feminism." Mary Ann Doane indirectly registers this dilemma for feminists when she explores the psychoanalytic notion of "fictions" or "illusions" of identity: "The attributes of agency, identity, and coherence are not absent from the definition of subjectivity but, instead, constantly re-

Now, in a postmodern period, as wary of real selves as real bodies, we cannot use any determinate sense of original or essential selves by which to mark (as we desperately need to do) our alienations. The most we seem able to perform is a scream against our constructions—to say they don't suit us. If we do not like more privileged constructions any better (masculine instead of feminine ones, for example) but desire to appear *outside the system* of currently available alternatives, then we are left indeterminate. Indeterminacy becomes, in this way, our mode of resistance to those determinate selves we know that we do not want to be.

This projection outside known systems seems at least obliquely spiritualizing (as it seems, to me, in Gallop and Haraway); in its move to exceed discourses we know, this projection outside can overtly employ (as Irigaray, to be sure, overtly employs) spiritual discourse (as I have defined it, discourse on escapes from discourse). This faith in escape for the sake of our bodies, as the necessary precondition for *nonalienated embodiment*, calls forth post-structuralist logic concerning materialism as a hidden God. That is to say, it parallels post-structuralist moves to believe in a materiality that, like God, escapes our constructions, while still rendering this 'matter on its own terms', like God, inaccessible to view.

Hope in Failure: Feminists' *Felix Culpa*

The spiritualizing going on around us in 'theory' involves us in failures of human meaning; it immerses us in (discursive) attempts to escape from discourse. No wonder we find dramatically reemerging in feminist forms the Christian doctrine of *felix culpa*, or "the happy fall"—the doctrine that proclaims that human failure makes possible a greater good. (For Christians, for example, humanity's fall makes possible the greater good of Christ's appearing.) Indeed, feminists of post-structuralist stripes are investing in failure for the sake of our future, for what failure might eventually make luminous by screening off our current sights. Now more than ever, post-structuralist feminists are losing their hope in 'positive' projects that directly deliver 'the' feminine difference and are placing hope, instead, in the failure of the dominant constructions that would seek to fix

---

ferred to as fictions or illusions. . . . It is this *illusion* of a coherent and controlling identity which becomes most important at the level of social subjectivity. And the woman does not even possess the same access to the *fiction* as the man." Doane's remarks imply that women are alienated, not from their 'own real selves', but from the empowering fictions that dominant culture offers dominant men (Doane, *Desire to Desire*, 11).

them as women.* Feminine specificity, given this scenario, has more to do with escape (what 'she' is not, what 'she' is elsewhere) than with essence (what 'she' is), for we need escapes from fixed constructions if we are to produce new bodies and selves.

Feminists, avowedly, have long desired the failure of (masculine) meanings. Yet, the advent of post-structuralist thought, as we know, has made feminists newly cautious toward, if not downright resistant to, any fixed *feminist* meanings. One senses this leeriness in Jacqueline Rose's 1983 essay "Femininity and Its Discontents." Arguing against what she saw at that time as "the present discarding of psychoanalysis in favour of forms of analysis felt as more material in their substance and immediately political in their effects," Rose was arguing for a psychoanalysis (namely, Freud's) that lets us put feminist hope in the failure of who we are as 'women' and 'men':

> The unconscious constantly reveals the "failure" of identity. Because there is no continuity of psychic life, so there is no stability of sexual identity, no position for women (or for men) which is ever simply achieved. . . . "Failure" is not a moment to be regretted in a process of adaptation. . . . Instead "failure" is something endlessly repeated and relived moment by moment throughout our individual histories. . . . Feminism's affinity with psychoanalysis rests above all, I would argue, with this recognition that there is a resistance to identity at the very heart of psychic life.[1]

Feminist post-structuralist theorizing is still full of attempts to "unthink" and "render impossible" the versions of bodies and selves that we have known, even the feminist versions we prefer.† Hence, Mary Ann Doane acknowledges that "all feminist positions are in some sense uninhabitable," echoing Elizabeth Weed's comments on the "impossible . . . relation of *women* to feminism."[2] Ellen Rooney, in a similar vein, seeks "the possibility of a political gesture that is not rooted in identity" (*CT*, 239). In fact, the desire to escape fixed gestures—toward politics or identities—runs so strong in these feminist channels that even materialist cau-

---

*I use *fix* in this sentence in two senses: dominant gender constructions attempt to "fix" women in order to "make them right" and proper in appearance, behavior, language, and occupation; dominant constructions attempt to "fix" women to assured and familiar positions in culture. This doubleness constitutes what we might call women's "fix" (their bind, and, sometimes, their addiction).

†Throughout his book *Altarity*, Mark Taylor associates post-structuralist "unthinking," "not knowing," and "saying the unsayable" with religious and theological categories. Since his book does not address materialism, he does not make these further links.

tions against escape end with imagining some vision of it. Donna Haraway, for example, in her effort to stress embodiment, seeks escape from
escapes like Christian "salvation history" (*CT*, 175). She ends her cyborg
essay, even so, by envisioning what reads like a feminist embrace of Christian Pentecost: "a dream *not of a common language*, but of a powerful infidel
heteroglossia . . . a feminist speaking in tongues" (*CT*, 204; my emphasis).
In "Post-Utopian Difference," Mary Ann Doane actually critiques *as utopian* Rose's feminist hope in failed identities. We can cling to "the constant
failure of sexual identity, its instability or even its impossibility," but we
must remember, Doane would caution, that this belief is a utopian gesture, for "identity in the realm of the social may be oppressive but insofar
as patriarchy seems to work . . . it [identity] cannot be seen either as a failure or an impossibility" (*CT*, 76). With this materialist caution in mind,
Doane ends her essay by seeming to reaffirm utopia (but utopian beliefs
recognized as utopian): "My critique of psychoanalysis is not a critique of
utopian thinking—to the contrary—but of its misrecognition (as authoritative science). . . . Utopias open up a space for non-essentialized identities—they authorize certain positions rather than others, certain politics
rather than others. A utopia is the sighting (in terms of the gaze) and siting
(in terms of emplacement) of another possibility. The chance of escaping
the same" (*CT*, 78).* Escapes remain crucial to Haraway and Doane, in
spite of their strong stands against some escapes: Both feminists desperately want out of the material relations we have known, even as both desperately desire new materialities we would embody. Unforeseen, and as
yet unrepresented, embodiments and "emplacements" (as Doane would
have it) are what they seek.

    Here is the crucial context in which to read Luce Irigaray. Gallop, as

---

*For a consideration of the theological roots and theological implications of partic-
ular utopian schemes, see Hawkins, *Getting Nowhere: Christian Hope and Utopian Dream*.
Hawkins helpfully reminds us of how the word *utopia* was conceived: "[Thomas More]
coined a word that withdrew with one hand the credibility it extended with the other.
He achieved this verbal sleight-of-hand by taking the Greek noun for "place," *topos*,
and prefixing it with a mysteriously ambivalent "u." His learned audience was quick
to enjoy the confusion, because More's prefix could be played out in either of two directions. It could be taken as the Greek "eu," meaning good, ideal, perfect, or, on the
other hand, taken as "ou," indicating an absence or deficiency. A linguistic hermaph-
rodite from birth, "utopia" might point either to the happy place of one's dreams ("eu-
topia") or to no place at all ("ou-topia"). Better yet, it might suggest both realities at
once" (5). Based on Hawkins's account, one could say that utopia is a knotting of the
good with the absent—a happy gap, until it meets fulfillment. For another theological
address to utopia, see "Critique and Justification of Utopia" by the German theologian
Paul Tillich.

usual, has put the matter well. In discussing Irigaray's focus on women's genital lips, she locates in Irigaray's theorizing "the tension between a feminist investment in the referential body and an aspiration to poetics" (*TTB*, 95) ("poetics" being Gallop's term for constructions). Irigaray's "referential illusion," Gallop claims, "might just save (post)modernist poetics from the absurd appearance of asserting the nonreferentiality of language and move it into a more complex encounter with *the anxiety produced by the absence of any certain access to the referent*" (*TTB*, 95–96; my emphasis). Aside from noting that if we substituted 'God' for "the referent," this last phrase could aptly apply to Victorian thinkers, I want to emphasize something that Gallop was among the first to notice: Irigaray poeticizes the body that many readers think she essentializes. This point looms radiant among Irigaray's post-structuralist supporters, though they often stress her "strategic" essentialism, arguing that she "risks" biological reference for the sake of making different bodies appear.[3] This slant is ultimately misleading, I believe. A stress on strategic essentialism has the rhetorical effect of reemphasizing Irigaray's closeness to the body rather than the ways in which she elaborately *mystifies* it—especially through blatant mystical conceptions. It is not that Irigaray is too close to the body in some assured, or even strategically essentialist, manner. It is perhaps the opposite: The impetus for Irigaray's "referential illusion" (a form of faith?) is her anxiety that we cannot, with certainty, anymore assume access to the referent—and some form of *access*, not just failure, is what she desires.

Far from alone, then, Irigaray is like Doane, like Haraway, like Gallop, in wanting to escape (back) to feminine bodies—to the bodily enigmas that, in Gallop's terms, exist "beyond/before language" by virtue of how they resist words' captures. Irigaray's uniqueness lies, if anywhere, in the explicitness with which she spiritualizes—not just poeticizes—the bodies she would grasp. Pointedly mystical moves, which effectively locate lack and God between 'woman's' genital lips (no small moves, these), make possible her bold belief in women's bodies that escape the dominant constructions that would suture them.* Irigaray, on some level, seems to understand, and even to dramatize, what I propose calling real-bodies

---

*I mean *suture* in both its ordinary language sense of "sewing up" and its more technical theoretical sense of "that moment when the subject inserts itself into the symbolic register in the guise of a signifier, and in so doing gains meaning at the expense of being." For the latter definition, see Silverman, *Subject of Semiotics*, 200. Both senses are appropriate for Irigaray because she associates women's oppression within the symbolic register (where her body appears only in terms of lack) with the "sewing up" of women's genital lips.

mysticism. This is the belief (not the certainty) that real bodies may exist on their own terms but that *we can reach them only by the same visionary means that separate us from their 'reality'*.

Real-Bodies Mysticism

For post-structuralist feminists, this separation from 'reality' remains one of the most familiar dilemmas—so much so that in the introduction to *Body/Politics: Women and the Discourses of Science*, Jacobus, Fox Keller, and Shuttleworth cite this dilemma as their central issue, offering the statement in this chapter's first epigraph. These feminists wish to hold in "tension" (and Gallop used precisely this word) discursive figures "and" material presences. This implied duality, however, cannot be so easily held, if imagined (in spite of the *and* that serves both to separate and to join these terms). Even in stating the problem, one can point *only through discourse* to that bodily aspect—"material presence or biological entity"—that exceeds, escapes, or stands partly separate from "a figure in discourse."

Materialism in its discursive shades has shadowed theorists for quite some time. One detects worry over things-in-themselves as early as Barthes's famous structuralist essay, "Myth Today." Concluding, Barthes wonders if we can know objects apart from the myths by which cultures grasp them:

> It seems that this is a difficulty pertaining to our times: there is as yet only one possible choice, and this choice can bear only on two equally extreme methods: either to posit a reality which is entirely permeable to history, and ideologize; or, conversely, to posit a reality which is *ultimately* impenetrable, irreducible, and, in this case, poetize. . . .
>
> The fact that we cannot manage to achieve more than an unstable grasp of reality doubtless gives the measure of our present alienation. . . . For if we penetrate the object, we liberate it but we destroy it; and if we acknowledge its full weight, we respect it, but we restore it to a state which is still mystified. It would seem that we are condemned for some time yet always to speak *excessively* about reality.[4]

Barthes is discussing what later becomes the debate between full-blown linguistic constructionists (who "posit a reality which is entirely permeable to history") and essentialists, or at least believers in objects that might, at some point, in some way, resist full linguistic construction (who "posit a reality which is *ultimately* impenetrable, irreducible"). His most important insight comes as he approaches his closing, when he recognizes that to pull apart an object's myths is to lose the very object itself ("we liberate it but we destroy it"), for *nothing that we can reach* remains beneath our demystifying penetrations. Extreme constructionism loses its object. Conversely, Barthes notes that to believe that the object does exist, somewhere on its own terms, is to leave it mystified or to mystify anew ("we respect it, but we restore it to a state which is still mystified"). Materialist respect for objects that exist apart from our myths can only serve to "poetize" and thus still "mystify" the very objects materialists or poets would want to deliver in "inalienable" form. Importantly, Barthes's use of *poetize* here should not be confused with Gallop's use of *poeticize*. For Gallop, *poeticize* refers to the use we make of language's metaphorical properties—its discursive figures. Barthes's *poetize* means nearly the opposite (if one could hold these concepts apart): We poetize when we (think we) point to a reality that exists outside our discursive figures. Truly, then, this distinction collapses, since we can only poetize by poeticizing in a mystical vein.

In fact, Barthes's end point—"that we are condemned for some time yet always to speak *excessively* about reality"—makes clear that every materialist *must* "poetize," must mystify, and even must make mystical, I would claim, the nondiscursive reality for which they would reserve some conceptual, discursive, and material space. On post-structuralist terrain, one cannot speak of "the tension between a feminist investment in the referential body and an aspiration to poetics," as Gallop does for Irigaray, without confessing that these two conceptions cannot rest side by side. One can only lean upon the other, and only one—"an aspiration to poetics"—can ever appear.* The most real, most referential thing, cannot be seen.

The legacy of post-structuralist dicta, warning that referents never appear, proves startling in its effects. Theorists have become so squeamish about pointing to bodies or reality outside of language that they have taken to submitting *the body itself* and *reality* to quotation marks. Here is an oxymoronic confession that they are pointing to an outside to language from within its domain. By contrast, the terms *material conditions, material effects,* and *material limits*—increasingly used in our critical climate—do not standardly appear with quotation marks. Even so, in the introduction

---

*This is a point that Kaja Silverman clarified in her 1981 essay, "Histoire d'O: The Construction of a Female Subject," when she coined a helpful formulation: "Discursive bodies lean upon real ones." Here was an early attempt to strike a path between full constructionism and biological essentialism, though Silverman's stress, understandably for the time at which she was writing, falls upon the cultural constructions that discursive bodies represent (Silverman, "Histoire d'O," 325).

to her book, *Uneven Developments: The Ideological Work of Gender in Mid-Victorian England*, Mary Poovey finds it necessary to qualify even *material conditions*:

> Despite my assumption that the conditions that produce both texts and (partly through them) individual subjects are material in the ever elusive last instance, I also maintain that this famous last instance *is* ever elusive—precisely because the material and economic relations of production can only make themselves known through representations. . . . I return in a moment to the compromise I have tried to strike in my organization of each chapter, but the effect of the self-consciousness I voice here will have to carry over into the rest of the book, where I occasionally represent the "real" as if it were a linear development that could shed both textualization and the quotation marks that signify that it is always a social construction.[5]

What is material, we note, has become perhaps the most "elusive" (and remains an "ever elusive") category in deconstructive thought. Representations are endlessly available, whereas materiality and bodies elude, demanding now belief, self-conscious confession, and quotation marks that the 'real' cannot shed.

In Haraway's 1988 essay, "Situated Knowledges: The Science Question in Feminism and the Privilege of Partial Perspective," she reveals a familiar nervousness about where this extreme constructionism—especially deconstruction—has left us vis-à-vis 'reality' (which Haraway, at the start, italicizes, letting italics drop as she states her desires):

> The strong programme in the sociology of knowledge joins with the lovely and nasty tools of semiology and deconstruction to insist on the rhetorical nature of truth, including scientific truth. . . . This is a terrifying view of the relationship of body and language for those of us who would still like to talk about *reality* with more confidence than we allow the Christian right's discussion of the Second Coming and their being raptured out of the final destruction of the world. We would like to think our appeals to real worlds are more than a desperate lurch away from cynicism and an act of faith like any other cult's. (SK, 185)

What makes Haraway nervous is twofold: (1) since deconstruction, we cannot intelligently talk about reality without sounding like (very conservative) religious believers whose appeals to hidden realities, beyond worldly constructions, must always constitute "an act of faith"; (2) we need to talk about reality, real bodies, and real worlds if we are to hold each other "responsible" (for Haraway, a key word) for how we learn to see a world of bodies and things that are agents themselves.

Haraway wants the fruits of real-bodies mysticism, minus mysticism.

She eschews any "act of faith" that relies on *escapes* from embodiment. She states: "To lose authoritative biological accounts of sex, which set up productive tensions with its binary pair, gender, seems to be to lose too much; it seems to be to lose not just analytic power within a particular Western tradition, but the body itself as anything but a blank page for social inscriptions, including those of biological discourse" (SK, 197). What Haraway wants is something very close to the "tension" that Gallop and the editors of *Body/Politics* outline: the tension between discursive figures and material presences. Not surprisingly, Haraway's statement of the problem, reminiscent of Gallop's and the editors', depends largely on an unexamined "and" (which she italicizes) that joins and separates both sides of the equation (and keeps both sides within the same sentence!):

> So, I think my problem, and "our" problem, is how to have *simultaneously* an account of radical historical contingency for all knowledge claims and knowing subjects, a critical practice for recognizing our own "semiotic technologies" for making meanings, *and* a no-nonsense commitment to faithful accounts of a "real" world, one that can be partially shared and friendly to earth-wide projects of finite freedom, adequate material abundance, modest meaning in suffering, and limited happiness. (SK, 187)

Perhaps Haraway is not telling us how to perform this tension—only stating it should be our goal. Still, I would argue that her call to "commitment to faithful accounts," particularly her listing of "earth-wide projects"— "*finite* freedom, *adequate* material abundance, *modest* meaning in suffering, and *limited* happiness" (my emphasis)—lends a clue: Post-structuralist humility will save the day and will enable a reliance on escape to sneak in through the back door.

What I mean is this: Haraway's stress on particularity, limits, modesty, finitude, accountability, responsibility, and noninnocence (central to her essay's embrace of things "partial") spells a twist that resembles Christian believers' required humility before God, since God represents a domain of possibility and agency beyond believers' control. With this panegyric to "partial perspective[s]," Haraway is able to stress the benefits of our acknowledging our limits, over and against our seeking forms of disembodied transcendence, for this human humility is what would make possible, in her scheme, a world (and bodies) that transcend(s) us. We limit ourselves so that our world (and our bodies) can escape us and return to us (at least in part) outside our constructions. In taking a stand against transcendence, Haraway thus makes a certain kind of transcendence possible. Small wonder that her essay ends by tying our humility to the possible appearance of something other than our selves:

The approach I am recommending is not a version of 'realism', which has proved a rather poor way of engaging with the world's active agency. . . . Ecofeminists have perhaps been most insistent on some version of the world as active subject, not as resource to be mapped and appropriated in bourgeois, Marxist, or masculinist projects. Acknowledging the agency of the world in knowledge makes room for some unsettling possibilities, including a sense of the world's independent sense of humour. Such a sense of humour is not comfortable for humanists and others committed to the world as resource. Richly evocative figures exist for feminist visualisations of the world as witty agent. . . . The Coyote or Trickster, embodied in American Southwest Indian accounts, suggests our situation when we give up mastery but keep searching for fidelity, knowing all the while we will be hoodwinked. I think these are useful myths for scientists who might be our allies. Feminist objectivity makes room for surprises and ironies at the heart of all knowledge production; we are not in charge of the world. . . . Perhaps our hopes for accountability, for politics, for ecofeminism, turn on revisioning the world as coding trickster with whom we must learn to converse. (SK, 199–201)

How far are we here from a Victorian version of a Christian God? Institutionally and practically, it appears we are quite far, so that Haraway might rightfully balk at the question. Discursively, however, some points of contact remain striking: Like God, the world is deemed an active subject with an independent sense of humor, which may prove uncomfortable to human projects; like God, the world demands that we "give up mastery but keep searching for fidelity, knowing all the while that we will be hoodwinked," for "we are not in charge of the world"; like God, the world demands that our hopes be expressed in conversations with what, or with someone who, remains outside our ability to bind everything with words.*

I have tried to show that Haraway speaks against transcendence on behalf of materialism. Yet, her very gestures that would script a post-structuralist materialism depend upon escapes that would return us to bodies that surprise us. I want to argue something similar for Gallop in *Thinking Through the Body*, for Gallop stresses that side of the duality that post-structuralists have only recently stressed: "the body as insubordinate to man-made meaning"; the body as "enigmatic because it is not a creation of the mind" (*TTB*, 18). This is no naive return to bodies, assuming linguistic, or material, transparency. Gallop rejects the notion that there

*As Robert Caserio has suggested to me, Browning offers some intriguing possibilities for imagining Victorian versions of God as a coding trickster. See, in particular, Browning's poem "Caliban Upon Setebos; or, Natural Theology in the Island." One might even notice that Caliban's natural theology meets and intersects with the theology of Browning's St. John (see "A Death in the Desert").

could appear "such a thing as a 'body itself', unmediated by textuality" (*TTB*, 93). What she does explore is the body's resistance to linguistic domination:

> The human being cannot help but try to make sense out of his own idiosyncratic body shape: tall or short, fat or thin, male or female, to name but a few of the least subtle morphological distinctions. Outside the theological model there is no possibility of verifying an interpretation: no author to have intended a sense in composing such a body. . . . By "body" I mean here: perceivable givens that the human being knows as "hers" without knowing their significance to her. In such a way a taste for a certain food or a certain color, a distaste for another, are pieces of the bodily enigma. We can, a posteriori, form an esthetic, consistent system of values (rules for Good Taste) to rationalize our insistent, idiosyncratic tastes. But the system is a guess at the puzzle, a response to the inscrutable given. (*TTB*, 12–13)

From the start, one might argue that Gallop has trouble pointing to "morphological distinctions"—"tall or short, fat or thin, [especially] male or female"—that are not already the result of culturally specific codes. This difficulty seems most dramatically apparent in her appeal to "a taste for a certain food or a certain color," as well as in a later list of tastes, predilections, and repulsions (which could be *fully* culturally induced in some cases, though perhaps not in all). Of course, what Gallop's trouble surrounding "morphological distinctions" points to is the issue I have been discussing all along: the difficulty of indicating in language whatever we want to designate as falling outside it.

Not surprisingly, Gallop seems most convincing on the body, from a deconstructive standpoint, at those points where she discourses on escapes from discourse, where the 'body' (in quotation marks, we note) "means all that in the organism which exceeds and antedates consciousness or reason or interpretation," where the 'body' means "perceivable givens that the human being knows as 'hers' without knowing their significance to her." This last phrase, in fact, sounds like Lacan on St. Theresa: "It is clear that the essential testimony of the mystics is that they are experiencing it [the '*jouissance* which goes beyond'] but know nothing about it."[6] True, Gallop defines the body against "theological models," linking theology to (beliefs, I guess, in) verifiable interpretations, puzzlemasters, correct divinations, and final guarantees of intended meaning— even though theology can only ever command faith in these things. Clearly, however, Gallop's antitheological return to the body proves itself a spiritualizing project of major magnitude. Precisely, as she puts it, the body is an "inscrutable given." The same gesture, then, that makes the body seem like it is solidly there, renders it elusive. The best argument for its material resistance to our domination is its propensity to escape our efforts at capture, for Gallop *defines* the body in terms of escape, the failure of meaning, and the impossibility of human sign systems ("that which *exceeds* and *antedates* consciousness or reason or interpretation"; my emphasis).* We believe, however, that the bodily puzzle remains as something that Gallop rather mystically calls "the mark of an enigmatic silence (sign of an impossible transcendence)" (*TTB*, 14).

"Mystic Unfathomable Visibilities"

This material perplexity that preoccupies Gallop and Haraway is emergent already in Thomas Carlyle. In fact, in Carlyle, this dilemma outlines the conceptual surprises we encounter now in feminists who would shed the linguistic garments that constrain them—but shed them through forms of *cloaking* and *concealment*. Carlyle, better than any theorist I know, represents the kind of spiritual materialism to which post-structuralist feminists are returning, both obliquely and overtly. In Carlyle, too, as in post-structuralists, *materialism has to do with concealment*: Carlyle's historical enigmas, akin to Gallop's bodily enigmas, show resistance to our conceptual control, thus heightening their existence apart from us. Most important of all, when we consult a Victorian like Carlyle who uses spiritual discourse openly, we can sense the collapse between 'spiritual' and 'material' borders in which post-structuralists, despite their deconstructions, invest so much distinction.†

---

*Interestingly, Gallop's own attempts to envision a penis that is not a phallus (a supreme hope in failure) can only be expressed in terms of escape. (Notice, for example, her use of ellipses in the passage below.) Reminiscent of Haraway and Doane, however, Gallop seeks escape from the oppression of (a dominant version of) transcendence that seeks to escape embodiment: "These questions bespeak a desire for the penis. Not the Paternal nor the Maternal Phallus. A desire that barely dares believe that there is a penis. That barely can see beyond the Phallus. But if there were a penis . . . one that could desire to penetrate another body, one that could want a woman, need a woman, not just a 'woman', but more excitingly, an 'other' body, not woman as the appropriate and appropriated phallic object, but an 'other body' . . . If there were a penis . . ." (*TTB*, 131).

†A book that touches in fascinating ways upon my study—that I take as confirmation—but that came too late to shape my thoughts is David Shaw's *Victorians and Mystery: Crises of Representation*. Though Shaw does not address materialism in the Marxist or post-structuralist senses that I adduce here (materialism and feminism are not a part of his project), his study adds rich layers to our knowledge of how a host of Victorians attached themselves to ineffabilities.

Given to us by Victorian scholars as the quintessential social prophet, Carlyle represents the secularized spirituality ("religion without theology") that peculiarly characterizes Victorian intellectuals' solutions to social problems. Carlyle is standardly deemed a transcendentalist, whose "social message," writes Richard Altick, is "the logical . . . derivation from his transcendental metaphysics and Calvinist heritage."[7] Even his "natural supernaturalism"—his secular focus on the natural world as sacred and revelatory—is still clearly marked by his transcendentalism: the natural *is* supernatural, for Carlyle.

The natural is supernatural, that is, in its wondrous inexplicability, where supernaturalism, we should notice, is defined as what we cannot fathom, what makes our ability to secure meaning fail. Nature is a discourse, a language even, that escapes the words and sentences that we know. Nature is a spiritual discourse:

> We speak of the Volume of Nature: and truly a Volume it is,—whose Author and Writer is God. To read it! Dost thou, does man, so much as well know the Alphabet thereof? With its Words, Sentences, and grand descriptive Pages, poetical and philosophical, spread out through Solar Systems, and Thousands of Years, we shall not try thee. It is a Volume written in celestial hieroglyphs, in the true Sacred-writing.[8]

In Gallop, material inexplicability—in the form of bodily "enigmas," with their status as "inscrutable givens"—offers proof of a *material* reality that stubbornly and importantly resists "domination" by "man-made meaning." In Carlyle, material inexplicability—in the form of natural enigmas, with their status as "inscrutable and certain" (Carlyle's phrase)—offers proof of a *spiritual* reality that stubbornly and importantly resists domination by man-made meaning. As in Gallop, in Carlyle, moreover, this "domination" by "man-made meaning" that material inexplicability resists is explicitly named as "science"; Gallop specifically associates what is "scientific" with what is "nonmystic" and "nonecstatic."*

*For Carlyle, consult a passage like the following from *Sartor Resartus*: "Have any deepest scientific individuals yet dived down to the foundations of the Universe, and gauged everything down there? . . . These scientific individuals have been nowhere but where we also are; have seen some handbreadths deeper than we see into the Deep that is infinite, without bottom as without shore" (194). For Gallop, see her discussion of Shere Hite's "science fantasy" that Gallop thinks pervades *The Hite Report*. For example, Gallop comments: "The major discrepancy between Hite and her subjects is that she, in search of scientific data, favors strong, clear, calculable responses whereas they, in quest of love and happiness, even power, are interested in diverse, less clearly measurable factors. This distinction determines a dynamic tension played out in *The Report* between the Woman whose voice Hite longs to hear and the women who actually

But how different is Gallop's hidden 'material' reality from Carlyle's hidden 'spiritual' one? If a 'reality' is imagined as hiding from our direct material access, does it matter if we conceptualize it as 'material' or 'spiritual'? Certainly these rhetorical differences can generate remarkably different systems of thought, which may in turn determine elaborately different politics. But do these conceptual differences between what we call 'spiritual' and 'material' always proceed in predictable directions? And do they hold up?

Some issues in Carlyle's *Past and Present* light up their collapse. This is a book as attentive to the need to escape intolerable material relations (produced by the Corn Laws and the Poor Law Amendment Act of 1834) as are feminist visions. This book, too, envisions an *alternative materiality*—but one that directs our hope to a historical past, not the future. The historical past presents itself as a beckoning *enigma*, a puzzle that promises a material presence to be approached and followed. Yet, troubling senses of inaccessibility appear wedded to Carlyle's hope in history: The Past is a "dim indubitable fact," whose dimness seems a function of approaching "a fact" that always recedes, "*far off* on the edge of *far* horizons, towards which we are to steer *incessantly* for life" (*PP*, 41; my emphasis).

For Carlyle, as much as for any post-structuralist, history has gotten difficult. Even written voices from the past repel in their "remote," "exotic," and "extraneous" characters, as Carlyle discovers when he reads the notebooks of a twelfth-century monk:

> A certain Jocelinus de Brakelonda, a natural-born Englishman, has left us an extremely foreign Book, which the labours of the Camden Society have brought to light in these days. Jocelin's Book, the "Chronicle," or private Boswellian Notebook, of Jocelin, a certain old St. Edmundsbury Monk and Boswell, now seven centuries old, how remote is it from us; exotic, extraneous; in all ways, coming far from abroad! The language of it is not foreign only but dead: Monk-Latin lies across not the British Channel, but the ninefold Stygian Marshes, Stream of Lethe, and one knows not where! Roman Latin itself, still alive for us in the Elysian Fields of Memory, is domestic in comparison. And then the ideas, life-furniture, whole workings and ways of this worthy Jocelin; covered deeper than Pompeii with the lava-ashes and inarticulate wreck of seven hundred years! (*PP*, 46)

The references here to "Stygian Marshes, Stream of Lethe," and "the Elysian Fields" suggest that material access to the past bears analogies to im-

---

speak. . . . In this scientific, nonmystic, nonecstatic sexuality, pleasure is allowed (it is, after all, a reasonable goal), but there is a premium on efficiency ('quickly') and predictable causality ('reliably')" (*TTB*, 85, 75).

possible spiritual journeys. The Past as "dim indubitable Fact" appears so exotic and remote, its escapes from us are mystical. But if its concealment makes history somewhat mystical, historical resistance to *our agendas* only heightens its existence apart from us. "We have a longing," writes Carlyle, "always, to cross-question him, to force from him an explanation of much"; "but no; Jocelin, though he talks with such clear familiarity, like a next-door neighbor, will not answer any question: that is the peculiarity of him, dead these six hundred and fifty years, and quite deaf to us, though still so audible!" (*PP*, 49). In history's character as "inscrutable and certain" (Carlyle's phrase), these *historical enigmas*, as one might call them, bear a discursive resemblance to the "bodily enigmas" that Gallop discusses, rather mystically, as "inscrutable givens." Because history resists us, because it is *not* transparent, it asserts, we believe, a materiality that exceeds us.

How fitting for Carlyle's sense of history, and for the post-structuralist debates that concern us, that Carlyle concludes his journey into the historical past with a monk's report of a bodily enigma. The story involves Abbot Samson's wish to glimpse the body of the martyr St. Edmund. Carlyle quotes his monk, Jocelin, on this secret sacred event, from which he, Jocelin, was unhappily excluded, hearing about it only through witnesses:

> These coverings being lifted off, they found now the Sacred Body all wrapt in linen. . . . But here the Abbot stopped; saying he durst not proceed farther, or look at the sacred flesh naked. . . . [Yet] proceeding, he touched the eyes; and the nose, which was very massive and prominent . . . and then he touched the breast and arms; and raising the left arm he touched the fingers, and placed his own fingers between the sacred fingers. And proceeding he found the feet standing stiff up, like the feet of a man dead yesterday; and he touched the toes and counted them. . . . And now it was agreed that the other Brethren should be called forward to see the miracles. (*PP*, 124)

Here is testimony: the most naked materiality seems the most holy, the most mysterious, the most difficult to grasp—something that Irigaray will powerfully demonstrate. In fact, the passage illuminates a difficulty more than it illuminates a body: the difficulty of grasping naked flesh. Where the description becomes most particular (the reference to the nose as massive), or most intent on the act of grasping (placing fingers between the sacred fingers, counting the toes), we receive the strongest sense of a bodily enigma that defies our captures. Carlyle caps this instructive scene with his own gloss on bodily enigmas: "Stupid blockheads, to reverence their St. Edmund's dead Body in this manner? Yes, brother;—and yet, on the whole, who knows how to reverence the Body of a Man? . . . For the Highest God dwells visible in that mystic unfathomable Visibility, which calls itself 'I' on the Earth" (*PP*, 126).

Surprisingly, we can couple Carlyle's spiritual materialism, so evident in this passage, with his own brand of full-blown constructionism. By doing so, we can understand why Gallop and Haraway, who seem primarily constructionists, participate in spiritual materialism. Carlyle's view of the body as a "mystic unfathomable Visibility" (a phrase that could describe post-structuralist conceptions of 'the body' apart from social constructions) points in two directions simultaneously: toward concealment and toward revelation. The interconnections between these terms prove quite intricate. What the body reveals most easily are the fabrications—in Carlyle's terms, the "garments" or "clothes"—by which we know it. This is, in large part, what his earlier book, *Sartor Resartus*, had explored: "The whole external Universe and what it holds is but Clothing," dressed up by society and religious institutions in every manner of word, symbol, and human conception.[9] Since, however, "the Tailor is not only a Man, but something of a Creator or Divinity," there is another side to the revelation of human constructions.[10] Every "garment" (every person or thing) reveals not only the set of human tailorings by which we know it, but it also *reveals* a divine *concealment*. What is revealed, what "*super*naturalism [brings] home to the very dullest," is concealment itself; and this concealment bespeaks a spiritual reality that "dwells *visible* in that *mystic unfathomable* Visibility" (*PP*, 126; my emphasis). Again, we graze post-structuralist formulations, except that it is spiritual discourse that renders the concealment post-structuralists stress as material. Thus, explains Gallop, "By 'body' I mean here: perceivable givens [Visibility] that the human being knows as 'hers' without knowing their significance to her [mystic, unfathomable]" (*TTB*, 13). Or, as Lacan will say: "The essential testimony of the mystics is that they are experiencing it but know nothing about it."

There is further evidence that Carlyle's spiritual materialism sits close to his own social constructionist tendencies. Having ended his historical review with a "mystic unfathomable Visibility" (St. Edmund's body), Carlyle closes book 2 of *Past and Present*, "The Ancient Monk," by taking a turn that looks like a version of extreme constructionism:

> What a singular shape of a Man, shape of a Time, have we in this Abbot Samson and his history; how strangely do modes, creeds, formularies, and the date and place of a man's birth, modify the figure of the man!

Formulas too, as we call them, have a *reality* in Human Life. They are real as the very *skin* and *muscular tissue* of a Man's Life; and a most blessed indispensable thing, so long as they have *vitality* withal, and are a *living* skin and tissue to him! . . .

And yet, again, when a man's Formulas become *dead* . . . till no *heart* any longer can be felt beating through them, so thick, callous, calcified are they . . . yes then, you may say, his usefulness once more is quite obstructed. (*PP*, 128)

Carlyle not only appears to be a precursor to post-structuralist analysts who would claim that everything is fashioned by discourse; he also sounds faintly like Althusser on how ideologies hail us into subjectivities. (Asks Carlyle: "This English Nationality . . . has it not made for thee a skin or second-skin, adhesive actually as thy natural skin? [*PP*, 129]). "Formulas" are real and inescapable (as are ideologies and subjectivities for Althusser). What we need, suggests Carlyle, are better formulas, since "blessed [is] he who has a skin and tissues, so it be a living one, and the heart-pulse everywhere discernible through it" (*PP*, 130–31). Happily, historical retrospection provides some: "Monarchism, Feudalism, with a real King Plantagenet, with real Abbots Samson, and their other living realities, how blessed!" (*PP*, 131). Seemingly, the *only* thing Carlyle can promise is other (possibly better) formulas, more distant and provocative.

Yet, Carlyle is not this fully constructionist, as we have seen. The clue to what might escape these formulas is his almost unnoticeable reference to "the heart-pulse," which he mentions twice: "When a man's Formulas become *dead* . . . till no *heart* any longer can be felt beating through them . . . his usefulness once more is quite obstructed"; "blessed he who has a skin and tissues, so it be a living one, and the heart-pulse everywhere discernible through it." This sense of something not commonly seen but *felt* beating or pulsing *through* skin is vital for Carlyle. This pulse, or beat, however, indicates a mysterious sign of a reality that can best prove its presence when it starts to *fail*—when "no *heart* any longer can be felt."*
For bodily and historical objects seem most real and most referential not

*Notice, for example, in the passages I have cited from Carlyle's *Past and Present*, how *dead* things—dead languages, dead bodies, dead Formulas, dead hearts—are largely what signify history and materiality as mystery: "The language of it is not foreign only but dead: Monk-Latin lies across not the British Channel, but the ninefold Stygian Marshes, Stream of Lethe, and one knows not where!"; "That is the peculiarity of [Jocelin], dead these six hundred and fifty years, and quite deaf to us, though still so audible!"; and, in a passage I did not cite, "the Body of one Dead;—a temple where the Hero-soul once was and now is not: Oh, all mystery, all pity, all mute *awe* and wonder" (*PP*, 126).

where they reveal something recognizable (which would only prove their capture by constructions) but where they conceal something from us.* These are concealments constructions cannot capture—except for mystical formulas, which tell us that there is something that cannot be told.

Irigaray's 'God' Between Their Lips: In Search of Symbolic Holes Women Can Feel

Here—on the question of perceivable concealments that only mystical formulas can capture—is the link to the deconstructive feminist Irigaray. For the sake of making different bodies appear, Irigaray renders these bodies opaque and seeks to lavish upon them concealments that they might wear. More arresting still, in offering us her spiritual materialism, Irigaray puts 'God' between women's lips.

By means of this puzzle I want to make bold that with all that has been written in reference to Irigaray, we have not fully realized the interest of her materialist dilemmas (for my purposes, her theories in *Speculum of the Other Woman* and *This Sex Which Is Not One*).† In fact, in a major study of Irigaray, Margaret Whitford confirms that materialist address to Irigaray is particularly needed now: "The question of Irigaray and materialism still awaits a thorough elucidation, which will take into account the fact that 'materialism' is a political term, over which there is contest for rights and

---

*Gallop says something quite close to this, in fact, when she discusses confusion and contradiction: "To read for and affirm confusion, contradiction is to insist on thinking in the body in history. Those confusions mark the sites where thinking is literally knotted to the subject's historical and material place" (*TTB*, 132). Scientists of every stripe would seem to know this knotting well, since they encounter the body and matter at those places where every known scientific formula or construction fails to explain what they are observing. It is precisely this failure, however, that convinces us that bodies and matter do push back against even our most precise formulations.

†There are several reasons why, for the purposes of this book, I am only addressing Irigaray's major early works, *Speculum of the Other Woman* and *This Sex Which Is Not One*. As will become apparent in my remarks below, I want to read Irigaray against the grain of Irigaray criticism by emphasizing Irigaray's *embrace* of lack as what makes her able to convert castration into (auto)eroticism. This Irigaray—"a feminist theologian of lack," as I will call her—is early Irigaray, the feminist who tangles with Freud and Lacan. Early Irigaray is also the theorist who most intently engages materialist issues "with" Marx. It seems to me the case as well that Irigaray's early theological writings—on Christian mysticism, especially—make the most dramatic links with Victorians (particularly with the Paul Emanuel character in Brontë's *Villette* and the St. Theresa figuration of Dorothea Brooke in *Middlemarch*). As a future endeavor, I would like to discuss the intersections between Irigaray's "sensible transcendental" and what in this book I deem, via Irigaray, "material opacity."

possession."* I concur with Whitford, and would add that Irigaray's materialist dilemmas are more nuanced than the few representations of them
have suggested. But this is true as well of her other assigned designations.
Irigaray has been called an essentialist, but, as I have already said, she may
be more aptly deemed a *believer*: She believes in bodies (and labors) whose
essence, if anything, is escape.† She has been called a "strategic" essentialist, but may be more fairly regarded as an *opaque essentialist*, and a very
mystical one at that, since mysticism, she asserts, "is the only place in the
history of the West in which woman speaks and acts so publicly" (*S*, 191).‡
She has been called a theorist of plenitude but may be more powerfully
read as a feminist theologian of lack, for whom the happy fall may be
found between a woman's lips—the same place, suggestively, she locates
'God'.§

By virtue of her stance as a believer, a mystic opaque essentialist, and
a feminist theologian of lack, I take Irigaray as the premiere test case for
spiritual materialism. Her theorizing, for a start, unambiguously exposes
how spiritual discourse engenders discourse on materialities that dominant constructions fail to capture. Yet Irigaray's happy fall is specific. She
puts a version of *felix culpa*, 'the happy fall' (lack, separation, failure) between the lips, representing the self-caress of the lips as made possible by

---

*See Whitford, 196n20. Readers of Irigaray are now fortunate to possess Whitford's
indispensable study, *Luce Irigaray: Philosophy in the Feminine*, a book that had not yet
appeared when I submitted this chapter as an article for publication. Whitford's is clearly
the most detailed study of Irigaray to date and a major contribution to our understanding of Irigaray as a philosopher of sexual difference. Although there is not much discussion in her book of Irigaray as materialist or even of Irigaray's theory of desire, I
find in Whitford important confirmation for a point that touches on the issues I address:
Irigaray, she argues, is trying "to effect change in the symbolic order. . . . She is not
pre-Lacanian, but post-Lacanian" (14). Whitford is superb on this point.

†For the essentialist designation see, for example, Monique Plaza, " 'Phallomorphic
Power' and the Psychology of 'Woman' "; and Toril Moi, *Sexual/Textual Politics*.

‡For the strategic essentialist reading of Irigaray, see Schor, "This Essentialism";
Fuss, *Essentially Speaking*; and Whitford, "Luce Irigaray and the Female Imaginary."

§In another major study of Irigaray, Elizabeth Grosz continually reads her against
the grain of loss. Discussing Irigaray on mother-daughter relations, for example, Grosz
examines the dynamics of "When Our Lips Speak Together" (the concluding essay to
This Sex Which Is Not One). Writes Grosz: "The 'we' here does not subsume or merge
one identity with another but fuses them without residue or loss to either. . . . This is
a space of exchange *without debt, without loss, without guilt*, a space women can inhabit
without giving up a part of themselves" (Grosz, *Sexual Subversions*, 126; my emphasis). In
fairness to Grosz, there are lines in this essay that could be read as Irigaray's desire to
escape lack and loss. I wish, nonetheless, to provide an alternative to this reading and,
indeed, will argue that even in this essay Irigaray conceives sex as fracture. (See Chapter
2 below.)

the slit, 'woman's' nothing, her (supposed) castration, that divides her. More intriguingly, Irigaray locates not only lack, but also 'God', between the lips, as I must explain. She *implants escape within the genitals* and makes what she terms "unformable apartness" (*S*, 235) their most essential biological feature. This is why, too, as much as Irigaray shares Marx's need for faith in 'natural' objects, 'matter on its own terms' before it is mystified through commodifications, her materialism breaks from Marx: She elaborately mystifies the female body, using blatantly mystical terms to bolster it against mystifications that are far more alienating than her own.

I want to convey how Irigaray's stance as an *opaque essentialist* (my term) is tied to her stance as a *feminist theologian of lack* (my term, again). At bottom lies my central claim: Irigaray wants to say that something of women's bodies is concealed without saying what this something is. This something, however, is closer to a crack, a seam, a slit, than it is to something we deem substantial. Irigaray's opaque essentialism, her tendency to make visible the body's opacity, thus enables her to perform two operations at once: She can complain against women's alienation from their bodies (by arguing that something is concealed by constructions); she can forge a deconstructive pact to leave the body's essence indeterminate (by arguing that what is concealed is a crack). What we might conclude from Irigaray's simultaneous embrace of alienation and indeterminacy is a maxim like this: Women are alienated not from some past body they have known but from a *future* body owed to them. These are bodies women have not yet been allowed to see, to fashion, or to listen for, even though these bodies *already* resist their dominant constructions, particularly where these bodies appear as holes in the dominant Symbolic.

My focus on holes should remind us that, for Irigaray, these materialist issues center on genitals—understandably so, since the body's genitals are still the prime site for the cultural readings that fashion boys and girls. Here is the import of Irigaray's famous, and much contested, figure of the lips: The lips represent Irigaray's address to the *matter* of castration. Do women, she seems to query, possess anything to be *seen materially* at the genital level? Or are "woman's erogenous zones," as their culture paints them, a "hole-envelope" (*TS*, 23)? It is a common mistake to begin discussion of Irigaray's lips with the tired, overworked issue of essentialism. Perhaps it is time to say directly that I want to make Irigaray ride new rims, on the lip of old extremities. This push appears in my portrait of her: Irigaray as opaque essentialist and feminist theologian of lack who puts 'God' between the lips. These formulations are of my own manufacture. I'm suggesting how to read her, moreover, in order to usher the question

of material concealments, perceivable concealments, into explicitly gendered domains. The question of castration, to which the lips speak, leads
us to a border we have not yet broached: What bodies in dominant Western culture are *privileged* to claim a material concealment?

We can probe this concern by reflecting on an issue that Irigaray would
know well. I am referring to Lacan on primary castration: the child's loss
of direct material access to its body when it enters language. One of Lacan's central insights and revisions of Freud, and one that shapes Lacan's
distinctive slant on human tragedy, is that both 'boys' and 'girls' lose unmediated contact with their bodies when they become speaking subjects,
caught in the "defiles" of signification. Lacan puts it this way: "What by
its very nature remains *concealed* from the subject [is] that self-sacrifice, *that
pound of flesh* which is mortgaged [*engagé*] in his relationship to the signifier" (my emphasis).[11]

Lacan links this "pound of flesh" to the production of sexual difference that attends the child's castration through language, for children do
not enter the Symbolic (language/law/culture) on equal terms. Cultural
readings clearly determine *how* bodies mortgage materiality for culture.
'Boys', by virtue of a cultural reading that assigns to their genitals *a valued
and visible materiality*, enter the Symbolic as privileged subjects who "sacrifice" their "pound of flesh" for Symbolic rites. 'Girls', by virtue of a cultural reading that assigns to their genitals *an unhappy lack and missing materiality*, enter the Symbolic as underprivileged subjects who "sacrifice"
their inferior bodies for inferior Symbolic rights. Indeed, these differential
doors to privilege are why so many post-structuralist feminists have argued that the phallus—the privileged signifier of what I am calling Symbolic rites—cannot be easily separated from the penis. Witness Kaja Silverman, who spells out the privilege that attends the boy's castration
through language:

> Lacan suggests . . . that the male subject "pays" for his symbolic privileges
> with a currency not available to the female subject—that he "mortgages" the
> penis for the phallus. In other words, during his entry into the symbolic order
> he gains access to those privileges which constitute the phallus, but forfeits
> direct access to his own sexuality, a forfeiture of which the penis is represen-
> tative. . . . What woman lacks within the Lacanian scheme is the phallus-as-
> lost-penis, the "amputated" or "castrated" appendage which assures the male
> subject access to the phallus-as-symbolic-legacy.[12]

Here is a material concealment, "a pound of flesh," worth its weight in
gold, since this particular material concealment (whatever the penis as a

pound of flesh might be if not "concealed" by discourse) can be cashed in for cultural coins.

Now we sense what lies at stake in achieving a certain *access to lack*, along with a material concealment one can point to, and why Irigaray might seek to acquire lack and concealment *on behalf of women*. What emerges from Silverman, so important for my argument, is precisely this: The phallus signifies lack and material concealment *while* transmitting privileges to dominant men that remain, perniciously, unavailable to women. Dominant men's associations with *veiled* lack appear to empower them; whereas women, who by assigned cultural readings *figure lack*, mortgage their bodies for the phallus (that is, for signification) free of charge, with no symbolic payoff. In this way, so perverse is the game, the Symbolic offers to dominant men the fabrication that they have lost nothing and that they are genitally superior to women, who are lacking, materially, the sign of success (the penis). This Symbolic myth, of course, offers *the* reading children learn to apply to their bodies ('he' has one, 'she' doesn't). To put it simply: Men's lack gets them privilege along with the means by which to veil their lack; women possess no empowering passage to the lack they are made *by the Symbolic* to wear. For according to dominant cultural constructions, the penis, against some feminists' splendid hopes for failure, is not deemed lost, or latent, or lacking—rather, 'woman' is, and her genitals are, too. What women are lacking, *within the Symbolic*, is the privilege of a material concealment.

Clearly, it would be in 'her' interests to unveil 'his' lack—to show that the fullness of the penis is a fraud, as Gallop, joined by Rose and others, tries to do.* But 'her' lack? Should 'she' reach for veils or for revelations? One might expect, under these circumstances, that Irigaray would offer to women their own plenitude—spectacular, pregnant, perhaps, in its fullness—and grant them something to be seen as genitals. The lips have surely been read this way, as part of a plurality of sex organs Irigaray wants to make visible. There is, however, another way to interpret her lips. By concentrating there, Irigaray attempts to gain a more empowered conduction both to materiality *and* to lack *at the same time*. We can read women's genital lips in the guise of a perceivable concealment: "As for

*See Gallop's "Of Phallic Proportions: Lacanian Conceit" in *The Daughter's Seduction* for her discussion of how Lacan purposely inflates the phallus as privileged signifier so as to underscore its fantastic status—a status that transcends and undermines the penis, for the penis falls short of these impossible qualities. See Jacqueline Rose's "Introduction-II" for her discussion of Lacan's attack on "the order of the visible" that would seem to privilege the penis.

woman, she touches herself in and of herself without any need for mediation, and before there is any way to distinguish activity from passivity. Woman 'touches herself' all the time, and moreover no one can forbid her to do so, for her genitals are formed of two lips in continuous contact. Thus, within herself, she is already two—but not divisible into one(s)—that caress each other" (*TS*, 24).

The lips tell us that something is there. The lips tell us that women's bodies are not the "hole-envelope" the Symbolic currently fashions them to be. The lips also say that the signal feature of what is there is what Irigaray calls "an unformable apartness" (lack, separation). This failure to fuse is a happy gap, a *felix culpa*, that was there "in the beginning," making the contact between lips possible. Irigaray here turns full face onto masculine theory by arresting Lacan's narrative with an image, with a material concealment of 'woman's' own.* "Reopen[ing] paths into . . . [a] logos that connotes [woman] as castrated" (*S*, 142), Irigaray makes visible what was supposed to remain invisible: 'woman's' genitals. Yet the lips wear their material concealment for all to see, for it is the lack of closure between her lips—'woman's' nothing-to-see—that forms "two lips in continuous contact," a nearness made possible by a space, a lack, a gap that allows 'woman' constantly to caress herself. This radical valuation of lips invests in 'woman's' slit—a dangerous expenditure. Nonetheless, castration, by this alternate logic of loss, converts to (auto)erotic pleasure.

Strangely, the question of belief enters in here, showcased in Derrida's passage on castration:

> "Woman"—her name made epoch—no more believes in castration's exact opposite, anti-castration, than she does in castration itself. . . . Unable to seduce or to give vent to desire without it, "woman" is in need of castration's effect. But evidently she does not believe in it. She who, unbelieving, still plays with castration, she is "woman." She takes aim and amuses herself (*en joue*) with it as she would with a new concept or structure of belief, but even as she plays she is gleefully anticipating her laughter, her mockery of man.[13]

The way Derrida poses castration in terms of *amusement* and *belief* suits Irigaray. This slant, in fact, may provide the terms for understanding that Irigaray does not refuse castration (a mistake Jacqueline Rose and others make in reading her) but refuses to believe in its standard associations with the female body. I want to underscore Derrida's notion that 'woman'

---

*I am obliquely making reference here to feminist film theory's founding moment in Laura Mulvey's famous essay, "Visual Pleasure and Narrative Cinema," where she asserts that (feminine) image arrests (masculine) narrative (Mulvey, *Visual and Other Pleasures*, 19–22).

"amuses herself . . . with [castration]." But if Derrida helps us to grasp
'woman' as an unbeliever, I will stress Irigaray's stance as a believer and
the new structure of belief she creates by "converting" castration into affirmation (not the same as anticastration). What Irigaray believes in, I will
argue, is a material concealment that she can simultaneously reveal and
preserve by making what she reveals a crack.

Irigaray's mystical, lyrical essay "La Mysterique" envisions how a divine resistance to familiar visibilities might operate to make a different
body seen, though seen opaquely. Here, we find Irigaray's most elaborate
demonstration of how she ties escapes back to feminine bodies: Irigaray
brilliantly imagines 'God' (using the term under erasure) between wom-
en's lips. In this way, she conducts us from a psychoanalytic landscape,
with its focus on the phallus, to a bodily landscape, with its focus on the
lips. She accomplishes this shift by passing us over a theological terrain
where 'God' casts 'His' lot with lack. To make this move, Irigaray must
be relying upon 'God' as the most respectable, and certainly most elegant,
absence in Judeo-Christian traditions. Even in the most incarnational
theologies—Catholicism, for example, which invests most heavily in the
body of Christ, endowed with sacramental mystery, nonetheless—'God'
is a sacred space, the one we must humbly allow, in the final analysis, to
remain resistant to us. As elegantly absent Person, or figure for material
concealment, 'God' designates whatever resists our attempts at securing
our bodies and world.

Visible concealment and escape once again become friends to bodies
that would make their opacities seen and known. Irigaray's own hope in
failure (for the sake of our bodies) appears when she stresses the need *as
subjects and objects* to escape from sight. "But as the eye is already guardian
to the reason," writes Irigaray, "the first necessity is to slip away unseen,"
"and in fact without seeing much either," for "her eye has become accus-
tomed to obvious 'truths' that actually hide what she is seeking" (S, 192–
93). Irigaray even directly invokes the opacity of objects, especially bodies, that we must learn to see. She speaks of "the opaque barrier that every
body presents to the light" (S, 193). She also quests in ways that touch
upon Haraway, Gallop, and Carlyle's tendencies to define matter *in terms
of* escape: "What if matter had always, already, had a part but was yet invisible, beyond the senses, moving in ways alien to any fixed reflection"
(S, 197). This passage makes "matter" sound indistinguishable from even
traditional explanations of 'God'.

If matter's opacity defies linguistic capture, then this is a defiance that
mysticism, with its stress on sacred silence or inarticulate utterance, is well

designed to make perceivable. Hence, Irigaray on the female mystic's failure to speak: "But she cannot specify exactly what she wants. Words begin
to fail her. She senses something *remains to be said* that resists all speech,
that can at best be stammered out. . . . So the best plan is to abstain from
all discourse, to keep quiet, or else utter only a sound so inarticulate that
it barely forms a *song*. While all the while keeping an attentive ear open for
any hint or tremor coming back" (*S*, 193). This is a particularly opaque
essentialism, if it can count as essentialism at all ("for it is no longer a matter of longing for some determinable attribute, some mode of essence,
some face of presence" [*S*, 193]). Irigaray's "attentive ear open for any hint
or tremor coming back," along with her "expectant expectancy, absence
of project and projections" (*S*, 194), may remind us of Gallop's "attempt
to listen to the material" apart "from an agenda for better control." Both
theorists stress escapes *on behalf of* "any hint or tremor coming back," and
on behalf of materialities that might resist our learned visions (note Irigaray's invocation of "song" and Gallop's stress on listening).

We need to come closer to something I have claimed: that Irigaray puts
'God' between women's lips. What is the clue to this puzzling assertion?
The hint, I suggest, is itself "the hint or tremor [that comes] back," that
tells us that some material resistance, some material escape, is taking place.
This "hint or tremor" of material escape Irigaray, I would offer, codes as
'God'; more substantial yet, she makes this tremor felt between a woman's
genital lips, implanting escape, as I earlier argued, within the genitals.
Thus, if Irigaray seeks, as she says, "the possibility of a different relation
to the transcendental" (*TS*, 153) then "God," she writes, "knows women
so well that he never touches them directly, but always in that fleeting
stealth of a fantasy that evades all representation: between two unities who
thus imperceptibly take pleasure in each other" (*S*, 236). This declaration
implies 'God's' touch between the autoerotic lips. Given the suggestion
that this touch is not direct but caught up, rather, in a "fleeting stealth,"
and given that the lips, as we know from Irigaray, touch by means of unformable apartness, 'God', by this logic, *becomes spacing.* 'God' is the gap,
at the gap, in the gap; 'God' is the gap of a woman's pleasure between the
lips, "opening up a crack in the cave (*une antr' ouverture*) so that she may
penetrate herself once more" (*S*, 192). 'God' is figured as the material resistance of 'woman's' body to representations that have neglected 'her'
pleasure. This material resistance eludes her in terms of specificities, but
she can perceive this resistance as concealed in mystical encounters.

I want to pierce the mystery of Irigaray's mysticism, to show how her
own mystical interests are strongly staked to lack: who wears it, who suf-

fers for it, and who envisions economies based upon it.* Mystical discourse, by this account, may provide for Irigaray a way of affirming, so as to use differently, the lack assigned to 'woman'. As much as women might like to flee God, Irigaray implies, they must retreat upon the mystical, because "this is the only place in the history of the West in which woman speaks and acts so publicly" (*S*, 191). We, as readers, then, are asked to enter into Irigaray's mystical discourse sympathetically, reverently—and, as women, even spiritual women, are so good at—expectantly.

Irigaray comes to a different 'God' and a different relationship between 'God' and 'woman' than traditional Christian theology has rendered. She speaks of "that most female of men, the Son"—Christ—a 'man' who lines up with 'woman'. In fact, this is what I mean in the introduction when I say, " 'God' figures a masculine body that wears its lack—its wounds unveiled—for all to see." For Irigaray plays with jubilation upon the mystic's holiness, celebrating 'his' holes that tell 'woman' glorious things about 'her' own:

> And that one man, at least, has understood her so well that he died in the most awful suffering. . . . And she never ceases to look upon his nakedness, open for all to see, upon the gashes in his virgin flesh. . . . Could it be true that not every wound need remain secret, that not every laceration was shameful? Could a sore be *holy*? Ecstasy is there in that glorious slit where she curls up as if in her nest, where she rests as if she had found her home—and He is also in her. . . . In this way, you see me and I see you, finally I see myself seeing you in this fathomless wound which is the source of our wondering comprehension and exhilaration. And to know myself I scarcely need a "soul," I have only to gaze upon the gaping space in your loving body. (*S*, 199–200)

This is Irigaray at her recapturing best, mapping lack onto the masculine body so that she can *afford* to reclaim lack for women. She makes the Christian tradition give back what Christ on the cross has borrowed from the feminine: a "gaping space" in the body worth gazing upon.† 'Wom-

---

*For other discussions of Irigaray's mysticism, see Moi, *Sexual/Textual Politics*, but especially Grosz, *Sexual Subversions*, 140–83.

†To be sure, the feminine gendering of Christ has appeared in Christian traditions, though it is often rendered by implication, not by statement. This is to say, when Christ is being sexualized in relationship to the Father, theologies—presumably, to avoid homosexual overtones—gender Christ as a Bride who takes the place of the Church (or Eve) on the marriage bed of the cross. Christ, in this way, can play the role of Bridegroom only by first becoming a Bride. Consider, for example, Augustine on the crucifixion: "[Christ] came to the marriage bed of the cross, and there, in mounting it, He consummated his marriage. And when He perceived the sighs of the creature, He lov-

an's' "slit," here pronounced "glorious," mirrors Christ's "fathomless wound." The wound itself acts as a mirror, enabling 'woman' to reflect upon her material folds. In this way, the wound tells all, making possible her peculiar ability to feel a hole she now inhabits *as* a mystery and *as* a revelation *in* a secret. The wound is a place (from which) to see a material opacity revealed by a gash.

Irigaray renders this mystical version of perceivable concealment as a fold, where "He is also in her": "She is closed over this mystery where the love placed within her is hidden, revealing itself in this secret of desire" (*S*, 200). This "secret of desire" shifts bodily boundaries even as the pronouns shift and bleed. The "He" who bleeds into "you" bleeds into "her," who bleeds into "me." Such a plea (and *pli*, in French, "a fold") for the other that folds the other into the lips requires, we can see, a 'God' who bleeds. Irigaray takes on castration, then, to its most excessive degree, complete with Freud's fatal look upon nakedness that reveals the "shameful" "secret" of the "gaping space"—a secret and a sacred lack that 'woman' shares with Christ, reminiscent of the mystics' stigmata that function as speaking wounds. Irigaray takes castration to the crypt, where she makes castration convert into autoerotic concealments. There might well be "exhilaration" in these bodies' hidden, but perceivable, material folds.

If Irigaray gets mystical when discussing sexual economies, she attempts to be pointedly materialist in her Marxist essays, in which she theorizes women's bodies as commodities ("Woman on the Market" and "Commodities Among Themselves" in *This Sex Which Is Not One*). In these essays, Irigaray appears to agree with Marx's critiques of capitalism as she fashions feminist analogies to his commodities analysis. While doing so, however, Irigaray conveniently forgets (or possibly does not realize) that she, in an essay like "La Mysterique," has repeated moves that Marx would censure. She proves particularly contradictory on the question of what Marx complains is "the mystical character of commodities"—the alienation of objects through abstractions. Indeed, Irigaray's contradictions on this question are so central to her own dramatic real-bodies mysticism that they provide a fitting climax to this chapter.

---

ingly gave himself up to the torment in the place of His bride . . . and He joined the woman to Himself for ever." The Victorian Coventry Patmore depends upon this same tradition in *The Unknown Eros*: "In season due, on His sweet-fearful bed, / Rock'd by an earthquake, curtain'd by eclipse, / Thou shared'st the spousal rapture of the sharp spear's head / And thy bliss pale / Wrought for our boon what Eve's did for our bale." Both passages are quoted from Abrams, *Natural Supernaturalism*, 45, 487n57.

Women do not exchange, they are exchanged: Irigaray begins "Women on the Market" with this fundamental and now familiar point, which she takes on loan from Lévi-Strauss.* This point, in fact, when she connects it to those she borrows from Marx on the bodies of commodities, forms the nerve of her feminist argument. Women, she asserts, when socialized into a 'normal' femininity, play the role of commodities in the dominant (masculine sexual) economy, metaphorically (and sometimes literally) bought and sold on the marriage market.† 'Woman's' "price," moreover, is set not according to her body's 'own properties' (an essential Irigarayan problem) but according to what counts in a phallic economy: 'woman's' ability to mirror men's "needs/desires" and thus to copy the "fabricated" standards set for women as reproductive and sexual vessels (*TS*, 176).

Like Marx, Irigaray, in her righteous anger over commodifications, leans heavily upon a natural/alienated opposition: "*A commodity—a woman —is divided into two irreconcilable 'bodies'*: her 'natural' body [notice Irigaray's use of quotation marks] and her socially valued, exchangeable body, which is a particularly mimetic expression of masculine values (*TS*, 180). The real surprise appears when Irigaray begins to depend upon Marx's critique of commodities' "mystical character"—though this surprise depends upon how one reads Irigaray's seeming essentialism. If one reads Irigaray as conventionally essentialist, one is not amazed that she laments with Marx that (the bodies of) commodities are treated as abstractions, abstractions that obscure their "coarse materiality":

> *Marx*. The value of commodities is the very opposite of the coarse materiality of their substance, not an atom of matter enters into its composition. Turn and examine a single commodity, by itself, as we will. Yet in so far as it remains an object of value, it seems impossible to grasp it.
>
> *Irigaray*. When women are exchanged, woman's body must be treated as an *abstraction*. The exchange operation cannot take place in terms of some intrinsic, immanent value of the commodity.
>
> *Marx*. The fact that it is value, is made manifest by its equality with the coat, just as the sheep's nature of a Christian is shown in his resemblance to the Lamb of God.
>
> *Irigaray*. Each commodity may become equivalent to every other from the viewpoint of that sublime standard. . . . They are exchanged by means of

*See, in particular, the first two pages of Irigaray's "Women on the Market" (*TS*, 170–71) for her repetition and questioning of Lévi-Strauss.

†Irigaray does not consider men's bodies as commodities. Considerations of nondominant men demand that we take up these complications.

the general equivalent—as Christians love each other in God, to borrow a
theological metaphor dear to Marx.

Marx. The mystical character of commodities does not originate, therefore,
in their use value.

Irigaray. This phenomenon has no analogy except in the religious world.

(*TS*, 175–76, 178, 181, 182–83)

Wedding her analysis to Marx, this stinging censure of making materialities mystical comes with contradictions from the author of "La Mysterique." Irigaray herself puts 'God' between the lips—a mystical abstraction of sublime proportions—in order to enable 'woman's' "coarse materiality" to appear, albeit opaquely. Her agreement with Marx, while
contradictory, is nonetheless wise. Believing along with Marx that use
values and real bodies do exist, though they are never seen truly unclothed
in capitalist economies, Irigaray can strongly register an alienation under
capitalism.

As I stressed earlier, before deconstruction, *alienation* was a concept
that marked a conflict with one's real body or one's real self; but since deconstruction, with its break from any notion of authentic selves or bodies,
we have found it less possible to use any determinate sense of original
selves or bodies by which we might mark our alienations. We are left with
conceiving alienation, then, as alienation from *new* possibilities, not from
original ones. This is an alienation from a future we might discover, not
from a familiar, essential past that we have known. This is an unhappy
alienation from what could prove a happier one. This is an alienation *from
whatever exists outside capitalism.* This alienation can best be marked, then,
by positing, *as a form of belief,* what must exist below, behind, or inside the
bodies that commodities are currently required to wear. This is real-
bodies mysticism Marxist-style, wherein one can only hope to split the
good mystical stuff (real bodies and their uses) from bad mysticism (the
commodification of bodies to masculine capitalist ends).

As is Irigaray's way, what she gives as complaint bleeds into possibility:

[A commodified] body becomes a transparent body, *pure phenomenality of
value.* But this transparency constitutes a supplement to the material opacity
of the commodity. (*TS*, 179)

The value of a woman [apart from her transparent value as commodity] always escapes: black continent, hole in the symbolic, breach in discourse. . . .
It is only in the operation of exchange among women that something of
this—something enigmatic, to be sure—can be felt. (*TS*, 176)

Irigaray's opposition, transparency/opacity, offers evidence once again that representations (here, commodifications) are particularly available ("transparent," in this case), while the bodies and objects that are made to wear these transparent supplements elude us through their "material opacity." For this reason, Irigaray must concern herself with making 'woman's' material opacity *seen* and *felt as opacity*. Of course, Irigaray well knows the complications that lie in wait: 'Woman's' (material) value may escape the Symbolic as a "hole," but, to a large extent, this escape is reappropriated *by* the Symbolic and made internal to the workings of the system. Thus 'woman's' value as a commodity seems to *include* her escapes from the system that contains her: 'Woman' gets commodified, bought and sold, as an enigma. Irigaray, however, cannot finally let herself believe in such a total containment. She invests, therefore, in 'woman's' hole. By so doing, she achieves two objectives: First, she registers resistance to totalizing masculine values (since she preserves the sense of 'woman's' escape from the dominant Symbolic); second, she forges hope for making women "feel" this "something enigmatic" in ways that might empower them, leading, as she says, to "a new critique of the political economy" (*TS*, 191).

Irigaray seeks, then, to give a form to "material opacity" that women can invest in for themselves, without falling back upon the masculine value of transparent selves that relate as rivals. It is not surprising that Irigaray believes "it is only in the operation of exchange among women that something of this—something enigmatic, to be sure—can be felt." Given the cultural and economic status of women as commodities exchanged among men, alternative exchanges between men and women are sometimes hard to see and feel.* Exchanges between women (or, as in mysticism, between the feminine mystic and 'God') can, at times, provide at least a partial isolation from the circuits of the masculine sexual economy and thus lend a more vivid backdrop against which to see a material opacity as opaque.

Perhaps for this reason, Irigaray ends her Marxist essays with the female homosexual's "inconceivable" desire for women. Here is an enigma that psychoanalysis—Freud, explicitly—has been made to feel as a "difficulty," she writes, "so foreign to his 'theory'" (*TS*, 195). "Hence the fault, the infraction, the misconduct, and the challenge that female ho-

---

*This problem of making *visible* and *readable* alternative exchanges runs parallel to the problem of fashioning for women a visible renunciation. How can their willing embrace of loss be read as resisting their prescribed role as 'woman', when read against the background of traditional coupling that enjoins this part upon them?

mosexuality entails" (*TS*, 194). The female homosexual writes a happy
fall for feminists since psychoanalysis under Freud is itself forced to feel
an opacity. As much as he attempts to force the explanation of the female
homosexual's "masculinity complex," Freud cannot, even by his own
terms, account for 'her' to his satisfaction. Women's desire, turned toward
one another, can *potentially* make them feel the Symbolic hole between
them, that each, as commodity, mirrors for the other. Feeling this hole,
they might erect for themselves their own material opacity that defies their
culture's attempts to deliver them as fully bought and sold. Something
might even accrue from this cipher—" a certain economy of abundance,"
says Irigaray, but an economy, I would add, that, according to her own
most cherished theories, is solidly based upon fracture and loss.

We must follow these issues to their destination. To do so will involve
us in the complicated circuits of the invisibilities of women's work and
Irigaray's attempts to address these forms of material concealment by
making desire a form of labor. We will have to take stock of how pleasurable loss can be produced between bodies, and, at the same time, attend
to the dangers of reproducing familiar fractures based upon inequities. We
will have to examine what Irigaray cannot see: how women are positioned
asymmetrically as commodities, so that exchanges between them are always susceptible to *partial* accounts along other axes (those of class, race,
religion, age, appearance, etc.). These implications raise serious questions
for alternative exchanges that would count so dramatically upon discernible loss.

To conclude, the fix for feminists is this: If escapes, though partial,
from dominant constructions do take place, if subordinates to systems are
never fully constrained by the boundaries that write their own relations,
what 'body' gets touched when the boundaries are broken? Is it enough to
believe—to have faith—that some freer body is being touched upon? Can
one touch a body that one must, in order to touch it, locate in the impossible place of a discourse that escapes the discourses that we know? Is this
necessary alienation of one's culturally constructed body—through an
other body that one cannot, must not, know by means of dominant constructions—the ultimate act of political, mystical autoeroticism? The
question remains (and I believe it bears a spiritual materialist stamp): How
can we bend ourselves toward the impossible bodies and selves we must
believe *now* that we can be? And how can we keep from fully arriving at
this material destination, so that we do not utterly overtake ourselves, capture ourselves, enslave ourselves, but continue to yearn after a telos that
recedes from our desire to fix it?

Chapter 2

Divine Loss: Irigaray's Erotics
of a Feminine Fracture

_~♫_

Shaving Lacan's Desire

shave vt. 1. to cut or scrape away a thin slice or slices from
2. to cut off (hair, esp. the beard) at the surface of the skin
3. to barely touch or to just miss touching in passing;
graze 4. [Colloq.] to lower (a price, etc.) by a slight margin
5. [Colloq.] *Commerce* to purchase (a note, draft, etc.) at a
discount greater than the legal or customary rate of interest.
shaveling n. [Now Rare] a person whose head is entirely or
partly shaved, esp. a priest or monk: used contemptuously.
shaver n. [Archaic] a person who is hard or grasping in bar-
gaining.
close shave n. [Colloq.] a narrow escape from danger.

—Webster's New World Dictionary

As if appropriating sorrow for sex, Irigaray converts lack into loss-
productive-of-pleasure. As if healing the subject's splits by caressing the
slit between her lips, Irigaray nurtures self-parting for pleasure. As if dis-
daining Lacan's tragic tone, contemptuous of his confidence that lack
must spell tragedy, Irigaray cradles the lack that Lacan deems "original
misery."* Irigaray, we may say, "shaves" his desire: She approaches his
lack to graze it in passing; she makes small cuts at the surface of his theory
(so much depends upon the space between the lips); she purchases desire

*Lacan, raised Catholic, is surely playing upon "the Fall" when he attributes to bi-
ological prematuration—the child's dependence at birth on its caretakers, which har-
bingers its primary loss of the mother—a status that, as Kate Millett has long com-
plained, Freud attributed to the castration complex. Stuart Schneiderman has written:
"Lacan was raised a Catholic; he did not practice Catholicism, but he was educated by

at a reduced rate (against his law); she eludes Lacan's tragedy by the narrowest margin as she grasps a hard bargain.

Lacan's tragic sense is now familiar. "The subject is split and the object is lost," says Juliet Mitchell, recapping Lacan in a motto or maxim.[1] Fracture and loss stand as twin pillars of Lacanian tragedy. They shadow the infant's development from birth, when the subject, sexed by the world outside it, is sent down the garden path of split destiny, seeking a lost complement it will find only in the glazed surface of romance. Suited up in the armor of its "outsides"—the mirror image it mistakenly takes for its bodily identity, and the language codes by which it is gendered and ushered into culture—the subject, separated from its first beloved (the body that mothered it), seeks satisfaction in substitutions. Desire is the lack that propels the subject along the track of substitutionary chains, never to arrive at a destination that satisfies its sense of "original misery."*

Lacan's dense explanations of desire, his thick attempts to show how desire differs from need, return us to lack's significant relation to material opacity. Something of human needs (what Kaja Silverman glosses as "organic reality") is alienated by needs' detour through language. "What is thus alienated in needs . . . cannot, by definition," says Lacan, "be articulated in demand" (*FS*, 80).† This something-of-needs, "obliterated" *by* articulation, by demand, can only "reappear" as a "*residue* which then pre-

---

the Jesuits and his theorizing bears the stamp of his own cultural heritage" (*Jacques Lacan*, 14).

*When I say "sexed by the world outside it," I am referring to the fact that the child's "sex" is determined at birth by a world outside the child; only later will this child, in its subjectivity, fulfill this "destiny" or refuse it (or make a series of negotiations with it, sometimes quite tangled ones, to be sure). By the same token, I am referring both to the child's mirror image and to the language it later acquires as "outsides" that shape it from its brink. On the question of split destiny, see Lacan, *Four Fundamental Concepts*, 204–5. On the mirror image, see "The Mirror Stage" (*E*, 1–7). On the question of language and its substitutionary chains, see "Agency of the Letter in the Unconscious" and "The Function and Field of Speech and Language in Psychoanalysis" (*E*, 146–78, 30–113).

†Silverman, *Subject of Semiotics*, 183. Elizabeth Grosz glosses "need" as "the experiential counterpart to nature"—what "comes as close to instincts as is possible in human existence"—"the requirements of brute survival"; "need requires real, tangible objects for its satisfaction" (Grosz, *Jacques Lacan*, 59–60). Demand, since it is addressed to the (m)other, is really asking for something other than particularities: It is asking for a proof of "love" and, thus, for an absolute, a plenitude that the (m)other does not have to give. Writes Lacan: "Demand in itself bears on something other than the satisfactions which it calls for. It is demand for a presence or an absence. This is manifest in the primordial relation to the mother, pregnant as it is with that Other to be situated *some way short* of any needs which it might gratify. . . . Hence it is that demand cancels out (*aufhebt*) the particularity of anything which might be granted by transmuting it into a

sents itself in man as *desire*" (*FS*, 80; my emphasis). Desire (lack) testifies
to an "abolished" material relation that reappears as "the force of pure
loss." States Lacan: "There is, then, a necessity for the particularity thus
abolished to reappear *beyond* demand. . . . In a reversal which is not a simple negation of negation, the force of pure loss arises from the relic of an
obliteration" (*FS*, 81). Desire, for Lacan, is a "residue" and a "relic" of
some material "obliteration" that cannot be spoken but that does re-
emerge as perceivable concealment, "reappear[ing]" "*beyond* demand."
Consonant with real-bodies mysticism, lack marks the spot.

No wonder Irigaray shaves desire by *embracing* lack, by making a
home for lack between lips. This "force of pure loss" testifies to a "residue," "a relic of an obliteration," for which Irigaray (as I earlier quoted)
"keep[s] an attentive ear open for any hint or tremor coming back" (*S*,
193). As if she could rewind a tape of broken glass, Irigaray asks us to hear
fractures and the relics of obliteration spun backwards into filaments,
crystal residues of organic reality. And yet, most significant for spiritual
materialism, desire is a search that can never go back without seeking "beyond."*

Elegant Absence and Courtly Love

For Lacan, the sexual relation is the lover's supreme dodge of this
seeking "beyond." Lacan strictly states that nothing will satisfy insatiable
longing—especially not sex or love. Taunting those who make sex suffice,
Lacan broadly questions, "For what is love other than banging one's head
against a wall, since there is no sexual relation?" (*FS*, 170). Lacan insists
that we cannot "disguise this gap" (*FS*, 81) between need and demand

---

proof of love, and the very satisfactions of need which it obtains are degraded (*sich er-
niedrigt*) as being no more than a crushing of the demand for love" (*FS*, 80–81).

*I do not by this move wish to collapse the "needs" of Lacan's discussion with the
something-of-women's-bodies for which Irigaray keeps an ear open, but, rather, to associate these "residues" with each other, which may be perceived (or so I imagine Irigaray imagines) in "the force of pure loss." If I am right about Irigaray's embracing
lack, here would lie an intriguing motivation. This is not to posit in Irigaray some utopian, wholesale return to pre-Oedipal organicism. Rather, I propose that she listens for
the body in the cracks of the Symbolic. Mysticism, I have claimed, is one way to perform this listening (mysticism as a discourse, a gesture, and an acting out, in which the
body complains—a point to which even Rose assents [*FS*, 52]). I strongly agree with
Whitford that Irigaray strategizes from within the Symbolic, but I am stressing that,
within its domain, Irigaray strains toward "abolished" materialities. For other readings
of attentive listening, see Whitford, *Luce Irigaray*, 39, 41.

with love's fantasy of two-become-one, substituting finite objects for the inaccessible, infinite object of desire.

In "God and the *Jouissance* of ~~The~~ Woman," followed by "A Love Letter," Lacan ridicules the man's fantasy that makes women wear the face of God for men.* Seeking to give his lack the slip, the man (em)beds in 'woman' his Other: whatever escapes him about himself, whatever might cradle his knowledge, stroke and hold his self-truth, which he then thinks he confronts and conquers in the sexual relation. As Carlyle writes in *Sartor Resartus*, humorously depicting men's "glowing Fantasy, the more fiery that it burnt under cover, as in a reverberating furnace": to such "young Forlorn[s] . . . all of the air [women] were, all Soul and Form; so lovely, like mysterious priestesses, in whose hand was the invisible Jacob's-ladder, whereby man might mount into very Heaven."[2] Seeking to rupture this masculine fantasy ("It is here that . . . severance is still needed" [FS, 154]), Lacan must address himself to "the good old God of all times," whose face 'woman' is required to wear. But here, Lacan reports, materialists do not fully grasp his attempt to "place God as third party . . . in this affair of human love" (FS, 141); they bristle at the tidings that God should be invoked at all. Lacan, as a consequence, must negotiate the tricky waters of what conventionally pass as separate seas: the fluid domains marked "philosophy" and "materialism":

> Some well-meaning people—always worse than those who mean badly— were surprised to have it reach them that I placed between man and woman a certain Other who seemed remarkably like the good old God of all times. They only heard it indirectly and became the willing bearers of the tidings. And my God, to put it aptly, these people belonged to the pure philosophical tradition, from among those who lay claim to materialism—which is precisely why I call it pure, since there is nothing more philosophical than materialism. Materialism feels itself obliged, God knows why, we can appropriately say, to be on guard against this God whom I have said to have dominated in philosophy the whole debate about love. Hence these people, to whose warm intervention I owed a replenished audience, were somewhat put out. (FS, 140)

Lacan clarifies his devotion to the Other by implying that the Other is not the "good old God" but rather the place of speech/language/the Symbolic that governs human subjects from their outsides. "The symbolic is the

---

*These essays, to be sure, have been discussed before, but never, to my knowledge, with a slant on Lacan's *materialist* motivations nor with an eye to his chiding of materialists in their purity, who, says Lacan, need to deal with "the good old God" if they would be sufficiently materialist.

support of that which was made into God" (*FS*, 154), presumably because it breaks over subjects from beyond their rims:

> For my part, it seems plain that the Other, put forward at the time of "The Agency of the Letter" (*Ecrits*, [1957]), as the place of speech, was a way, I can't say of laicising, but of exorcising our good old God. After all, there are many people who compliment me for having managed to establish in one of my last seminars that God does not exist. Obviously they hear—they hear, but unfortunately they understand, and what they understand is a little hasty.
>
> Today, however, my objective is rather to show you precisely in what he exists, this good old God. The mode in which he exists may well not please everyone, especially not the theologians who, as I have been saying for a long time, are far more capable than I am of doing without his existence. Unfortunately I am not quite in the same position because I am dealing with the Other. (*FS*, 140–41)*

"God has not made his exit," says Lacan, since 'woman' is still made to bear his place, for "when one is a man, one sees in one's partner what can serve, narcissistically, to act as one's own support" (*FS*, 154, 157). What 'man' seems to finger in 'woman', what she becomes a "symptom" of, and why he tries to finesse what he feels with the "good old God," is his own hole, his impossible conquest of a lost complement.† It is the Symbolic that poses this impassable barrier to completion, as if, by means of the cultural garments the Symbolic requires men and women to wear, they cannot get naked. No wonder the epitome of finesse in this game is courtly love, where *obstacle* is thematized and, therefore, throned by means of fantasy, accepted as an expected limit so as to protect the man against the failure of the sexual relation. Says Lacan:

> [Courtly love] is an altogether refined way of making up for the absence of sexual relation by pretending that it is we who put an obstacle to it. It is truly the most staggering thing that has ever been tried. . . . For the man, whose lady was entirely, in the most servile sense of the term, his female subject, courtly love is the only way of coming off elegantly from the absence of the sexual relation. (*FS*, 141)

This far into his essay, Lacan plays his role of cynic, exposing what snares human subjects into fantasy. Yet rounding the bend of courtly love, he falls into the lap of the mystics. Startling his reader by a sudden shift in tone, he now affirms the mystics' caress of something that looks like ma-

*Notice the stress on hearing in this passage: an example here of the *in*attentive ear.
†For a discussion of 'woman' as "symptom" see "Seminar of 21 January 1975" (*FS*, 168).

terial opacity. Here is how the exorcist of "the good old God" arrives, unexpectedly, back at God's hands: He suddenly gets materialist over women's "exclus[ion] by the nature of things which is the nature of words" (*FS*, 144). That is to say, in recognizing that the phallic function can define itself only by producing 'woman' as exception, as photographic negative to the man, Lacan seems to pay *materialist respect* to what might be the *material remainder* of a woman, which language (and even women) cannot speak:

> It none the less remains that if she is excluded by the nature of things, it is precisely that in being not all, she has, in relation to what the phallic function designates of *jouissance*, a supplementary *jouissance*.
>
> Note that I said *supplementary*. Had I said *complementary*, where would we be! We'd fall right back into the all. . . .
>
> There is a *jouissance* proper to her, to this 'her' which does not exist and which signifies nothing. There is a *jouissance* proper to her and of which she herself may know nothing, except that she experiences it—that much she does know. She knows it of course when it happens. (*FS*, 144–45)

The mystics suggest themselves to Lacan as those who "sense that there must be a *jouissance* which goes beyond," for "that is what we call a mystic" (*FS*, 147). Beginning with a joke, Lacan shades into what unfolds as his serious appreciation of mysticism:

> Naturally we ended up in Christianity by inventing a God such that it is he who comes!
>
> All the same there is a bit of a link when you read certain genuine people who might just happen to be women. . . . The mystical is by no means that which is not political. It is something serious, which a few people teach us about, and most often women or highly gifted people like Saint John of the Cross—since, when you are male, you don't have to put yourself on the side of Aφx [all]. You can also put yourself on the side of not-all. There are men who are just as good as women. It does happen. And who therefore feel just as good. Despite, I won't say their phallus, despite what encumbers them on that score, they get the idea, they sense that there must be a *jouissance* which goes beyond. That is what we call a mystic. . . .
>
> It is the same as for Saint Theresa—you only have to go and look at Bernini's statue in Rome to understand immediately that she's coming, there is no doubt about it. And what is her *jouissance*, her *coming* from? It is clear that the essential testimony of the mystics is that they are experiencing it but know nothing about it. (*FS*, 146–47)

The mystics, male and female, lining up "on the side of not-all," allow themselves to be shaken and split by a lack-turned-opacity, obscure pleasure that refuses translucence.* Lacan concludes with a joke that, again, returns him to God. Not the "good old God," but a 'God' who courts women's *jouissance* as women's material complaint against constructions:

> These mystical ejaculations are neither idle gossip nor mere verbiage, in fact they are the best thing you can read—note right at the bottom of the page, *Add the* Ecrits *of Jacques Lacan*, which is of the same order. Given which, naturally you are all going to be convinced that I believe in God. I believe in the *jouissance* of the woman in so far as it is something more. . . . Might not this *jouissance* which one experiences and knows nothing of, be that which puts us on the path of ex-istence? And why not interpret one face of the Other, the God face, as supported by feminine *jouissance*? (*FS*, 147)

Lacan's gambit is clever. Men can be mystics and so can Jacques Lacan. His passage, however, exceeds his cleverness. Read generously, it may bespeak his desire to depart from phallocentrism and the binding anguish of its conventions. At the very least, Lacan seems eager not to be abandoned by women and mystics who go (and come) beyond. Here is 'woman', then, 'woman' along with her mystic partners, who are on her "side," teaching men to find pleasure in lack. This is to read Lacan straight-faced, of course, to grant him his "ejaculation," not his joke.†

As is her way, Irigaray complains most against Lacan when she most closely follows him. Thus she makes her displeasure known at Lacan's assigning pleasure to a statue: "In Rome? So far away? To look? At a statue? Of a saint? Sculpted by a man? What pleasure are we talking about? Whose pleasure? For where the pleasure of the Theresa in question is concerned, her own writings are perhaps more telling" (*TS*, 91).‡ Along the axis of

---

*In Roland Barthes's *The Pleasure of the Text* (written roughly at the same time that Lacan was giving this seminar, 1972–73), *jouissance* is, by definition, "unspeakable," in contrast to pleasure, when pleasure is defined as "contentment." (Though here we must recall Richard Howard's "Note on the [English] Text": "Barthes himself declares the choice between pleasure and the more ravishing term to be precarious, revocable, the discourse incomplete" [v].) Barthes even cites Lacan as his authority: "I refer to Lacan ('What one must bear in mind is that [*jouissance*] is forbidden to the speaker, as such, or else that it cannot be spoken except between the lines')" (21). I am on my way to a definition of feminine *jouissance* as *desire-pleasure*: desire with the face of pleasure; contentment cracked by pleasurable longing; a lacking that is a way of having.

†In many ways, this is the problem—the possibilities and dangers of men's crossing over to the side of 'woman'—that grounds Alice Jardine's investigations in *Gynesis: Configurations of Woman and Modernity*. See also Whitford's worries about Derrida (*Luce Irigaray*, 126–35).

‡Jacqueline Rose also tries to move the discussion into the domain of St. Theresa's writings: "And if we cut across for a moment from Lacan's appeal to her image as executed by the man, to St. Theresa's own writings, to her commentary on 'The Song of

access, Irigaray splits from Lacan. Nurtured, seemingly, at the breast/
phallus of Lacanian psychoanalysis, Irigaray broke with Lacan in 1974 and
has since established herself as one of Lacan's foremost challengers. She
reads him straight-faced when he is joking, mocks him—as if she could
make him her shaveling—when she repeats him. Irigaray generally cas-
tigates Lacan, as if he were a sly gynecologist: hand-in-glove with the
man's Symbolic fantasies that Lacan would say require rupture. Most dramatically, Irigaray accuses *Lacan* of making 'woman' wear the face of God
for men—now as proof of the body's enjoyment and proof of the speaking subject's relation to the material world:

> Men cannot do without that state as proof of the existence of a relation be-
> tween body and soul. As symptom of the existence of a "substantive com-
> ponent," of a "substantive union between soul and body," whose function is
> ensured by the "enjoying substance."
>
> As no intelligible entity alone can carry out this proof or test, respon-
> sibility for it has to be left to the domain of sensation. For example, to the
> pleasure of woman. Awoman [sic]. A body-matter marked by their signi-
> fiers, a prop for their soul-fantasies. . . .
>
> It helps them bear what is intolerable in their world as speaking beings,
> to have a soul foreign to that world. . . . It is *necessary* that the fusion of the
> soul—fantasmatic—and the body—transcribed from language—be accom-
> plished with the help of their "instruments": in feminine sexual plea-
> sure. . . .
>
> From this point on, does not that ineffable, ecstatic pleasure take the
> place, for men, of a Supreme Being . . . ? With the requirement, for them,
> that it be discreet enough not to disturb them in the logic of their desire. (*TS*,
> 96–97)*

Lacan, says Irigaray, even "silences" (as if he has slipped his hands over)
'woman's' *jouissance* in the very act of posing its "discovery." Irigaray on
Lacan on 'woman': "Pleasure without pleasure: the shock of a remainder
of 'silent' body-matter that shakes her at intervals, in the interstices, but
of which she remains ignorant. 'Saying' nothing of this pleasure after all,
thus not enjoying it" (*TS*, 96). Here are the clues that Irigaray, too, reads
Lacan's gesture toward the mystics as *materialist*, at least in part: "the shock

---

Songs,' we find its sexuality in the form of a disturbance" (*FS*, 52). Stephen Heath may
be taken as a fellow critic of Lacan on St. Theresa, Gallop a defender. See Heath, "Difference," and Gallop on Heath in *Daughter's Seduction*, 43–55.

*This is a passage from Irigaray's essay, "Cosi Fan Tutti" (*TS*, 86–105), her critique
of Lacan's *Encore* essays on 'woman'. The quotations that appear in her passage are her
citations of Lacan.

of a *remainder* of 'silent' *body-matter"* (my emphasis) forms this "pleasure without pleasure" that disturbs her.

Though it might appear that Irigaray also rails against Lacan for assigning an opacity to women's pleasure, she is really provoked by something subtler: that Lacan takes in stride the limit that he hits.* Lacan is not shaken by his inability to locate women's pleasure. There is no reason, no way, he would say, to pursue this limit (a *jouissance* that goes beyond) beyond the limits of discourse (as we know it). This impossible status of 'woman' and 'woman's' pleasure—the good news, something of her "escapes," the bad news, 'she' does not fully know it nor does 'she' exist—provides the limit to Lacanian theory at the same time that it sketches women's fix. In its role as limit, the concept of this *jouissance* touches upon something Lacan calls the Real (the unapproachable, ungraspable, algebraic x).† In the inaccessibility of 'her' *jouissance*, Irigaray senses hints of courtly love and Lacan as courtly lover: "There is no longer any need, then, for her to be there to court him. The ritual of courtly love can be played out in language alone. One style is enough" (*TS*, 104). Irigaray, ever elsewhere than at home in the discourse that Lacan takes to be the only discourse, states her protest: "To the objection that this discourse is per-

*This confidence is most evident in Lacan's theorization of the mirror stage, a "jubilance" that perhaps anticipates a mastery that he does *not* possess in reference to 'the woman.' We may note, for example, in his writings on the mirror stage, his admission of wonder at this little drama: "Its repetition," he writes, "has often made me reflect upon the startling spectacle of the infant in front of the mirror" (*E*, 1). This passage displays Lacan's intriguing reflections as he gazes into the riddle of the child's mirror stage, guessing at the meaning of this "startling spectacle." His guessing reveals him as a jubilant theorist, coming into his own, as does the mirror stage child who "overcomes in a flutter of jubilant activity, the obstructions of his support and, fixing his attitude in a slightly leaning-forward position, in order to hold it in his gaze, brings back an instantaneous aspect of the image" (*E*, 1–2). Well might Lacan be jubilant, then, if faced with a contradiction placed before him (and placed there by Freud), he succeeds in filling in the "gaps left by Freud's varied and contradictory notions of the ego" (Ragland-Sullivan, *Jacques Lacan*, 16). It is an open question as to what extent this same confidence (or lack thereof) imbues his address to the problem of 'woman'—another gap bequeathed him by Freud.

†Alan Sheridan, Lacan's translator for *Ecrits: A Selection*, glosses the Real in such a way that its links to "material opacity" are striking: "The real in its 'raw' state (in the case of the subject, for instance, the organism and its biological needs), may only be supposed, it is an algebraic x" (*E*, x). It is "that before which the imaginary faltered, that over which the symbolic stumbles, that which is refractory, resistant. Hence the formula: 'the real is the impossible.' " In a statement that takes us back to the discussion of need/demand/desire, Sheridan concludes his gloss by defining the Real as "the ineliminable residue of all articulation, the foreclosed element": "the umbilical cord of the symbolic."

haps not all there is, the response will be that it is women who are 'not-all' " (*TS*, 88).

Given that they both leap toward God and mystics, and given that Irigaray's celebration of a lack-turned-opacity already seeps through Lacan's address to mysticism, what razor-cuts between these theorists is not so much a theoretical difference—for their theories take them to the same spiritual materialist ledge. A difference in *urgency* cracks their congruence. Irigaray urgently desires to pursue beyond the limit of not speaking—to *listen* to Theresa, her writings, her words, Irigaray so "attentive to the hint or tremor coming back" that she wants women to *touch* it for themselves. Lacan's relaxed confidence concerning mystic silence could never suit Irigaray's investment. For her, there can be no taking-for-granted that somewhere, elsewhere, women find their pleasure. If lack is turned toward material opacity by the mystics, then Irigaray wants it seen, heard, and felt as opaque material pleasure. Of course, Irigaray, ultimately, can only write a theory of these matters. Even as she makes us hear the words of mystics, she can conduct us only to the threshold of what we might feel beyond the fall of words.

We are back, then, to Irigaray shaving desire. Irigaray's trick is to steal Lacan's (theory of) desire: she shaves it (and, thus, puts a new face on it) and claims it as 'woman's' own. The new face she puts on desire is pleasure. The way she does this, as we have seen, is by focusing on an image that does not appear in the subject's official story of desire.* At the lips, that is, Irigaray finds a figure for a touch that is a mirroring touch: an identification that enjoys its own splitting, a failure to fuse that enjoys impossibility: "Thus, within herself, she is already two—but not divisible into one(s)—that caress each other" (*TS*, 24). The mirrored images of the genital lips reconceptualize the mathematics of division. Clear accounts escape precise calculation here, and all because of a division (between lips) that does not divide clearly.† If Lacan's version of desire is a division and a lack—and one that "costs" the subject—then Irigaray shaves desire in that other sense of "shave" as well: "to lower (a price, etc.) by a slight margin"; "to purchase (a note, draft, etc.) at a discount greater than the legal or customary rate of interest" (*Webster's New World Dictionary*). Irigaray

*See footnote on p. 31.

†The difficult logic of division toward which Irigaray leans can be found as well in "When Our Lips Speak Together": Irigaray wants to convey a separation that does not allow precise distinctions but that does not leave exchangers indistinct. She writes: "Open your lips; don't open them simply. . . . We never separate simply. . . . One cannot be distinguished from the other; which does not mean that they are indistinct" (*TS*, 209).

has cut the cost of desire against the Lacanian law of tragedy. Irigaray's "feminine" desire, in this respect, is not a wholly other desire, but a different orientation to lack that makes desire its own kind of pleasure. Feminine desire, as Irigaray fashions it, is (masculine) desire with a different valence and a different tension.* It is a lacking, unveiled, that is also a having. In this sense, feminine desire *is jouissance*—a restless pleasure that is not limited to a single object or a single organ. Perhaps, most importantly, Irigaray imagines this pleasuring (around the crack of desire) as a lacking *shared between* desiring bodies. By virtue of this move—a relocation of lack and open holes to the space between bodies—'woman' ceases to *be* a lack or a "hole-envelope": "With you, I don't have any ['holes']. We are not lacks, voids awaiting sustenance, plenitude, fulfillment from the other" (*TS*, 209).

'God', in Irigaray's theories, plays a vital role in this regard. 'God', as we have seen, is figured as the material resistance of women's bodies to the cultural constructions that have barred women's pleasure. More daring yet, because Irigaray locates this material resistance (this opacity) in 'woman's' hole (where she is said to lack), 'God', not 'woman', is a crack, a lack, a gap—the fracture we need for conceiving new pleasures. In this respect, 'God' is the wound of our relations but also the only hope for the lack that, fracturing us, allows us to touch ourselves. But 'God' is more than divine lack or an elegant figure for material opacities. In Irigaray's rendering, 'God' also figures the body of a lover who, while coming close to 'woman', nurtures the fracture that keeps "him" from possessing "her": "Thus 'God' will prove to have been her best lover since he separates her from herself only by the space of her *jouissance* where she finds Him/herself. To infinity perhaps, but in the serenity of the spacing that is thus projected by/in her pleasure" (*S*, 201). What looks like Irigaray's vision of lovers reveals her potent fracture of dyads (mother/child, husband/wife, two genders, two lovers). Irigaray, I suggest, splinters dyads and their unities into excess when she slips 'God', and thus "infinity," between one and two. Here the necessity of conceiving two mirrors dramatically appears. Positioned, culturally, as a mirror to men, 'woman', when turned upon herself or her feminine other (Christ, for example), figures the turning of mirror upon mirror. Here, between mirrors, images are split from themselves to infinity. There are many pleasures and feminine bodies between the mirrors, in the gap of (her) desire. If she infi-

---

*I am using the sense of *valence* from the Latin, *valere*, "to be strong." *Webster's Seventh Collegiate Dictionary* defines it this way: "the relative capacity to unite, react, or interact (as with antigens or a biological substrate)."

nitely approaches her other, she comes nearer—as if she is always dividing the remaining distance between them—infinitely approaching, never reaching, becoming asymptotic (asymptote: "tangent to a curve at infinity").*

Sex, then, is fracture. Sex, understood as bodies at a brink, demands the attempt to keep closing the gap while nurturing the lack. This contradiction, lying at the heart of sex, stimulates ill-conceived attempts to close the space that shapes its burn—a movement which, if two could perform it, would annihilate otherness, make sex void. Irigaray's erotics of fracture, conversely, counsels the embrace of this space that makes the sexual relation (im)possible: "The sky isn't up there: it's between us" (*TS*, 213).† That is to say, Irigaray's own solution to the sexual relation is a form of courtly love (!). She seeks to cure the sexual relation by putting *her own* obstacles to it, Irigaray "coming off elegantly," as Lacan accuses courtly lovers, "from the absence of [the] sexual relation." Irigaray, in fact, is devoted to courtly love's elegant absence. She affirms the obstacle and deems it 'God', so that the obstacle is a fracture is a lover who spreads for 'woman' 'his' own gash.‡

Webster's New World Dictionary. If this approach without arrival sounds like Barthes's *A Lover's Discourse*, it is important to recall that Irigaray's *Speculum* preceded Barthes's book by three years and that *This Sex Which Is Not One* was published in the same year (1977). It seems possible, nonetheless, that Irigaray was influenced by Barthes in her erotics, especially by *The Pleasure of the Text* (published one year before *Speculum* was published). Consider Barthes's statement: "What pleasure wants is the site of a loss, the seam, the cut, the deflation, the *dissolve* which seizes the subject in the midst of bliss" (*Pleasure*, 7). Or, again: "Neither culture nor its destruction is erotic: it is the seam between them, the fault, the flaw, which becomes so." On a later page he illustrates his point by imagining a glimpse of flesh, a body revealed in a moment of gaping, a body as the gap between clothed borders. Writes Barthes: "Is not the most erotic portion of the body *where the garment gapes*? . . . the intermittence of skin flashing between two articles of clothing (trousers and sweater), between two edges (the open-necked shirt, the glove and the sleeve); it is this flash itself which seduces, or rather: the staging of an appearance-as-disappearance" (9–10).

†This sense of spacing leads to statements that stress the open-endedness of desire, or desire as restless pleasure: "This does not mean that we are focused on consuming, consummation, fulfillment. . . . Are we unsatisfied? Yes, if that means we are never finished. If our pleasure consists in moving, being moved, endlessly. Always in motion: openness is never spent nor sated" (*TS*, 210). Irigaray approaches this same question from a different angle in "This Sex Which Is Not One": "[Women's] desire is often interpreted, and feared, as a sort of insatiable hunger, a voracity that will swallow you whole. Whereas it really involves a different economy more than anything else, one that upsets the linearity of a project, undermines the goal-object of a desire" (*TS*, 29–30).

‡Here, it seems to me, is the problem with relying on Irigaray's later theological writings, which are not as imbued with what I am reading as Irigaray's conversion of castration into (auto)eroticism, via her play on gashes and wounds. And yet, it seems

Cleaving (to) the glassed surface of mirrors, Irigaray imagines mystics, too, in terms of courtly love. She writes, with incandescence, a seemingly heterosexual embrace that is modeled on a feminine erotics of fracture. For if Irigaray preserves 'God' as 'he', she does so only by conceiving
the pleasures of the sexual relation as a "lesbian" tryst: 'Her' (auto)-
eroticism swells to recognition by touching 'his' body that mirrors 'her'
wounds:*

> And she never ceases to look upon his nakedness, open for all to see, upon
> the gashes in his virgin flesh. . . . And to know myself I scarcely need a
> "soul," I have only to gaze upon the gaping space in your loving body. (*S*,
> 199–200)

> For this most secret virginity of the "soul" surrenders only to one who also
> freely offers the self in all its nakedness. This most private chamber opens
> only to one who is indebted to no possession for potency. . . . Thus I am to
> you as you are to me, mine is yours and yours mine, I know you as you know
> me, you take pleasure with me as with you I take pleasure in the rejoicing of
> this reciprocal living—and identifying—together. (*S*, 196)

> Thus (re)assured of the complicity of this all-powerful partner, they/she
> play(s) at courtship, kneeling in self-abasement at one moment, adorning
> themselves with gold and diamonds the next, touching, smelling, listening,
> seeing, embrac(s)ing each other, devouring, penetrating, entering, consum-
> ing, melting each other. She is trusting as a dove, arrogant as a queen, proud
> in her nakedness, bursting with the joy of such exchanges. Her divine com-
> panion never tires of praising her and encouraging her (auto)eroticism that
> has so miraculously been rediscovered. (*S*, 201–2)

striking to me that even in her new work on angels Irigaray has remained fixed on (what
I am calling) "God between the lips." Consider the following passage, in which 'God'
is implied between angels who seem so close to her earlier figuration of women's genital
lips: "Two angels who face one another—this event could only take place here. They
turn toward one another, guarding and calling the divine presence between them. . . .
Face-to-face, they stand in almost timid contemplation, intent on something that has
yet to come, yet to be situated, not yet inscribed, written, spoken. . . . They halt the
return from sameness to sameness, before any determination or opposition of presence
can be made. . . . Neither like nor other, they guard and await the mystery of a divine
presence that has yet to be made flesh. Alike and different, they face each other, near
enough and far enough for the future to still be on hold." We should notice, once again,
Irigaray's attention to materiality ("has yet to be made flesh"), which she continues to
invoke throughout her essay: "Something lives there out of site, or perhaps between
sites, some airy, mobile and yet material structure serving to bear presence" (*Sexes and
Genealogies*, 44–45).

*On pp. 54–56, I will discuss the problems in Irigaray's work surrounding the terms
lesbian, autoeroticism, heteroeroticism, and *homoeroticism.*

These exchanges figure forth, with much luxuriance, Irigaray's theory of feminine mirroring. These passages read as 'woman' reclaiming the Son's mirroring exchange with the Father: "All mine are thine, and thine are mine. . . . as thou, Father, art in me, and I in thee, that they also may be one in us. . . . I in them, and thou in me" (John 17:10, 21, 23). The Gospel of John's signal feature is a God whose 'self' appears as an (auto)erotics of fracture—a set of relations within the Godhead, systematized by the doctrine of the Trinity. Dare we suggest, then, borrowing Irigaray's words for the purpose, that God, like a woman, "always remains several, but ['he'] is kept from dispersion because the other is already within ['him'] and is autoerotically familiar to ['him']" (*TS*, 31)? And perhaps God, too, "derives pleasure from what is so near that ['he'] cannot have it, nor have ['himself']"?

What are the properties of autoeroticism, the implications of feminine fractures?

Properties of Autoeroticism: Implications of Mystical Accounts

Defying calculation, which measures accumulations, installing infinity between the numbers one and two (and thus between dyads—lovers or lips), Irigaray works against familiar values of possession and property. She exploits this defiance by imagining a nearness "within" and "between":

> Woman always remains several, but she is kept from dispersion because the other is already within her and is autoerotically familiar to her. Which is not to say that she appropriates the other for herself, that she reduces it to her own property. Ownership and property are doubtless quite foreign to the feminine. At least sexually. But not *nearness*. Nearness so pronounced that it makes all discrimination of identity, and thus all forms of property, impossible. Woman derives pleasure from what is *so near that she cannot have it, nor have herself*. She herself enters into a ceaseless exchange of herself with the other without any possibility of identifying either. (*TS*, 31)

As if converting the 'God' relation to exchange between women (or, at least, to exchange between 'woman' and her 'other'), Irigaray seems to fashion 'the other', as she fashioned 'God', as a roiled, if semiliquid, barrier that rebuffs any efforts to fuse body-envelopes. The other even makes her obscure to herself, making self-possession "impossible" but self-pleasure ecstatically near in adiaphanous pleats. Opacity, by Irigaray's estimation, stops "ownership" in the gap, making 'woman' unable to close upon an other ("what is *so near that she cannot have it*"), or even upon her own identity ("*nor have herself*"). 'Woman', in this way, "puts into question all prevailing economies" (*TS*, 31).

Yet, as if the smoke of Irigaray's hazy borders trips alarms, political dangers emerge from these conceptions. When Irigaray, attempting to undermine capitalist notions of property (patriarchal ones, too), stresses lack/loss/spacing/'God'/escape, she repeats the Christian values of dispossession and deferral. These Christian values, so familiar to us now, have been made powerfully to support, in some countries, in certain periods, capitalist dynamics (we'll visit Weber on precisely this point). Does Irigaray, then, when she counsels nurturing lack between bodies, and when she celebrates a desire that makes lacking a way of having, unwittingly reinforce economies that have endlessly deferred the pleasure of only some of their constituents? Isn't it often the same constituents whose pleasure is put off?

These questions crucially ask, as Irigaray set out to ask in *Speculum*, who bears the burden of lack in a system—who gets to have pleasure; who has to defer it; whose pleasure counts on someone else's loss. We know that Irigaray locates political ground on this point, since her project begins with who lacks what and who veils lack instead of owning up to it. Her unusual strategy, I would warn—foregrounding a happy lack that women should not conceal but embrace and pursue—can politically run aground on the very differences and splits between women that enable them to feel each other as opacities. The danger remains that hierarchical differences between women (race/class, for example) might perform much of the work of splitting women from each other so that, pursuing nearness, they might be withheld from each other for pleasure. Irigaray tends to veil what performs the necessary cracking between women's bodies, positioned as each other's mirrors. She tends, that is (as is relentlessly noticed in a myriad of feminists), to lean too heavily upon "female sameness." If we feel that this blindness to difference is nothing new, constituting the same old complaint, almost now too easy to repeat, we need to understand why Irigaray wishes to write an alternate version of sameness. Her wish has everything to do, oddly, with the *other's opacity* (the other's inaccessible difference) that cuts a slit between her lips: "the other . . . within her . . . [who] is autoerotically familiar to her."

Mirroring between women, as Irigaray conceives it, enables them, first and foremost, to stroke their own opacity. Not surprisingly, given her reliance on the female homosexual in her Marxist essays, Irigaray has envisioned "tactical strikes" that may look to some readers like lesbian separatism: "For women . . . ," she writes, "to keep themselves apart from men long enough to learn to defend their desire . . . to discover the love of other women while sheltered from men's imperious choices . . . these are certainly indispensable stages in the escape from their proletarization on the exchange market" (*TS*, 33). Her widely read essay, "When Our Lips Speak Together," can surely be read as a lesbian lyric. Yet her constant attacks on masculine sameness make trouble for theorizing *homo*sexuality, unless an alternate sameness can be written.

Irigaray appears to have this divergent doubling in mind, witnessed by a section in her essay on Freud, "Female Sameness." Here, for the first time, she argues against Freud on the female homosexual's masculinity complex: "Nothing of the special nature of desire *between women* has been unveiled or stated. That a woman might desire a woman 'like' herself, someone of the 'same' sex, that she might also have auto- and homo-sexual appetites, is simply incomprehensible to Freud" (*S*, 101). Irigaray seems to refer to desire between women who are similarly signed as 'feminine,' who, being similarly dressed in lack, might identify with, as well as desire, a 'feminine' other.* What strikes in her remarks is how quickly homosexuality is joined, or even supplanted, by *auto*eroticism—to the extent that "auto" begins to precede "homo" in her remarks ("she might also have auto- and homo-sexual appetites").†

Two motivations foster this slide. On the one hand, Irigaray wants to make lesbianism a special subset of autoeroticism, for what concerns her is not so much "women-among-themselves" (always for her a strategy,

---

*The problem becomes, of course, how to define "feminine" other. Could a "feminine" man, for example, suit Irigaray's sense of "a woman 'like' herself, someone of the 'same' sex"? One would think that the immediate answer for Irigaray would be no. Christ and 'God', however, who return a woman to her "auto-sexual appetites," both appear as "he" in her writings, and Irigaray explicitly deems Christ "that most female of *men*, the Son" (*S*, 199; my emphasis). I experiment with these possibilities in my reading of *Villette*, most dramatically, and to a lesser extent in my remarks on *Middlemarch*.

†In her article "The Lesbian, the Mother, the Heterosexual Lover: Irigaray's Recodings of Difference," Christine Holmlund argues for three phases in Irigaray's work structured around "three central female figures," "moving from the lesbian to the mother and the daughter to the female lover in a heterosexual couple" (286). "The first phase," Holmlund argues, "includes the early, densely written, deconstructions of male philosophers (*Speculum* and *Ce Sexe*)." I would reply that this tidy breakdown, although an interesting speculation, is far too neat for Irigaray. Her early work, focused on the genital lips and on desire between women, has more to do with (auto)eroticism than it does with lesbianism. Irigaray's chief concern (in *Speculum* and *This Sex*) is allowing women to touch "their own" bodies and "their own" desire in the heteroerotic relation (of which lesbianism is actually *a subset*, I will argue).

not a goal) but putting women in touch with their "self-affection" from which they are "irremediably cut off" (*TS*, 133). On the other hand, Irigaray wants to make lesbianism and autoeroticism special subsets of *het-ero*eroticism, since difference not sameness, fracture not fusion, form the dynamics of her erotics. Irigaray seeks a true "hetero"—not our culture's "normal heterosexuality," by means of which the exchange of women, from man to man, constitutes the ultimate "hom(m)o-sexuality" (men touching men through the bodies of women).* Her concern for an "auto" that is "homo" but still "hetero" (!) leads her to the ledge of an oxymoron: *a fractured sameness*—unspeakable, but felt as a self-caress by the other at hand: "a self-same that would be 'other' than the one that dominates the phallocentric economy of discourse and signifiers" (*S*, 102, n. 105). "It will be read," Irigaray continues, "by half-opening the 'volume' else-where and otherwise" (*S*, 102, n. 105). Astonishingly, what opens up the space of desire in the auto-, homo- relations between women is, for Irigaray, too (despite her charge against "hom[m]o-sexuality"), another woman's body. Nowhere is this fertile contradiction in Irigaray more apparent than in (Irigaray's fantasy of?) the little girl's fantasy to have a girl baby with the mother:

> The wish for that girl child conceived with the mother would signify for the little girl a desire to *repeat and represent* her own birth and the separation of her "body" from the mother's. Engendering a girl's body, bringing a third woman's body into play, would allow her to identify both herself and her mother as sexuate women's bodies. As *two* women, defining each other as both like and unlike, thanks to a third "body" that both by common consent wish to be "female." (*S*, 35)

Irigaray's articulation among women of "both like and unlike" (women touching women and touching themselves through the bodies of women)

*In "Women on the Market" and "Commodities Among Themselves," Irigaray speaks of "the reign of 'ho(m)mo-sexuality,'" punning, of course, on the French word *homme* ("man"). There, she writes: "Thus all economic organization is homosexual [*sic*]. That of desire as well, even the desire for women. Woman exists only as an occasion for meditation, transaction, transition, transference, between man and his fellow man, indeed between man and himself" (*TS*, 193). Her discussion of this "reign" is linked to the thesis that guides us through *Speculum*: The dominant Symbolic is a masculine Imaginary, by virtue of which men only ever see *themselves*. By contrast, Irigaray wants feminine mirroring (a feminine Imaginary) to form the basis of a different Symbolic. Though Irigaray exempts from her censure "the 'other' homosexual relations, masculine ones," some readers may feel that she too quickly drops her neologism ("ho[m]mo-sexual") and uses the standard "homosexual" to designate her object of critique.

presents heady possibilities for scripting desire between women, but also theoretical and political dilemmas.*

Where there's bleeding, there's often pain, yet Irigaray's lacking bleeds with joy. For Jacqueline Rose, this celebration of bleeding boundaries poses problems. Rose pins Irigaray when she criticizes the politics of a sexuality "from which any idea of the psychic as an area of difficulty has been dropped."[3] Rose reads Irigaray's mirroring as "untroubled psychic unity," putting Irigaray's count at one (in spite of the title to Irigaray's book).[4] Rose, nonetheless, presents the problem generally, and in a way that highlights the political stake in her concern: "Perhaps for women it is of particular importance that we find a language which allows us to recognise our part in intolerable structures—but in a way that renders us neither the pure victims nor the sole agents of our distress."† Ironically, this language that would implicate women may be spoken with mirrors—perhaps only with mirrors. Shaving Lacan's desire in her looking glasses, Irigaray projects psychic difficulty onto mirrors and so produces feminine mirroring not as fusion but as radical implication. "Implication" is a(c)count between one and two, suggesting that neither "untroubled psychic unity" (Rose's phrase) nor perfect separation can be gained: "Woman derives pleasure from what is so near that she cannot have it, nor have herself" (Irigaray).

"Implication" is a word that appears with astounding frequency in recent critical theory; yet few have explicitly theorized its use. Here is a term that could possibly open a more communal, even politicized space in Irigaray, for, appropriately, "implication" gathers the strands of intimate involvement, incriminating involvement, entanglement (from the archaic sense, "interweaving, entwining"), and indirect indication (*American Heritage Dictionary*). Insofar as feminine mirroring kisses the glass of (auto)eroticism, "intimate involvement" aptly renders its implications. Feminine mirroring, in its most utopian light (the only light by which Rose can see it), also imagines a collectivity that proceeds not by fusion but by entanglement, where infinity, I have said, hangs in the crease be-

---

*As this book goes to press, I want to point to a recent publication—Helena Michie's *Sororophobia: Differences Among Women in Literature and Culture*—that makes the concerns I am about to raise its focus. Michie even briefly addresses Irigaray (in her introduction and conclusion) and deems her a theorist who does not attend to women's differences. Though we clearly share this view (with many other feminists, too, I might add), I try to set my own complaint against the background of Irigaray's more promising forays into what I deem her theories of "fractured sameness" and radical "implication."

†Rose, *Sexuality in the Field of Vision*, 14. One notes that Rose herself, at the level of pronouns ("our," "us"), is forced into the kind of homogeneity she is seeking to attack.

tween one and two.* Indirection, fittingly, for this sense of entanglement, connotes Irigaray's refusal to give precise accounts of mirror images.

By contrast, "implication"'s *incriminating* shades seem, on the surface, less applicable to Irigaray: the senses of complicity, guilt, even plotting. And yet, as has become familiar to feminists, too often 'the other woman' in the mirror bleeds for 'us', instead of (with) 'us'; 'we other women' bleed for 'them' instead of (with) 'them'.† In this sense, 'the other woman's' placement *implies* 'us'; 'our' positions determine and sustain 'her' own, as 'our' images split from each other along the axes of class, religion, race, attraction, attractiveness, age, etc. Spivak—recall her famous essay on Kristeva, "French Feminism in an International Frame"— was among the first post-structuralist feminists to read women's mirrorings as fractured by their differences. Echoing Spivak, Gallop, in turn, explored the simultaneous distance and proximity between (desiring) women by underscoring "the feminist socioeconomic rift . . . [the] resemblance and difference between the bourgeoise woman writer and the other woman who may be our mother, lover, cleaning woman, or secretary."‡ The mirroring relation must be read, then, as chipped by guilt, pity, desire, aggression, sympathy. 'We' are plotted both with 'the other' and in the plots against 'her'. By looking in 'her' mirror, 'we' may, in Rose's terms, "recognize our part in intolerable structures." If other women are not quite 'me', being so near that 'they' cannot have 'me', 'they' are also so near 'me' that 'they' can no longer have 'themselves'. Feminine mirroring uncovers the fallacy of any economy that counts on discrete free individuals. Feminine mirroring, one might say, "speaks" a

---

*Irigaray's notion of feminine mirroring may help us to avoid what reads as a lump-collectivity in the work of Fredric Jameson (see his notions of collectivity in *The Political Unconscious: Narrative as a Socially Symbolic Act*).

†One (you, we) can clearly get a sense of the pronoun problems encountered here. Any given woman can be simultaneously "the other woman" (in one respect, or in one sign 'she' wears) and part of the 'we' that excludes her as 'other' (a lesbian woman in a group of straight women, or a black feminist in a group of white feminists—to offer standard examples). In this respect, of course, the multitude of differences 'one' might wear as signs in a moment (Nebraskan, Hindu, adolescent, straight, attractive, etc.) may make any sense of 'we/them' seem impossible, even absurd. And yet, as 'we' know, *in any given context*, certain of 'our' signs seem more dramatic than others, more determinative for 'our' sense of inclusion or exclusion. This ungraspable multitude of signs, worn in a moment, is another sense of material opacity, as 'I' discuss below.

‡Gallop, "Annie Leclerc," 153–54. Not surprisingly, Michie, too, interprets the status of 'the other woman' in Spivak and Gallop, though at greater length than I do here, in *Sororophobia*. The scenario with which she ends her book nicely illustrates what I would theorize as "radical implication."

difference where there was thought to be sameness and speaks implications where there was thought to be difference.

Irigaray's mirroring as "implication" finds support in two essays that, together, form a feminist primer on women's differences: Biddy Martin and Chandra Mohanty's "Feminist Politics: What's Home Got to Do with It?" based on Minnie Bruce Pratt's sterling essay, "Identity: Skin/Blood/ Heart." Analyzing Pratt's autobiography, Martin and Mohanty reconceptualize relations of female sameness. They begin by lamenting the white-bread, homogenizing tendencies in Western bourgeois feminism, which "[add] on difference without leaving the comfort of home."[5] Yet they also find deficient the deconstructive turnstile politics of indeterminacy, since "the claim to a lack of identity or positionality is itself based on privilege, on a refusal to accept responsibility for one's implication in actual historical or social relations."[6] They appear, in this way, to theorize implication, exploring the shifting valuations and boundaries of "home" in Pratt's story, highlighting her entanglement in specific oppressions:

"I will try to be at the edge between my fear and outside, on the edge at my skin, listening, asking what new thing will I hear, will I see, will I let myself feel, beyond the fear," she writes. It is her situation on the edge that expresses the desire and the possibility of breaking through the narrow circle called home without pretense that she can or should "jump out of her skin" or deny her past.

Later they quote from Pratt's autobiography:

When, after Greensboro, I groped toward an understanding of injustice done to others, injustice done outside my narrow circle of being, and to folks not like me, I began to grasp, through my own experience, something of what that injustice might be. . . . But I did not feel that my new understanding simply moved me into a place where I joined others to struggle *with* them against common injustices. Because *I* was implicated in the doing of some of these injustices, and I held myself, and my people, responsible.[7]

Pratt's comments suggest the political expediency of holding to identity fictions ("myself, and my people") so as not to efface our view of other bodies upon which unjust social fictions have been written. By fingering these "formulas," as it were, not only might we feel the force of these fictions (which we help to sustain, after all), we might also feel the pulse of opacity beneath them. Irigaray's feminine mirroring, if conceived as radical implication, might theorize a seam between bodies close enough to make them intimate with each other's opacities ("what new thing will I hear, will I see, will I let myself feel") and close enough to incriminate them in one another's fictions (but, still, "without the pretense that [I] can or should 'jump out of [my] skin' ").

To perform this work, we would have to twist in an incriminating direction this bid that Irigaray makes for pleasure: "Each will not in fact have known the identity of the other, has thus lost self-identity *except for a hint of an imprint* that each keeps in order the better to intertwine" (*S*, 196; my emphasis). Irigaray seems to imagine that bodies intertwine themselves (better) through their "hints" of "imprints." They feel each other's opacities by feeling their *failure* fully to capture each other—since the "hint of an imprint that each keeps" acts as a barrier to fusion. Here might lie 'God' of a slightly different order than Irigaray conceives: 'God' as the (infinite) *set of imprints of others* who split us from ourselves and from each other, by making us feel what our fictions can't secure. Between two (or more) who exchange and produce their pleasure through their fractures *lie these many other bodies*, whose social fictions, which themselves cannot even finally be secured, make the two who exchange who they are. This 'God', in this respect, not only intimates us to each other; this 'God' incriminates us in our pleasures by making us feel a material opacity. This version of opacity, like vapor against the haze of night, might cause us to feel along bodily walls for what is concealed in our private exchanges: the many bodies between and around us, bodies that cut us into identity and that keep torn open the space of our desire. Only such an opaque intimation ("the hint of an imprint") assures that when the other (woman) bleeds we feel it.

Chapter 3

Lacking/Labor: "Labour Is Ever an Imprisoned God"

Irigaray's Anticapital

Irigaray cracks another door to guilt, though she herself opens it only part way: she raises the issues of capital gains and women's labor, but solely in ways that make women compatriots. Her writings sharpen perspectives, nonetheless, on how Victorian women might accumulate losses as erotic gains and how they might forge their desire as their labor, or at least as their vocation.

Since women's unpaid sexual labor (at home and at work) has barely received notice from theorists, Irigaray appears unique, if not eccentric, when she seems to suggest that *desire between women* produces something unaccounted by capitalist and Marxist standards.* Her chief provocation to established Marxist theories is to posit a different kind of productivity—one that remains at least partially beyond the brink of capitalist production and exchange.† "Anticapital" will be my name for this different

*Paid sexual labor—prostitution—has received much attention, of course. And unpaid sexual labor has been duly noted as a necessary topic to address, but usually in the context of theorists' confessions that they will not address it. See my remarks on Delphy, for example, on p. 65. A notable exception is Gayle Rubin in her famous essay, "The Traffic in Women: Notes on the 'Political Economy' of Sex." Quite striking as well at this point in time is the fact that, with so much attention being paid to Irigaray's writings, critics who address her Marxist theories seem to fall into two distinct groups: those who dismiss these essays with only a surface address to her words on the page, and those who summarize Irigaray's points, with little or no interpretive nuance.

†Recall that Marx defines productive labor as labor that directly produces surplus value and capital.

productivity, by which gain is supplanted by acquisitions of pleasurable loss.* Irigaray shows herself backlit, then, by another shade of spiritual materialism: those forms of women's unwaged labor that remain materially concealed *as labor* and that remain materially unaccounted for by wages.

Irigaray, in this way, concentrates on what appears only at the limits of Marx's theory, since his labor theory of value examines only those exchanges *measured* by a wage. Recalling her tangle with Lacan at his limits, Irigaray's passion for pressing beyond established brinks forces her necessary break from Marx: she must break beyond his calculations.† Just as Irigaray ignores (or sometimes scorns) Lacan's passion for schemata, graphs, set theories, and equations, she nowhere comments on Marx's calculations. In his essay on commodities, Marx proves to be a strict accountant, following out in mathematical detail the capitalist logic of value and determining the points at which this logic slips. Irigaray, by contrast, does not calculate the "surplus value" that men extract from women (though she uses this term), because no known method of accounting can grasp it.‡

Domestic and sexual labor for men is unwaged and unseen—not viewed, that is, as constituting labor. Irigaray, of course, is far from alone in her focus on women's concealed forms of labor. A broader, heated context exists for feminist materialist analysis of work that uncovers both capitalist and Marxist limits. Take, for example, the ongoing domestic labor

---

*Though this conception may bring to mind Bataille in "The Notion of Expenditure"—and Irigaray, I believe, has been influenced by Bataille in ways we must come to understand and discuss—my stress on anticapital (which I claim for Irigaray) involves *productive* loss and, perhaps more oddly, *accumulations* of loss. In Bataille, the sense is different, insofar as he examines "the principle of loss" in the guise of "unproductive expenditures: luxury, mourning, war, cults, the construction of sumptuary monuments, games, spectacles, arts, perverse sexual activity (i.e., deflected from genital finality)" (362). (See also Bataille's explanations of "*potlatch*" in the same essay.) What Irigaray does share with Bataille, I imagine, is the notion of "possessor[s]" "*at the mercy of a need for limitless loss*" (367).

†See Stuart Schneiderman (*Jacques Lacan*) on Lacan's use of set theory and Stephen Melville ("Psychoanalysis and the Place of *Jouissance*") on Lacan's use of graphs and schemata.

‡In her study on Victorian single women, Martha Vicinus confirms that one cannot even calculate how many women have their labor extracted for free: "As late as 1901 only 45.5 percent of spinsters over forty-five were occupied in some form of paid employment; 54.5 percent were listed as retired or unoccupied. How many of this 54.5 percent wanted to work or *worked without pay for their families* or worked part time is impossible to calculate" (*Independent Women*, 27–28; my emphasis).

debates that specifically address invisible labors and the versions of "productivity" that define them. All of the debates' participants share a fundamental observation as their starting point: the labor specific to women in capitalism receives no account in orthodox Marxism.* Moreover, the domestic-labor debates often stall on a central question—is domestic labor productive or unproductive for capitalism?—since on this question of productivity hangs the visible status of women's work as exploited.†

According to Paul Smith, in his essay "Domestic Labour and Marx's Theory of Value," women's domestic labor is *not* productive labor, since it is "concrete labour" (cooking, cleaning, child care, etc.) that "produce[s] use values for immediate consumption."‡ Though domestic labor may be functional for the smooth operation of capital, domestic labor remains *external* to the circuits of capitalist production and exchange. The proof of this externality, argues Smith, is that "domestic labour cannot be expressed in a definite magnitude of value."[1] Though "concrete," "immediate," and unquestionably there, it cannot be measured.

Smith, like Lacan, invokes a systematic exclusion of women's specificities, suggesting—too indifferently for feminists?—that measurements, like words, cannot encompass categories that, by definition, remain outside the signifying systems that comprehend them only in the negative ("not-man," "not-man's work"). Feminist responses to Lacan, as we have seen, and to Marxists like Smith, turn on making these exclusions "appear," on giving material (and sometimes mystical for the sake of material) form to their appearance. In the domestic labor debates, these

---

*Increasingly, however, the discussions of women and men with regard to the international division of labor are complicating both these questions and accounts. See Lim, "Capitalism, Imperialism, and Patriarchy"; Haraway, "Manifesto for Cyborgs"; and Spivak, "Political Economy of Women."

†Christine Delphy relates this anecdote, indicating what is at stake in the claim that one is exploited: "At this time (between 1968 and 1970) I was taking part in one of the two groups which initially helped create the new feminist movement in France. I was very annoyed—and I was not alone, though like the hero of Catch 22 I thought I was being personally got at!—by one of the men in this mixed group. He claimed that the oppression of women could not be equal in importance to that of the proletariat since, he said, although women were oppressed, they were not 'exploited.' I was well aware that there was something wrong with this formulation. In that group at least we recognized that women earn half as much as men and work twice as hard: but apparently their oppression nevertheless had, in theory, no economic dimension!" (*Close to Home*, 15).

‡See Paul Smith, "Domestic Labour and Marx's Theory of Value," 204. Although Smith is by self-designation a "post-Marxist" theorist, on this issue he represents an orthodox Marxist view.

efforts turn on productions of the term "productivity." Maria Dalla Costa, for instance, champions her unorthodox view by broadening "productivity" to include productions she deems to be "indirect."* What domestic labor "indirectly" produces, Dalla Costa argues, is the commodity "labour power." To the extent that domestic labor reproduces the necessary conditions for producing labor power, domestic labor contributes to this commodity's exchange value, and thus, indirectly, to surplus value.

Although Christine Delphy also begins by defining women's housework as exploited, unaccounted, unpaid labor, she takes another tack altogether in *Close to Home: A Materialist Analysis of Women's Oppression.* Terming herself a feminist materialist rather than a Marxist, since there can be no account in Marxism of "the exploitation of the unwaged," Delphy does not concern herself with productivity *in relation to capitalism.*[2] Instead, she theorizes what she terms "the domestic mode of production": a separate system of production, circulation, and consumption but one that "meets" and "interpenetrates" the capitalist mode of production.[3] It is precisely domestic labor's *nonmarket value,* Delphy claims, that *causes* its unpaidness. In the domestic mode of production, consumption is not fully separate from production (the family consumes the meal the domestic laborer has just produced). Circulation, moreover, takes the form of transmitting patrimony—family property and possessions—from one generation to the next. In this way, women's frequent positions as noninheriting, unpaid workers in the domestic mode of production "reconstitute" certain relations within capitalism: namely, divisions into possessors and nonpossessors.

Delphy theorizes, then, a productivity that is forged *outside of capitalism's visible circuits of exchange.* Her link to Irigaray, on this point, is crucial. True, the possibility of connecting Delphy to Irigaray seems, on the surface, slim: Delphy mentions Irigaray in footnotes, charging her with "idealist problematics," and, predictably, with essentialism (Delphy signs herself a strict constructionist).[4] Strange, then, that Irigaray and Delphy join hands across the body of Marxism, for Irigaray, like Delphy, concerns herself with a different kind of productivity from the one Marx examined. Like Delphy, Irigaray protests Marx's labor theory of value that, by its focus on work for wages, privileges the analysis of men's exploitation. Irigaray and Delphy both examine women not only as those who do not pos-

*For other views in these debates, see Margaret Benston, "The Political Economy of Women's Liberation"; Lise Vogel, "The Earthly Family"; Angela Davis, "The Approaching Obsolescence of Housework"; Eli Zaretsky, *Capitalism, the Family and Personal Life*; and Heidi Hartmann, "The Unhappy Marriage of Marxism and Feminism."

sess property but also as those who are themselves possessed (since, for Irigaray, women *are* commodities).*

Both theorists, led by these lines of attack, seem to stress women's ties to each other *as a class*, oppressed through the domestic and sexual labor they perform for men. Notwithstanding the different placements of working-class women and bourgeois women (usually designated "bourgeois," says Delphy, with reference to their husbands' class positions), women mirror for each other their roles as sexual objects.† This stress on the mutual recognition of women around their unacknowledged sexual labors *joins* Delphy to Irigaray at the precise location of their theoretical *splitting*: they join hands across women's bodies. Although she confesses that sexuality remains "outside the field of my analysis," Delphy emphasizes that "*all* the aspects attached to sexuality are as important and as *material* as economic oppression."[5] (And here we note, again, that what escapes Marxist theory is something quite material.) For Delphy, sexuality locates an undeniable site of class struggle. Irigaray makes this particular site the focus for her reading of Marx.

In fact, Irigaray's clever, full-bodied analogy to Marx's treatise on

---

*Indeed, Delphy's argument that bourgeois women are not bourgeois hinges on this point: "The fact that they exercise, or seem to exercise, certain bourgeois prerogatives arouses indignation because they are seen as doing this unjustifiably, i.e. they are usurping a position. And not only are they usurping it and posing as bourgeois (thereby escaping their 'normal' treatment), but it is precisely because they are the property of bourgeois men (because they are possessions and *not* bourgeois) that they can pose as bourgeois and deny the fact that they are possessions!" (*Close to Home*, 123). One can immediately understand this point with regard to Victorian women, since the struggle over married women's property rights comprised a key campaign waged by Barbara Bodichon and others. The final Married Women's Property Act did not pass until 1893. In her introduction to *Barbara Bodichon and the Langham Place Group*, Candida Ann Lacey dramatizes this point: "In accordance with English Common Law, the husband had absolute control over his wife's property and her earnings; she was unable to dispose of her possessions without his consent; if her property was stolen, *he* was the victim of the theft; the legal custody of her children, too, belonged to him. . . . Mrs. Gaskell, for example, received none of the income from her writing but had to depend on her husband giving her a small allowance" (4).

†Many critics read Irigaray as treating women as a class, which she does seem to be doing at times since she does not make many distinctions between women who wear the 'woman' sign. Officially, however, she claims otherwise: "But women do not constitute, strictly speaking, a class, and their dispersion among several classes makes their political struggle complex, their demands sometimes contradictory" (*TS*, 32). Delphy firmly stresses women's common oppression as a class. Her discussions of bourgeois women, while crucial for understanding that women's class positions are often double, do not adequately address unmarried women or lesbians, whose class positions may not be referenced through a man (or at least, not directly).

commodities leads to her discussion of the economy of *"(so-called) masculine sexuality"* (*TS*, 184), which leads her directly back to desire. Irigaray scorns this masculine economy for its drives toward accumulation rather than use, for "the economy of desire—of exchange," she writes, "is man's business" (*TS*, 188). There are two points to note here. First, Irigaray uses "desire" and "exchange" interchangeably, as glosses on each other, making desire a central issue in how bodies exchange and are exchanged. Second, Irigaray regards accumulation, a calculable wealth, as the telos of masculine capitalist desire.

Expectedly, Irigaray critiques this endless, open-ended pursuit, characteristic of insatiable desire, which forms, simultaneously, the dynamic of capitalist accumulation and the drive of masculine sexual conquest:

> Wealth amounts to a subordination of the use of things to their accumulation. . . . What he desires is to have them all. To "accumulate" them, to be able to count off his conquests, seductions, possessions, both sequentially and cumulatively, as measure or standard(s).
>
> All but one? For if the series could be closed, value might well lie, as Marx says, in the relation among them rather than in the relation to a standard that remains external to them—whether gold or phallus. (*TS*, 174)

She is using Marx here to criticize extreme goal-driven desire, such as masculine and capitalist thrusts together display. She is also, through Marx, making evident that masculine capitalist desire *needs a lack always ahead of it* ("all but one?") in order to pursue its goals ("to have them all"), its standards ("gold or phallus"), and its pleasures ("conquests, seductions, possessions"). But here another swerve from Marx occurs. For Irigaray, we have seen, theorizes (and needs to theorize) an endless approach between women (or between men and women) without a(r)rival, without fusion, without conquest, without possession. The way she figures this endless approach is to imagine nonclosure (an "all but one?" drive) *between* two bodies who pleasure each other. She has stolen, then—herself something of a corporate raider—the dynamism, the excitement, the restlessness of capitalism, while reconceiving its central aim. In this way, the teleological thrust of masculine capitalist desire (along with its dynamic excitement) gets repeated and *redirected* as an endless approach that is headed toward an infinite space *between (not ahead)*—an approach pursued by those who pleasure themselves through a lack. This infinite-space-between-not-ahead is Irigaray's 'God'—'God' who "separates [woman] from herself . . . to infinity perhaps, but in the serenity of the spacing that is thus projected by/in her pleasure" (*S*, 201). She has put a version of capitalist desire between women's lips, and this capitalist desire, with its aim redirected to accumulating loss, is Irigaray's 'God'! This is Irigaray, as we have seen, about the business of courtly love, "pretending that it is we who put an obstacle to it," while pretending (here with Marx) to find its dynamics inimical to feminist materialist principles.

What does prove inimical to these principles is what engenders Irigaray's rage: women's nonparticipation in the lack they are made, materially and conceptually, to supply: "This means that the division of 'labor'—sexual labor in particular—requires that woman maintain in her own body the material substratum of the object of desire, but that she herself never have access to desire. The economy of desire—of exchange— is man's business" (*TS*, 188). The question of access arises once again. It is the axis along which Irigaray splits not only from Lacan but also from Marx. Irigaray is asking: Can women escape their constructions as commodities? Can women as 'woman' hold some different relation to desire, so that desire, lacking, produces something *for* themselves?*

Desire between women who feel lack between them, who turn their lack into "elegant absence," might spell the limits—so Irigaray imagines—of capitalist exchanges that can be precisely measured. Women as 'woman', positioned at the limits of received accounts, may already be forging, Irigaray envisions, an alternative economy of exchange "without accounts." She says "without accounts" since such exchanges could be measured only if we refer to economies from which these women-as-'woman' already (though only ever partially) escape. Such a spiritualization of economy, to the extent that it relies on escape and elsewhere, takes us back to desire at the mirrors. If women through their work of desire *for each other*, or for something beyond the gendered accounts that we currently know, "maintain," as Irigaray would have us believe, " 'another' kind of commerce, among themselves," "without accounts . . . without

---

*One might wish to explore what Irigaray does not investigate: to what extent a woman can require that another woman "maintain in her own body the material substratum of the object of desire, but that she herself never have access to desire." Some recent writings on butch/femme relations in lesbian communities have begun to raise these issues in sophisticated ways. See, for example, Joan Nestle, ed., *The Persistent Desire: A Femme-Butch Reader*. One line of investigation might suggest that, contrary to some feminist critiques of butch/femme (especially from the 1970's and 1980's), femme women may experience, quite powerfully, the possibility of having bold access to the lack that they supply for their butch partners, even while they maintain in their own bodies "the material substratum of the object of desire." A reading of Hollibaugh and Moraga's essay in Nestle's volume ("What We're Rollin' Around in Bed With: Sexual Silences in Feminism: A Conversation Toward Ending Them") might support such a claim, though the authors do not discuss their issues in these terms.

additions and accumulations . . . without sequence or number" (*TS*, 196–97), then this work of desire constitutes a different kind of productivity—a productivity that, at least partially, remains outside of capitalist productions. Women's work of desire thus produces a kind of *anticapital*, by Irigaray's description: a set of losses that accumulate through approaches without (ar)rivals. "It is only in the operation of exchange among women that something of this—something enigmatic, to be sure—can be felt."

We are back to where I ended Chapter 1, having taken a glide from opacity to lack to labor, having gleaned the logic of relations among these three terms. Now we are ready to see how Irigaray might cast lines to Victorian writers, who routinely, as we know, spiritualized labor and who often figured labor as a cure for their anguished concerns with desire and, even more overtly, with pleasure. In making this move, we transit into less generally Christian, and more specifically Protestant, purviews. With this transit, the scorn of accumulation shifts, the trust in capitalist ventures grows, and the reliance on mysticism wavers or wanes—though Brontë and Eliot break this contract.

Weber and Carlyle: Gospels of Work

Weber is an obvious place to begin—a chronological halfway house, one might say, between Irigaray and Carlyle. Not only does Weber elucidate the logic of capitalist accumulation to which Carlyle seeks an alternative; he also reveals the religious dynamics of accumulation *through* desire, which Irigaray, we have seen, rejects, then transforms into her version of wealth *as* desire.

Weber, for a start, locks our sights on a category which we have seen Irigaray resist: calculations. Beginning with a definition of capitalism that makes it not a greed for gain but a rational, calculated pursuit of profit through economic exchange, Weber ties its development to the evolution of rational bookkeeping in his two-part article, *The Protestant Ethic and the Spirit of Capitalism* (1904–5). Whereas Irigaray would wish to capture the capitalist drive without its acquisitions and make women, in particular, alive to material pleasure, Weber describes what she would reverse: he asserts that capitalism, early on, required a restless drive toward acquisition, combined with a disciplined indifference to the material pleasures that such a drive must bring. To Weber's mind, "a Protestant ethic" has historically provided capitalism's required combination of passionate accumulation and extreme frugality. This apparent contradiction, in fact, forms the linchpin of Weber's argument, taking the reader beyond his initial empirical observation that Protestants in Germany, in marked distinction to Catholics, were especially tied to economic rationalism.*

The difference between Protestants and Catholics, in this regard, finds explanation, Weber suggests, in the different character of their religious beliefs and not solely in historical and political factors. Conducting his own interrogation of spiritual and material borders, Weber rejects what he deems Marxism's oversimplified distinction between material base and superstructure—a rejection shared not only by Irigaray but also by Marxist thinkers such as Althusser.† Weber, then, seeks to determine "whether and to what extent religious forces have taken part in the qualitative formation and the quantitative expansion of [the] spirit [of capitalism] over the world" and "what concrete aspects of our capitalistic culture can be traced to them" (*PE*, 91). His study, ultimately, points to the "tremendous confusion of interdependent influences between the material basis, the forms of social and political organization, and the ideas current in the time of the Reformation" (*PE*, 91). At one time, he argues, capitalism needed religion's support to produce subjects compatible with its aims, even if the time for such necessary collaboration has by this time passed (for so Weber argues); Irigaray, of course, imagines that revised and radicalized religious concepts might now strike against such collaborations and compatibilities.

In making distinctions between various Protestant traditions, Weber must theorize something that Irigaray, late in the twentieth century, is still struggling to emphasize on behalf of feminists: the crucial role played by interpretations of *opaque and visible gains from labors*. The story of the Protestant ethic and the spirit of capitalism, as Weber tells it, turns on the shift from accepting opaque gains from labor to wanting them made visible and, more important, cumulative as signs of God's favor. In the push toward visibility, then—not, in this case, a visible opacity—lies the seed of a wish for material accumulation.‡ This push, along with the seed it bears,

---

*Weber's essay finds its ground in calculations of its own: He ties his analysis to empirical observations—"a glance at the occupational statistics of any country of mixed religious composition brings [it] to light with remarkable frequency" (*PE*, 35)—of the greater number of German Protestants, as opposed to Catholics, who are business leaders, owners of capital, and commercially trained personnel.

†See Althusser's discussion of Ideological State Apparatuses (1969) in *Lenin and Philosophy*.

‡Obviously, the suppressed wish for pleasure plays a major role here (at the very least through a pleasure in accumulation) though the pleasure logic must work its way out in the form of a seeming bid against it.

is something Weber traces as the shift from Luther's conception of callings to Calvin's more complicated doctrine of election.

With Luther and the Reformation, Weber argues, there developed the concept of "a calling" as one's divinely ordained duty in the world. Since the reformers deemed monastic life a selfish withdrawal from labor and the world, they regarded the Christian's labor in a calling as brotherly love. For Luther, this calling was "traditionalistic": God placed Christians in particular stations, and there each Christian was humbly to remain. For Calvin, says Weber, one's calling in life was far less certain because of what he believed was God's "election." Before the foundation of the world, God elected an unknown portion of humanity for salvation; for this elect, Christ died on the cross. Calvin held that believers could never know their status with certainty; the elect comprise God's "Invisible Church" and may not be marked by any externals—only by their blessed status after death. Calvin's followers, according to Weber, could not abide such a tense uncertainty—an opacity that might be covering over an ultimate loss— and so they began to stress "the recognizability of the state of grace" (*PE*, 110).

What resulted were attempts to possess election's "signs": worldly activity and worldly success. In this way, says Weber, not only was an unequal distribution of goods ordained by God—a belief clearly convenient for capitalism—but "asceticism was carried out of monastic cells into everyday life" (*PE*, 181). Here emerge the outlines of the Victorian worry over pleasure as something opposed to Christian labor. Weber writes:

> Contrary to many popular ideas, the end of this asceticism was to be able to lead an alert, intelligent life: the most urgent task the destruction of spontaneous, impulsive enjoyment, the most important means was to bring order into the conduct of its adherents. . . . By founding its ethic in the doctrine of predestination, it substituted for the spiritual aristocracy of monks outside of and above the world the spiritual aristocracy of the predestined saints of God within the world. (*PE*, 119, 121)

Bourgeois Christians, by this account, could make a bid for aristocracy, climbing the ladder of spiritual status as they "acquired" their way up the rungs of rising class position—a bid that Eliot criticizes through the character of Bulstrode in *Middlemarch*. The disciplined order that attended Christians' upward mobility necessitated, in its turn, anxieties about "impulsive enjoyment" that might short-circuit the drive to rise above. A moral accounting accompanied the rational orders of business, so that "the process of sanctifying life could thus almost take on the character of a business enterprise" (*PE*, 124). Furthermore, it is no great step, Weber implies, from the belief in labor as ascetic technique that could prove one's election (thus lessening opacity) to the belief that God might open the channels of profit for the ones he elects. From the much invoked parable of increasing the talent that God has entrusted—which Brontë invokes and reworks in *Villette*—to "the clean and solid comfort of the middle-class home as an ideal" (*PE*, 171), the Protestant ethic, Weber argues, stimulated narratives of a rise in "status" from "low to at least middle-class."*

Weber halts this story of an upward climb, however, to deliver a surprise that Irigaray would appreciate: the constant danger of this Protestant ethic to religion itself. In a striking passage quoted by Weber, John Wesley voices the contradictions inherent in the ascetic drive towards acquisition:

> I fear, wherever riches have increased, the essence of religion has decreased in the same proportion. Therefore I do not see how it is possible, in the nature of things, for any revival of true religion to continue long. For religion must necessarily produce both industry and frugality, and these cannot but produce riches. But as riches increase, so will pride, anger, and love of the world in all its branches. How then is it possible that Methodism, that is, a religion of the heart, though it flourishes now as a green bay tree, should continue in this state? . . . Is there no way to prevent this—this continual decay of pure religion? (quoted in *PE*, 175)

Weber here stages the kind of contradiction he is so good at spotting: the contradiction of a Protestant asceticism that, when most vigorously pursued, most vigorously converts to asceticism's opposite. Seen in this light, the Protestant ethic always enacts its own contradictions between "frugality" and "riches," "purity" and "decay," biting its tail in its drive towards "industry." Nor is it difficult to detect in this scheme a contradiction Protestants themselves were bound to notice: between the drive of their industrious Christianity and the dynamics of the older New Testament tradition that stood against wealth and even ownership. Not surprisingly, charity schemes, as ways of purifying this religion of accumulation, took on great importance in Victorian Methodism and Evangelicalism.

Another "solution" was to make labor an end in itself: to make accumulation and the visible signs of election retreat from view in the face of labor's visible badge of grace. This was the Victorian gospel of work, which has been a staple trope of Victorian studies for decades now. In his

---

*Here for orthodox Marxists, of course, is a problem with Weber: his use of the terms "status" and "low" derails his examination from the Marxian concern with class, not status, divisions in capitalism.

classic study, *The Victorian Frame of Mind*, Walter Houghton tells us that
"except for 'God,' the most popular word in the Victorian vocabulary
must have been 'work.'"[6] So closely was the concept of work connected
to both the articulation of 'God' and the smooth operation of the industrial
machine that work became a religious construct. "All true Work is Religion," for Carlyle (*PP*, 201).* As doubt about one's election impelled Cal-
vinists to work, so doubt about the very existence of the supernatural pro-
pelled the Victorian inheritors of a Puritan past. Yet, as Weber demonstrates was the case in ascetic Protestant sects, so, too, in mainstream
Victorian writers, such as Carlyle, Ruskin, and the Catholic Newman,
work was constructed as pleasure's opposite, the opposite of "the lust of
the moment."[7] What better parable to invoke, moreover, than the parable
of the rich man, Dives, who is banished from Abraham's bosom because
he made, in the words of Newman, "a sort of science of sensuality" while
the poor man, Lazarus, lay begging at his gate?†

If these writers customarily split work from pleasure, they also split
work from desire. But since Carlyle is the preeminent Victorian example
of this gospel of work, we should be struck by how his writings turn remarkably round on him, revealing that he (like Irigaray writing so many
years after him) deifies work that *is* desire. Consider this passage from
Carlyle's "Labour" (*Past and Present*):

> It has been written, "an endless significance lies in Work"; a man perfects
> himself by working. Foul jungles are cleared away, fair seedfields rise in-
> stead, and stately cities; and withal the man himself first ceases to be a jungle
> and foul unwholesome desert thereby. Consider how, even in the meanest
> sorts of Labour, the whole soul of a man is composed into a kind of real har-
> mony, the instant he sets himself to work! Doubt, Desire, Sorrow, Remorse,
> Indignation, Despair itself, all these like hell-dogs lie beleaguering the soul
> of the poor dayworker, as of every man: but he bends himself with free val-
> our against his task, and all these are stilled, all these shrink murmuring far
> off into their caves. The man is now a man. The blessed glow of Labour in
> him, is it not as purifying fire, wherein all poison is burnt up, and of sour
> smoke itself there is made bright blessed flame! (*PP*, 196)

Although Carlyle lists "Desire" as a "hell-dog," capitalism clearly feeds
on the purposeful activity of the flame that he enthusiastically designates

*Engels writes directly of Carlyle's "worship of labor." See his "Review of Thomas
Carlyle's *Past and Present*."

†Newman, *Sermons and Discourses*, vol. 2, 156–60. We will see how the parable of
Dives and Lazarus returns in Brontë's letters, but in such a way as to scold Charlotte's
object of affection and desire (her Belgian professor) for not responding to her sensual
needs.

"Labour." Carlyle, then, as we have seen with Irigaray, is enamored of capitalism's dynamic energy. Yet, clearly worried about its effects, he would seek to redirect the pursuit of profit towards a perpetuation of *labor*. For labor, consonant with the harmony it is thought to fashion among the men of all classes, creates inner harmony within the individual man, clearing away the uncontrolled growth that is said to characterize the man as a "jungle" (as if his work saves him from being an African while men are hard at work subjugating Africa). He further distances labor from the sexual tinge of the jungle (a kind of breeding gone wild) and from the "foul unwholesome desert" (a seedless, impotent place). The passage resounds, then, with sexual worry in the form of answers to it, though sexual connotations remain quite strong: labor produces man as man by "a purifying fire" that, for Carlyle, is seemingly other than desire and that produces such wholesome (though sexual?) results as causing "fair seedfields rise" and hell-dogs to shrink back into their caves (a Miltonic reference to female sexuality?). While leveling class distinctions in his euphoric praise of work, masking, we might note, the real exploitation of the "poor day-worker," Carlyle also draws a tight circle around men, making man-to-man work a compensation for averted sexuality.

Trying to keep his "flame" free not only from sexual contamination, therefore, but also from the taint of desire, Carlyle uses the figure of the "bright blessed flame" of labor in its spiritual sense: a restless seeking of "God the World-Worker" (*PP*, 170). In fact, although work, at first glance, appears merely to function as a "practical" "fact" (something we can grasp with surety amidst doubts), work, as Carlyle begins to unfold it, begins to mediate between worldly and spiritual materialisms. Work is the "practical material" means by which to fight the *bad materialism* of capitalism's "earthly Profit-and-Loss economy" for the sake of the *good materialism* of "God the World-Worker." Carlyle's spiritual materialism, such as we explored in Chapter 1, comes even more directly to the fore when he glosses this bad materialism as "temporary Semblances" (seen but untrue) and this good materialism as "eternal Substance" (true but unseen) (*PP*, 18). As Carlyle continues to preach labor's virtue, we see a spiritual materialist dynamic so prominent in Irigaray's theories as well: work collapses into desire, and this work of desire collapses into God. Carlyle, that is, concentrates his most intense focus on the spiritual "force" behind work (desire) and its spiritual telos (God). Desire is spiritually ordained, since it constitutes the "god-given Force" that "rises" "from the inmost heart of the Worker" (*PP*, 197). This "Force for Work," Carlyle says, "burns like a painfully smouldering fire, giving thee no rest till thou unfold it" (*PP*, 201). Labor, as the telos of this burning fire, this "Force for Work," is itself "the one God's voice we have heard" (*PP*, 170) and the "truest emblem there is of God" (*PP*, 170). Carlyle even makes Labor seem as if it *is* God—or at least, a god—when he pits "godlike Labour," "which is yet to be the King of this Earth" (*PP*, 170) against "brutal Mammonism." For "Labour," Carlyle writes, "is ever an imprisoned god, writhing unconsciously or consciously to escape out of Mammonism" (*PP*, 207)—as if Labour itself were a material opacity, "an imprisoned [material] god" whom we must *desire* (in order) to set free. Indeed, Carlyle would have all workers burn for this imprisoned god—for Labor—and through "the real desire to . . . work," do what Carlyle imagines can be done: "bod[y] forth the form of Things Unseen" (*PP*, 205).

For Irigaray, too, as we have discovered, a 'God'-ordained desire performs the work of "bod[ying] forth the form of Things Unseen." What is unseen, what she would body forth, is bodily opacity and its appearance, psychically, as "the force of pure loss."* Desire, that is, when pursued as labor, produces the visible form of loss, which can then be employed for productions of pleasure. We have seen that Irigaray captures the restless, insatiable drives of capitalist dynamics and places this dynamic force of loss between lovers, or between women, or between women lovers. Brontë and Eliot perform something similar when they make the labor of women's desire the imprisoned god they seek to body forth.†

*Here we must recall that Lacan's notion of the "particularity" of need, which gets "abolished" by its detour through signification, reappears "beyond demand" as "the force of pure loss" (desire).

†In *Desire and Domestic Fiction*, Nancy Armstrong also considers the Brontës as producing new figures for desire: "The new territories of the self that the Brontës sought to represent were *the unseen desires of women.* To represent the passions they claimed Austen had failed to reveal, the Brontës borrowed supernatural figures from fairy tale and figures of passion from romance; they made these materials represent the *unseen but very real emotional power of women*" (192; my emphasis). Strikingly, Armstrong's comments here, like my own, hover about an unseen real that clearly fascinates the Brontë sisters. Whereas Armstrong concentrates on the Brontës' sources in fairy tale and romance, I would underscore Charlotte's overwhelming reliance on Scripture (especially in *Villette*) for supernatural figures of passion. And though Armstrong's address to the question of labor (so insightful throughout her book) has dropped out altogether here, I would stress how the Brontë novels (again, *Villette*, so dramatically) co-fashion work with desire. For another recent discussion of Charlotte Brontë in relation to Victorian discourses on desire, see Mary Poovey, "Speaking of the Body: Mid-Victorian Constructions of Female Desire." Although this essay largely addresses the prostitute as the chief example of a contradictory representation of female desire, Poovey stresses that "literature was the nineteenth-century . . . genre that most readily accommodated mid-Victorian women's efforts to represent female sexual desire" (38). More telling, to

Victorian Women Essayists: A Plea to Carlyle's "God of Labour"

Work was an issue separate from women, or so one might conclude, since Victorian men generally distinguished between "work" (God's call to labor in the world) and feminine "missions" (that befit bourgeois ladies stationed at home). If Carlyle, for example, did not address women separately from men, it's because he did not address women at all. His supposedly generic use of "man" remained gender specific to men, as Carlyle makes clear in his praise of work as a harmonizing force—"the man is now a man"—and in his appeal, at the close of *Past and Present*, to "one grand Host" of workers: "Ploughers, Spinners, Builders; Prophets, Poets, Kings; Brindleys and Goethes, Odins and Arkwrights; all martyrs, and noble men, and gods are one grand Host. . . . Noble every soldier in it; sacred, and alone noble" (*PP*, 294).

Ruskin, by contrast, did address both women and men. And the differences between them, according to Ruskin, could not be more obvious: men work, while women (denigrated to their positions of queenly elevation) support men's quests in the world. In his by-now-infamous lecture, "Of Queens' Gardens," Ruskin underscores familiar Victorian rationales for why women should work for men at home. Not so curiously, these rationales center on a peculiarly Victorian bourgeois rendition of courtly love. Ruskin argues for *chivalry at home* as the best safeguard against domestic anarchy. 'Woman' is to be for 'man' (her bourgeois knight) not his slave but the queen of his household, for "where that true faith and captivity ['of blind service to his lady'] are not, all wayward and wicked passion must be" (QG, 141). Here the aristocratic discourse of courtly love, itself always a discourse on desire, fashions the bourgeois household as a harbor *from* the vagaries of passion—as if to substantiate Lacan's charge that the sexual relation seeks to dodge desire.* Confirming

my mind, Poovey's specific example (*Jane Eyre*)—buttressed by no others—is a novel so thoroughly shaped by a religious plot and by what Poovey herself underscores as "a religious vocabulary . . . [that] allow[s] Brontë] to preserve both sides of the contradictory image of woman at once" (42).

*James Kavanaugh, in a bold reading of *Wuthering Heights*, makes critical observations about the capitalist dynamic that could nicely apply to a reading of Ruskin's anxieties here and to the hopes of the Victorian women essayists to follow (see *Emily Brontë*, 92–93). Most importantly, Kavanaugh suggests that "the membrane" separating the industrial and domestic spheres is "too permeable," tending "to bring the disruptive need for dynamic individual growth into the family, and the disruptive need for col-

as well Irigaray's complaint that "the ritual of courtly love can be played out in language alone," in which "one style is enough" (*TS*, 104), Ruskin informs us that woman may be educated, but "all such knowledge should be given her as may enable her to understand, and even to aid, the work of men" (QG, 150); or, "speaking broadly, a man ought to know any language or science he learns, thoroughly; while a woman ought to know the same language or science only so far as may enable her to sympathize in her husband's pleasures, and in those of his best friends" (QG, 154).* A man at home with himself, his pleasure, and his fellow men.

What a woman's pleasures might be, or how her pleasures might find articulation along with her work, Ruskin does not address. He warns, rather, against a threat that may befall the educated woman at home, for theology, he says, is the "one dangerous science for women" (QG, 152). Why this should be so he does not directly say, though we can guess why Ruskin would try to bar women from one of the most powerful discursive domains of the Victorian period. He simply takes refuge in a curiously excessive diatribe against women's participation in theology:

> Strangest of all, that they should think they were led by the Spirit of the Comforter into habits of mind which have become in them the unmixed elements of home discomfort; and that they dare to turn the household gods of Christianity into ugly idols of their own—spiritual dolls for them to dress according to their caprice, and from which their husbands must turn away in grieved contempt, lest they should be shrieked at for breaking them. (QG, 153)

This passage represents only a portion of a longer section in which Ruskin himself shrieks about women's daring to "profanely touch" the science of theology, each sentence beginning with "Strange." Not only are women accused by Ruskin of making God in their own image, projecting God onto their mirrors (wearing the face of God for themselves?). They are also charged with dressing "spiritual dolls" according to their "caprice" (desire?). In this society, it is still men who "break" (in on) 'woman', especially when 'she' seeks to be at home with herself, her caprice, and her family of fellow dolls.

Ruskin is clearly anxious that women might discover in theology

---

lective support into the market-place" (95). Kavanaugh's reference to "the membrane" separating spheres of influence is something I develop fully in my reading of the *Middlemarch* "hymen." See Chapters 6 and 7 below.

*As we shall see, these are statements well suited to the character of Casaubon in *Middlemarch*.

some means by which they might (un)dress themselves.* Was he thinking of those women in Victorian women's movements who, by the aid of theological arguments and biblical metaphors, wrote passionately on behalf of women's right to work in a wider sphere? What space for women in this gospel of work did Victorian women try to force open? How did they assert their material claims in the discourses available to Victorian women? And how did they address or neglect the issues of work and desire, and work and class divisions?

As readers, we may feel poised at this point to imagine that Victorian women essayists could form the perfect bridge to the novelists by providing predictions of Irigaray's labor theories and revising those of Carlyle and Ruskin. Unfortunately, we will not find the going so easy or neat as this. In fact, to read these essayists is perhaps to conclude that Irigaray, Brontë, and Eliot look to be as much—if not more—the heirs to Carlyle, who ignored the question of women's work, as they are to the women who argued so vigorously for inclusion among the bearers of Carlyle's "bright blessed flame" of labor.

The issue of inclusion actually holds the key for understanding such a knotted logic. The essayists' (fairly) progressive arguments on behalf of (largely) bourgeois women force their essays down certain paths of persuasion: Treading carefully, and even somewhat lightly, they argue for women's inclusion in the wider world of work, asserting that women would take "home elements" with them as they join (keeping, in this way, their femininity and well-ordered families intact). As a consequence, the essayists do not provide the sly, biting depictions of cultural inequities we find in the writings of Irigaray and in the novels of Brontë and Eliot—not to mention bold depictions of women taking their pleasure with women. Indeed, Irigaray, Brontë, and Eliot all dramatize why conventional notions of inclusion do not work for women in the bourgeois realm of work; why women cannot just be "counted in" when they retain their specificities as women or wear class markers different from the dominant class. This is why—their interest in the *dilemma* of inclusion—a certain kind of labor must concern them: namely, a woman-to-woman exchange. These fascinations make them seem heirs to Carlyle because they so fervently

*Ruskin even warns against a second threat, in addition to theology, associated with a "morbid thirst": "I enter not now into any question of choice of books; only let us be sure that her books are not heaped up in her lap as they fall out of the package of the circulating library, wet with the last and lightest spray of the fountain of folly" (QG, 155). Ruskin's worry spills over his text as sexual innuendos proliferate, suggesting that women's laps might be wetted by (other women's?) books that veritably throw themselves at women readers "as they fall out of the package of the circulating library."

stress desire as a form of labor that lands one in the lap of God, bonds one to similarly gendered partners (lands one, that is, in the laps of other women), and bodies forth the form of things unseen.*

Why, then, given such conclusions, should we concern ourselves with Victorian women essayists? In large part, given their more conventional slant on inclusion, they form the perfect backdrop against which to see and understand how Irigaray, Brontë, and Eliot prove the more sufficient and exemplary pleaders to Carlyle's "God of Labour." But this assertion is somewhat disingenuous, even so; for it does not take enough account of how crucial a contribution to Victorian debates on women's work these essayists make—how much of the ground they cover must be traced by the novelists, too, even if the novelists cut a different path along it. The struggles we find in these essays, then, over the role of charitable work, the desire for professions and independent advance, and the insertion of others into bourgeois families all emerge as central issues in *Villette* and *Middlemarch*. Most important of all, the necessity of making a case for women's work by means of "god-talk" is something shared, to a striking degree, by all of these women.

Three Victorian essayists, in particular, make strong appeals to free the imprisoned god of women's labor: Anna Jameson, Barbara Bodichon, and Josephine Butler constitute a spectrum of (bourgeois) perspectives.†

---

*Ruskin is not the only writer to focus on what takes place in women's laps (see my immediately preceding note). Eliot, in *Middlemarch*, makes the novel's most dramatic scene one in which Dorothea's hand rests "on Rosamond's lap, though the hand underneath it was withdrawn." Hands on hands, hands on laps, and the "rising sobs" shared between women form the peculiar erotics of that scene, as we shall see.

†I certainly make no pretense here to an exhaustive study of the issues that surrounded the Victorian debates on "women and work" or the persons who engaged them. I select Jameson, Bodichon, and Butler for their diverse but overlapping concerns, and I confine myself to their ideas as expressed in the essays they produced—as opposed to their commitments as activists on several fronts (Bodichon and Butler, in particular). In a book recently published, *Victorian Feminists*, Barbara Caine takes a similar tack as she makes four key Victorian feminists the focus of her study (Butler among them). Caine explains her strategy: "This focus is in some ways a narrow one, but it allows for a detailed analysis of the intricacies of feminist ideas and beliefs which is not possible if one focuses on whole movements or on particular campaigns" (3). Caine is most anxious to establish the range of perspectives these feminists forged on "the situation of women, the nature of femininity, [and] the basis of sexual oppression" (3). For a helpful discussion of the term *feminist* as it applies to these Victorian essayists, see Caine, 4–7. For the movement side of Victorian feminism, see Patricia Hollis, ed., *Women in Public, 1850–1900: Documents of the Victorian Women's Movement*; Susan Kingsley Kent, *Sex and Suffrage in Britain, 1860–1914*; Ray Strachey, *The Cause; A Short History of the Women's Movement in Great Britain*; and Philippa Levine, *Victorian Feminism, 1850–1900*. In the discussions of women and work from this period, it is helpful to

Jameson, the most conservative, sketches a proposal that, in many respects, Eliot interrogates throughout *Middlemarch*: a scheme for women's unpaid, charitable vocations as Protestant sisters of mercy—a plan that moves women out of the home but not yet into the mainstream work force alongside men. By contrast, Bodichon, a key contributor to Victorian feminism, argues passionately for women's paid participation in "professions"—a possibility that Brontë, too, explores in *Villette*—thus staking a claim for women as working participants with men (in the bourgeoisie). Only Butler takes up, in any measure, an issue that Irigaray, Brontë, and Eliot elaborately hold in common: the issue of *whose work determines their invisibility* in capitalist accounts. For Butler, this issue takes the form of her address to prostitution and directs her attention, though somewhat indirectly, to the class relations among working-class women and "ladies."*

Anna Jameson authored two lectures—"Sisters of Charity, Catholic and Protestant, Abroad and at Home" and "The Communion of Labor," a follow-up to the first—which, we are told, were "delivered privately" in 1855 and 1856 and were "printed by desire." Jameson offers a plea for women's labor that is bound to a set of contradictory fears. On the one hand, Jameson fears divisions between men and women, lest women be ghettoized by "separate laws concerning women, as such" (*SC*, 162) and

---

keep in mind the important role of the census findings from 1851 that revealed a large surplus of unmarried women (half a million) who became, for many activists, the perfect justification for pleas on behalf of women's labor. For the worried lament that greeted these findings, read W. R. Greg's famous essay, "Why Are Women Redundant?"

*I find it difficult to choose between *middle-class* and *bourgeois* for the terms of this study. Along with many materialist scholars, I recognize the need to reexamine the strict Marxist division between working-class and bourgeois, given the vast number of "white collar" and "professional" workers (with the many ranks among them) now working for multinational capitalism. I find the distinction between "white collar proletariats" and "white collar representatives of capital" an extremely useful one at times. Even so, this being said, and it being likely that in some other context I would decide the matter differently, for the terms of this book I will purposely adhere to a division even Marx mitigated somewhat with his theory of the middle-class, petit bourgeois sector of professionals. My reason for designating middle-class professional bodies (the women writers I consider, for example) "bourgeois" is to mark, in the strongest terms, the way in which certain categories of work would seem to position their workers as representatives of capital (and steep them in certain sets of values), even if the individuals who fill these positions work against this grain. The more troubled questions of class identifications and splittings between women (and men) of seemingly different class positions and of the extent to which women can ever truly be bourgeois comprise a major focus for my study.

lest they lose the all-important support of (what she represents as) reasonable men. This fear of divisions between men and women leads her,
however, to divide between them. What divides them is money—for
Jameson grants to men the roles of paid laborers and paid professionals,
while she grants to women the roles of married and unmarried "nuns."
In fact, on first inspection, Jameson's views do not seem far removed from
Ruskin's theory of complements: distinct but inseparable roles for the
sexes, which she describes as "not the *division*, but the *communion* of labor"
(*SC*, 26). As a sign of a second intriguing contradiction, Jameson so ea-
gerly seeks the communion of women with men that she forges a plan for
a sisterhood. Underlying this sex segregation, nonetheless, runs Jameson's fear of women among themselves. Hence her anxious ridicule of a
Swedish woman's plan to found "a sort of universal feminine coalition":

> Her plan virtually excluded the cooperation of the masculine brain, thus di-
> viding what Nature herself has decreed should never be disunited without
> mischief, the element of *power* and the element of *love*. The idea was simply
> absurd and necessarily impracticable. Such an association of one half of the
> human species in an attitude of independence as regards the other, would
> have excited a spirit of antagonism in the men; and among the women,
> would have speedily degenerated into a gossiping, scribbling, stitching com-
> munity, unstable as water. (*SC*, 140–41)

Women among themselves, it would seem, cannot be trusted: love without power, unstable, too fluid. A sexual worry appears to inform this belief as well. The author, in another context, asserts that she is "no friend
to nunneries," since among the bad things bred by "any large number of
women shut up together in one locality" may be found "sick disordered
fancies" (*SC*, 70).*

"The great unacknowledged law of the Creator," as Jameson repre-

---

*Martha Vicinus's book, *Independent Women: Work and Community for Single Women,
1850–1920*, provides the best discussion to date of Victorian women's residential institutions. In fact, she points out that "Jameson's lecture brought to the attention of a
larger audience what religious women had been doing for years": "As far back as 1840
the Quaker Elizabeth Fry had founded the Institution for Nursing Sisters, which
trained respectable religious women to nurse the poor. The high-church Oxford Movement leaders John Henry Newman and E. B. Pusey had openly advocated, and then
assisted in, the revival of Anglican sisterhoods in the 1840s" (46). Vicinus is particularly
helpful for distinguishing differences between Evangelical, Dissenting, and High
Church sisterhoods (of which the last attracted the most bourgeois women to its ranks).
She also confirms the view we see Jameson expressing: "Although the single woman's
sexuality—active, failed, or denied—was most frequently discussed in code, it was always an issue for the opponents of women's single-sex communities and institutions"
(32).

sents it, that women should work alongside men, not in fully separate spheres, brings the author to the occasion for her essay. For Jameson has discovered that "the problem [of women's work] . . . has been partially solved by another church in other countries" (*SC*, 37). She refers to the Catholic church's institutions of charitable women, by which Catholic women "of all classes" have open to them a religious vocation in the social sphere, nursing the ill in hospitals and prisons, caring for orphans, teaching children, and even providing day-care for the children of poor working women. Jameson's enthusiasm—"I am anxious to show you the immense results of a well-organized system of work for women" (*SC*, 38)—inspires her short history of various charitable orders from the seventh century to the 1820s, when a Protestant community of the Sisters of Charity was formed on the Rhine (Florence Nightingale trained there). She records their way of life—not secluded in cloisters, not bound by vows of celibacy, but united under communal rules and often garbed in particular dress. Such opportunities to devote themselves to serious vocations outside the home, Jameson suggests, explain why so many educated women convert to Catholicism. Jameson urges that English Protestants appropriate this successful Catholic model, just as Protestants long ago appropriated Catholic cathedrals and colleges "for pious ends."

Indeed, the justification for such an extension of the domestic collective into the world may be found, argues Jameson, at the foot of the cross, in the words of Jesus to John and Mary: "When from the cross those memorable words were uttered by our Lord, 'Behold thy Mother! Behold thy Son!' do you think they were addressed only to the two desolate mourners who then and there wept at his feet? No—they were spoken, like all his words, to the wide universe, to all humanity, to all time!" (*SC*, 28). Christ provides the focus for a crossing—in this instance, not a crossing between genders but a crossing over and between family borders. Jameson imagines a domestic collectivity. Yet the implications of such configurations—here, quite seriously, an infinity of others between one and two—exceed the traditional conception of home that Jameson never truly questions. Additionally, though she offers this religious model to women of all classes, Jameson (like Irigaray, in this regard) tends to privilege a single class by not seriously addressing any others. If anything, at times, she paints the working class as ill-behaved and claims, at one point, that low hospital wages prohibit the hiring of "a better class of women" (*SC*, 103). Jameson is clearly most comfortable with "women of refined habits . . . holding a certain position in society" (*SC*, 112) who, to the amazement yet admiration of all around them, make a vocation of charitable endeavors. Here lies the benefit of having something that one can give up: against the backdrop of one's class condescension—sacrificing time and labor, that is, for the classes "below"—one's renunciation can be read more easily as "freely" chosen, instead of as one's duty towards men. That is to say, since this is a labor model of "sacrifice" and "charity" (unpaid) it works most persuasively as a means for bourgeois women to make their Christian renunciations visible. It comes as no surprise, then, that the book's title page is followed by a verse tribute to Florence Nightingale. Nor are we surprised that towards the end of the second lecture, "The Communion of Labor," Jameson presents an impassioned defense of "service without pay":

> The idea in this country that every thing has a money value, to be calculated to a farthing, according to the state of the market, is so ingrained into us, that the softest sympathies and highest duties, and dearest privileges of Christians, are never supposed to be attainable unless sold and paid for by the week, or month, or year. This is so much the case, that those who visit the poor people can hardly banish from their minds the conviction that there is some interested motive, some concealed, selfish object in doing so. Yet if once brought to believe that there is really only the wish for their good, how beautiful and how blessed becomes the intercourse! The two meanest forms of sensuality and selfishness in our lower classes, the love of money and the love of drink, are best combated by the combined religious and feminine influence. (*SC*, 276)

Covering over bourgeois support of money values and capitalist markets, Jameson constructs "our lower classes" as a group in league with the capitalist machine, insofar as they love the money that capitalism "calculate[s] to a farthing." By contrast, those who can afford to give, not sell, their time are linked with "the softest sympathies and highest duties, and dearest privileges of Christians." Thus Jameson elevates charity, and by implication those classes who perform it, above paid labor. Though she seeks to establish institutions that would enable poor women (working-class women and prostitutes) to join the ranks of the unpaid (!) by providing them with room and board and charitable vocation, this rise up to the "dearest privileges of Christians" would still stand them, presumably, on a lower step than their more refined sisters.*

*Even though "enormous numbers of women volunteered" for these services, so that "they were the largely unpaid foundation of the social service system" (Vicinus, 22–23), class distinctions between women were often dramatically maintained in religious communities. As Vicinus relates: "Poorer women were encouraged to become lay sisters, doing much of the daily drudgery of the community, while the better off became choir sisters (occasionally bringing their maids with them to serve as lay sisters)" (55).

Jameson's essay points up the contradictions that attend an appeal for women's unpaid participation in a wider sphere of service. On the most obvious level, the unpaid status of these charitable vocations represents no economic advance over women's unpaid status as domestic and sexual laborers in their homes. Women, by this plan, are merely offered a sphere of activity outside of the family—admittedly, an advance for bourgeois women—in which to perform the kinds of labors they perform in their homes (caring for children, nursing the ill, etc.). Neither financial nor sexual independence for unmarried women results from this arrangement, since they would have to remain celibate, while leading lives of charitable service in exchange for room and board.* The only real gain for women in this plan accrues to bourgeois married women who, "holding a certain position in society," might discover opportunities in a realm beyond their homes, where they might practice a recognizable renunciation.†

Barbara Leigh Smith Bodichon, like Jameson, makes use of theological arguments and scriptures to support an appeal that, unlike Jameson's, takes the issue of women's work beyond the realm of charitable institutions. Though she frequently uses the general term "work," Bodichon specifically argues for women's paid participation in "professions" as doctors, shopkeepers, accountants, mechanics—work that will provide women with what she refers to as "livelihoods." The founder of the *English Women's Journal* (1857), an active campaigner for key pieces of legislation affecting women, and one of George Eliot's most trusted friends after they met in the 1850s, Bodichon, Gillian Beer suspects, was a likely model for Dorothea in *Middlemarch*.‡ In her influential tract *Women and Work*, written in 1857, Bodichon makes women's dignity before God the

*Vicinus's discussion of the celibacy issue in religious communities highlights its contradictions: "A single woman was trapped in a paradox: the price of independence was the reinforcement of sexual stereotyping. Her personal ambition had to be hidden from herself and society under the cloak of self-sacrifice" (16). This bind is precisely what makes the "heroines" of *Villette* and *Middlemarch* such instructive studies in an autoeroticism born of lack.

†Sophia Jex-Blake, founder of the London Medical School for Women, stands as a particularly dramatic example of the problems women faced if they sought paid labor. Margaret Todd, in *The Life of Sophia Jex-Blake*, quotes this woman's father from a letter: "I have only this moment heard you contemplate being *paid* for the tutorship. It would be quite beneath you, darling, and I *cannot consent* to it. Take the post as one of honour and usefulness, and I shall be glad. . . . But to be *paid* for the work would be to alter the thing *completely*, and would lower you sadly in the eyes of almost everybody" (67, 68–69).

‡For Bodichon's unorthodox childhood, her social ostracism, and her central role in campaigns for women's property rights and the right to vote, see Hester Burton, *Barbara Bodichon, 1827–1891*, but especially Sheila R. Herstein, *A Mid-Victorian Feminist: Barbara Leigh Smith Bodichon*. For Beer's comment, see *George Eliot*, 165.

keynote of her plea for women's labor. The title page of an American edition bears a quotation from the apostle Paul—"For there is neither Jew nor
Greek, there is neither bond nor free, there is neither male nor female, for
ye are all one in Christ Jesus." As if to underscore its leveling of class and
gender distinctions, Bodichon pairs the apostle's language with an excerpt
from Elizabeth Barrett Browning: 'woman' should work, "otherwise she
drops / At once below the dignity of man / Accepting serfdom."*

Not surprisingly, Bodichon strategically appeals to the Christian
principles of her audience. What better way to gain sympathy for liberal
treatment of women than to pit Muslim countries against the Christian
countries of the United States and Great Britain on the issue of women's
rights? The Christian countries, through their superior religions, she implies, have acknowledged, in contrast to Muslim countries, that "women
are God's children equally with men" (*WW*, 13). This accepted religious
principle must now gain full play by making women equal partners in the
world of work. Bodichon makes her readers take note that "the men of

---

*Ironically, the American edition's introduction (1859) to Bodichon's essay, written
by an American woman, trots out and reinforces the most damaging divisions that exist
along lines of gender, race, and class. After a long preamble, for example, on the need
for American girls to receive in-depth training in the domestic arts, so as to make of
each "a qualified housewife," the author pens an extraordinary passage that could not
be less in keeping with the spirit in which Bodichon quotes St. Paul: "We must, year
after year, receive into our families demi-savages—foreign people, ignorant of our
modes of life, grown up in habits adverse to them. We must skillfully teach, firmly
discipline, and patiently bear with them. We must do this for the love of God and our
neighbor—*and for self preservation*; and when this, perchance, is done, we must see them
pass off into their vocation, married life, and take to our homes a new raw force! We
know nothing of Southern life from observation, but we have no reason to believe that
the Southern mistress of slaves has an easier task than the matron of the free North"
(*WW*, 7). That the "Southern mistress of slaves" may be so comfortably compared with
"the matron of the free North" says much about conditions of domestic servants—
unmistakably constructed as outsiders to the family in the designations "demi-savage"
and "foreign." And though the biblical injunction of love for God and neighbor provides the rationale for this supposedly selfless education of one's servants, the italicized
phrase ("*and for self preservation*") bears the single greatest emphasis in the passage. But
this is not the only such juncture in the introductory essay that jars against everything
Bodichon will urge. In counterdistinction to Bodichon's stress on women's participation in professions, the author emphasizes marriage and family as woman's vocation
("We are not among those who claim or desire the right of suffrage for women. We
believe that her exemption from direct political duties is a privilege and blessing to her"
[*WW*, 8]). It is of greatest import, it would seem, to educate women in the "admin-
istration of the family" so that we will no longer "see husbands obstructed, teased, dis-
appointed, accepting life in a boarding-house as a refuge from homes which their young
dreams had glorified with domestic happiness, found too late not to be the 'Bliss that
has survived the fall' " (*WW*, 8–9). In the American edition, Bodichon's essay comes
on the heels of such injunctions almost as an attempt to counteract its introduction.

those races ['the Moors, Turks, and other Mohammedans of Algeria'] keep their women entirely immured and entirely ignorant, and all their prejudices as husbands and Mohammedans are strongly against even allowing them to leave their houses" (*WW*, 25). Presumably, any reader who would condemn Mohammedans for immuring women would follow the logic of the (Christian) girl's "religious and inquiring mind" which seeks a wider domain beyond her home life.

As part of Bodichon's strategic appeals, she suggests that women will become "more strongly feminine" by serious work, on the logic that "you do not call a lioness unfeminine, though she is different in size and strength from the domestic cat, or mouse" (*WW*, 21).* A more promising rumination takes her closer to interests we have seen in Irigaray, and will encounter again in the novels. Bodichon speculates that with women's professionalization new associations of women might be formed. Such associations might take the form of practicing medicine in groups with one another, of opening shops together, or, more interesting yet, of working and caring for their families cooperatively. Writes Bodichon: "Some reformers in England think that if women entered professions, some association of families together would probably take place, and the woman born with a natural gift for managing domestic concerns would arrange for the association, leaving the Doctor her time, and the newspaper editors free from the cares of cooking and cleaning" (*WW*, 19). Of course, for all of the possibilities this plan might offer, Bodichon does not speculate on the hierarchical or nonhierarchical structuring of such associations between domestic laborers (in this scheme, professionals?) and professional women.

At the time she is writing, the few cooperative ventures open to women are religious sisterhoods and schools. Bodichon, like Jameson, sees this promise of work for women as a prime reason why women join the Catholic church. Like Jameson's, Bodichon's essay grounds its claims in theological injunctions about women's status. It is *God's command* that no Christian be idle; professions save women's souls from the devil and serve to strengthen them more than marriage does; work in the world enables women "to stand as dignified rational beings before God" (*WW*, 30). Not without purpose does Bodichon bend Christ's Golden Rule in the direction of women's oppression: "Oh, girls, who are now suffering in this battle, remember your sufferings when you have children, and do unto

---

*By comparison, Emily Davies, Bodichon's contemporary, makes a more timid plea: "It is certainly not easy to see why it should be unfeminine for a girl to sit in her father's office, under his immediate eye (and protection, if needed) gradually acquiring some experience" (*Thoughts*, 11).

them as you would you had been done unto!" (*WW*, 21). Bodichon's special appeal to Christ is also characteristic of many Victorian feminists, as
we shall see with Butler. Twisting a scene from the gospels, Bodichon has
Christ hopefully engaging a woman whom he thinks might be "a new
worker for the truth" (*WW*, 29). With clear disappointment (Bodichon's
interest becomes apparent here) Christ discovers that this worker is
blinded by domestic concerns, for she has called to him: "Blessed is the
womb that bare thee, and the paps which thou hast sucked"—a line that
in the Bible bears no trace of censure.

Finally, Bodichon ends her essay with remarks that rebut Jameson's
praise of unpaid service:

> Money is only a convenient representative of desirable things. It would be
> well if all should part with what they make, or what they do well for money;
> they will then know that some really want what they produce. What they
> produce will go to the right people, and they, the producers, will gain a
> power; for money is a power. . . . If for your needlework you get money,
> you know that your work goes to some one who wants it. You are not always
> sure of that if you give it away. . . . To make all work done for money hon-
> orable, is what we should strive for. To insist on work for love of Christ only,
> to cry up gratuitous work, is a profound and mischievous mistake. It tends
> to lessen the dignity of necessary labor; as if work done for daily bread could
> not be done for love of Christ too! (*WW*, 33)

There is no glorification of unpaid, charitable labor here, or of the refined
Christian women who undertake it. Bodichon argues that money is "a
power," though she clearly downplays its role as capital in markets of exchange, stressing instead its representative role as a sign of the buyer's
(even spiritual) appreciation ("you know that your work goes to some one
who wants it"). Perhaps Bodichon wants to preserve some sense of charitable accomplishment on the part of women, even as she wishes to see
them paid, since she imagines that the buyer's desire lets a woman know
to what extent the product of her labor is valued. By Bodichon's logic,
monetary exchange is a proof of *use* value that women "producers"
should not give up—for the love of Christ!

Bodichon senses the new independence that women's access to money
might bring. Expressing none of Jameson's worries that money obscures
the love of Christ, Bodichon anticipates women's fuller, which is to say
dignified, participation in the masculine economy. But what about
working-class women and prostitutes? Does their work serve the general
goal of independence for women? Do they in any way reveal the hopes of
bourgeois women to close the door on troubling reflections: for example,
reflections on women professionals who might still serve as unpaid do-

mestic and sexual workers in the private sphere while they serve as paid professionals in the public domain? Bodichon does not answer such questions. Josephine Butler begins to do so, once again using spiritual tropes.

Scholars most often mention Butler in the context of Victorian prostitution, for in 1870 she founded the Ladies' National Association for the Repeal of the Contagious Diseases Acts (those acts by which women living in specified garrison towns could be declared prostitutes and forcibly examined for venereal disease).* An Evangelical Christian, Butler published many books and articles, ranging from such titles as *Catherine of Siena* and *Salvation Army in Switzerland*, to *Women's Work and Women's Culture* (1869). Butler edited this latter book and wrote the long introductory essay that opens the volume.

Clearly, Butler is the one among the three essayists who, in discussing women's work, gives the greatest attention to inter-class relations and invisible labors. In fact, quite a bit like Brontë and Eliot, Butler offers surprising forecasts of Irigaray's views and turns them, as Brontë and Eliot do, towards a developing theorization of women's class fractures. Not only does she offer a version of Irigaray's analysis of the economy of "(so-called) masculine sexuality," but she also, amidst her conventional views, forces her reader to focus on bodies who operate as an excluded term in official accounts of the labor force. This consideration opens the door (actually, the closet) to Butler's scrutiny of domestic borders, which begins to allow her, though in tentative ways, to envision how others might penetrate the home. Though Butler stresses that hers are not solely "women's questions" and that she is not interested in blaming men—for "the evils in society . . . [are] the result of accident, and of the halting and unequal progress in society"—Butler, nonetheless, claims that men have failed Christian teachings and that "ladies" have often supported only parts of women's movements (*WWC*, iii, ix). Presumably with such men and women in mind, she suggests that the Scriptures, history, and human life all teach that "the class . . . which deprives, oppresses, or denies," in the end, suffers most—and here, we must note, she uses "class" to refer to gender divisions as well as to divisions in social stratification.

Though this statement—the oppressor suffers most—sounds like discursive mystification, the impact of the passage and of the essay as a whole has a surprisingly different character. One can interpret this assertion along the lines of Martin and Mohanty's "Feminist Politics: What's Home Got to Do with It?" They discuss the "price at which secure places are

---

*For discussions of Butler's activism and ideas, see A. S. G. Butler, *Portrait of Josephine Butler*; Judith Walkowitz, *Prostitution and Victorian Society: Women, Class, and the State*; and Barbara Caine, *Victorian Feminists*.

bought" and the pain of the bourgeois woman who must realize "that home was an illusion of coherence and safety based on the exclusion of specific histories of oppression and resistance."[8] Butler warns any would-be oppressors that though "God's kindness is in reserve" for all the oppressed whom she finds in the Bible ("the labourer deprived of just wages, the wronged widow, the neglected orphan" [xi]), one cannot rely on such claims while the impoverished classes (again, she refers to women as a class) live in despair.

Butler reserves her passion, however, for discussing prostitution—which, strikingly, she never names.* This discussion begins amidst her analysis of census findings and women workers—what the census reveals and what it leaves out of view:

> Nor does the census include among these breadwinners the armies of women, counted by the thousands in all our towns and cities, who are forced downwards to the paths of hell, by the pressure from above, through the shutting up of avenues to a livelihood by means of trade monopolies among men, and through the absence of any instruction or apprenticeship to qualify them for employment. Of this class of persons, and of this sorest of human griefs, we are never forgetful; no, not for a day. I speak for myself and for other *women* at least, my fellow-workers. The subject was thought too painful an one to be specifically treated in a volume for general reading . . . *there is no analogy whatever among men, however miserable certain classes of men may be, to the wholesale destruction which goes on from year to year among women*—destruction of bodies, of consciences, of souls. . . . At present, and indeed ever since the world began, this class of people have been generally left out of account in all theories of life, and in the framing of legislative and social measures, except so far as society has had to be protected against them . . . and so far as individual missionary efforts have attempted to restore a few of the fallen. (*WWC*, xvi-xvii)

Butler pinpoints here a class bottom that also comprises a sexual "hell." These are the "soldiers" in Carlyle's Host—"armies of women," Butler terms them—who do not get mentioned and who open indecorous holes in Carlyle's holy array. (Though "breadwinners" in Butler's eyes, these are the women who, for Coventry Patmore, have "spoiled the bread and spill'd the wine," according to his metaphor of a ruined Eucharist.)† If

---

*On Victorian prostitution, see Walkowitz, *Prostitution*; Poovey, "Speaking of the Body"; and the Victorian William Acton, *Prostitution*.

†Quoted in QG, 142. There, Ruskin writes: "Know you not those lovely lines—I would they were learned by all youthful ladies of England,—'Ah, wasteful woman!—she who may / On her sweet self set her own price, / Knowing he cannot choose but pay, / How has she cheapened Paradise! / How given for nought her priceless gift, / How spoiled the bread and spilled the wine, / Which spent with due respective thrift, /

anything has "cheapen'd Paradise," however, it is that "pressure from above"—"the shutting up of avenues to a livelihood by means of trade monopolies among men"—that has "forced [these women] downwards to the paths of hell." Where one would expect to find heaven in opposition to hell, one discovers, here, in heaven's place, "trade monopolies among men," as if Paradise itself has been displaced by financial fraternities. This latter phrase, by which Butler charges that the masculine work force has closed ranks on women ("shutting up . . . avenues"), calls to mind Irigaray's formulations of the traffic in women and women's consequent exclusion from making exchange.

As Butler presents it, this is explicitly a women's issue: "I speak for myself and for other *women* at least, my fellow-workers. . . . These our fellow-women are not forgotten by us." The hints of feminine mirroring (such as Irigaray might recognize) arise when Butler includes all classes of women in this lament. Invisibility (prostitution) lies at the center of women's specificity, since "*there is no analogy whatever among men.*" The question of invisibility and further, stronger implications of feminine mirroring surface as Butler's passage continues:

> I think that any theory of life, or of public arrangements is thoroughly un-scientific, as well as unchristian, which leaves this mass of people out of account, which deals with it as a fact which must be endured, but which must be as much as possible pushed into a corner, and fenced round so as to annoy and hurt the rest of the community as little as possible. Such economy resembles that of an indolent housewife who is aware of a certain chamber in her house which is full of the accumulated dirt of years, but which she fears to look into, hopeless of any possible cleansing, and the door of which she keeps carefully closed, content so long as the rest of the dwelling is not fatally infected by the presence of the evil. (*WWC*, xvii)

The "fallen" who "pursu[e] this calling"—Butler terms prostitution a "calling"—appear as a blank in society's account books, evincing, for Butler, an unscientific, unchristian "economy" (an interesting double-

---

Had made brutes men, and men divine!' " In Irigaray's terms, this woman's sin is obviously that she, as commodity, takes herself to market ("on her sweet self set her own price"). The lines are extraordinary, as is Ruskin's choice to quote them. 'Woman's' sexuality, joined to her divinity ("her priceless [sexual] gift" imagined *as* the eucharistic bread and wine), is contaminated by her self-controlled economy of desire (read: prostitution) expressed in capitalistic terms. Women who are sexually "wasteful" are imagined by Patmore *as capitalists*; they spoil the Paradise they might otherwise create if instead they would save their consumers ("knowing he cannot choose but pay") from the reckless desire that threatens to swamp the Protestant ethic—an ethic ("due respective thrift") that, according to Weber, is the very engine of capitalist accumulation.

barreled pejorative). Now comes Butler's fascinating analogy of the lazy housewife who "fears to look into" a chamber of her house, fearing, it would seem, her implication in "the accumulated dirt of years." That Butler should choose a feminine figure proves especially crucial. The housewife analogy implicates women of all classes in their "sisters'" plight. No clear separation can be made from "fallen" women who, after all, inhabit one's chambers (closet housewives?). As with Irigaray's feminine mirroring, the housewife is brought dangerously near to "the other within," who can be closed in upon ("the door of [the chamber] she keeps carefully closed") but not overtaken ("hopeless of any possible cleansing").

We may graft another reading onto Butler's housewife. Given the context of Butler's discussion and her passion "to restore a few of the fallen" (as we know from her efforts to repeal the Contagious Diseases Acts), Christ's parable of the woman's lost coin may linger in the background of Butler's passage. In this parable, God's passion for the unredeemed is compared to the ardor of a woman who, presumably not daunted by "the accumulated dirt of years," sweeps every corner of her house in search of a single lost coin: Christ/God is a housewife. Though the standard dogma on Christ has always been his downward mobility (he "made himself of no reputation, and took upon him the form of a servant" [Philippians 2:7]), to figure "that most female of men" as domestic would seem, for many, to be stooping too low. Yet Butler stresses that on the issue of prostitution "Christ's teaching in this particular does not seem to sanction . . . a measure of ignorance or of refinement" (*WWC*, xxii).

The resonance of Butler's analysis of prostitution carries over into her discussion of domesticity. Butler has in mind something more threatening than Jameson's injunction to extend home outward into society (of course, for Butler, too, "women instinctively create a home around themselves"): Butler imagines an insertion of others into the family.

> Our English homes, which we continue to boast of as the strongholds of all virtue, might seem to be the least appropriate portion of the world to single out for warning. Doubtless there is goodness among them, and much wickedness outside. Yet I believe that a voice might justly say to them, as that of the angel of the Church of Thyatira, "Nevertheless I have somewhat against thee." . . . I believe we have flattered ourselves by thinking that our homes must have an influence for good, far and wide, if we simply continue good and pure, and keep within doors and enjoy our sacred seclusion. I think more is required of us than this, at least at the present age. The French speak of a selfishness *à deux*. . . . I think means might be found, where there is a will, to break down in a measure where there is such a separation, and to give

forth more freely of the strength and comfort and sweetness of family life to the homeless and solitary and sinful. I have seen a family of children grow up all the more tender and considerate because their parents housed with them for years a harmless lunatic, a stranger, whose simple and happy belief that he was an important member of the family was often the subject of innocent mirth. I have seen a marked elevation of sentiment and growth of Christian feeling among a household of servants, dating from the reception into the house of a poor outcast who died among them, instead of in the hospital, tenderly waited upon by them in turns. (*WWC*, xxxix–xl)

Butler, characteristically, grounds her suggestion with a tag from Scripture—here the warning from the Book of Revelation ("I have somewhat against thee"). She proceeds, nonetheless, to soften this beginning by presenting cheerful versions of infusing home life with the world of poor people, "lunatics" (if "harmless"), strangers, and outcasts.* This is Butler's attempt, sentimentalized as it is, to give an account between one and two—to insert others into/between a selfishness *à deux*. Though she fears that these may "seem extreme measures," the strategy to contain Victorian others remains all too apparent: *domesticate others* to avert the threat of "Revolution" at "Home."† Yet even such a domesticating measure—an insertion of the other within—might bear a greater potential to disturb than Butler realizes. The identification of the other as self-same never occurs without some splitting. Others are never fully "taken in" by such tender schemes.

Butler herself ends her essay with an instance of splitting: between Christ and the apostle Paul, between "essential Christianity" and the teachings of the Church—the kind of religious revision that Irigaray seeks to make especially radical. For Butler, splitting occurs along the axis of

---

*Interestingly enough, when it came to their lack of property rights, married women shared the same status as lunatics and criminals.

†In Butler's essay, a discussion of "Revolution" (frequently capitalized in her essay, as is "Home") takes center stage. She begins by outlining the different strategies the two parties advocated for averting Revolution in 1832. Some men counseled extending privilege to calm dissatisfaction. Others advised to keep it tightly confined to the "upper classes," lest the very extension of privilege engender Revolution. With these points expounded, the stage is set for Butler's analogy: "The majority of Englishmen have, I believe, at this day, a secret dread lest the granting of the claims which are just now put forward by women should revolutionize society. . . . the fear that to grant what they are asking would revolutionize our *Homes*. This is indeed a serious question; for I believe that Home is the nursery of all virtue, the fountain-head of all true affection, and the main source of the strength of our nation. . . . It is from the heart of my beloved home, with my children around me, that I speak; wherefore I trust I shall be believed to be free from indifference to the fear that our homes may be revolutionized or destroyed" (*WWC*, xxv–xxvii).

women. The treatment of women reveals the faultlines between, on the one hand, the historically relative (and less than enlightened) teachings of Paul and the Church through the ages, and, on the other hand, the eternal teachings of perfect equality characteristic of Christ and true Christianity. The Church "falls" on its sin against women. Thus Butler: "In the darkest ages of the Church there have been women whose whole lives were a protest against the capricious and various teachings of the Church concerning women, and who consequently endured a life-long martyrdom" (*WWC*, liv). In fact, sin and the curse of sweat and toil, resulting from the fall, are linked to the social and political abuse of women, since women in the work force could help to ease the burden of labor.

Butler trades on 'woman' as redeemer, yet bends this redemption in the direction of a woman's equal right to work. She even provides a feminist twist on Calvin's notion of "invisible Church" by imagining an elect within a wider domain of Christians. Like Calvin's followers, however, Butler is anxious to establish how this elect might be recognized: the "silent minority," who truly are the Church, are those who have proven their escape from the warp of unenlightened dogmas by believing in and fighting for various equalities. This minority includes God's enslaved and would-be escapees. Butler, for this reason, gives the example of the slaves who, she asserts, "crouching among the sugar-canes [Butler's own construction from a height] . . . secretly searched throughout the Bible for arguments against slavery" (*WWC*, lv) and, in spite of passages that might be misinterpreted(!), found arguments for their own equality under Christ. In particular, and significant for Butler's argument, the slaves found their hope and frightened their masters "through a steady gaze fixed on Christ himself." Once again, Christ is constructed as the pivot, as the mirror for women and those put low. Something of their suffering and their own implication in the suffering around them returns to them in the gaze fixed on Christ. Spreading along a spectrum of workers, this multiple return on investments in the mirror fractures, for Butler, any sense of the Christian's isolation from labor struggle. Women's labor is ever an imprisoned god, hung between the poles of (un)realized aspirations and (un)paid necessities. It "writh[es] consciously or unconsciously to escape"—for the love of Christ.

Interlude

~❧

Religion taught me sacred escapes. I was a lesbian girl of thirteen, looking down the barrel of gender not gently aimed at my head, looking for a way to stay sane in a teenage world I thought would eat me alive. I was undeniably bent from my gender. In my early years I was willing to wear only the dress my wise mother called my "sword dress" (so named for the sword on its belt). At thirteen, I was looking for a way to stay bent but still be approved.

It is a wonderfully contradictory manner, of course, in which bending proceeds. For what else can you call it but "contradiction" when you simultaneously take as your role models Mary Tyler Moore and Barnabas Collins from *Dark Shadows*—the good girl and the good vampire? Like Barnabas (my dominant model), I held myself a tragic figure with a tragic secret that would keep me, like him, from winning the girl I loved—the good girl (that other figure of my self). In this split, I cherished two specific desperations: one for goodness, the other for girls. Desperately, like Mary, I wanted to be good, and by the most conventional societal standards. Though too early yet for the army TV slogan, "Be all that you can be" (sold to me, when I did hear it, by the black NBA stars I also wanted to be), that sound bite captures the gist of my agenda: I *raged* to be good—in school, in sports, in music, in "niceness" (a category unto itself in junior high). The only credential for goodness I was missing was religion (raised Unitarian, I thought I was devoid of it). Religion would be the climax, more powerful because deferred, to my climb toward self-perfection.

But another agenda crossed this move. I sought a safe space to hide

out from boys and bond with girls while my confusion settled or sent me
screaming into the night. Rescue came in the surprising form of Evangelicals and, as luck would have it, an all-girl prayer meeting held in my
junior high cafeteria at formica tables and attended by the most beautiful,
most engaging older girls that I could imagine. Heaven was taking shape.
I could stay bent a long time in this mode. I did, in fact, through high
school and college. Against all expectations, in fact, conservative religion—the kind that has you hiding tracts in people's shoes and bedclothes,
Bible verses under their placemats or in their pants pockets—helped me
bend *away* from my gender during my formative sexual years. Through
its consistent sex segregation—a move to keep girls safe from sex and
drawn tight by the strings of their gender—conservative religion empowered me as a teacher of women.

The crux of my story turns this contradiction to the negative: the religion that fed my lesbian passion and made me a teenage oxymoron—a
girl leader—simultaneously drew the string on both these pursuits that it
had so enabled. A leader and a lover of women, through religion and with
its permission, I could consummate with its blessing neither of my aims:
I could not become an Evangelical pastor; I could not with God's approval,
or so they told me, marry a woman. My solution was to go to divinity
school, where it seemed many students were enacting gender experimen-
tally. Among images that stay with me boldly: a black man in a pink party
gown came to the Eucharist and was served the blood of Christ by a
woman. Religion was bending something in that place.

Notice, first, that conservative religion (Evangelicalism, no less) afforded me the chance to escape some aspects of my gender assignment and
allowed me, up to a point, to develop my lesbian passion. Consider, second, this designation: "my lesbian passion." I need now to say that, when
at thirteen I desired other girls, I did not desire them as if I were a lesbian—
though "lesbian" is the standard cultural label for what I was feeling, since
I was indeed desiring these girls, blatantly so, in a sexual way. What *I*
thought I was doing was pursuing girls as any boy might, since in my subjectivity I was Barnabas Collins, a masculine subject who pursued women
with a secret sense of tragic limitation and resulting wounds. Importantly,
and this begins to lead me to a third point, the more radical forms of religion I encountered at divinity school (particularly in a course, "Ethics
and the Family," taught by a nun) convinced me that I could love God
along with, and even through, women. When I dared to consummate that
passion, I began to take to myself, though with hesitation, the label upon

which my culture and lover jointly insisted—the label, "lesbian"—as if it were a sword dress I must wear, a label waiting for me at the brink, a label that would form me from the outside in.*

I can put it this way: becoming a lesbian *feminized* me, since on some level I had to admit that, at least in the eyes of those around me, my lover included, I was a woman loving a woman.† The result was an unexpected mirror event: Through my more openly feminine lover, I embraced my gendered relation to lack—something I had always felt as degrading, in spite of my occasional spectacular moments as Mary Tyler Moore. For the first time I could feel both the force of this wound and the force of this wound's surprising implications. Exchanging lack with her, I could freely grieve my crippled relations to the world of material opportunity. I could also realize that caressing lack is a possible way of producing a pleasure that remains perceptibly connected to other bodies and their wounds. From even our most private encounters, we found that sex can open a door, or at least a cut, onto concealed incriminations.

*Since first writing these pages, I have read Judith Butler on the topic of lesbian identity categories in her essay "Imitation and Gender Insubordination." It strikes me that my reluctance to wear the label "lesbian" and my eventual submission to its terms (experienced, initially, as another kind of sword dress) bear out several of her central claims, particularly when she argues that " 'to be' lesbian seems to be more than a simple injunction to become who or what I already am," "for it is a production," she says, "usually in response to a request" (13). Though I also take Butler's point that "identity categories tend to be instruments of regulatory regimes" (13), I am interested to explore the results—among them, a different kind of pleasure—of wounding myself with this cultural tag. I should add that I am intrigued to find in Butler's pages the term "opacity," of which I make much in this book. She uses the term to emphasize that identity categories do not magically reveal a self that had remained hidden: "If I claim to be a lesbian, I 'come out' only to produce a new and different 'closet.' The 'you' to whom I come out now has access to a different region of opacity. . . . In this sense, *outness* can only produce a new opacity" (15–16). Again, I want to explore the potential of these seeming negatives. Of course, Butler herself appears to affirm this opacity to some degree: "Or is this very deferral of the signified *to be valued*," she asks, "precisely because the term now takes on a life that cannot be, can never be, permanently controlled?" (16). My book is centrally concerned with this value, but also with opacity's relation to concealment of class relations.

†I do not wish to imply that every woman in similar circumstances would have to admit that she is a woman loving a woman; it is certainly possible in these relations to cross-gender oneself with some consistency, and to live out with women masculine and/or heterosexual fantasies. There was something about my lover's insistence, and my own relation to dominant structures, that formed this particular imperative for me.

Part II

Chapter 4

Recollecting Charlotte Brontë

≈

Dead Emanuel: "The Relic of an Obliteration"

With a steady gaze fixed on Christ, her vision bent on a Bridegroom vanishing just beyond her narrative verge, Brontë seeks at least to shadow the imprisoned 'God' of women's labor—for her, like Irigaray, a labor of desire. *Villette*, that is, depends upon 'God' as an elegant absence. Paul Emanuel (Emmanuel: "God with us": a name for Christ in the Gospel of Matthew) is the heroine's lover, who installs lack within their love and who is himself an elegant absence by the novel's end. Sent by his employers for three years (like Christ who harrows hell for three days) to a place called Basseterre (French for "low earth"), Paul is apparently shipwrecked off the coast of Europe on his voyage home.* As a figure for Christ, Paul stands as the telescopic endpoint—more of a gathering point perhaps—of the novel's scenes of desire between women, representing a hetero-

*In the Christian tradition, the three days between Christ's crucifixion and resurrection are conceived of as the period of his "harrowing hell," when "he went and preached unto the spirits in prison" (1 Peter 3:19). (*Webster's New World Dictionary* lists an entry for *harrow hell*: "[Archaic] to enter hell and rescue the righteous: said of Christ.") The tradition of Christ as divine Bridegroom arises particularly from Jesus' words in Matthew 9:15: "Can the children of the bridechamber mourn, as long as the bridegroom is with them? but the days will come, when the bridegroom shall be taken from them, and then shall they fast." See also John 3:28–30; Revelation 21:2, 9 and 22:17; Isaiah 62:5; Psalms 19:5. At the end of *Villette*, after a multitude of biblical allusions that point to Paul as Christ (many of which I will cite along the way), Lucy thinks, as she hears Paul approach, that she hears the steps of the "master-carpenter" and that Paul when she sees him is "bright" in "bridegroom-mood" (579). All references to *Villette* are from the Penguin edition unless otherwise specified.

erotic relation deftly modeled on feminine fractures. The mystic's courtly love with 'God' emerges, therefore, in Brontë's *Villette*. It is as if we see in a silvered surface, scratched by silver wounds, a mirrored wound turned upon a wound.

In fact, as dead Emanuel, Paul, in Lucy's memory, becomes "the relic of an obliteration" (to recall Lacan's phrase).* Brontë's novel ends, to be sure, with a bold display of material concealment: the lover who "enrolls" Lucy's desire, who makes her autoerotics her labor, himself disappears, creased into the text, in a way that not even the reader can discern, making the telos of *Villette* an opacity. Paul even figures the material resistance of *Lucy's* body to the structures and relations that have neglected her pleasure. What remains in view, at the close, is Lucy's longing, the fulfillment of which now lies submerged (as if it were veiled by the weight of waters) but visible to the reader (and to Lucy) in a shroud.†

Brontë's most striking version of "the force of pure loss" is death. This loss, seemingly ultimate, pushes to perimeters Irigaray's affirmation of deferral. Can the space that *death* opens open commerce with pleasure? How vast can the space between lovers grow, before the pleasures of approach dissolve, unsustained? In scouting the pain and desire linked to death, trying to understand it in spiritual terms as a God-ordained loss (and even a labor), Brontë uses a framework familiar to Victorian readers: Lucy writes a spiritual autobiography.

Brontë's confrontation with the pain of loss, however, offended atheists and Christians alike:

*For my discussion of "the relic of an obliteration" and "the force of pure loss" (which I mention below), see the beginning of Chapter 2.

†Patrick Brontë's anxiety over the ending of *Villette* exemplifies the response of many Victorian readers. Writes Mrs. Gaskell, relating what Charlotte had told her: "Mr. Brontë was anxious that her new tale should end well, as he disliked novels which left a melancholy impression upon the mind; and he requested her to make her hero and heroine (like the heroes and heroines in fairy tales) 'marry, and live very happily ever after.' But the idea of M. Paul Emanuel's death at sea was stamped on her imagination till it assumed the distinct force of reality, and she could no more alter her fictitious ending than if they had been facts which she was relating. All she could do in compliance with her father's wish was so to veil the fate in oracular words as to leave it to the character and discernment of her readers to interpret her meaning" (*Life of Charlotte Brontë*, 479). Indeed, the extent to which Victorian readers did not wish to interpret Lucy as left a maiden is evident in the fact, as Charles Burkhart informs us, that "her immediate public seems to have read what it wanted to into her ambiguities; Mrs. Oliphant, writing later in the century, says that 'the ultimate fate of M. Paul, left uncertain at the conclusion, was debated in a hundred circles with greater vehemence than many a national problem'" (*Charlotte Brontë*, 102).

An atmosphere of pain hangs about the whole, forbidding that repose which we hold to be essential to the true presentment of any large portion of life and experience. . . . The religion she invokes is itself but a dark and doubtful refuge from the pain which compels the invocation. (Harriet Martineau, *Daily News*, Feb. 3, 1853)

Faith is indeed a very prominent feature in Miss Snowe's mind; more a religious than a theological faith; more a trust, a sentiment, and a hope, than a clearly-defined belief that could be stated in propositions. . . . We are sure that it is not in any high sense Christian. It may, however, be a genuine effusion from an overstrained endurance. (*The Spectator*, Feb. 12, 1853)

We are not at all proud of [Lucy Snowe] as a representative of our reformed faith. (Anne Mozley, *Christian Remembrancer*, Apr. 1853)[1]

Those who were not inclined to accept religious "answers"—as in the first quotation, for example—deemed *Villette* irredeemably dark, since the novel's only proposed "solution" to Lucy's misery is a religious, and hence unacceptable, one. For many Christians, Brontë's religious solution proved more despairing than the torment it should have soothed. Lucy Snowe is resigned to hope at parting with her lover, but this resigned faith does not proclaim God's victory over pain. The novel's hope, then, did not ease either type of unsettled reader. In our own time, of course, shaped by modernist and postmodernist sensibilities, we tend to find depictions of pain and incompletion less unnerving than some attempts at hope. We feel more comfortable analyzing how ideals fail to withstand the force of disruptions than following a faith into the dim reaches of its optimism.*

The difficulty of wrapping our minds around *Villette* remains, therefore. Sexual and spiritual concerns in the novel interrupt each other to such

---

*An obvious and important exception to this characterization are those contemporary feminist critics who, in many respects, have been Brontë's most optimistic readers—at least with regard to the ending of *Villette*. And yet, though they celebrate Lucy's independence at the end of the novel, they generally, for the sake of their optimism, mitigate any emphasis on Lucy's pain. Gilbert and Gubar are the prime example, going so far as to suggest that "it is Lucy's unconscious and unspeakable will that Madame Walravens enacts when she sends Paul on a typically witchy quest for treasure in (of all places) *Basse/terre*" (*Madwoman*, 431), for "it is only in his absence that [Lucy] can exert herself fully to exercise her own powers" (438). See also Auerbach, *Communities of Women*, 112–13; Moglen, *Charlotte Brontë*, 227–29; Platt, "How Feminist Is *Villette*?" 20–26; and Tayler, *Holy Ghosts*, 278–81. Kathleen Blake, in her study of feminine self-postponement, takes a different tack, stressing not Lucy's independence without Paul but her "laboriously evolved ability to profit by pain" (*Love and the Woman Question*, 72). Blake is reaching toward an aspect of *Villette* that I explore as Lucy's autoerotics of labor.

a degree that we might find it difficult to determine whether Brontë addresses a sexual or a theological problem when she opens onto death. Stuart Schneiderman, in *Jacques Lacan: The Death of an Intellectual Hero*, probes at length "something that analysts, among others, have never wanted to look at very closely: death and its symbolization."[2] Insisting on death's analytic importance, he recalls a memory of Lacan, relayed to him by Robert Jay Lifton:

> Lifton met Lacan at Yale in 1975 and asked him about the symbolization of death. He proposed this as an alternative to the classical psychoanalytic symbolization that centers on sex and sexual relations. Why couldn't there be another system of symbolization besides the one focused on male and female principles? That other symbolization would be of continuity and discontinuity or better, he added, continuity and death. Lacan responded: "I am a Liftonian." Of course, everyone thought this to be a facetious remark, a kind of mock praise. And yet it was not characteristic of Lacan to give compliments, and besides he knew better than most that there is always truth in wit.
>
> What Lacan said next makes this clear. He stated that he was a Freudian and that the Freudian approach emphasized sex, adding that he was probably too old to change. He thought that Lifton's approach might be just as valid as his own, since there was more than one path that research could follow. Perhaps they would end at the same place.[3]

Brontë's novel undresses sex and death side by side. The novel's odd rhetoric of gaps, holes, hollows, thirstings, and crucifixions suggests that "partings" of various kinds comprise the losses, but also the pleasures, of sex and death. Parting in *Villette* vibrates, even, to a double valence: the sexual dilemma of the parting inscribed in one's desire, and the spiritual (though still clearly sexual) problem of the parting that results from a lover's death.

Perhaps the novel's most complicated knot involves the sexual economics of its form, for here the encounter between Victorian spiritual discourse and contemporary psychoanalysis occurs most dramatically. Crucial reasons exist why, in the case of *Villette*, we cannot be too quick to condemn the impetus to psychoanalyze Lucy Snowe—nor, more importantly, can we escape it. For her alienations, her partings from self, are not concealed in Brontë's novel but, rather, are put on textual display as the novel's main point. *Villette*, after all, thematizes how Lucy "misses" herself. Yet these very depictions of Lucy—along with the novel's complete cast of characters—come to us through Lucy herself, through her own told tale. *Villette* is Lucy Snowe and only Lucy Snowe. The clue, then, rests with *Villette*'s narration. What gets rendered as the unconscious of the character Lucy Snowe cannot be separated from whatever this novel knows on other terms than its narrator's stated understandings. What Brontë, along with her culture, cannot say or speak directly—either because she knows it unconsciously or because it would be too risky to say— becomes *visible* in *Villette* as the *unconscious* of Lucy Snowe as narrator. *Villette*, then, begs a psychoanalysis of the narrating character because of the way it foregrounds Lucy's seductive disjunctions, her reluctance in telling, *as* the tale that is being told.*

Specifically, it is by arching us back upon 'God' that *Villette* crosscuts psychoanalysis. Lucy's spiritual autobiography allows Brontë, at the very least, to search desire's dynamics, for Lucy traces each Christian's duty to internalize, to repeat in her flesh, a teleology that makes a sacred map of desire: the drive of Christian history from Adam and Eve's union with God, to the divisions of desire that resulted from the fall, to every lack's fulfillment, at history's end, when Christ weds the Church in apocalyptic marriage—a moment that, *in* history, never comes, since its arrival, by definition, will be outside. Lucy's tendency to carve her plot according to this well-known spiritual formula must lead to her recognition of desire, which betrothal to Christ *promises* but cannot in this life prove to satisfy. Such a "fall" into the relays of desire's insatiability is dictated, then, by the very form of Lucy's narration, the form that Brontë has Lucy use for ordering her remembrance.†

---

*Villette has long been subjected to psychoanalytic ponderings of various shades— in fact, long before critical theorists began to pore over Brontë's novel. At first, attention was focused on psychoanalyzing the author, whose life seemed ripe for interpretations of sexual repression and the ill effects of a missing mother. Later, Lucy Snowe herself became a figure for repressed sexuality and emotional reticence. Since psychoanalyzing both authors and characters has in recent years come under attack, current criticism has taken for its focus the marked reticence, yet strange eruptions, of the text itself. Although there are good reasons for critical shifts away from psychoanalyzing authors and characters—since such attempts rarely take into account the constructedness of the author's life and the character's "existence"—I am trying to show why, in the case of *Villette*, we cannot make clean cuts between character, narrator, and author. An obvious example (and an early one) of psychoanalyzing the author is Rosamond Langbridge's *Charlotte Brontë: A Psychological Study* (1929). Examples of the second approach, which even so do not leave the first approach behind, are Robert Keefe's *Charlotte Brontë's World of Death* and Helene Moglen's *Charlotte Brontë: The Self Conceived*. Mary Jacobus, "The Buried Letter: Feminism and Romanticism in *Villette*," and Christina Crosby, "Charlotte Brontë's Haunted Text," provide excellent examples of a focus on the eruptions of the text.

†The deferral built into betrothal to Christ is such a well-established theological point that even Christian narratives that do not take the form of autobiography often bend or break their forms to preserve this theology. Notice, for example, that in

Inspecting remembrance, Stuart Schneiderman has remarked that "in analysis one rewrites one's history"—something one could easily claim for spiritual autobiography, with its backward constructions of God's designs.* As Lacan has emphasized, it is not the accuracy of this account that matters but the act of putting one's past into words. Lucy's retelling of her past, for instance, reveals her present concerns of aloneness. Through her spiritual autobiography, the older Lucy, who rewrites the events of her younger life, resembles an analysand before the screen of her reader/analyst, telling these events (in past tense) with the immediacy and anticipation of her younger self. The form of *Villette* even positions the reader to interpret the strange blanks of Lucy's discourse, for Lucy herself directly addresses the reader at junctures. The only action the reader/analyst may not perform is to intervene directly in the telling of the tale or to terminate analysis (which even so, according to Lacanian theory, involves the analysand's judgment; the analyst merely agrees to terminate). What constitutes something like the narrator's transference onto her reader/analyst is resolved only at the novel's end, where Lucy's narration, of her own accord, literally dissolves. Importantly, at this point, the narrator, implying Paul Emanuel's shipwreck, realizes that her earlier "transference" *onto Paul* was transferred somewhere else by his death. To be sure, the narrator, as if mounting Paul on the cross of a shipwreck, depicts him as her divine Bridegroom. This Christ, as Lucy, looking back, depicts him, even appears something of an analyst/screen for her younger, earlier transference (he was "the subject who is supposed to know," in Lacan's phraseology). The narrator's remembrance, before the screen of her reader, of her earlier

---

book 1 of Spenser's *Faerie Queene*, the anticipated consummation between the Red Cross Knight and Una does not take place. Thus this romance does not conclude as one would expect a romance to conclude: with betrothal, marriage, and consummation. Una and the Red Cross Knight are betrothed, yet he returns to the court of Gloriana. One important reason for this ending is the need, on the allegorical level, for Christ (Red Cross Knight) and the Church (Una) to remain betrothed but not wed—this marriage can be fulfilled only at the end of time.

*Schneiderman, *Jacques Lacan*, 71. My claim should not elide the obvious differences between spiritual autobiography, with its rather neat turns, and analytic narrative, with its halting and not quite progressive movements. Rather, we should not fail to notice that Brontë's adaptation of a spiritual plot for Lucy's narration allows Brontë's text to present in a relatively coherent, orderly form what an analytic narrative would present in a more incoherent, interruptive form. There are crucial points of overlap, nonetheless: namely, similar concerns to recount all "temptations" to substitute finite objects for the infinite object of desire, and to accept ultimately, radically, the deferral of desire's fulfillment.

transference onto a character (a character, that is, in the plot of her desire), doubles the narrative's analytic complexities.*

The figure of such an analyst-Christ is not so strange. Schneiderman explains the transference as a passion that the analyst suffers:

> An analysis does not begin with the analyst promising a cure or even suggesting that in most cases of the same sort a cure is something that can be expected. The question of the beginning of a psychoanalysis is whether the analyst accepts or refuses the patient's suffering. . . . When I talk of accepting suffering, I mean quite simply that the analyst ought to recognize the validity of the experience of suffering. It is not a foreign element in the patient's life, but essential to the patient's existence. . . .
>
> So when the analyst accepts his patient's suffering, this also means that he *permits himself to be implicated in whatever it is that has produced that suffering*—this through the transference, which Lacan said was something that analysts have to suffer, as a passion.[4] (my emphasis)

Accepting the suffering of Lucy Snowe, permitting himself "to be implicated in whatever it is that has produced [it]," Paul, as the character-analyst, cuts a figure for our own response—our engagement with the suffering told to us as readers. And who better to suffer this passion than Paul, whose biblical surname Lucy unearths by the strong resemblance (she imagines) she sees (and needs to see) between Paul and Christ?

With respect to Lucy's dead Emanuel, her analyst might perform another function. As Lacan has stated, accentuating the analyst's nonintervention: "The analyst intervenes concretely in the dialectic of analysis by

---

*I use the term "transference" here in the Lacanian sense of "the subject who is supposed to know" (*Four Fundamental Concepts*, 232). In this sense, I examine the narrator's transference onto the reader as the one she supposes to hold the mastery of self-understanding and spiritual insight. I examine as well young Lucy's transference onto Paul Emanuel as the one she presumed to know her desire. And though Lacan states "now, he does not present himself as a god, he is not God for his patient," it is from this point of extreme supposition (as if it is its closest equivalent) that Lacan must disentangle the analyst ("So what does this trust signify? Around what does it turn?" 230). He explains: "The question is first, for each subject, where he takes his bearings from when applying to the subject who is supposed to know. Whenever this function may be, for the subject, embodied in some individual, whether or not an analyst, the transference, according to the definition I have given you of it, is established" (*Four Fundamental Concepts*, 233). Jane Gallop, in *Reading Lacan*, discusses "*something like a* 'transference' at play between reader and text" (30). In Gallop's examination, her concern is the reader's transference onto the text—that is to say, the reader's supposition of the mastery of the text. My examination of transference in *Villette* attacks this question from the opposite angle, focusing on (what gets represented here as) Lucy's suppositions of mastery in Paul and in her reader.

pretending he is dead, by cadaverizing his position" (*E*, 140). For Lacan, the analyst "makes death present." This cadaverizing of the analyst's position, making his intervention his burial, proves remarkably apt for *Villette*. Having her take for the plot of her retelling the believer's apocalyptic marriage to Christ, Brontë shows Lucy as shaping a tale of a *transferred transference*. Since Jesus was destined to disappear when his disciples most presumed his mastery, he left them to focus on the void of their desire (his empty tomb) and to follow the subject presumed to know toward an indefinite realm beyond.* Schneiderman, discussing Lacan's use of set theory, provides a fascinating bridge to *Villette*:

> In Lacan's theory the empty set has more than one manifestation: what comes to mind most immediately is the empty grave, the empty tomb. . . . The empty grave is important . . . because of its symbolization of the place against which we have to confront the dead. If the dead were at home in their graves, then they would be buried, classed, and we would be finished with them. If the grave is empty, we have to deal with them. The empty grave has a significant role in the story of Christ as well as in that of Hamlet. . . . Also, there are two central figures in Freudian theory who are noteworthy for not having been buried, for having disappeared without a trace: Oedipus and Moses.[5]

We will see that Brontë meditated on Moses in "La mort de Moïse" (one of her Belgian devoirs for Heger). In *Villette*, it is Paul's disappearance *off the coast* that presumably leaves an empty grave and certainly leaves the narrator focused on a brink.

By these developments, *Villette* confirms that the believer's God-given work in this world is, above all, the work of desire—the work of believing in and hastening unseen material relations, sexual and economic. Speculating on economies of loss, *Villette* shifts away from Weber's concern with pleasure's deferral and shifts, instead, toward erotic formulations of deferral as pleasure. In reading *Villette*'s evasive end, I will try to make a case for a sexual and economic "rise" that does not repeat a Calvinist success scheme. Instead, this rise in fortune makes (auto)eroticism, fed by loss, the biblical talent that Lucy must increase for the sake of her master.†

---

*John 16:28–29: " 'I came forth from the Father, and am come into the world: again, I leave the world, and go to the Father.' His disciples said unto him, 'Lo, now speakest thou plainly, and speakest no proverb.' "

†It is the complicated *intersection* between these categories—spirituality and sexuality, work and desire—that Brontë critics have not yet addressed. The most dramatic gap in critics' address to *Villette* involves the materialist (but also, to my mind, sexual and spiritual) issues of Lucy's labor. Very few studies—among the few, Judith Newton's in *Feminist Criticism and Social Change*, edited by Judith Newton and Deborah Ro-

Parting Words

I have said that *Villette*'s narration discloses an older woman's capture before her reader/analyst of her past relations, as a younger woman, with a man she remembers as an analyst/Christ. In this sense, *Villette* is twice layered with Lucy's past and present. Tripling this relation, Brontë surely transferred onto Lucy her own sexual and theological partings, along with

---

senfelt—have introduced questions of class position and labor struggle, both of which, as I will argue, appear so prominently in the narrative of Lucy's economic rise. It seems to be the case that *Villette*'s long, important history of psychological readings has occluded Brontë's steady engagement with labor—her rich understanding of how work plays so complexly upon psychic investments and sexual dynamics.

On the bright side of *Villette*'s critical history, the early feminist attention to the novel's representations of rage and rebellion (studies as different from each other as those by Gilbert and Gubar and Mary Jacobus) broke the surface of the text's odd fissures and evident repressions. The excellent studies of love's deferral and the sexual haunting of Lucy by the nun, opening further windows onto narrative instabilities (see Kathleen Blake, *Love and the Woman Question* and Christina Crosby, "Charlotte Brontë's Haunted Text"), were accompanied by impressively detailed studies on repression and eroticism (see John Maynard, *Charlotte Brontë and Sexuality*, and John Kucich, *Repression in Victorian Fiction*). Yet, along the way, what was getting lost, with such superb focus on textual disruption and sexual repression, was not only Brontë's interest in labor but also her dramatic use of spiritual language and plot. Many of the best studies on *Villette* skirt the crucial issue of how Brontë's spiritual interests impinge upon her fictions, or pause in a few places only to suggest that these interests form the conservative aspects of this novelist's otherwise subversive writings.

In fact, when I wrote my dissertation chapter on Brontë's *Villette* in 1985 (Stockton, "Spiritual Discourse and the Work of Desire") there did not exist a single study that discussed in any measure the pervasive biblical allusiveness of *Villette*. Until Irene Tayler's *Holy Ghosts*, Barry Qualls was the one critic who had discussed in any detail the representation of Paul Emanuel as divine Bridegroom. Yet Qualls—perhaps because he reads Lucy's journey as "a journey towards the acceptance of renunciation which is the lot of Everyman" (*Secular Pilgrims*, 77)—does not address sexual issues. Tayler, by contrast, stresses Paul's role in "rousing [Lucy's] long-buried fires" (*Holy Ghosts*, 246). I have been struck by Tayler's careful reading of the novel's biblical allusions, since she and I have produced, independently of one another, catalogues of *Villette*'s biblical materials that in large part correspond to and confirm one another. Not surprisingly, even so, we take our readings in different directions. Whereas I see Brontë's spiritual discourse as confirming Lucy's sexual desire and wedding it to Lucy's vocation of autoeroticism, with which Paul leaves her at the novel's end, Tayler emphasizes Paul's role in "protect[ing Lucy] from the treacherous seductions of the flesh" (246); he helps her, Tayler argues, to put passion to rest by "bury[ing]. . . carnal desires" (252) that would interfere with her divine vocation of teaching and feminine creativity. Tayler tends, therefore, to split off spirituality from sexuality and to make sexuality that which Lucy must sacrifice in order to be, like Brontë, God's "wise virgin" with her "lamp 'chastely lucent'" (274). The novel's constant attention to scenes of desire between women and to the erotics of women's class fractures do not comprise a focus for Tayler.

her dread of desire's suspense. For loss, and the fear of loss, initiate the Brontë outpourings that so well match post-structuralists' interests in desire.

Parting, in the sense of separation from loved ones, has long been acknowledged a quintessential Brontëan concern. Her letters catalogue a series of traumas that include the deaths of her mother, brother, and four sisters, and a devastating rejection from Constantin Heger, a married professor with whom she fell in love while studying in Belgium. This much any Brontë reader knows. What we must uncover again—for tucked in its sorrows are her longings for women—is the parting, in the sense of negotiating with a part, that attended Brontë's several separations. This parting is the part of lover, or, at the very least, a body at the brink of loves.

Brontë's letters to Ellen Nussey demonstrate the subtly sexualized part she was writing for herself, particularly in her role as a spiritual sister who feared separation from God and her "helpmate." When Brontë pours forth her fears to Ellen, she falls into passion. Overtly, Brontë imparts her struggle to overcome her "melancholy state" and to hope, with Ellen's help, more surely in God:

> If I could always live with you, if your lips and mine could at the same time drink the same draught at the same pure fountain of mercy, I hope, I trust, I might one day become better, far better than my evil wandering thoughts, my corrupt heart, cold to the spirit and warm to the flesh, will now permit me to be. I often plan the pleasant life which we might lead together, strengthening each other in that power of self-denial, that hallowed and glowing devotion which the past Saints of God often attained to. My eyes fill with tears when I contrast the bliss of such a state, brightened with hopes of the future, with the melancholy state I now live in . . . longing for holiness which I shall never, never attain.[6]

The sustenance of the Scriptures, the image of the fountain, the hope for a hope, the longing for holiness, and especially the need for a spiritual helpmate all run charged, feverish lines through Brontë's letters (as well as through *Villette*). Brontë perceived a critical connection between spiritual health and passionate sisterhood. Yet, it is spiritual *failure* that occasions, (blessedly?) necessitates, the homoerotic relation with Ellen that Brontë imagines might spiritually heal her, as if she might find God between their lips. Her sexualized tone leaves each line swollen with longing, especially since thirst in Brontë's corpus prominently signifies sexual desire: "if your lips and mine could at the same time drink the same draught at the same pure fountain of mercy, I hope, I trust."

For some of Brontë's earlier critics, this tone raises worries. Anxious to ease the concern he stirs up, Charles Burkhart, in *Charlotte Brontë: A Psychosexual Study of Her Novels*, addresses this "trouble":

> As a schoolgirl [Charlotte] developed a greater-than-schoolgirl crush, yet still no more than a normal abnormality, on Ellen Nussey: ". . . don't desert me—don't be horrified at me, you know what I am—I wish I could see you, my darling, I have lavished the warmest affections of a very hot, tenacious heart upon you—if you grow cold—it's over."[7]

Following his discussion of Charlotte's "strong masculine streak" and her tendency to describe her male characters in female terms, Burkhart reassures us (with no more than a normal abnormality of expression?): "She was not in any imbalanced way lesbian, or masculine, or sadistic." Burkhart (and his associative chains) aside, however one wishes to read their relations, Charlotte's outpourings to Ellen shaped for her a sexual discourse that still could be read by peers (and probably by Charlotte) as "spiritual." One could read Charlotte's passions toward Ellen as bolstering a safe context for desire, while nurturing some sense of "self-affection." Or, one could read these passions as "lesbian," forced by cultural dictates to pass on to heteroeroticism.

Brontë's preference for friendship over passionate love (already a spurious division for her) evinces, in part, her reluctance toward men. Whereas "profound, intense affection" (between women companions, in particular) provided requited, lasting love (or so she thought), intense passion for men represented "no desirable feeling":

> In the first place, it seldom or never meets with a requital; and, in the second place, if it did, the feeling would be only temporary: it would last the honeymoon, and then, perhaps, give place to disgust, or indifference, worse perhaps than disgust. Certainly this would be the case on the man's part; and on the woman's—God help her, if she is left to love passionately and alone.[8]

Brontë was concerned with love's temporality—how love works itself out through time, and how time's transmutations play, precariously, with passions. We encounter this concern in her letters to Ellen, though mostly she fears separation from Ellen through that inevitable vagary of time, the loss we call "death." In one letter, she bares presentiments that greatly beset her in Ellen's sickness: "When I parted from you near White-lee Bar, I had a more sorrowful feeling than ever I experienced before in our temporary separations. . . . I certainly had a feeling that the time of our reunion had never been so indefinite or so distant as then."[9]

In the former letter the tension is of a different kind, fixed, as it is, on the evanescence of love with men, a fleeting quality time will unmask. Brontë's assumption that the man would soon grow indifferent to love—she deems this "the man's part"—while the woman would be left alone in her passion, reveals the extent to which she feared not desire but rejection. This desire surfaces in what were Brontë's dreams of "the 'great love,' the sexuality that overwhelms and solves all of life's problems."[10] Only in her fictional world does Brontë encounter such a "great love," a love at once sexual and faithful; but by the time of *Villette*, her last complete novel, Brontë makes the lover, Paul Emanuel, a tyrannical Christ, who in living up to his biblical name, *must* leave Lucy (God help her) "to love passionately and alone." In this novel, Brontë seems bent on redeeming the terrors of love's deferral by *affirming* them. Having Lucy picture her absent lover as a lover-Christ was one way of securing such redemption—Brontë's remarkable rendition of Irigaray's approach ever nearer without a(r)rival. The clue to this divine securement lies already in Brontë's letter, seen in this sentence: "Certainly this would be the case on the man's part; and on the woman's—God help her, if she is left to love passionately and alone." Breaking the expected parallel construction, "man's part . . . woman's part," Brontë substitutes "God" for woman's "part," and substitutes a conditional clause for a declamation, interjecting a divine blank between a woman and her allotted fate that perhaps, with God's help, does not arrive.

It is not particularly new to suggest that in the fictional creation of Paul Emanuel, Brontë transformed her devastating separation from her Belgian teacher—"I think, however long I live, I shall not forget what the parting with M. Heger cost me" ("parting" in the double sense of separation and playing the part of devoted student only).* What needs to be expressed is how this transformation (Heger into Paul) represents, in the words of Irigaray, "an articulation between autoeroticism and heteroeroticism," so that *Villette*'s scenes of desire between women form preludes

---

*Shorter, *Letters* 1: 227. Helene Moglen (*Charlotte Brontë*, 192–93) and Barbara and Gareth Lloyd Evans (*Everyman's Companion to the Brontës*, 107) both make the point that the character of Graham Bretton was based on George Smith, Brontë's publisher, whom she may have wished to marry. Nonetheless, in the intensity of the emotional investment, in the representation of this investment as idolatry, and in the recurrent focus on Lucy's letters from Graham, we may recognize a reworking of the relationship with Heger. Furthermore, her splitting of the Heger relationship into Lucy's two different attractions, to Graham and Paul, respectively, afforded Brontë the chance to represent her experience of rejection with Heger while imagining what a love with him might have been like.

to a "great love" modeled on Lucy's relations with women. For if Brontë's devastation of desire with Heger explains the impetus for her novel's transformations, her partings from her sisters (through their deaths) explain how she discovered shades of "clean" pain and affirmative loss. Brontë, I suspect, may have used the experience of her sisters' deaths in 1848–49—along with the god-talk that carried her through—to rework her parting from Heger, and even from Branwell, her brother, into Lucy's loss of Paul. *Villette*'s display of a dead Emanuel may be nourished by the partings Brontë found that she could manage more successfully—cadaverous gapings that at least felt good as "the relics" of requited love. The grip of her feared abandonment by men thus gets broken, and written, as Christ's *required* departure, leaving her not in desperation but in hotter shades of anticipation.

It was on an unconscious level, most likely, that Brontë first understood her idol worship of Heger:

> Day and night I find neither rest nor peace. If I sleep I am disturbed by tormenting dreams in which I see you, always severe, always grave, always incensed against me. . . . If my master withdraws his friendship from me entirely I shall be altogether without hope; if he gives me a little—just a little— I shall be satisfied—happy; I shall have a reason for living on, for working. Monsieur, the poor have not need of much to sustain them—they ask only for the crumbs that fall from the rich man's table.[11]

Brontë made a god of Heger, an elevation witnessed not only by her confessions of dependence but also by her reference to Jesus' parable of the rich man and Lazarus. In Jesus' story, a poor beggar lies at a rich man's gate, "desiring to be fed with the crumbs which fell from the rich man's table" (Luke 16:21). When both men die, the beggar, Lazarus, is carried by angels to Abraham's bosom (a figure for heaven), while the rich man goes to hell. Did Brontë link herself with the beggar, and Heger with the rich man who meets his just reward? Or did she perhaps confuse Luke's parable with the versions of this scriptural lesson in the gospels of Matthew and Mark? In the latter books, a gentile woman, seeking Jesus' attention, pleads that even "the dogs eat of the crumbs which fall from their masters' table" (Matthew 15:27), to which Jesus replies: "O woman, great is thy faith: be it unto thee even as thou wilt" (or "as you desire," according to the Revised Standard Version). The context of Brontë's letter—a plea to one she considers her savior (whom she may coax to meet her desire)—would suggest that she held this last version in mind. Yet, Brontë's words are virtually a direct quotation from Luke, thus tainting Heger with the rich man's indifference (and unenviable fate). This blending of allusions, such that one cannot confidently locate the biblical source, implies worry on Brontë's part that Heger might prove an unworthy redeemer.

There is another relation to Heger, as the class relations of the biblical story also suggest. The story of Brontë's idolatry is also the tale of her attempt to rise out of the position of governess to teacher—and beyond, in Brontë's mind, to writer. Heger symbolized this passage to bourgeois independence in the realm of work. The many devoirs she wrote for her professor—the majority on Old Testament or religious themes—represented not only labors of love but also the means by which Charlotte might be groomed for new professional parts. In this serious respect, Heger's indifference after their parting signified no reason "for living on, for working." By the time Brontë wrote letters to Heger, her plans to open a school with her sisters had fallen through, and they were again in quest of schemes for circumventing the position of governess.

By her final letters, Brontë's desperation and her rousing acknowledgment of loss increased, indicating, once again, how her "failure" fired her expressions. Now she more consciously rebelled against her "slavery" to what she called "a fixed and dominant idea which lords it over the mind." She registered longing at every bend in her protest against it:

> One is ready to do anything to find peace once more . . . but I have been able to conquer neither my regrets nor my impatience. That, indeed, is humiliating—to be unable to control one's own thoughts, to be the slave of a regret, of a memory, the slave of a fixed and dominant idea which lords it over the mind. Why cannot I have just as much friendship for you, as you have for me—neither more nor less? . . . Fever claims me—I lose appetite and sleep—I pine away.[12]

One of Brontë's poems delivers her conviction that she wasted her devotion:

> But once a year he heard a whisper low and dreary
>   Appealing for aid, entreating some reply;
> Only when sick, soul-worn, and torture-weary,
>   Breathed I that prayer, heaved I that sigh.
> He was mute as is the grave, he stood stirless as a tower;
>   At last I looked up and saw I prayed to stone:
> I asked help of that which to help had no power,
>   I sought love where love was utterly unknown.[13]

What most impresses is Brontë's blatant attempt to paint Heger's indifference as *impotence*, so that her inability to "move" him (emotionally, sexually) becomes his inability to "move" ("he stood stirless as a tower"). Her requests of him are prayers "to stone," offering the oxymoron of Heger's hard impotence—perhaps the perfect contradictory image for a pagan idol, who seduces his devotees to false climax. Again, Brontë turns to Scripture in the cleft of failure, venting passion: the second stanza surely alludes to John, chapter 5, in which we are told that yearly "a great multitude of impotent folk, of blind, halt, withered" lay by a certain pool, waiting for God's angel to stir healing waters. This allusion—with Brontë's unmistakable stress on deferral—reappears prominently in *Villette*, along with a God (this time, Paul) as "mute as is the grave." Here, the allusion underscores what Brontë considered false powers—Heger's inability to render sexual and economic aid; there, in *Villette*, deferral and a mute God leave Lucy to her (own) pleasures in her (own) school.

Brontë's sharp disappointment in Heger was not the only pain from parting she suffered. Several partings splay her letters: temporary separations from Ellen, due to their living apart; the excruciating separation from Heger, caused, so Charlotte tells it, by the failure of his love; the equally excruciating separations from her siblings, caused by early deaths. A distinction between these partings runs through them. In the case of what she deemed failed love, Brontë knew no means by which to affirm the pain of separation that she suffered. Neither did she know how to manage a part that she might play in relation to this loss. Her use of spiritual talk in these cases—dramatically seen in her letters to Heger—allows for a biblical indictment of idolatry and her idol's impotence, but for nothing more hopeful, for nothing that would fashion affirmative longing from the cut of desire. In the case of death, however, if the separation bore no trace for her of the failure of love, Brontë found she could use Christian discourse: conceptions of eternity that defer reunion to some other place and time. For this deferral she had a name, a conception which trapped, then even sustained it.

Not surprisingly, the death of her brother was something that Brontë could not embrace with hope, for his parting combined the pain of failed love with the grief of death. Of the Brontë sisters, Charlotte had formed the closest ties to their brother, Branwell. She, perhaps more than anyone else, knew all that was wasted in the spiral of Branwell's self-destruction. The tone of Charlotte's letters after his death reveals deep resentment and a sense of her brother's betrayal of her love:

> I do not weep from a sense of bereavement—there is no prop withdrawn, no consolation torn away, no dear companion lost—but for the wreck of talent, the ruin of promise, the untimely dreary extinction of what might have been

a burning and a shining light. My brother was a year my junior. I had aspirations and ambitions for him once, long ago—they have perished mourn-
fully. *Nothing remains of him* but a memory of errors and sufferings. There is
such a bitterness of pity for his life and death, such a yearning for the emp-
tiness of his whole existence as I cannot describe. (my emphasis)[14]

Brontë experienced irredeemable, or what one might call "unclean," pain
in her lost relationships with Heger and Branwell. Memories made bitter
by failed expectations or the inevitable letdown of romantic fantasy were
all that remained when Heger stopped writing and Branwell died. She had
idolized both—hence my designation of her emotion as "unclean," in the
Old Testament sense applied to an altar to a pagan god. Differently from
Heger, Branwell, too, had represented for Charlotte the possibility of
professionalism—not a passage to her own profession but her vicarious
participation in what she hoped would be Branwell's achievements. As her
letters reveal, Branwell, as the family's only son, was the child chosen for
professional preparations. In a strange sense, then, as her letter suggests,
Charlotte's desire to work was attached to Branwell's possibilities ("I had
aspirations and ambitions for him once"). Heger, and Branwell toward his
end, had not pursued her in such a way as to mark with pleasure the obstacle that makes relations possible—the void that she might take up and
hold as the "remainder" of a body materially concealed (in Belgium or in
heaven). This pain of loss might have stood as "a relic" of material pursuits now "obliterated." As it was, the pain of these separations refused
any comfort. Brontë could not warm her faith around them.

Within eight months of Branwell's death, Brontë's two remaining sisters died. Though this loss of her literary companions was severe—now
she lost her partners in work—Brontë's letters reveal that the pain of these
partings could more adequately, if still incompletely, be embraced by
hope:

> We are very calm at present. Why should we be otherwise? . . . We feel [Em-
> ily] is at peace. . . . We saw her taken from life in its prime. But it is God's
> will, and the place where she is gone is better than she has left. God has sus-
> tained me, in a way that I marvel at, through such agony as I had not con-
> ceived.[15]

> [Anne] died without severe struggle, resigned, trusting in God—thankful for
> release from a suffering life—deeply assured that a better existence lay before
> her. . . . I let Anne go to God, and felt He had a right to her.[16]

Though one might suspect a certain forced quality in the resignation, here
there is not the same regret that relationships did not deliver up their pur-

suits. The felt loss is "clean": suffering emerges soothed by Charlotte's sense of a nearness. The empty spaces left by these deaths bore witness to palpable (if obliterated) pleasures. The pain was the very mark of a pleasure removed but somehow alive in its trace.

True, her letters following these deaths, indeed the letters that Brontë wrote throughout her remaining years of life, reveal her struggles to cope with aloneness. Though her moods swung darkly, between dark and darker poles, she may have found, nonetheless, a way to proceed from *Villette*'s backward glance. For, less than two years after the publication of *Villette*, and less than a year before her death, Brontë married a clergyman whom she loved mostly out of pity. Patrick Brontë vehemently opposed the marriage, at least in part because Arthur Bell Nicholls was a Puseyite—an Anglican who believed that the Church of England should reclaim its roots in Rome (a strange echo of the Catholic Paul Emanuel). Her father's opposition was so intense, in fact, that at the last minute before Charlotte's wedding he refused to attend. Ironically, this refusal paid fitting tribute to *Villette*'s "articulation between autoeroticism and heteroeroticism": Charlotte was given away to her husband by another woman, her friend Margaret Wooler.[17] Thus the deed was done and a worrisome step undertaken. As Charlotte wrote to a friend:

> There has been heavy anxiety—but I begin to hope all will end for the best.
> My expectations however are very subdued—very different, I dare say, to
> what yours were before you were married. Care and Fear stand so close to
> Hope, I sometimes scarcely can see her for the shadows they cast. And yet I
> am thankful too, and the doubtful Future must be left with Providence.[18]

What is the shape of such a "Providence"? And how is a seemingly personal yet ambiguous conviction such as this theologically based?

The "Fine Religious Feeling" of an Absence

Exactly what brand or blends of theologies Brontë held we cannot be certain. We do know that Patrick Brontë, Charlotte's father, was sympathetic to Wesleyan Nonconformity and "belonged to a closely-knit group of Yorkshire Evangelicals," Yorkshire being the location where the Evangelical movement first appeared in England.[19] The parish of Haworth, in which Patrick Brontë was established as perpetual curate from 1820 until his death in 1861, had acquired note as a frequent spot on the Wesley brothers' preaching circuit. One of the curates before Patrick's time "ranked third in the Methodist hierarchy, after John and Charles Wesley," and saw to it that many famous evangelists preached in the Haworth pulpit.[20] Deemed "a religion of the heart," as Elisabeth Jay informs us, Evangelicalism stressed the life of the individual and thus viewed the individual believer as enacting the drama of apocalypse in daily life. Even so, it was Charlotte's Aunt Branwell who was most adamant in the Brontë household on matters of religious indoctrination. Among the doctrines she would have preached to the children were these: "the concept of the natural depravity of man, the need for a saving relation to God, the relative unimportance of systematic theology, and the insistence on a few simple ideas, such as the view that all pleasure is evil, the notion that all life here must be directed to the ultimate end of salvation, and the idea that only a life of restraint, abnegation, and submission to duty will have any chance of reaching that end."[21] As for Patrick, though a strong adherent to the basic doctrines of the Church of England, he manifested in his ministry an emphasis on the individual: "He was not interested in the niceties of doctrine per se so much as in the actual application of Christian principles in his own daily life and in that of his parishioners."[22]

In her own doctrinal views, Charlotte Brontë was less explicit and probably less orthodox than her father; she was surely less "enthusiastic" than her aunt. J. M. Baillie, in an early article, "Religion and the Brontës" (1931), is "concerned . . . to ask how [the Brontë sisters] came to be so little affected by the religious movement of their time."[23] He refers, of course, to the spread of Evangelicalism and the Oxford Movement. Other critics, however, suggest that in *Jane Eyre*, particularly, Brontë both responds to and critiques Evangelical Christianity, having put aside the Evangelical views of her youth to pursue a more Latitudinarian direction.[24]

These views, in the end, are not contradictory. Baillie may be generally right, in the sense that both Charlotte and Emily color their protagonists' faiths with fierce, inward, independent qualities. On the surface, these independent versions of faith seem far removed from doctrinal disputes; yet these "inward" revisions, I suggest, are themselves refinements of the Evangelical, Methodist, Calvinist, and even Catholic doctrines that surrounded the Brontës' daily conversation and reading. It is characteristic of Charlotte, at least, to bend the spiritual talk that she borrows by taking it, strangely, at its word. By taking certain doctrines to the letter, she locates the points at which these doctrines convert to new, unimagined possibilities. This tendency leads one critic, in an article on *Jane Eyre*'s "dubious" religious sense, to claim with dismay: "[Jane] employs terms from the Eucharist not out of sacramental respect but out of a desire to dramatize her emotional dependence."[25] Perhaps Queen Victoria's banal praise of *Jane Eyre*'s "fine religious feeling" offers a surprisingly apt phrase. For the difficulty of Brontë's views resides in her concern to foreground (what she regards as) "feeling" against the drapes of God's obscurity.

Mrs. Gaskell, Charlotte's biographer, is the source of a much-quoted conversation that suggests what might result from God's peculiar inaccessibility:

> We talked about the different courses through which life ran. [Charlotte] said, in her own composed manner, as if she had accepted the theory as a fact, that she believed some were appointed beforehand to sorrow and much disappointment; that it did not fall to the lot of all—as Scripture told us—to have their lines fall in pleasant places. . . . She said she was trying to school herself against ever anticipating any pleasure; that it was better to be brave and submit faithfully; there was some good reason, which we should know in time, why sorrow and disappointment were to be the lot of some on earth. It was better to acknowledge this, and face out the truth in a religious faith.[26]

Though religion clearly offers consolation, God, in Brontë's view, eludes comprehension, leaving the believer in the dread suspense of faith. Passages such as this perhaps make clear why Brontë held to political conservatism, since she was skeptical of reforms that would redress God-appointed inequities. She extrapolates this belief, moreover, from her own class-induced ills—for example, her limited anticipations of pleasure, since clergymen's daughters most often found employment as governesses, situated, immured, in bourgeois families. As a woman so immured, Brontë (though her novels often indicate otherwise) seems to affirm the Calvinist ideology that God, not sexual and political economies, sustains these disappointments of pleasure. Such passages have led to speculations that Brontë adhered to grim Calvinist views, though critics mostly stress as evidence Brontë's despair, not her politics of economic reform. Thus Baillie, sounding much like Brontë's Victorian critics, proffers the opinion that "none of her friends, her letters, or her poems suggest that she had either the capacity for or the experience of cheerful hope or joyousness which are undoubtedly characteristic of Christianity at its best."[27]

Demonstrating the most extreme speculations, Rosamond Langbridge ties Charlotte's experience with Heger to her "crawling, imitative creed, which . . . filled her with despair":

> It is most significant to see her predominant and fixed idea of M. Heger as "always severe, always incensed against her" (that image which haunted her dreams and depressed her vitality because, do what she might, she could not

win from him that exacting form of appreciation which was unconsciously the only kind she wanted), transferring itself to her conception of God, the professor of her spiritual exercises, and casting an ever-deepening shadow on her esteem and judgment of herself. Nor did it stop short here. The Calvinistic Saviour of the Brontës' world had always been a gloomy and eclectic Person of unappeasable severity and chronic habit of fault-finding, but now it became impossible to do anything up to His lofty standard and almost impossible to propitiate or please Him.[28]

Charlotte, we know, was frequently haunted by the thought that "ghastly Calvinistic doctrines are true," and that "if the Doctrine of Calvin be true I am already an outcast."[29] The chief sources of her fear were twofold: her worry that she could not demonstrate moral and spiritual perfection ("if Christian perfections be necessary to Salvation, I shall never be saved") combined with her belief that her own desire was not meant to be fulfilled ("she believed some were appointed beforehand to sorrow and much disappointment"). Yet if she feared Calvin might be right, she also hoped his scheme was wrong. Her novels provide eloquent evidence of a hope against Calvin.

It is ultimately imprecise, then, for Langbridge to speak of Brontë's "Calvinistic Saviour" as "a gloomy and eclectic Person of unappeasable severity." *Villette* indicates that Brontë was sinking the ship of this doctrine, while holding aloft, floating "him" just above or below the broken surface of watery mirrors, a more merciful God. The portrait of Paul as tyrannically tender speaks directly to Brontë's transformations. Paul's disruptive technique, which chases Lucy's desire out into clearings, transforms the "chronic habit of fault-finding" that perhaps epitomized her Calvinistic Savior.* Even the arbitrary whim of this God to appoint "sor-

---

*More than one feminist critic has acknowledged that, although he is depicted as a Catholic tyrant, Paul affects Lucy in ways that are other than strictly tyrannical. Thus Gilbert and Gubar assert, on the one hand, that "Paul . . . wants Lucy to join the ranks of Milton's dutiful daughters by executing his commands either as a secretary who transcribes his performances or as a writer who will improvise in French on prescribed subjects" (*Madwoman*, 429). On the other hand, over and against what they refer to as Paul's "petty tyrannies," Gilbert and Gubar admit that "his very faults . . . make it impossible for Lucy to see him as anything other than an equal" (428); for this reason, they argue, Paul "recognizes Lucy's capacity for passion because of his own fiery nature." We may conclude that it is their profoundly ambivalent interpretation of Paul that leads these writers, in a remarkably detailed reading of *Villette*, to devote surprisingly little space to discussion of this prominent "anti-hero" (their phrase). See also Blake on Paul's "indirect good to Lucy" (*Love and the Woman Question*, 67, 71) and Karen Chase (*Eros and Psyche*) on "the very force of [Paul's] antagonism . . . [that] makes him an agent for [Lucy's] change" (69). Moglen also argues that "[Paul] sparks [Lucy] to growth" (*Charlotte Brontë*, 218, 214–29)—a view Tayler likewise champions throughout her reading.

row and much disappointment"—appointments that seem to assign class standing—reappear, reworked, in *Villette*. Paul reverses Lucy's class inequities, *in spite of* Lucy's preordained fate to meet with "sorrow and much disappointment." Brontë achieves this revision by adhering to an orthodox formula: the savior's ability to erase God's judgment (here class standing) by his willingness to suffer with those put low.

If it is too simplistic to read Brontë as grimly Calvinistic, it is insufficient to read her as strictly anti-Catholic. This claim will seem harder to support in light of Lucy's ire toward Catholics. Yet, what Brontë detected as Catholic sensuality both attracted and repelled her; indeed, this might explain her attempted distinctions between the novel's Catholics: between Paul Emanuel's beckoning passion and Madame Beck's sensual indulgence. Perhaps Brontë distrusted the tangible qualities of Catholic sacramentalism, believing this easy promise of presence was sure to disappoint. Her hatred of hypocrisy was surely strong, and she apparently felt that the supposedly immediate audience with God that Catholics enjoyed was unduly controlled by human priests—a priesthood, Lucy remarks in *Villette*, that "might march straight on and straight upward to an all-dominating eminence." Gilbert and Gubar claim that Lucy sees the church as "a patriarchal structure with the power to imprison her."[30] This reading suggests that it was the prominent institutional scaffolding of the church, as much as anything else, that disturbed her.* It may even be possible that Brontë used the Catholic setting of *Villette* as an opportunity to criticize, under the veil of anti-Catholicism, institutional aspects of the Anglican church she found incompatible with "inward" faith—even though this inwardness was itself produced by Protestant institutions.

It is significant, then, that Brontë, a devout Christian, strongly critiqued *both* Evangelicalism and Catholicism, for J. Hillis Miller reminds us that in nineteenth-century England Evangelicalism and the Catholic revival were "belated attempts to stop the 'melancholy, long, withdrawing roar' of the sea of faith."[31] Miller explains that this period was characterized not so much by God's death as by God's inaccessibility: "God still lives, but, as Hölderlin said, he lives 'above our heads, up there in a different world.' . . . God keeps himself hidden."[32] The Reformation itself, Miller argues, had played a decisive, though not immediate, role in weakening the doctrine of the incarnation, particularly as it receives expression in the Protestant Eucharist:

*Terry Eagleton (*Myths of Power: A Marxist Study of the Brontës*) picks up on this criticism as well when he notes: "Religion can clearly be *too* worldly; and this is true in *Villette* of Roman Catholicism, whose clergy are condemned as 'mitred aspirants for this world's kingdoms'" (67).

Instead of being the literal transubstantiation of bread and wine into the body and blood of Christ, the Eucharist came more and more to be seen in the Zwinglian or Calvinistic manner. To these reformers the bread and wine are mere signs commemorating the historical fact that Christ was once, long ago, present on earth: "This do in remembrance of me." Instead of being a sharing in the immediate presence of Christ, the communion service becomes the expression of an absence.[33]

These observations apply with special force to *Villette*. By depicting Paul as a *remembered incarnation* by the novel's end, Brontë's text conveys the enigma of inaccessible presence. So many of the phrases, in fact, that pass as theological in her novel—"a blank," "a Presence nameless," "attesting trace," "somewhere," even "elsewhere"—demonstrate how Brontë challenges absolutes in order to affirm an Absolute experienced as infinitely deferred from a present standpoint.

J. Hillis Miller asserts that, in the face of God's absence, the Victorian Romantics (Browning, Emily Brontë, Arnold, and Hopkins, for his purposes) sought "to re-establish communication" by "[defining] the artist as the creator or discoverer of hitherto unapprehended symbols . . . which establish a new relation, across the gap, between man and God."[34] In *The Secular Pilgrims of Victorian Fiction*, Barry Qualls seems to agree, for he suggests that before the nineteenth-century novelists, the Romantics "transmuted . . . spiritual biography into *Bildungsroman*."* Such a transmutation was tied to their revision of God: "From the being outside and beyond man, ordering all life, God comes down to nature and retreats to the world within, to the inner life where He—or the experience of 'God'—comes to stand for order, creativity, imagination."[35] Qualls considers the Victorians inheritors of both the religious tradition of Bunyan's spiritual biography and the Romantics' revision of this tradition. What the Victorians did with this inheritance was to change the focus from "a world elsewhere" (the phrase Qualls uses for the spiritual realm) to a "world of 'human interest and business,' of ordinary life."[36]

Undoubtedly, Brontë draws upon Bunyan's spiritual biography. Just as surely, she situates her fiction in the everyday realm of human affairs. But having said this, we must acknowledge two caveats. Unlike the Romantics, as Miller describes them, Brontë does not so much seek to close the gap between God and human beings as she attempts to affirm this gap

---

*Qualls, *Secular Pilgrims*, ix. Terry Eagleton, in "The Structure of Charlotte Brontë's Fiction," briefly notes "that Charlotte tends in puritan fashion to conceive of 'real life' biography as plot and fable" (*Myths of Power*, 91). Tayler discusses biblical imagery in detail but does not address Brontë's use of the Puritan autobiographical form.

as her "cure." Nor is it accurate to state, as Qualls does, that "a heaven beyond is not [Lucy's] focus."[37] Lucy's focus "elsewhere," I suggest, is precisely the means by which she is shown as accepting the incompletion of desire. For the pleasures of work depend in *Villette* on the pain of parting and, further, on the strange pursuits set in motion by divine obstacles and divine blanks.

Chapter 5

Working for God Autoerotically:
Approaching the Bridegroom Without
A(r)rival in Brontë's *Villette*

~✎

Employment as a Watcher of Women's Suffering

Comprising a rush on autoeroticism, Lucy's story of class "fall" and "rise" is punctuated by mirror-attractions. As Irigaray would predict, these mirrorings function as erotic exchange. As Irigaray might not foresee, they also function *vocationally* for Lucy, letting her touch upon a series of vocations that may or may not be available to her—roles as bourgeois housewife, wealthy widow, kept coquette, actress, capitalist career-woman, nun, and master-teacher. These body-echoes dramatize Lucy's ambiguous class position as one who fell from the bourgeoisie (her secret family sorrow) and as one who sought to "rise" in economic, as well as sexual, terms. Through embrace with her narrative's characters, Lucy shows how she affected class privileges (and even class worries) like those which, she hints, once rightfully pertained to her. Lucy's echoing reflections of these women demonstrate, then, how she made her way sexually and vocationally through the looking glass.

The start of Lucy's story—the Polly Home and Miss Marchmont episodes—inaugurates her mirroring and splitting, setting in motion her doll- and mirror-games. To her reader, she hints at her former class position, even while relating her "fall" into nursemaid's work for these mistresses—one a bourgeois child (as Lucy once was) and one a bourgeois older woman (as, we later learn, Lucy now is). In relation to her doubles, Polly Home and Miss Marchmont, the narrator shapes a set of strange attractions. Both echoes, we discover, rendered young Lucy "autoerotically familiar to herself" (Irigaray's phrase) even as the narrator begins to turn in upon the folds of her desire—and, just as crucially, her labor history—through the act of narrating past relations. We know the narrative is retrospective from its use of past tense and certain signal phrases ("when I was a girl") that suggest an older narrator. We do not yet know the extent of retrospection, or whether Lucy tells her story from a stance of economic success or financial pain.

If we sense something skewed in Lucy's portraits of Polly, we are apt to link these apparent distortions to an "unreliable" narrator.* I have already connected this "unreliability" to the peculiar analytic effect of Lucy's spiritual tale, stressing that what Lucy is shown as telling reveals as much, if not more, about the narrator as the events do about the character. Now I want to stress that narrator and character are unhitched by time. As a consequence, this temporally spaced repetition of one Lucy by the other reveals the narrator's attempts at first to cover over and, later, to name a still disturbing work of desire. In following out this two-tiered story, I will render narrative events in the past tense so as to convey the sense of recollection. In this way, I hope to underscore the reader's role as analyst, as one who hears a linear unfolding of the past, and who must simultaneously discern its revelations and omissions.

The novel begins with numerous hints about "unsettled sadness" in Lucy's family, the clues pointing vaguely to death, or financial disaster, or both. The narrator reveals her past status as a disadvantaged relative by making reference to *Pilgrim's Progress*, suggesting that she seeks to understand her past as a spiritual journey that demands dispossession. In this way, her visit to her bourgeois relatives, who "had been residents there for generations, and bore, indeed, the name of their birthplace—Bretton of Bretton" (61)—may be marked as "a sojourn" before inevitable exile (into work). Writes Lucy: "My visits to [my godmother] resembled the sojourn of Christian and Hopeful beside a certain pleasant stream. . . . I

---

*Remarking on the "faults" of Brontë's *Villette*, Charles Burkhart writes: "There are other faults, such as mischievous use of narrative viewpoint, exaggerations and sermons, but they are only nubs or knots in the solid strong texture of the novel" (*Charlotte Brontë*, 100). Generally, however, the opinions comprising this critical debate range from those who see the narrator as basically mature and objective ("in Lucy's case, the primary perspective is the objective one of her sombre maturity" [Maynard, *Charlotte Brontë*, 165]) to those who see a development in the narrator herself ("the unreliable narrator has been replaced by one who confronts her reader directly . . . she achieves with Brontë herself the maturity of her creator's art" [Moglen, *Charlotte Brontë*, 225]). For essays that further sharpen the issues surrounding *Villette*'s narration and the question of the narrator's unreliability, see Janice Carlisle, "The Face in the Mirror: *Villette* and the Conventions of Autobiography"; Brenda R. Silver, "The Reflecting Reader in *Villette*"; and Karen Lawrence, "The Cypher: Disclosure and Reticence in *Villette*."

liked peace so well, and sought stimulus so little, that when the latter came
I almost felt it a disturbance, and wished rather it had still held aloof" (62).
In the fluid equilibrium that Lucy describes, we discern the outlines of a
Christian teleology: a movement from a home where "the soul" is not di-
vided (hence Lucy's happy stasis) to a "fall" into self-division and desire.*

This fall begins with Polly's arrival and Lucy's growing perception of
gender roles, since, in Christian schemes, humanity's fall into work and
desire is attended by the sharpened split between "the sexes."† Represented almost as displaced self-consciousness, young Lucy's growing observation of her context is biblically coded as her reading of "signs." The
narrator crucially remembers herself as having been a watcher of passions
and sufferings. When she discovered a child's bedding in her room, Lucy
remembers asking herself: "Of what are these things the signs and to-
kens?" (62). The narrator borrows this focus on "signs"—the first of
many borrowings, some rather subtle—from the Gospel of John. Her dependence on this particular gospel suits her concern with the meanings of
"home" and "exile" in her story, for John's gospel of sacraments and signs
begins with the proclamation that "[Jesus] came unto his own, and his
own received him not" (John 1:11; the Revised Standard Version reads
"came unto his home"). John's is also the gospel that renders God's own
'self' as parted from within—containing the I/thou confusions that Irigaray mimics in her mystical discourse.

Lucy's reading of "signs" informed her that a second guest was coming to Bretton. This specific memory initiates an elaborate game of dolly
in the narrative. Polly Home, a motherless child with domestic surname,

---

*For a detailed discussion of Christian teleologies, particularly in neoplatonized tra-
ditions, which he believes profoundly influenced canonical Romantic literature, see
M. H. Abrams, *Natural Supernaturalism*. Abrams details three major turns in the Christian teleology: union with God in the Garden of Eden; the fall into wandering desire
and self-consciousness (signaled by a split between "the sexes"); reunion with God
through the agency of Christ (represented as the apocalyptic nuptials between Christ
and Christ's Bride, the Church).

A recent publication—Christina Crosby's *The Ends of History: Victorians and "The
Woman Question"*—adds new understanding to how *Villette* "invites a typological reading" and "does so according to a traditional exegetical procedure well-known and
widely practised in Victorian England" (114, 113). Crosby is particularly suggestive in
her discussion of those passages in *Villette* that "induce skipping" (the extended per-
sonifications), showing that *Villette* is "wildly excessive allegory" (135–36).

†I must stress that it is a particularly neoplatonized Christian tradition, not necessarily Scripture itself, that depicts 'man' as primary. For a detailed reading of Genesis
1–3, which argues the undifferentiated status of the first earth creature created by God,
see Mieke Bal, "Sexuality, Sin, and Sorrow: The Emergence of Female Character (A
Reading of Genesis 1–3)."

whom Lucy regarded as "a mere doll" and who regarded Lucy, in return, as "the girl," becomes a doll/double upon whom the narrator plays out her memories of pain and desire. Here is a first glimpse at what increasingly looks like the narrator's way of understanding, while still obscuring, what may have been her slavery—here, quite literally, her servanthood—to her own passion.* For though the narrator claims that, even then, she distinguished herself from this excited "creature" ("'a very unique child,' thought I") Lucy's narration, from her memory of their corresponding accommodations ("in addition to my own French bed in its shady recess, appeared in a corner a small crib . . . and in addition to my mahogany chest of drawers, I saw a tiny rosewood chest" [62]) to her memory of Polly's reference to shared space ("'no need to say good night, since we sleep in the same chamber'"), serves to implicate Lucy—both narrator and character—in Polly's vagaries. One could even read Lucy's curious depiction of "Polly" as parrotlike ("how is papa's little Polly? . . . How is Polly's papa?") as the narrator's defense against the threat of Polly's doubling. This defense works by suggesting that Polly doubled everyone around her, not just Lucy. As evidence of Polly's mimicry, the narrator notes that Polly's affectionate name for Graham—"my dear boy"—was "adopted in imitation of his mother." And Polly, according to Lucy's telling, also "learned to mimic" Graham's friends, whom "she had never seen," being able "completely to realize their aspect, manners, and dispositions" (83).

More curious still is the way in which Lucy's depiction of Polly prepares for this child's doubling of the later figure, Paul (her name, Paulina, is surely a clue). Lucy performs this anticipation by making Polly a parody of Christ. These peculiar references begin with a portrayal of Polly at the washstand: "Behold! there she was risen and mounted on a stool near the wash-stand, with pains and difficulty inclining the ewer (which she could not lift) so as to pour its contents into the basin" (66). The biblical word

---

*Helene Moglen has similarly noted Lucy's defenses: "As Lucy tells Polly's story, revealing the nature of her identification with the child, as we remark upon the things she chooses *not* to tell us, we first divine the traces of Lucy's singularly defended and complex personality" (*Charlotte Brontë*, 197). Yet Moglen's detailed and insightful reading of the Bretton material is at times difficult to follow, since she often neglects to distinguish between which feelings and strategies belong to the narrator and which to young Lucy. Maynard's reading evinces an opposite tendency. He clearly distinguishes between narrator and character—"the mature Lucy reveals the hidden participation in Polly's feelings that the young Lucy of the time couldn't acknowledge" (182)—but does not suggest that the narrator cannot yet acknowledge her participation in Polly's feelings.

of wonder, "Behold!" (in the gospels it sometimes announces the Christ) is followed by Lucy's parodic rendition of Polly's crucifixion.* The phrase "risen and mounted" may allude to Christ's salvific display on the cross, prefigured in the Old Testament type of the brazen serpent set upon a pole (cf. Numbers 21:8,9 and John 3:14). Polly, however, is "risen and mounted" on a stool, not a cross. As for her wounds, Lucy sketches them in miniature: as stigmata Polly suffered from sewing a handkerchief ("pricking herself ever and anon, marking the cambric with a track of minute red dots" [73]). This detail is joined by Polly's baleful call to her father, which Lucy recounts as "a sort of 'Why hast thou forsaken me?'" By means of this characterization, Lucy conveys Polly's dramatic taste for martyrdom by dramatically *imagining* between Polly's lips Christ's words, spoken to his father, on the cross (cf. Mark 15:34). Lucy even parodies Polly's attempts to render her emotions by citing Scripture (as Lucy herself does throughout her narration):

> "Poor Jacob!" she would sometimes say, with quivering lips. "How he loved his son Joseph! As much," she once added—"as much, Graham, as I love you: if you were to die" (and she re-opened the book, sought the verse, and read), "I should 'refuse to be comforted, and go down into the grave to your mourning.'" (87)

These scriptural allusions accrue throughout *Villette* but grow less parodic when, as narrator, Lucy applies them to her own pain. (Polly's citation of this Scripture, for instance, as remembered by Lucy, prefigures the narrator's close to her story: Just as Joseph was not really dead in the biblical story, at the end of *Villette* M. Emanuel may in some sense be alive—or resurrected—though concealed from Lucy's view.) Here the narrator's parody of Polly's fears for Graham's death (and of the reading Polly fashions for this death from Scripture) could be read as expressing the narrator's discomfort with grief. Such a mocking of Polly's pain as the petite crucifixion of a doll can be seen as the narrator's unwillingness, at this point, to enter into the passions of suffering.

Another significant aspect to the narrator's doll game remains. I have said that Polly may figure for the narrator the bourgeois child that Lucy once was. We should also realize that Polly figures the bourgeois housewife that Lucy suggests she never thought she could be. Judith Newton

---

*"Behold the Lamb of God!" (John 1:36); "Behold your King!" (John 19:14); "Behold my servant, whom I have chosen; my beloved, in whom my soul is well pleased: I will put my spirit upon him, and he shall shew judgment to the Gentiles" (Matthew 12:18).

has catalogued the ways in which Polly (age six) plays the role of sacrificing "upper-middle-class housewife" to Graham Bretton (a boy of sixteen)
as she waits on him, shares his interests, and encourages his work.* I
would add that one sees in Paulina a female version of Paul Emanuel's later
"sacrifice" for *Lucy's* work. In the portrait of Paulina, however—as opposed to the portrait of Paul—Christian service collapses into, and thus
becomes indistinguishable from, the sacrifice expected of the bourgeois
woman. The narrating Lucy does not find herself in this ambiguously
"privileged" figure of the wife—as if this vocation were simultaneously
above her class and below her dignity.

Lucy's narration of the miniature mating games played out between
Paulina and Graham makes clear that she discerns (at least retrospectively)
the rise and fall of chivalric elevation, which so easily betrays a woman to
denigration. She relates Polly's own indignation when Graham "lifted
[Polly] up on high" (75) with his hand held over his head. This biblical
phrase—"lifted up on high"—refers, once again, to the elevation of
Christ, but signals only indignity for Polly. Here is another indication that
Christ-likeness functions for women as a gender prescription, not as a vol-
untary spiritual devotion. Lucy identifies further indignities of the sexual
exchange: She notes that Graham demanded kisses in payment for gifts he
gave to Polly and openly informed her, "I reckon on being able to get out
of you a little of that precious commodity called amusement" (74). If
Lucy remembers that she held herself aloof from these mating games
(though she was fourteen), her narrative hints at her awareness of the servanthood inscribed in the bourgeois woman's domesticity: She remembers that Graham teased Polly that "when he had a house of his own, she
should be his housekeeper, and perhaps—if she showed any culinary genius—his cook" (80–81).

This superimposition of the servant's role on the bourgeois woman is
precisely the point at which Polly, again, in the older Lucy's narrative,
mirrors young Lucy's class position, since Lucy herself is shown as a kind
of substitute servant for Polly's "nurse-girl." This substitution was initiated the night of Polly's arrival, and, significantly, the substitution of
Lucy for Harriet revolved around the issue of beds. As Lucy retells it:

> Ere long, a voice, issuing from the corner, demanded—
>   "May the bell be rung for Harriet?"
> I rang; the nurse was summoned and came.

*See Judith Newton on this point ("*Villette*," in Newton and Rosenfelt, *Feminist
Criticism*, 105).

> "Harriet, I must be put to bed," said her little mistress. "You must ask where my bed is."
>
> Harriet signified that she had already made that inquiry.
>
> "Ask if you sleep with me, Harriet."
>
> "No, missy," said the nurse: "You are to share this young lady's room," designating me. (65)

Shortly after this passage, we learn that Harriet left to visit friends, leaving Lucy as Polly's "companion" (and dresser, it seems). Harriet returned, as Lucy tells it, only at the end of the Polly Home episode.

Lucy's narrative, in this way, shows her as *playing* nurse-girl before she became one. But as is true of the class mirrorings this position entails, there is a display of Lucy's self-touching through her position as Polly's companion (as a substitute watcher, one could say, of Polly's grief at her parting from Graham):

> I saw the little thing shiver. "Come to me," I said, wishing, yet scarcely hoping, that she would comply: for she was a most strange, capricious, little creature, and especially whimsical with me. She came, however, instantly, like a small ghost gliding over the carpet. I took her in. She was chill; I warmed her in my arms. She trembled nervously; I soothed her. Thus tranquillized and cherished she at last slumbered. (92)

This is the first clear instance of a female embrace in *Villette*. It seems a particularly Irigarayan fiction of a feminine mirroring: one that makes women familiar to themselves by passing them through an other's opacity. For one gets the sense that, in Polly, Lucy held an opacity, "a small ghost" that she took into her arms. The autoerotic suggestions of Lucy's holding Polly, touching upon her own desire, are implicit in Lucy's reference to "wishing, yet scarcely hoping" and in the sense that Miss Snowe, embracing her doll, was warming, in part, her own chill, caressing her need to be "tranquillized and cherished." Lucy doubly embraced in Paulina the class privilege out of which she had fallen and the domestic service into which she would fall.

In her tale of Miss Marchmont, Lucy's mirror-game elaborately continues. This portrait of "a maiden lady of our neighborhood," wealthy, well-situated, impotent, gray-haired, fashions another reflection for Lucy, but one we can discern *only* retrospectively. For not until the following chapter do we learn that the narrator herself is gray-, even white-haired. As Polly was a double for young Lucy (the character) in the narrator's game of dolls, so Miss Marchmont is a double for older Lucy (the narrator) in Lucy's narrative game of mirrors: Miss Marchmont becomes a narrator within Lucy's narrative, telling a retrospective story of her own. As with the doubling that involves Polly, the trace of a servant's image remains on the representation of the mirror-attraction, splitting these female doubles along the axis of class. Lucy represents her "fall" into work—"self-reliance and exertion were forced upon me by circumstances, as they are upon thousands besides"—as her substitution for Miss Marchmont's former nursemaid:

> It seemed that a maid, or rather companion, who had waited on her for some years, was about to be married; and she, hearing of my bereaved lot, had sent for me, with the idea that I might supply this person's place. She made the proposal to me after tea, as she and I sat alone by her fireside.
>
> "It will not be an easy life," said she candidly, "for I require a good deal of attention, and you will be much confined; yet, perhaps, contrasted with the existence you have lately led, it may appear tolerable." (95)

This recollection resonates, richly, with erotic associations: from the slippage that occurs between "maid" and "companion" (the latter sounds more ambiguous jobwise and carries associations of companion in marriage), to the companion's reason for termination (she leaves her position to marry—someone else), to "the proposal" Miss Marchmont makes to Lucy (to enter, by substitution, into intimacy), to the fireside setting (firelight will soon recur with striking erotic suggestion). Lucy's details of their "sort of intimacy" strengthen her narrative's intimations of autoerotic resemblance between employer and "the watcher of suffering":

> Two hot, close rooms thus became my world; and a crippled old woman, my mistress, my friend, my all. Her service was my duty—her pain, my suffering—her relief, my hope—her anger, my punishment—her regard, my reward. . . . She gave me the originality of her character to study: the steadiness of her virtues, I will add, the power of her passions, to admire, the truth of her feelings to trust. All these things she had, for these things I clung to her. (97)

Lucy's portrayal of their cohabitation is sharply striated by the class lines drawn between them ("her service was my duty—her pain, my suffering"). Even so, Lucy's employment as companion clove her own passage to pain, to desires that attended (another woman's memories of) parting. Miss Marchmont transfixed young Lucy with remembrance—even as, at the novel's end, the reader can discern that the narrator all along has been fixed on her memory of parting from Paul.

Lucy's narrative plays complexly on a looking back that is, actually, a looking forward. When she narrates, with emotion, her final vigil with

her elderly patient (in a storm of keen, shrieking winds), this remembered
night-watch points forward, narratively, to the novel's closing tempest.
And yet, chronologically, the novel's closing tempest lies closer to the narrator's present circumstances than does her vigil with her dying mistress.
Important clues to that final narration lie embedded in this first night-
watch, the memory of which presumably spreads a wound that plagues
the narrating Lucy. Lucy even renders this death-bed vigil as an apocalypse: the Christian's internalized "end of the world," which takes the believer out of history in order to wed her, finally, to Christ. Miss Marchmont lay at a crossroads, at the portal of death, looking backwards
through extraordinary love, wedded to loss. Her recollection, folded into
Lucy's retrospection, signals the pleasure to be gained (by Lucy) in narrating a naming of (her own) desire:

> "I love Memory to-night," she said: "I prize her as my best friend. She is just
> now giving me a deep delight; she is bringing back to my heart, in warm and
> beautiful life, realities—not mere empty ideas—but what were once realities,
> and that I long have thought decayed, dissolved, mixed in with grave-mould.
> I possess just now the hours, the thoughts, the hopes of my youth. I renew
> the love of my life—its only love—almost its only affection. . . . While I
> loved, and while I was loved, what an existence I enjoyed! . . . Through that
> year my heart lived with Frank's heart. . . . If few women have suffered as I
> did in his loss, few have enjoyed what I did in his love. . . . It was such a love
> as honoured, protected, and elevated, no less than it gladdened her to whom
> it was given. . . . I do not know," she continued, after a pause: "I cannot—
> *cannot* see the reason; yet at this hour I can say with sincerity, what I never
> tried to say before—Inscrutable God, Thy will be done! And at this moment
> I can believe that death will restore me to Frank. I never believed it till now."
> (98–99)

Memory itself proved a feminine lover, delivering a dying woman to herself with "deep delight." Reported as a kind of material return to "realities—not mere empty ideas" ("I possess just now the hours, the thoughts,
the hopes of my youth"), Memory effected an analytic resurrection of
buried desire. In her retroactive capture of parting, Miss Marchmont re-
shaped anticipation; embracing Frank's void, she discovered a longing that
concludes beyond edges, materially occluded but visible as hidden.

   Here is that "articulation between autoeroticism and heteroeroticism" that Brontë's life and novels fashion from extraordinary loss, exorbitant privation. These autoerotic intimations are theologically linked
to advent, to crucifixion, even to apocalyptic consummation in Miss
Marchmont's tale of her fiancé's death (like Paul, Frank died en route to

his lover). On a "Christmas Eve," Miss Marchmont had awaited her lover's advent, sexualized in her telling as if to convey the treacherous excitements of sexual desire. Her story of that evening, as she told it to Lucy, began with a remarkably immediate "glassing," as if converting obstacle to ecstasy, and proceeded towards a coming that never arrived:

> I sat down to wait. Once more I see that moment. . . . I see and feel the soft firelight warming me, playing on my silk dress, and fitfully showing me my own young figure in a glass. . . . I wait, with some impatience in my pulse, but no doubt in my breast. . . . The moon was mounting high. . . . Would he for once fail me? No—not even for once; and now he was coming—and coming fast—to atone for lost time. (99–100)

Miss Marchmont rendered her desire in blatantly spatial terms; Frank was riding nearer, nearer, nearer . . . then a blank:

> I saw the horse; I heard it stamp—I saw at least a mass; I heard a clamour. *Was* it a horse? or what heavy, dragging thing was it, crossing, strangely dark, the lawn? How could I name that thing in the moonlight before me? or how could I utter the feeling which rose in my soul? (100)

Miss Marchmont portrayed her suspension in desire—resulting from Frank's approach without arrival—as a problem of naming. Some "thing," "strangely dark," "crossing" familiar space so as to render all familiarity opaque, defied attempts at naming. Miss Marchmont summoned the rhetoric of crucifixion—here without the parody that Lucy, as narrator, uses on Polly—as a means of representing the gash of desire. Miss Marchmont recalled for Lucy how this opacity had embraced her, until its alien quality had become transmuted into a kind of pietà:

> But I was kneeling down in the snow beside something that lay there—something that I had seen dragged along the ground—something that sighed, that groaned on my breast, as I lifted and drew it to me. He was not dead; he was not quite unconscious. I had him carried in; I refused to be ordered about and thrust from him. I was quite collected enough, not only to be my own mistress, but the mistress of others. They had begun by trying to treat me as a child, as they always do with people struck by God's hand; but I gave place to none except the surgeon; and when he had done what he could, I took my dying Frank to myself. He had strength to fold me in his arms; he had power to speak my name; he heard me as I prayed over him very softly; he felt me as I tenderly and fondly comforted him.
>
> "Maria," he said, "I am dying in Paradise." He spent his last breath in faithful words for me. When the dawn of Christmas morning broke, my Frank was with God. (100–101)

Miss Marchmont's narration reverberated with Augustine's tradition of Christ's mounting the cross as a marriage bed. Her own stress fell on approach to the marriage bed of consummation that culminates, dramatically, in crucifixion, locating the material fulfillment of the abandoned believer beyond the brink of bodies.

Miss Marchmont recalled that her servants had tried to intervene between her and her dying "thing," but that she had rejected their (duteous!) attempts to "treat me like a child," having preferred contact with the opaque object of suffering. And yet, of course, Miss Marchmont was telling her life's great passion to her nursemaid, Lucy, as if to affirm the indispensable role of a watcher of sorrow—the analyst/nursemaid paid to acknowledge the patient's suffering. Lucy's role as this analyst figure is underlined by what she recalls as her mistress's final question: "What do you think, Lucy, of these things? Be my chaplain and tell me."* Lucy's memory of her response, moreover, "I had no words," is the perfect theological/psychoanalytic response. This bewildered silence—a fitting quiescence on the part of the analyst—was "the answer" Miss Marchmont had "never tried to say before": "We should acknowledge God merciful, but not always for us comprehensible. We should accept our own lot whatever it be, and try to render happy that of others. Should we not?" This resignation, platitudinous as it is—reminiscent of Brontë's remark about the pain and disappointment life allots to some—effects, nonetheless, the blankening of God that charges *Villette*.†

Exile and Ecstasy: Taking a Part(ing)

The next step in Lucy's spiritual tale occasions a twist on vocation as substitution. Upon her employer's death, looking "like an over-wrought servant," Lucy recalls that she went "to see and consult an old servant of our family; once my nurse, now housekeeper at a grand mansion not far from Miss Marchmont's" (103). This is a small but arresting detail in what Lucy depicts as her vocational "turning." This remembered incident represents a looking glass cracked, again, by class. Here the "old servant of our family, once my nurse" reflects for the narrator that she, Lucy, in one

---

*For a discussion of the nursemaid as a figure for the paid analyst, see Gallop, "Keys to Dora," in *Daughter's Seduction*, 141–43. See also Peter Stallybrass and Allon White, "Below Stairs: The Maid and the Family Romance," 162–63.

†My reading takes obvious issue with Gilbert and Gubar's contention that Miss Marchmont "is in effect a nun, but a nun who receives no religious consolation, since she can neither understand nor condone the ways of God" (*Madwoman*, 406).

respect, mirrored Polly's class position, for she was once a girl with a nurse. Simultaneously, Lucy's echo of her nurse signals that, in another respect, Lucy was split from the bourgeoisie, for Lucy, too, served as a nurse to a mistress in a mansion. Ultimately, then, this mirroring, as Lucy in later life depicts it, bore the quality of a self-consultation. Lucy consulted a figure for herself, touched upon her fall into servanthood, before her vocational opportunities took a turn.

Expectedly, Lucy represents this turning in terms that suit her spiritual stance: " 'Leave this wilderness,' it was said to me, 'and go out hence' " (104). This language of exile (God's words to Abraham) enables the narrator's retrospective reading of her vocational ambitions as the believer's necessary wandering in suffering, self-consciousness, and desire. Here is an instance of how alienation, even in the biblical guise of exile, is best recognized from some future standpoint. Lucy's narrative itself offers figures for the act of retrospection. Lucy tells the reader how she casually discovered that Englishwomen were finding congenial positions as nurses in foreign families. This fortuitous discovery causes Lucy to comment that "I stored up this piece of casual information, as careful housewives store seemingly worthless shreds and fragments for which their prescient minds anticipate a possible use some day" (105). In a novel in which an old woman remembers through immediate narration and anticipation, this statement may figure how subjects unconsciously anticipate revisionary recovery of their lives. Storing up the shreds and fragments of their present, they prepare for a future backward glance that assigns meaning to disordered selection. In this sense, one lives always anticipating one's retrospection.

Particularly fitting, the narrator, two paragraphs later, breaks her narrative in order to present herself in parentheses: "(for I speak of a time gone by: my hair which till a late period withstood the frosts of time, lies now, at last white, under a white cap, like snow beneath snow)" (105). This casual piece of information, stored up by Lucy's text, lends a suggestion of just how retroactive is her telling, causing us to meditate, retrospectively, on the mirroring relation between Lucy and her mistress. One also senses here, via the pun "snow beneath snow," the analytic quality of spiritual autobiography: the narrating Lucy—seemingly present, more available to the reader—lies beneath the more distant Snowe, whose body and relations (now obliterated by the passing of time) must be *re-*created for the sake of the narrator's present concerns. No wonder this story can so accurately prophesy its unfolding events. It is told by one who knows the ending, though she knows in a "factual," not an "analytic" sense. The shreds and fragments young Lucy is shown to have stored along the way are themselves imbued with the narrator's present; they are represented as touched upon *only* by the narrator's present impetus to write her life as her spiritual history.

Brontë's act of writing according to spiritual paradigms brings us to Lucy's exilic allusions. Since exile for Moses (but also for Christ) prepares for future ecstasy, Lucy's depiction of her journey to London as a journey to Babylon (the biblical land of Israel's exile) enables her depictions of visionary ecstasy in urban excitement. The interest for *Villette* in one of Brontë's devoirs for Heger, "La mort de Moïse" ("The Death of Moses"), lies in its themes of present exile and future (though presently deferred) fulfillment. Brontë represents the "mystic cloud which veils Jehovah" as commanding Moses: "Look towards the South, towards the regions of Gilead and Manasseh, towards Jericho the city of palm trees, towards the far-off sea. That is the land which I promised to Abraham and his seed for ever; I have shown it to thee but thou shalt not enter it." Though Moses feels "the bitter regrets of the man condemned to die at the moment when life offers him most charms," Brontë assures us that "a new impression, powerful in quite another fashion, had taken possession of his soul." He is graced to envision Israel's future, consummated by the Messiah's advent (a consummation inextricably tied to crucifixion in the Christian tradition). This hope provides such a "moment of ecstasy" that Moses, she writes, "ceased to live."[1]

Not only does this essay bear implications for Lucy's later ecstasy with Paul (a moment she was condemned to outlive), it also casts her vocational ambitions in a biblical light. Her overview of the city recalls Moses' vision toward the south from Mount Nebo:

> Finding myself before St. Paul's, I went in; I mounted to the dome: I saw thence London, with its river, and its bridges, and its churches; I saw antique Westminster, and the green Temple Gardens, with sun upon them, and a glad, blue sky of early spring above; and, between them and it, not too dense a cloud of haze.
>
> Descending, I went wandering whither chance might lead, in a still ecstacy of freedom and enjoyment; and I got—I know not how—I got into the heart of city life. I saw and felt London at last: I got into the Strand; I went up Cornhill; I mixed with the life passing along; I dared the perils of crossings. To do this, and to do it utterly alone, gave me, perhaps an irrational, but a real pleasure. Since those days, I have seen the West-end, the parks, the fine squares; but I love the city far better. The city seems so much more in earnest: its business, its rush, its roar, are such serious things, sights, and

sounds. The city is getting its living—the West-end but enjoying its pleasure.
At the West-end you may be amused, but in the city you are deeply excited.
    Faint, at last, and hungry (it was years since I had felt such healthy hun-
ger), I returned, about two o'clock, to my dark, old, and quiet inn. (109)

This oddly ecstatic passage may register Lucy's desire to labor at the heart
of London's business—and, perhaps, to glean the capital that feeds London pleasures. And though she constructs work and desire as excitements
opposed to the search for pleasure (City business vs. West End amusement), her entire narration bespeaks her desire to link work with pleasure,
to see work *as* pleasure—as self-pleasure, even ("to do this, and to do it
utterly alone").

    This possible relation—work as pleasure—is buried through much of
Lucy's narration. Consistently, she splits off work from pleasure, affirming the Protestant valuation of work, while scorning what she deems the
Catholic indulgence of sensual pleasure. Her description of Madame
Beck's summer festival affirms this dichotomy while subtly confusing it,
since Lucy was induced, by the Catholic Paul Emanuel, to take a part for
pleasure in the fête. Before Lucy narrates the fête, however, she tells how
she came to be an English teacher at the pensionnat. In a crucial way, Lucy's reluctance to take the part of teacher (for her, a class ascent) matches
her reluctance to take part in the fête's "comic trifle." Her acceptance of
both parts foretells the marriage between work and pleasure that her final
narration dramatically effects.

    The story of Lucy's vocational transition from nursemaid to teacher
proves, not surprisingly, one of substitution. Replacing at first the drunk
Mrs. Sweeny, Lucy, we are told, took a hybrid position "between gou-
vernante and lady's-maid." Not long after, Madame Beck abruptly requested Lucy to substitute for the English master. Lucy paints herself as
having lacked ambition—"I shrunk into my sloth, like a snail into its
shell. . . . I was capable of sitting twenty years teaching infants the horn-
book"—also as having sought to avoid pain, not to gain the luxury of
pleasure: "My work had neither charm for my taste, nor hold on my interest . . . the negation of severe suffering was the nearest approach to
happiness I expected to know" (139–40). Only at *Villette*'s apocalyptic
conclusion do suffering and happiness, work and pleasure, prove congenial bedfellows.

    At this point, Madame Beck provided the impetus for Lucy to fall
more completely into work, even as Lucy rose in expectations: "[Madame
Beck], without more ado, made me relinquish thimble and needle; my

hand was taken into hers, and I was conducted down stairs" (140). This resultant turn in Lucy's class position is rendered in her memory as Madame Beck's requirement that she surpass the ineffectual Miss Turner—a teacher Madame Beck described as having "no more command over [the students] than a servant from the kitchen would have had" (141). But if Lucy remembers that she succeeded where the "slavish" Miss Turner had failed, she also represents her employer, Madame Beck, as the educational version of a capitalist exploiter: "From that day I ceased to be a nursery-governess, and became English teacher. Madame raised my salary; but she got thrice the work out of me she had extracted from Mr. Wilson, at half the expense" (144). The imprint of her fall from the bourgeoisie thus sticks to Lucy, even as she supposedly rises in ambivalent response to Madame Beck.*

Lucy's narration of the fête proves complex in her introduction of Paul Emanuel, whose Catholic passion she wants to contrast with Catholic sensuality. There may be an even subtler contrast being drawn, one that may license Lucy's erotic fractures with the female characters of her memory, who perhaps, in ways yet to be realized, culminate in Paul. Lucy begins remembering the fête by presenting the kind of woman she is not:

> The Parisienne . . . was prodigal and profligate (in disposition, that is: as to action, I do not know). That latter quality showed its snake-head to me but once, peering out very cautiously. A curious kind of reptile it seemed, judging from the glimpse I got; its novelty whetted my curiosity: if it would have come out boldly, perhaps I might philosophically have stood my ground, and coolly surveyed the long thing from forked tongue to scaly tail-tip; but it merely rustled in the leaves of a bad novel; and, on encountering a hasty and ill-advised demonstration of wrath, recoiled and vanished, hissing. She hated me from that day. (194–95)

The innuendos here—profligacy, a snakish advance glimpsed just once, whetted curiosity (from her tongue to her tail-tip) that must be put to rest by its conversion into wrath, and the specter of inferior novelistic possibilities—all point to lesbianism.† Presumably, by making this version of

---

*Passages like these demonstrate that if Brontë did adhere to Calvinist views of predetermined fates (which we cannot be sure she did), such adherence did not keep her from making astute critiques of sociopolitical economies.

†In her article "Passion Between Women in the Victorian Novel," Sarah Putzell-Korab notes Victorians' associations of lesbianism with the French novel. She writes: "In 1901 the British medical journal *The Lancet* smugly announced, 'As yet in this country the novelist . . . has not arrived at the treatment in romance of . . . Sapphism,' which it groups with other 'diseases . . . found in French novels.' Opinion has not significantly altered since then. In 1956 Jeanette Foster remarked that until the end of the

desire between women retreat, hissing, from her narrative, Lucy clears a space for her approved erotic startle, grasped through other women as she makes her way to Paul. Of course, Paul himself, as Lucy represents him directing the play, leads her through the bodies of women to new heights ("a trance to the seventh heaven") of sexual possibility.

It is not surprising, then, that Lucy depicts his demand that she "take a part" in the fête as Paul's sexualized invasion of her "sanctuary" ("firm, fast, straight—right on through vestibule, along corridor . . . strode a step, quick, regular, intent" [201]). The tremendously intricate narration that ensues reveals Paul as goad, who, precisely by virtue of his style of interaction, sets in motion the contradictions of Lucy's desire. On the one hand, the reader, with feminist critics, may detest (what Lucy depicts as) Paul's tyranny and his constant attacks on "vile *amour-propre*"—"that base quality," he claimed, "of which women have so much." This attack on a woman's "self-respect" and "self-love" (her autoeroticism?) seems sexist to an extreme. But Paul's offensive against "the proper love" of women's self-respect may also be read as something else, something other than re-sistance to their autoeroticism: an attack against the self-respecting femi-nine elevation the culture deems "propre" for Victorian women. Indeed, his provocations, as Lucy recounts them, differed greatly from Graham Bretton's denigration of Polly when he raised her up in chivalrous con-tempt. Jane Gallop's remarks on Lacan may be strangely germane:

> Not simply a philosopher, but, artfully, a performer, he is no mere father fig-ure out to purvey the truth of his authority; he also comes out seeking his pleasure in a relation that the phallocentric universe does not circumscribe. To designate Lacan at his most stimulating and forceful is to call him some-thing more than just phallo-centric. He is also phallo-eccentric. Or, in more pointed language, he is a prick. . . .
>
> Unlike phallocentrism which locates itself in a clear-cut polemic field where opposition conditions a certain good and evil, the prick is "beyond good and evil," "beyond the phallus." Phallocentrism and the polemic are masculine, upright matters.
>
> The prick, in some crazy way, is feminine. The prick does not play by the rules; he (she) is a narcissistic tease who persuades by means of attraction

---

nineteenth century the presentation of lesbianism in literature was 'nearly an exclusive product of France.' . . . At most, Nina Auerbach's 1978 study, *Communities of Women*, acknowledges lesbianism as 'a silent possibility in two or three of the novels.' This 'si-lent possibility' deserves further consideration, however, because educated Victorians were aware of it from their reading of French novels, and it is referred to in English literature" (180). Putzell-Korab discusses this "silent possibility" in her article, provid-ing a brief discussion of *Villette* in which, she, too, cites the passage on the Parisienne.

and resistance, not by orderly systematic discourse. The prick, which as male organ might be expected to epitomize masculinity, lays bare its desire.[2]

There is no better reading of Lucy on Paul than Gallop on Lacan. In a bizarre relation of anticipation and retroaction, the Paul Emanuel of Lucy's narrative progressively resembles the French psychoanalyst. Indeed, Stuart Schneiderman's description of Lacan fits Paul remarkably well: he was "raised a Catholic . . . [and] educated by Jesuits"; "he did not seek respectability—he sought respect"; "people were in awe of him and approached him with a mixture of fear and reverence"; he "managed to create a reputation for being strange, bizarre, insolent, and at times outrageous"; he "was also known as an extremely generous man . . . he often showed a degree of hospitality quite out of character in his city, [and] his devotion and dedication to his patients had few limits."[3] As Lacan has claimed, moreover, that "the analytic maieutic adopts a round-about approach that amounts in fact to inducing in the subject a controlled paranoia" (*E*, 15), so Paul is shown to have produced in Lucy something similar, having hoped, it seems, for Lucy's failure to sustain her facade of "vile *amour-propre*." "Christ," in *Villette*, proves to be a prick for the sake of Lucy's pleasure.

Paul's treatment of Lucy as she learned her lines for the play figures such *induced paranoia*, a disturbance that strikes at the root of a woman's denigrating heights. Lucy recalls that Paul locked her in the "solitary and lofty attic" (an elevation) where the "objects . . . discomposed me more, perhaps, than it would be wise to say." Here, too, trapped in seclusion, she recalls how she began to lose her taste for withdrawal and sacrifice: "A *pâté*, or a square of cake, it seemed to me would come very *apropos*; and as my relish for these dainties increased, it began to appear somewhat hard that I should pass my holiday, fasting and in prison" (203–5). As if to convey that ecstasy proceeds from exile—or that autoeroticism proceeds from *attacks* on "vile *amour-propre*"—Lucy recalls that Paul, soon after, broke in upon the attic, at which point, she tells us, in "an inverse repetition of the impetus which had brought me up into the attic, [he] instantly took me down—down—down to the very kitchen . . . superintended my repast, and almost forced upon me more than I could swallow" (206).

Paul, like Lacan, for all his phallic thunder, sided with the "not-all"; his getting Lucy to "take a part" was a way of getting her to take back a lack. The role that Paul induced Lucy to play—a "butterfly, talker, and traitor" (a prick?)—well suited this strategy. Playing such a "narcissistic tease" (Gallop's term), Lucy could woo Ginevra in the play in a manner that "in some crazy way, is feminine." Lucy took this subversive route.

She created a costume of indefinite sexual signification when she overlaid her customary feminine dress with masculine signs (vest, collar, cravat, paletôt). As this oddly vested creature, Lucy recalls she made love to Ginevra; and what had been her initial reluctance gave way as she recklessly redesigned her "part":

> Now I know I acted as if wishful and resolute to win and conquer. Ginevra seconded me; between us we half-changed the nature of the *rôle*, gilding it from top to toe. . . . I know not what possessed me either; but somehow, my longing was to eclipse the "Ours": *i.e.*, Dr. John. Ginevra was tender; how could I be otherwise than chivalric? Retaining the letter, I recklessly altered the spirit of the *rôle*. Without heart, without interest, I could not play it at all. It must be played—in went the yearned-for seasoning—thus flavoured, I played it with relish. What I felt that night, and what I did, I no more expected to feel and do, than to be lifted in a trance to the seventh heaven. (210–11)

Lucy appears to have earned self-affection by making a pass at heteroeroticism. The play reveals what is literally a feminine embrace with a vengeance, aimed as it is at a(r)rival ("my longing was to eclipse the 'Ours': *i.e.*, Dr. John"). By making love to another woman, Lucy, as she renders it, became autoerotically familiar to herself ("I acted to please myself"), having touched upon (her own) longing and (her own) coquetry that she later acted out with Paul. Before the drama, Paul had instructed Lucy along with the other girls "to penetrate herself well with a sense of her personal *in*significance" (209; my emphasis).* This command, which only a prick could pass along, urges self-penetration with a lack. Yet, throughout *Villette*, as in Irigaray, too, self-puncture with the soft or sharp edges of obstacles allows a woman to feel her own desire. Lucy's caress of her "personal insignificance"—the greatest obstacle to her class climb— enables her pleasure of parting from herself, of slipping another part "between" herself and Ginevra. Strikingly, the narrator associates her sexual assertion that evening ("what I felt that night, and what I did") with a particularly mystical move: "a trance to the seventh heaven."† Ecstasy and exile meet each other here, for Lucy's entire narration is structured on the spiritual tenet that an exile into work and desire vows ecstasy.

*The enigmatic if not offensive quality of this comment may be the reason that the Penguin edition of *Villette* mistakenly substitutes "significance" for "insignificance," thus softening the blow of Paul's seemingly outrageous instructions to his female players. See the Clarendon edition, 195.

†In her devoir "La Mort de Moïse," Brontë uses the term "seventh heaven" in apposition to the phrase "the very throne of the eternal."

Coquetry and Capitalism

Lucy's tendency to read her life in biblical terms—exile and the promise of ecstatic rise—enables her to portray her ambitions as "authorized"
rather than interested ("I am a rising character: once an old lady's companion, then a nursery-governess, now a school-teacher" [394]). For this
reason, we should not be surprised that Lucy's denial of ambition accompanies her anxious portraits of ambitious desire in both its sexual and economic forms. Predictably, her portraits of Ginevra Fanshawe (as coquette)
and Madame Beck (as capitalist educator) spell Lucy's denegation of likeness. As always, however, the differences Lucy asserts are belied by her
narrative's mirrors. For later, we learn that Lucy was called a coquette by
Paul and became a Madame Beck when she became the owner (by substitution!) of a school for girls. Significantly, in light of Lucy's eventual
relation to capitalism, Lucy's narrative connects both Ginevra and Madame Beck to trading elements.

As one might expect from her customary split between work and
pleasure, Lucy paints Ginevra as "a child of pleasure"—"work or suffering found her listless" (211). We are clearly expected from this observation
to construct Lucy and coquettish Ginevra at the opposite ends of a work/
pleasure spectrum. The narrator now repeats her contrast between a Catholic penchant for pleasure and a Protestant commitment to work, and renders this conflict most humorously when she recalls how she "drubbed"
Ginevra as a "John Knox to a Mary Stuart"(408)! But even this bold conflict cannot hold. When Lucy tells the reader, "I stood and let [Ginevra's]
self-love have its feast and triumph: curious to see how much it could swallow" (214), she uses the very language that describes her moment of pleasure when Paul Emanuel led her from the attic and fed her to the brink of
satisfaction ("almost forced upon me more than I could swallow"). These
and other touches force us to link Lucy to Ginevra, even as the narrator
strenuously denies any such resemblance.

This unacknowledged likeness even emerges in the odd way that Lucy
repeats certain features of the "trading element in [Ginevra's] composition." Ginevra, we learn, was the daughter of a man whose family connections were unquestionably good (Lucy's were too) but who had little
money (Lucy's own bind). Against this background, Lucy disdains Ginevra's resourcefulness, her knack for acquiring commodities she could
not afford on her own, even though Lucy's narrative reveals that her own
dresses were bought by the Brettons, and that, later, Paul Emanuel "gave"

her a school. One could even argue that Ginevra's stated purpose—"I will never be a bourgeois wife, not me!" (156)—speaks for Lucy's implied refusal, throughout her narrative, of the married role, as if both women's ambitions require their rejection of wifehood.

Ginevra's coquetry (in dictionary terms, "the act of trifling or dallying") reveals her as knowing how the sexual game is played. It is precisely her savvy as a sexual trader ("I heard her adjudge to every jewel its price"), and her ability to manipulate masculine stakes, that makes her coquetry a sign of her commercial interest and skill ("Are you disposed to barter?" she asks Lucy Snowe; later she declares, "I have got my portion!"). Ginevra knows how to market herself as a "charming commodity" and a "flashing gem" (Lucy's phrases), using her own commodification as capital by which to invest (in) herself.

Lucy's ties to coquetry and commercialism prove more attenuated than Ginevra's sly self-commodifications. True, the novel insists on their embraces—their wooing at the fête, their walking arm-in-arm, their spontaneous waltzing—moments that unquestionably force Lucy's contact with her own coquetry and her potential for commodification on "the market." Lucy's tendency, nonetheless, to portray herself as the "gentleman" with Ginevra suggests that, in recalling these embraces, she seeks to shun the woman's position in the trade (something Brontë found extremely degrading). Even so, Lucy's denial of her attraction to Ginevra ("Take yourself away. I have no pleasure in looking at you or your *parure* [set of jewels]" [153]) is dashed with the way she comments, throughout, on Ginevra's beauty and the way she recalls how she interposed Ginevra between herself and Paul—as if one could touch upon Lucy Snowe only through Ginevra Fanshawe.

Madame Beck, "the bourgeoise," stimulates Lucy's more serious reservations regarding ambition and private ownership. She particularly unleashes the anxiety (probably shared by Brontë) that access to capital short-circuits loss that cannot be denied. Madame Beck's sensual indulgence, her prurience really, *frugally* controls the production and circulation of commodities (girls) in Madame's school/factory. Here, we note, Brontë makes Madame Beck's Catholic sensuality serve a kind of Protestant frugality and capitalist accumulation—just as, by a reverse impetus, she eventually makes Lucy's Protestant work ethic blossom into a kind of Catholic sacramentalism. More than that, the narrator associates surveillance—for her a central aspect of Catholic control—with Madame Beck's form of capitalist possession. From her first appearance in Lucy's narrative, Madame Beck is linked to gazing and sizing up. Her spying, we learn, takes place through keyholes or "from some aperture or summit of observation, through parted bough or open window" (182). Much as we are asked to deplore surveillance, to associate it with ambitious deceit, we soon realize Lucy's implication in Madame Beck's practice, for Lucy, too, often spied through keyholes; and, later, an "aperture" furthers her remarkable sexual ambitions.

In fact, Lucy's affiliations with her archrival, Madame Beck, go deeper than surveillance. Through Madame Beck, Lucy confronted, indirectly, her own aspirations for control and even ownership. Each woman gazed upon the other's surveillance, and each used mirrors to perform this indirection. In one recollection, Lucy reveals the gazing game and the sexual-economic stakes of its play:

> I will not deny that it was with a secret glee I watched her. Had I been a gentleman, I believe madame would have found favour in my eyes, she was so handy, neat, thorough in all she did. . . . I stood, in short, fascinated; but it was necessary to make an effort to break this spell: a retreat must be beaten. The searcher might have turned and caught me; there would have been nothing for it then but a scene, and she and I would have had to come all at once, with a sudden clash, to a thorough knowledge of each other: down would have gone conventionalities, away—swept disguises, and *I* should have looked into her eyes, and *she* into mine—we should have known that we could work together no more, and parted in this life for ever. (186)

A certain fascination bound Lucy to her mistress. But the retreat required here also figures the convoluted mediations required for Lucy's telling: the series of surveillant attractions, which the narrator continually sets up but denies, enables Lucy's simultaneous avowal ("I will not deny") and disguise ("had I been a gentleman") of her desire for women ("to come all at once, with a sudden clash, to a thorough knowledge of each other").

Even though Lucy's split from Madame Beck lies along the lines of class and access to capital, recalling class divisions between Lucy and her other female "superiors," Lucy clearly admires her adversary, even when she most sarcastically renders Madame Beck's achievements. Unlike her other mistresses whose access to capital arises through patrimony (or marriage), Madame Beck's capital comes from her work. Perhaps this is why Lucy paints Madame Beck as masculine: "At that instant, she did not wear a woman's aspect, but rather a man's. Power of a particular kind strongly limned itself in all her traits, and that power was not *my* kind of power: neither sympathy, nor congeniality, nor submission, were the emotions it awakened" (141).* According to Lucy's portrait, Madame Beck ran a met-

---

*Vashti, of course, is another threatening figure of aggressive desire, though one far more in touch with suffering and the gaping of desire than Madame Beck is shown to

onymic economy, whereby she was constantly firing and hiring, substituting one employee for another, in search of the best value for her money (on the side, she and the Jesuit Père Silas were "nursing . . . the West Indian estate" to which Paul Emanuel was later exiled). Lucy was a worker in this establishment. Yet her praise of Madame Beck's management—she conceived "her own system for managing and regulating this mass of machinery," "a real business to fill her time"—may signal Lucy's identification with the owner of a school, such as Lucy may still be at the point that she narrates.

Significant, however, for her representations of "order and industry," Lucy attributes system breakdowns in Madame Beck's machine to uncontrollable pain and desire. For the woman to whom "interest was . . . the alpha and omega of her life" (a biblical allusion that opposes Madame Beck to Paul), pain is a gaping that one should always veil. Lucy renders this resistance—and Madame Beck's imperviousness to piercing—by alluding to the crucifixion (one in a series of crucifixion references): "No force or mass of suffering concentrated in one heart had power to pierce hers. Not the agony in Gethsemane, not the death on Calvary, could have wrung from her eyes one tear" (137).

Desire's equally troublesome rupture is brought comically to the surface by tales of Madame's children. Désirée, whose name signatures the "farce" of her mother's desire, was a child entirely out of control ("'Quel poison que cet enfant là!' were the expressions dedicated to her, alike in kitchen and in school-room" [157]). As if proving Lacan's assertion that desire is bound to loss, Madame's Désirée, Lucy informs us, "stole and hid." Lucy first mentions a stolen "brooch"—that prominent symbol of female sexuality—and the hiding-place for such stolen goods as "some hole in the garden-wall" (an appropriate postlapsarian reference). By her customary surveillance, Madame Beck wished to "cure" her Désirée of the "evil spirits" with which she "overflowed," for Madame, Lucy notes, "had not rectitude of soul to confront the child with her vices" (158). Al-

---

be. Vashti, in fact, embodies the cut of pain and desire, which makes of her a kind of devil. Lucy writes: "Behold! I found upon her something neither of woman nor of man: in each of her eyes sat a devil. . . . How wildly they shook her with their passions of the pit! . . . Swordsmen thrust through, and dying in their blood on the arena sand; bulls goring horses disembowelled, make a meeker vision for the public—a milder condiment for a people's palate—than Vashti torn by seven devils. . . . I have said that she does not *resent* her grief. No; the weakness of that word would make it a lie. To her, what hurts becomes immediately embodied" (339–40). Lucy's narration, nonetheless, registers her strange attraction to this figure: "The strong magnetism of genius drew my heart out of its wonted orbit; the sunflower turned from the south to a fierce light, not solar—a rushing, red, cometary light—hot on vision and to sensation" (340–41).

though Madame Beck's self-possession epitomizes the control for which Lucy had been striving, the narrator ridicules this sublimation as spiritual renunciation: "Brava! once more, Madame Beck. I saw you matched against an Apollyon of a predilection; you fought a good fight, and you overcame!" (171).

Lucy parts from Madame Beck amidst the corridors of pain and desire. Even in moments when Madame Beck models Lucy's class rise toward the bourgeoisie, Lucy's narration skews this Weberian plan for success ("Courage, Lucy Snowe! With self-denial and economy now . . . an object in life need not fail you" [450]) toward a clasp of pain and incompletion:

> When I shall have saved one thousand francs, I will take a tenement with one large room, and two or three smaller ones, furnish the first with a few benches and desks, a black tableau, an estrade for myself; upon it a chair and table, with a sponge and some white chalks; begin with taking day-pupils, and so work my way upwards. Madame Beck's commencement was—as I have heard her say—from no higher starting-point, and where is she now? All these premises and this garden are hers, bought with her money. . . .
>
> [But] it is right to look our life-accounts bravely in the face now and then, and settle them honestly. And he is a poor self-swindler who lies to himself while he reckons the items, and sets down under the head happiness that which is misery. . . . Falsify; insert "privilege" where you should have written "pain"; and see if your mighty creditor will allow the fraud to pass, or accept the coin with which you would cheat him. Offer to the strongest— if the darkest angel of God's host—water, when he has asked blood—will he take it? Not a whole pale sea for one red drop. I settled another account. (450–51)

This is an extraordinary passage, shifting from Lucy's plan for capital gains to her settling of a different account with her creditor. Here pain, like desire at other moments, functions as a kind of anticapital that opposes "privilege" and the upward way. Lucy's seemingly Weberian rise to a school of her own is wedded, eventually, to a sea of blood, which only 'God' can part for pleasure.

Divine Pursuits of a None

In *Villette*'s rare economy of loss, the *fulfillment* of thirsting becomes attached to crucifixion images. More striking still, crucifixion images blend cuts and holes that signify pain with blanks and voids that signify sexual and economic fortune. The curious shift away from a customary sexual economics is dramatically borne out by the novel's love plot: Lucy's shift from Graham to Paul, or, as it takes on its spiritual proportions, Lucy's swerve from the false promise of pagan idolatry toward the sterner pleasures of devotion to Christ. The hinge between the idol and the analyst/Christ is the figure of the nun. She is the narrative's sign of a self-knot: Lucy's temptation to substitute finite objects for the infinite object of desire. To *resist* the haunting of desire is thus to be menaced by no one—that is to say, by none. To take on the haunting, along with its menace, already begins to redeem deferral.

Volume 1 of Lucy's narrative traces phase one of a Christian teleology: a "fall" from unity and happy stasis into the divisions of work and desire. Lucy marks this phase by her movement out of the Brettons' "peaceful boredom" into more intense forms of watching suffering, first as an unofficial nursemaid to Polly, then as a paid "companion" to Miss Marchmont. Lucy's memory continues to chart this gradual "fall" by depicting her career moves as a series of substitutionary parts, ranging from lady's maid to governess to teacher—all of which increasingly demanded that Lucy take part in the passions played around her. Her role in the drama of Madame Beck's fête—undertaken at the instigation of Paul—represented, as Lucy conveys it from a distance, the culmination of this initial part-ing.

As if to mark the right-angled turn of the Christian paradigm from its first phase into its second of divisions, the novel puts abrupt closure to Lucy's first installment: Volume 1 ends with a blackout. After the excitement of the fête, Lucy tells us, she performed, for a last time, her role as a watcher of women's suffering. During a long vacation, she was charged with the care of a crétin, since "no substitute to fill [the] office [of nurse] had been provided" (229). Though here, once again, the role of substitute fell upon Lucy, this time she found it unendurable. She had thus sought relief in a Catholic confessional—yet another sign that Brontë associates Catholicism not only with sensuality but with the dynamism of desire itself. Upon leaving the church, Lucy recalls, she had fainted from weariness. "Immeshed in a network of turns unknown . . . [she] seemed to pitch headlong down an abyss." Here Lucy's narrative marks a turning-point.

The novel's second volume begins with the chapter "Auld Lang Syne," since Lucy awakened to the Bretton home she knew in her youth (now reconvened on foreign soil, as if the Bretton *home* had been exiled).*

---

*As Lucy remarks: "Had [a Genius] borne me over land and ocean, and laid me quietly down beside a hearth of Old England? But no; I knew the fire of that hearth burned before its Lares no more—it went out long ago, and the household gods had been carried elsewhere" (240).

The *act* of conveying this retrospect unfolds depths in Lucy's past, for now her words reveal what she has never confessed: She, like Polly, had been smitten by Graham:

> Striving to take each new discovery as quietly as I could, I whispered to my-self—
> "Ah! that portrait [of Graham] used to hang in the breakfast-room. . . . I well remember how I used to mount a music-stool for the purpose of un-hooking it, holding it in my hand, and searching into those bonny wells of eyes. . . ." I hardly believed fancy could improve on the curve of that mouth, or of the chin. (243)*

The narrating Lucy is now able to name what she could not have told us when she began narration. Now, in fact, the narrating Lucy steps in sud-denly to make confession: much earlier she had realized that Madame Beck's Dr. John was the Graham of her adolescence (information she has withheld from the reader, even as she withheld it then from members of the pensionnat):

> I first recognized him on that occasion, noted several chapters back, when my unguardedly-fixed attention had drawn on me the mortification of an im-plied rebuke. . . . To *say* anything on the subject, to *hint* at my discovery, had not suited my habits of thought, or assimilated with my system of feeling. On the contrary, I had preferred to keep the matter to myself. I liked entering his presence covered with a cloud he had not seen through, while he stood before me under a ray of special illumination. (248)

Not only does her implication in Madame Beck's surveillance seem sub-stantiated by this admission—Lucy enjoyed the power of her gaze—it also illustrates the ambiguity of this narrator's candor. More intriguing yet, her pointed self-possession, as the narrator fashions it, was enabled by her strategic manipulation of opacity—her own opacity, which she wore as a shield while she advanced: "I liked entering his presence covered with a cloud he had not seen through."

---

*Interestingly, Lucy's focus on Graham's mouth and chin as the locus of her own fancy will find an important echo in *Middlemarch*: for Dorothea, the fact that Will's "mouth and chin [had] a more prominent and threatening aspect than belonged to the type of [his] grandmother's miniature" becomes a complex index to her growing erotic investment in both men *and* women. Here, in the passage from *Villette*, the image of "those bonny wells of eyes" may carry a stronger charge for Lucy than her mention of Graham's mouth and chin, since water and well imagery swells to such major propor-tions by the end of the book, especially with Lucy's drugged quest for the "huge stone-basin—that basin I knew, and beside which I had often stood—deep-set in the tree-shadows, brimming with cool water, clear, with a green, leafy, rushy bed" (547).

At this point, biblical references to thirsting begin to proliferate. Lucy recounts her caution in rediscovering the Brettons, lest she feel too much and risk rejection: "Let me be content with a temperate draught of this living stream: let me not run athirst, and apply passionately to its welcome waters" (251). This "living stream," which grows in significance throughout Lucy's story, alludes to John's Gospel (4:10), where Jesus offers a Samaritan woman "living water." The tenor of Jesus' offer suggests that "everlasting life" makes itself available to those who, as Lucy then refused to do, "apply passionately to its welcome waters." Lucy, despite the tenor of this allusion, preached herself a sermon to stamp out feelings and wait in patience for God's healing angel to stir stagnant waters: "Thousands lie round the pool, weeping and despairing, to see it, through slow years, stagnant" (252). Taking her text from John 5 (the passage alluded to in Brontë's poem), Lucy stresses the endless deferrals of God's timing ("long are the 'times' of Heaven") yet does not perceive what Brontë would expect her readers to know: Jesus makes the visiting angel obsolete by healing people directly. This scriptural reference even reveals the requirement for healing as desire for immediate material change: "When Jesus saw him lie, and knew that he had been now a long time in that case, he saith unto him, 'Wilt thou be made whole? . . . Rise, take up thy bed, and walk.' And immediately the man was made whole, and he took up his bed, and walked" (John 5:6,8,9). As Lucy proceeds to tell her tale, she progressively depicts Paul as the goad who chased her into assertive health by chasing her into the fracture of desire ("wilt thou be made hole?").

Lucy renders her fascination with Graham as the chief obstruction to assertive health, painting this romantic fantasy for a "rising" character as a "fond idolatry," the very conclusion Brontë came to about her relations with M. Heger. Early on, Lucy tells us she was "driven to compare his beamy head . . . to that of the 'golden image' which Nebuchadnezzar the king had set up." Lucy confesses that God's manna faded when compared with the "morsel of real solid joy" that Graham's letters provided—and here she biblically renders these letters as "the wild savoury mess of the hunter" Esau, who, like Graham, was red-haired. Characteristically, the scriptural reference contains the judgment, for Esau may have provided "savoury meat," yet he, being one day faint with hunger, sold his God-given birthright to obtain a pottage of lentils (Genesis 25:29–34). Behind the depiction of Lucy's hungering lies the narrator's developing recognition: as Esau sold his birthright, his dignity, his lordship, so Lucy, as she depicts Paul as having warned her, lay in danger of selling her dignity for the false elevation of wifehood.

In the thick of accounting how she idolized Graham, Lucy shows that her yearnings were haunted by a ghostly nun.* The emergence of the nun begins to shift narrative weight from satisfaction to crucifixion. Seen first when Lucy received Graham's letter, the nun may then have symbolized Lucy's broken vow to remain aloof from sexual desire, since this nun, by legend, transgressed the seemingly fixed borders between sexual wants and spiritual laws. The garden behind the pensionnat with its *"l'allée défendue"* ("forbidden alley") provided the setting for the legend of the nun, "buried alive, for some sin against her vow." Lucy, at first, claims that she dismissed "the romantic rubbish" attached to the garden, unaware that she, too, made it sexual. In particular, her description of the "forbidden alley" could be seen to trace a genital cleft: "As the walk was narrow, and the neglected shrubs were grown very thick and close on each side, weaving overhead a roof of branch and leaf which the sun's rays penetrated but in rare chequers, this alley was seldom entered even during the day, and after dusk was carefully shunned" (174). Being initially unable to admit that she then desired attachment, the narrator, early in the novel, describes her solitary "tryst" in *l'allée défendue*: "I became a frequenter of this strait and narrow path [Matthew 7:14]. . . . I cleared away the relics of past autumns, choking up a rustic seat at the far end. . . . I made this seat clean" (174). The clearing of "relics" and the cleaning of the seat suggest the Old Testament practice of transforming a pagan worship site into a sacred spot for Yahweh (cf. Joshua 24:1–28). Lucy, therefore, not only portrays "this strait and narrow path" in ways that invoke female genitals—making the path that Christian women should tread their own forbidden alleys—she also recalls that she cleared her own space in this (genital) cleft. This action befits her story's later stress upon divinely ordained autoeroticism (a solitary "tryst"?).†

---

*Until Robert B. Heilman's treatment of the nun as a psychologically significant feature of *Villette* ("Charlotte Brontë's 'New' Gothic"), it was commonplace to assert (as some critics still do—see Barbara Lloyd Evans and Gareth Lloyd Evans, *Everyman's Companion to the Brontës*, 277) that this gothic subplot was beneath Brontë's talent. Following Heilman's work, many critics have argued that the nun is literally "beneath" Lucy Snowe, representing as she does a signal feature of Lucy's buried emotions. Christina Crosby's richer interpretation reads the nun as a specter of indeterminacy that haunts Brontë's text, though I would stress the conflation of sexual and spiritual indeterminacies that the nun represents. Tayler's reading comes closest to my own (*Holy Ghosts*, 257–61).

†Brontë's tendency to create detailed, if oblique, figures for female genitals and genital pleasure can be seen at several points in *Villette*. Consider, for example, this description that begins her chapter "Vashti": "Conceive a dell, deep-hollowed in forest secrecy; it lies in dimness and mist: its turf dank, its herbage pale and humid. A storm

Even the novel's early passages, particularly ones concerning the garden, lean towards images of crucifixion, where piercing figures the painful incompletions of sexual longing: on some nights, Lucy narrates, "the spectacle of clouds, split and pierced by white and blinding bolts," "stirred up a craving cry I could not satisfy" (175–76). For this reason, Lucy, "after the manner of Jael to Sisera" (an image she takes from the Book of Judges), had attempted to drive a spiritual nail through her sexual longings. Though crucifixion here would murder desire, it only serves to testify that what gets crucified rises again: "Unlike Sisera, they [her longings] did not die: they were but transiently stunned, and at intervals would turn on the nail with a rebellious wrench; then did the temples bleed, and the brain thrill to its core" (176).

Lucy's memories clearly reveal that she could not evade the garden's love rites. The nun, she relates, having first appeared when she opened Graham's letter, appeared a second time when Lucy was dressing for a night out with Graham. The nun simultaneously signaled Lucy's idolatry of Graham, by which she was seeking sexual satisfaction, and her fear of leading a loverless life. But these last associations begin to shade the nun towards some incompletion, some none, that the narrator still denies. What may most haunt older Lucy, the narrator, as it haunted Lucy then, is not so much her idolatrous attempt to fill her void—she knew even then her feelings for Graham had no healing potential—but the haunting suspicion that no filling of her void is possible. Such an unshakable incompletion would comprise her unacknowledged self-(k)not—a cipher that doggedly obstructs all efforts to secure the "savoury meat" that would satisfy. Young Lucy significantly buried Graham's letters, evidence of the incompletion of desire, in a "hole" at the foot of "Methuselah, the pear tree" in *l'allée défendue* (a serious version of Désirée's comically rendered burials). As if to underscore gaping desire, the narrator recalls that, at this point, the nun appeared a third time. Not surprisingly, with the letters buried, the next time Lucy spotted the nun she was with the one who, all along, was inciting her desire.

Paul Emanuel is the goad of Lucy's narrative. He appears simultaneously as the master analyst and as the Christ of her story. By attacking

---

or axe makes a wide gap amongst the oak-trees; the breeze sweeps in; the sun looks down; the sad, cold dell, becomes a deep cup of lustre; high summer pours her blue glory and her golden light out of that beauteous sky, which till now the starved hollow never saw" (334). We should notice the crucial role played by the making of the gap that opens a space for "lustre." Later, I will discuss Brontë's figures of the "deep-set basin," "the narrow, irregular aperture visible between the stems of the lindens" and the moon's "pearly front" as references to genitals.

"*amour-propre*" and inducing in Lucy a "controlled paranoia," Paul incited new heights of outburst.* These patterns of incitement steam through Lucy's story, whether the issue is Lucy's coquetry ("You alluring little coquette!" Paul hisses) or Lucy's "scarlet" dress (" 'Pink! pink!' I threw in") or Paul's outrageous comments about "unfeminine knowledge" and "women of intellect." Here, for example, Lucy shows Paul at his goading best, for though the narrator tells her reader that she did not possess "the noble hunger for science in the abstract," she immediately reverses herself in the next line: "Yet when M. Paul sneered at me, I wanted to possess them more fully; his injustice stirred in me ambitious wishes. . . . Whatever my powers—feminine or the contrary—God had given them, and I felt resolute to be ashamed of no faculty of His bestowal" (440). Although Paul did not play Lucy's analyst in the sense of offering her "the pure mirror of an unruffled surface," through his constant ruptures of her settled exterior he did "bring into play the subject's aggressivity," as an analyst would (*E*, 15, 14). In his penchant for cloaking his opinions in ludicrous bombast, Paul effected another analytic goal: that of sending back to the subject her message in inverted form (*E*, 15). The result, according to Lucy's narrative, is that Lucy confirmed her "ambitious wishes" as given by God and, by force of her representation, as stirred up by God's goading servant.

Of course, Scripture itself could affirm this analytic slant to Lucy's Christ—the gospel portraits of Jesus' aggressive penetration of minds, his ability to tease out the secrets of even the most resistant hearts. One can discern this tradition progressively surging in *Villette*, as the narrator progressively names her desire. At one juncture, Lucy reveals that Paul's insights initially spooked her:

> He had the terrible unerring penetration of instinct, and pierced in its hiding-place the last lurking thought of the heart. . . . No calamity so accursed but M. Emanuel could pity and forgive, if it were acknowledged candidly; but

*I am reading against the grain of many Brontë critics here. Maynard reads Paul as sexually repressed, though he claims that Paul does grow into an "emotional and sexual maturity" through his relationship with Lucy: "Despite all M. Paul's positive qualities, Lucy is not entirely wrong in her early complaints about him. His willful, angry, bossing qualities are the expression of his desire to deal with sexual feeling by suppressing it. His jealousy reveals his interest in Lucy, but it sometimes takes the form of trying to drive her back away from her opening life" (Maynard, *Charlotte Brontë*, 197). Crosby also reads Paul as "determined to repress his desires" ("Charlotte Brontë's Haunted Text," 711); and Blom adds that "[Paul] assumes that in the female such passion is indicative of evil" ("Charlotte Brontë," 97). For a reading of Paul as reactionary and tyrannical, see Patricia Beer, *Reader I Married Him*, 104, 105, 126; and Kate Millett, *Sexual Politics*, 140–48.

where his questioning eyes met dishonest denial . . . he could exultantly snatch the screen from poor shrinking wretches, passionately hurry them to the summit of the mount of exposure, and there show them . . . the spawn of that horrid Truth which cannot be looked on unveiled. (423–24)

This passage offers yet another view of a piercing that is joined to the embrace of "horrid truth." The real significance of Paul's surveillance, along with his exposure of denial, is that these are typically divine characteristics. In fact, this description seems closely modeled on a well-known passage from the book of Hebrews:

For the word of God is quick, and powerful, and sharper than any two-edged sword, piercing even to the dividing asunder of soul and spirit, and of the joints and marrow, and is a discerner of the thoughts and intents of the heart. Neither is there any creature that is not manifest in his sight: but all things are naked and opened unto the eyes of him with whom we have to do. . . . For we have not an high priest which cannot be touched with the feeling of our infirmities; but was in all points tempted like as we are, yet without sin. Let us therefore come boldly unto the throne of grace, that we may obtain mercy, and find grace to help in time of need. (Hebrews 4:12–13, 15–16).

Only gradually does Paul's stern, Old Testament penetration (with its focus on eyes) give way in Lucy's narrative to the merciful (even feminine) New Testament portraits of Jesus. Through her memories of Paul, the narrator continues to shape an understanding of how God's severity and mercy are entwined. As she narrates the spring outing he directed, Lucy constructs the pastoral side to Paul's personality:

On the green swell of ground surrounding this well, we were ordered to be seated, monsieur taking his place in our midst, and suffering us to gather in a knot round him. Those who liked him more than they feared, came close, and these were chiefly little ones. . . . He began to tell us a story. Well could he narrate: in such a diction as children love, and learned men emulate; a diction simple in its strength, and strong in its simplicity. . . . His mind was indeed my library, and whenever it was opened to me, I entered bliss. (471–72)

Lucy's memory of Paul becomes curative. Her description of how they gathered in a "knot" on a "green swell of ground surrounding [a] well" entangles allusions to burial and pregnancy, to thirst and satisfaction. Paul has begun to resemble, in Irigaray's words, "that most female of men, the Son." Indeed, Paul's feminine ways are shaped by the narrating Lucy at various junctures: on the spring outing, she recalls, she observed Paul "crossing himself as devoutly as a woman" (474); in another context: "he was as capricious as women are said to be"; the "core [of his heart]," Lucy remembers, "was a place, tender beyond a man's tenderness; a place that humbled him to little children, that bound him to girls and women; to whom, rebel as he would, he could not disown his affinity" (425–26). Lucy's remembered relation to Paul echoes, then, her many mirrored relations with women. Consonant with her portrait of Paul's divine discernment, Paul announces their "affinity" to Lucy:

> I was conscious of rapport between you and myself. . . . We are alike—there is affinity. Do you see it, mademoiselle, when you look in the glass? Do you observe that your forehead is shaped like mine—that your eyes are cut like mine? Do you hear that you have some of my tones of voice? . . . I perceive all this, and believe that you were born under my star. Yes, you were born under my star! Tremble! for where that is the case with mortals, the threads of their destinies are difficult to disentangle; knottings and catchings occur— sudden breaks leave damage in the web. (457)

Unlike the narrator's earlier denial of her entanglements with Polly, Ginevra, and Madame Beck, Paul's recognition, in its forceful language, is implicitly sanctioned by Lucy's narrative.* His allusion to "knottings" demonstrates that Paul embraced something like Irigaray's "characteristics of fluids": "those rubbings between two infinitely near neighbors that create a dynamics"; "dynamics of the near and not of the proper . . . which makes the distinction between the one and the other problematical" (*TS*, 79, 111). As proof of this sympathetic tangle, Lucy relates that she and Paul together glimpsed the nun—that enigmatic sign of a self-knot.

As one would expect from his biblical name, Paul Emanuel became Lucy's model of one who had jousted loss and deferral. Lucy's confrontation with Paul's own loss instigates her tale of the grotesque Malevola (the Catholic Madame Walravens). If Lucy skews her portrait of Paul towards divinity, she depicts Malevola as more than demonic: a bad sex dream. This "Cunegonde, the sorceress" ("cunt-gone?" puns John Maynard)[4] signifies for Lucy the terror of sex threatened by absence. Over and against Malevola's threat, stood Paul Emanuel, separated from her granddaughter, Justine Marie, when his rich banker father left "debts and destitution" after his death. Denied the chance to marry Paul, since he had now fallen beneath the daughter of a jewelry merchant, Justine Marie was

---

*Christina Crosby briefly mentions this doubling, in which "Paul is Lucy's Imaginary Other," but she does not attribute any particular significance to this doubling relation, other than to note that this is "yet another image in the series refracted throughout the text" ("Charlotte Brontë's Haunted Text," 712). She does not discuss Lucy's Imaginary relation to Polly.

exiled and, after, died in a convent (another nun bound to incompletions). Malevola figures a capitalist drive that crucifies lovers. Paul Emanuel figures the lover crucified by capitalism: first, by the capitalistic failures of his father, then by those of his lover's father, whose debts and obligations Paul assumed. Having lost his "nun," first to the vicissitudes of capitalist desire and, then, to death (as Lucy, later, lost Paul), he stands as the figure of a lover deferred. Given Paul's stance as one left fixed on material concealment, we should not be surprised that Lucy recalls sharing with Paul a minimalist creed—"God be merciful to me, a sinner!" This is a creed written around an almost absent assertion, befitting Paul's near erasure of God as "that mighty unseen centre incomprehensible, irrealizable, with strange mental effort only divined" (517).

Exchanging Christ: The Perils of Paulina

Lucy's narrative does not merely give us in Paul Emanuel a version of Christ. Her story also gives us in Paulina Home a female Paul and a female Christ. Brontë, in this way, dramatizes the class and gender requirements for representing divine lovers. Early in the novel, the narrator parodies Polly Home's sufferings as petite crucifixions. Later in the novel, when Paulina Mary Home de Bassompierre reappears, Lucy no longer parodies Polly as a miniature martyr. As Paul's mind opened a divine repository ("his mind was indeed my library, and whenever it was open to me, I entered bliss"), so Paulina's discussions with Graham revealed her "suggestive, persuasive, magic accent that opened a scarce known treasure-house within" (518). As Paul enabled Lucy to unearth a buried store of feelings, so Paulina, too, tapped Graham's deeper consciousness: "While he was looking at [Paulina], recollections would seem to be suddenly quickened to his mind" (519). In sum, "of [Graham's] happiness [Paulina] was the corner stone" (532), where "corner stone" (in Scripture, a figure for Christ) grounds the edifice of Paulina's divinity.

The portrayal of Polly as a female Christ evinces, I suspect, Brontë's unabated need to write a woman-to-woman relation, even when representing divine love. In this sense, Paul as a feminized Bridegroom is not enough. A female Christ figure enables something different: a meditation upon women's relations to crucifixion and to the redemptive possibilities of sacrifice. In a slightly different vein, Paulina as a Christ figure represents one who, like Paul, confronted the agony of parting and lived to see its translation to fulfillment, for Paulina, Lucy claims, led a charmed life.

Lucy's portrait of Paulina has decidedly prelapsarian qualities. It is as if Lucy looks back before Polly's pain (and her own?) to find a trace, pull a thread, of Eden. This Edenic reversal of suffering may explain why Paulina is variously described as a fairy, "a strange little mortal," and an Undine (a water sylph who marries a mortal). She was enveloped so securely in fortune that Paulina only changed "homes." As Lucy concludes: "Some lives *are* thus blessed: it is God's will: it is the attesting trace and lingering evidence of Eden. Other lives run from the first another course. Other travellers encounter weather fitful and gusty, wild and variable—breast adverse winds, are belated and overtaken by the early closing winter night. Neither can this happen without the sanction of God" (468). A typical Brontëan resignation underlies Lucy's cheer: she reads as differences in Providential design what might be otherwise read as class differences. "The lingering evidence of Eden" that Lucy detects in Polly owes largely to the fact that the loss Paulina suffered as a girl did not entail, as it did for Lucy, a fall in class position. At one point the narrator herself makes this note, when she poses in her mind a question she would like to put to Graham: "Had Lucy been intrinsically the same, but possessing the additional advantages of wealth and station, would your manner to her, your value for her have been quite what they actually were?" (401). Paulina's stance as the bourgeois woman Lucy would have been (had Lucy escaped financial tragedy) causes the narrator to recognize Paulina as her (displaced) double: "I wondered to find my thoughts hers: there are certain things in which we so rarely meet with our double that it seems a miracle when that chance befalls" (361).

Polly's charmed existence was not the only aspect of bourgeois positioning that Lucy might have known. For if Polly's life was charmed, it was also exchanged. This is the downside of bourgeois womanhood—a "privilege" that Lucy "happily" escaped by having no dowry, no prospects to market. Here lie two problems for Lucy's portrait of Paulina Home as a female Christ: first, Polly's charms easily collapse back into portraits of domesticated angels ("This was not an opaque vase, of material however costly, but a lamp chastely lucent, guarding from extinction, yet not hiding from worship, a flame vital and vestal" [359]); second, Polly's entrance on the marriage market makes "Christ" an object of exchange.*

---

*We might notice that Polly's status as domestic angel is announced by her transparent form ("a lamp chastely lucent"), making both her blessing and her curse her lack of opacity ("this was not an opaque vase").

Neither of these problems plagues the portrait of Paul Emanuel, for such are the difficulties of rendering a savior to be read as a woman. Insofar as sacrifice *defines* bourgeois womanhood, it is precarious, if not impossible, to read a female character primarily as a Christ and only secondarily as a woman. This is where the character of Paul can succeed: his sacrificing gestures must be read as Christ-like since they cannot be read as masculine. In the process of lining up with the "not-all" (to invoke Lacan's mystics) "he" can be *seen* as crossing to lack.

Even so, in spite of Paulina's failed divinity, something of her sexual exchange gets transformed. The gem imagery from her scenes of transfer from her father to her husband—her father calls her "my little jewel," "my little treasure," "the only pearl I have"—returns, reconceived, by the end of *Villette*.* In the long night swirl of an opium dream, where foliage gems and voices drop from the heavens into glades, Lucy's intense concern with apocalypse, her investment in Paul as divine Bridegroom, and her major references to autoeroticism converge and hang, suspended, in a vigil.

Apocalypse and Autoeroticism

Brontë was haunted by suspense and "dead blank[s]" in her parting from Heger. She never could be sure that relief, in the form of a word from him, would come her way. This dread of blank intervals is carefully reworked at the end of *Villette*. Lucy's suspension in the woman's waiting game—in Lucy's words, "a doubtful hope of bliss to come, not now, but at a day and hour unlooked for. . . . a worse boon than despair" (542)—is recast as the Christian's stance before apocalypse: hoping, through lack, for eventual fulfillment, welcoming lack as the promise of fulfillment. By this spiritual casting, the older Lucy telling the story (and Brontë along with her?) makes sense of desire's (seemingly infinite) interval of incompletion.

---

*The implicit violence of sexual exchange is curiously transferred to the body of the suitor, enacted in a ritual blood-letting, humorously orchestrated by Polly herself. From an Irigarayan perspective this transfer, though violent, is still a "hom(m)osexual" encounter, allowing men to touch each other through a woman's body. In *Villette* we read: "'Graham, stretch out your right hand. Papa, put out yours. Now, let them touch. Papa, don't be stiff, close your fingers; be pliant—there! But that is not a clasp—it is a grasp! Papa, you grasp like a vice. You crush Graham's hand to the bone; you hurt him!' He must have hurt him; for he wore a massive ring, set round with brilliants, of which the sharp facets cut into Graham's flesh and drew blood: but pain only made Dr. John laugh, as anxiety had made him smile" (530–31).

The scenes that prepare for apocalyptic climax wed apocalypse to autoeroticism.* The chief scene conjures Lucy's tour of Villette's night festival—a journey inspired by an opium cocktail, which Madame Beck served to her rival as a means of keeping Lucy confined. The opium produced the opposite effect, converting confinement into escape: Lucy wandered, drugged, through Villette. Lucy, in these scenes, betrays a strange connection to objects, as if she needs and wishes to see them newly materialize. Through her skewed defamiliarizations, these objects even seem examples of "mystic unfathomable Visibilities." Fittingly, then, Lucy's escape is her private apocalypse, a narcotic twist on John's Revelation. Countless images overflow the pages of John as if to dominate Lucy's somnambulism: rushing waters, trumpets, gates, light, music, and stars. Yet even this biblical slate of images warps in autoerotic waves.

As if confirming the Lacanian tenet that "the expression of a desire must always be sought in a dream," (*E*, 58), Lucy reckons how, in visionary mode, she anticipated her journey's destination: "a huge stone-basin—that basin I knew, and beside which I had often stood—deep-set in the tree-shadows, brimming with cool water, clear, with a green, leafy, rushy bed" (547). Recalling, faintly, Lucy's parody of Polly at the washstand, this image of Lucy standing at the basin conveys more than thirsting. The "deep-set" basin ("that basin I knew") figures something like Christ's "living water," deep-set in a well, brimming from a seemingly genital bed: described as "green, leafy, [and] rushy." No wonder Lucy saw herself barred from the park that contained the basin; no wonder she realized that the only way to gain her entrance was through an (Irigarayan) slit: "a gap in the paling . . . *the narrow, irregular aperture* visible between the stems of the lindens, planted orderly as a colonade" (my emphasis). That Lucy claimed this "gap" for herself, on behalf of her desire, may be further implied by her observation that "a man could not have made his way through that aperture, nor could a stout woman, perhaps not Madame Beck; but I thought I might: I fancied I should like to try, and once within, at this hour the whole park would be mine—the moonlight, midnight park!" (547).

Following her account of her anticipation, Lucy renders her escape from the "convent" (Madame Beck's school) in present tense: "I cross the threshold and . . . wonder at the strange ease with which this prison has been forced" (a reference to the apostles being suddenly sprung from prison by an angel [Acts 5:19ff.]). Apocalyptic references now begin in

*David Shaw, in his discussion of *Villette* (*Victorians and Mystery*), concentrates on these scenes but addresses neither their sexual nor their religious allusions.

earnest, losing none of their sexual valence. The "sky bears the aspect of a world's death," Lucy recalls, switching next to past tense: "Light broke, movement gathered, chimes pealed—to what was I coming?" What Lucy comes to is her mind's transformation of the fête into something like a holy city, an Egyptian version of the new Jerusalem (cf. Revelation 21, 22):

> In a land of enchantment, a garden most gorgeous, a plain sprinkled with colored meteors, a forest with sparks of purple and ruby and golden fire gemming the foliage; a region, not of trees and shadow, but of strangest architectural wealth—of altar and of temple, of pyramid, obelisk, and sphynx; incredible to say, the wonders and the symbols of Egypt teemed throughout the park of Villette. (550)

The suggestion of colored stones and the "golden fire gemming the foliage" directly recall the new Jerusalem ("garnished with all manner of precious stones" [Revelation 21:19]). Now Lucy's telling is gathering up the gems of women's sexual exchange into folds of a gorgeous enchantment.

Lucy's acquisition of pleasure remains the plot of her desire. Her goal remains the stone-basin: "With the passionate thirst of unconscious fever . . . I still secretly and chiefly longed to come on that circular mirror of crystal, and surprise the moon glassing therein her pearly front" (551). Lucy's line crowns a set of dense associations, attaching thirst to longing, to a mirror, to water, and, finally, to the moon. Using an image that resembles the Irigarayan lips-as-mirrors, Lucy concludes with an ambiguously sexual/genital reference to the moon's "pearly front." Lucy's desire to surprise the moon in an act of "glassing"—a verb that makes reflection active—suggests her wish to catch the moon in a self-caressing pose, as well as her longing to gaze upon herself. As is claimed of desire's indirections, Lucy was "hindered from pursuing it direct: now a sight, and now a sound, called me aside, luring me down this *alley* and down that" (my emphasis). When she stood on the brink of the basin, on the very verge of arrival, she was swept up, and swept along, in unspeakable pleasures:

> Already I saw the thick-planted trees which framed this tremulous and rippled glass [of the stone-basin], when, choiring out of a glade to the right, broke such a sound as I thought might be heard if Heaven were to open— such a sound, perhaps as *was* heard above the plain of Bethlehem, on the night of glad tidings.
>   The song, the sweet music, rose afar, but rushing swiftly on faststrengthening pinions—there swept through these shades so full a storm of

harmonies that, had no tree been near against which to lean, I think I must have dropped. Voices were there, it seemed to me unnumbered; instruments varied and countless—bugle, horn and trumpet I knew. The effect was as a sea breaking into song with all its waves. (552)

Lucy conveys her intent pursuit of self-sexual pleasure by thickening her descriptions of apocalyptic sensuality. With the scene "framed" around the "tremulous and rippled glass" of the basin—described so as to catch it in spasm—the passage convulses with the sudden "choiring out of a glade," intensified next by "a storm of harmonies," "rushing" so as to make the reader swoon from the force of Lucy's prose. This vision borrows images, first of all, from the Book of Revelation, where Christ's voice is "a trumpet" and "the sound of many waters" (1:10,15), and where, greater than Lucy's crystal mirror of water, may be found "before the throne . . . a sea of glass like unto crystal" (4:6). Lucy explicitly refers to the choir "heard above the plain of Bethlehem" (cf. Luke 2:13–15). Tellingly, therefore, Lucy has conflated allusions to the advent (Christ's betrothal to humanity) with allusions to apocalypse (the event that foresees this betrothal's completion). In this way, she sidesteps the crucifixion that weds and parts these moments in history.

Crucifixion, however, cannot be held off in the text of *Villette*. The gaping wound of crucifixion (a hole in expectation) must also be realized. This crucifixion is doubly represented—for Paul first, then for Lucy. Paul's crucifixion, as Lucy portrays it, was plotted by a Catholic capitalist junta: the unholy trinity of Madame Beck, Madame Walravens, and the Jesuit Père Silas. Now we learn that Madame Walravens had once "been rich . . . and though for the present without the command of money, was likely one day to be rich again" (559). We have returned to the story of class fall and rise—one that gauges anxiety over a woman's rising back to bourgeois ranks. Madame's class travels involved sending a "competent and upright agent," a "steward," to Basseterre for a three-year attempt to revive her "large estate, received in dowry on her husband's failure." Lucy thus pictures her lover as a Christ crucified by the Catholic church's capitalist ventures and forced to harrow hell for three years (not three days) by visiting a large estate in Basseterre (a figure for hell). Brontë, through her narrator, in this way may displace anxiety over Protestant links to capitalism by writing a set of Catholic monsters whose capital gains kill "Christ."

Lucy's portrayal of her own crucifixion follows her portrait of the junta's play for Paul. Lucy had mistakenly believed Paul betrothed to the young woman by his side at the festival. Linking the threat of capitalism (and, here, colonialism, too) with her fear of how bourgeois women are sexually exchanged, Lucy narrates how she fantasized a pact between Paul and the Catholic junta: "I gathered that while M. Paul should be absent, working for others, these others, not quite ungrateful, would guard for him the treasure he left in Europe. Let him bring them an Indian fortune; they would give him in return a young bride and a rich inheritance" (565). Lucy's mistaken rivalry is informed by her own impossibility of being exchanged. As a result, Lucy sounded the depths of a pain (an unclean pain) that signaled rejection:

> I extended my grasp and took it all in. . . . I invoked Conviction to nail upon me the certainty, abhorred while embraced, to fix it with the strongest spikes her strongest strokes could drive; and when the iron had entered well my soul, I stood up, as I thought renovated. . . . And then—something tore me so cruelly under my shawl, something so dug into my side, a vulture so strong in beak and talon, I must be alone to grapple with it. I think I never felt jealousy till now. . . . This was an outrage. (566–67)

The parodic references to Polly's pain as petite crucifixion encircle Lucy now, as she represents her own presumed loss, and its attendant jealousy, as a crucifixion with nails and spikes (along with reference to the side-piercing spear). In light of the tradition that Christ mounted the cross as a marriage bed, on which to suffer passion and torment, we note with interest Lucy's remark that "nothing remained now but to take my freedom [of having discovered her pain] to my chamber, to carry it with me to my bed and see what I could make of it" (566).* Though, on one level, Lucy carried the wrong pain to bed—Paul was not betrothed—on another level she discovered, once there, the pain of a self-knot that required her embrace:

> My head reeled, for by the faint night-lamp, I saw stretched on my bed the old phantom—the NUN. . . . I defied spectra. In a moment, without exclamation, I had rushed on the haunted couch; nothing leaped out, or sprang, or stirred; all the movement was mine, so was all the life, the reality, the substance, the force; as my instinct felt. I tore her up—the incubus! I held her on high—the goblin! I shook her loose—the mystery! And down she fell—down all round me—down in shreds and fragments—and I trode upon her. (569)

Rushing forth from Lucy's telling is the most violent embrace of *Villette*. Retold, it is an autoerotic moment, for Lucy remembers "the move-

---

*For an exploration of Christ mounting the cross as a marriage bed, see the footnote on page 34.

ment was mine" and suggests, fetchingly, a self-embrace by the pun on her name, "I shook her loose." Far from destroying this sign of her lack, try though she did, Lucy recalls that she was bequeathed these "shreds and fragments," which "fell—down all round me," by a fop who used them for his masquerade. The phrase "shreds and fragments" should remind us of the narrator's earlier claim that she stored up "pieces of casual information . . . seemingly worthless shreds and fragments" for which she "anticipate[d] a possible use some day." It is as if the narrator discovers in the nun a figure for how she has gripped her own story and how the opaque bits and pieces of her narrative are falling down around her. Lucy's words also reveal what, through narration, she is coming to accept: behind the nun, the haunting sign of an absence, was a man; or, as Lacan asserts, "The phallus can only play its role when veiled." Lucy's uncovering of de Hamal's phallic farce—his lack disguised by the veil of the nun—does not dismiss the crack of her desire. Thus she recalls that, far from removing the nun from her bed, she "thrust [these vestments] beneath [her] pillow" and "deeply slept" (570).

Following her encounter with the nun—a moment analogous to the blackout that closes volume 1—Lucy's spiritual autobiography takes a final right-angled turn. The Bridegroom passages emerge full-blown. Lucy, we are told, mistook Paul's footsteps for those of "the master-carpenter"; and still thinking Paul was engaged to be married, she perceived that Paul was bright in "bridegroom-mood." Wrong though both assumptions were at the time, they secure the present narrator's reading of Paul Emanuel as the Christ, who told his followers: "Can the children of the bridechamber mourn, as long as the bridegroom is with them? but the days will come, when the bridegroom shall be taken from them, and then shall they fast" (Matthew 9:15). As befits the banquet preceding the fast, Lucy shows herself as having glimpsed the impossible, ungraspable, algebraic x of sexual satisfaction: "Once haply in life, one golden gift falls prone in the lap" (579).* This glimpse of material satisfaction soon falls into blankness once again.

By proceeding to narrate intensely happy memories, which depict her transference onto Paul of hopes for material succor, Lucy must inevitably arrive at naming what she has always feared: "that rude agony of rupture at the close . . . absence interposes her barrier!" (578). That she must greet this deferral, and discover her transference transferred beyond her own

*For discussion of the algebraic x and its link to the Lacanian Real, see the footnote on page 48.

brink, is ordained for Lucy by the spiritual plot of her autobiography: the divine Bridegroom is destined to disappear when the Bride anticipates consummation. This consummation of the approach ever nearer is deferred until an unknown hour; only then, and elsewhere, will this longed-for completion be fully (and materially) realized. Meanwhile, the Bride possesses only the promise of return and must content herself with the Bridegroom's pledge of "interest." By recollecting Paul as divine Bridegroom, the narrator shows her strategy for accepting, as an old woman (herself a Miss Marchmont), her lover's disappearance and death.

The Bridegroom memory performs another spiritual materialist task. The narrator scripts, in Paul's support of Lucy's vocation, divine support for her pleasure in work. Lucy's portrait of her home/school in the Faubourg Clotilde, which Paul had prepared for her, carries associations with a (feminine) body and a (feminine) sexuality ("'Dare you take the freedom of going all over the house?' I inquired. 'Yes, I dare,' said he, quietly" [585]). Around a french window, there were "tendrils, and green leaves, kissing the glass"; the parlor's "delicate walls were tinged like a blush"; there was a "half-open, crimson-silk door" to this interior; and outdoors, Lucy narrates, "In a large garden near us, a jet rose from a well, and a pale statue leaned over the play of waters" (584, 588). Paul's legacy to Lucy, as she tells it, was not only their authorized union, but for Lucy, *upon Paul's departure, an authorized eroticism*—a self-caress within a pink interior and, outdoors, a play among waters from a well.

Lucy's Bridegroom memory could in this way be spoken by Irigaray's sexually generous 'God': "Thus 'God' will prove to have been her best lover since he separates her from herself only by that space of her *jouissance* where she finds Him/herself. To infinity perhaps, but in the serenity of the spacing that is thus projected by/in her pleasure" (*S*, 201). Even so, a significant separation between Brontë's and Irigaray's lovers may seem to insist itself. This distinction highlights Brontë's grounding in the Christian tradition and particularly her concern with the parting that is death: the lovers are separated *from each other* "to infinity." Such a literal absence of the lover—though even for Brontë this absence figures something looming beyond the literal—might seem, on the surface, foreign to Irigaray's celebration of her lovers' rapport around a crack. And yet in Irigaray's "When Our Lips Speak Together," we discover a passage that approaches Brontë's sense of parting—and approaches her sense of self-touching through parting—that she conveys at the close of *Villette*. Irigaray writes:

> But how can we stay alive when we are far apart? . . . How can I wait for you
> to return if when you're far away from me you cannot also be near? If I have
> nothing palpable to help me recall in the here and now the touch of our bod-
> ies. Open to the infinity of our separation, wrapped up in the intangible sen-
> sation of absence, how can we continue to live as ourselves? . . . We must
> learn to speak to each other so that we can embrace from afar. When I touch
> myself, I am surely remembering you. (*TS*, 215)

What remains serene and stunning is the extent to which a Christian Victorian woman turns parting toward pleasure ("when I touch myself, I am
surely remembering you") by appropriating the trope of apocalyptic marriage.

Paul, then, was separated from Lucy "to infinity":

> "You shall live here and have a school; you shall employ yourself while I am
> away; you shall think of me sometimes; you shall mind your health and hap-
> piness for my sake, and when I come back—" There he left a blank. I prom-
> ised to do all he told me. I promised to work hard and willingly. "I will be
> your faithful steward," I said; "I trust at your coming the account will be
> ready. . . ." He was my king; royal for me had been that hand's bounty; to
> offer homage was both a joy and a duty. (587)

The motif of the master's departure, and the faithful steward's hastening
the master's return, is clearly biblical. It parallels the faithful steward parable (Matthew 25:14–30) by which Jesus sharpened his disciples' readiness
for his return at any hour. This indeterminate union, rendered by Lucy's
word "blank," again points up a material realm that cannot be grasped,
being figured simply as the elsewhere of a woman's desire. Once again,
we may set Lucy's memory side by side Irigaray's vision: "Thus (re)-
assured of the complicity of this all-powerful partner, they/she play(s) at
courtship. . . . She is trusting as a dove, arrogant as a queen. . . . Her divine companion never tires of praising her and encouraging her
(auto)eroticism that has so miraculously been rediscovered" (*S*, 201–2).
Villette achieves precisely this feat: this autoeroticism *is* the labor, the labor
of desire, with which Paul entrusted Lucy. Suspended in stewardship, she
took Paul's place as her lover (she's now a lover to herself) as well as his
place as "owner" of her school.

The vexed question of Lucy's ownership taps another aspect of Jesus'
parable with respect to capitalism. This biblical story has often been used
to champion the Protestant valuation of work and the Protestant valuation
of returns-on-work-with-interest: the master grants the steward capital,
which the steward invests to yield an increase. Weber would add that plea-

sure is importantly deferred in this scheme, so that accumulation without depletion can be achieved and rendered, precisely, by accounts. Lucy's depiction of her stewardship for Paul both does and does not bear out these relations. To be sure, Lucy was given a school in which to invest (in) herself. She did:

> I commenced my school; I worked—I worked hard. I deemed myself the steward of his property, and determined, God willing, to render a good account. Pupils came—burghers at first—a higher class ere long. About the middle of the second year an unexpected chance threw into my hands an additional hundred pounds. . . . With this hundred pounds I ventured to take the house adjoining mine. I would not leave that which M. Paul had chosen, in which he had left, and where he expected again to find me. My externat became a pensionnat; that also prospered. (593–94)

This much matches Weber's expectations: it suggests that the labor of desire befits bourgeois properties and, also, accumulations. Yet, what appeared to belong to Lucy was not her own. Nor did it belong to Paul: "He was hardly the man to become a proprietor; I more than suspected in him a lamentable *absence of the saving faculty; he could get, but not keep*; he needed a treasurer. The tenement, then, belonged to a citizen in the Basse-Ville" (589; my emphasis).

The increase Paul expected was the increase of Lucy's *pleasure*, not her property, through her desire to work at self-employment. The lush passages in the Faubourg Clotilde suggest these pleasures. If this labor signals self-sexual pleasures, at least in Lucy's telling, it was sustained by desire's *deferrals*: "The spring which moved my energies lay far away beyond the seas, in an Indian isle. At parting, I had been left a legacy; such a thought for the present, such a hope for the future, such a motive for persevering, a laborious, an enterprising, a patient and a brave course—I *could* not flag" (594). Lucy depicts an economy of deferral, yet an economy where deferral becomes its own form of pleasure, and desire, clearly, its own form of labor. In fact, Paul Emanuel, sentenced by the Catholic junta to Basseterre, figures, remarkably, Carlyle's "imprisoned god" of Labor, whom, Carlyle says, we should work to body forth. Lucy's unflagging desire to work seems to body Paul forth in absentia, and to body forth his material concealment *with pleasure* for Lucy: "M. Emanuel was away three years. Reader, they were the three happiest years of my life" (593). This pleasure can aptly be deemed "anticapital," so clearly comprised and buoyed, as it is, by accumulated loss ("'and when I come back—'there he left a blank"). This "force of pure loss" is a residue of a vanished materiality: Paul himself. This is why Lucy's anticapital cannot receive account: it is bound to an opaque material fulfillment.

Indeed, approaching the Bridegroom without a(r)rival, the narrator loses her account altogether. No longer an employed watcher of suffering, she has risen to the wages of her "own" pain and pleasure, so that now, like Miss Marchmont, Lucy can claim her "own" dispossession. The same keen Banshee winds that arose when her mistress died accompanied Lucy's night-watch for Paul. The sexual intensity ("it will rise—it will swell") this memory still carries emerges in the narrator's shift to present tense:

> And now the three years are past: M. Emanuel's return is fixed. . . . My school flourishes, my house is ready. . . . The sun passes the equinox; the days shorten, the leaves grow sere; but—he is coming. . . .
> The wind shifts to the west. Peace, peace, Banshee—"keening" at every window! It will rise—it will swell—it shrieks out long: wander as I may through the house this night, I cannot lull the blast. (595–96)

Though Lucy had told us enough to suggest Paul's death by shipwreck, her ambiguous climax, announced by Jesus' words ("Peace, be still!"), does not directly tell us whether Lucy heard this voice or felt the hush of the winds when it came. What we as readers hit is a "pause": "Here pause: pause at once. There is enough said" (596). The narrating Lucy, by this barrier, by this curtain thrown down upon her scene, makes visible the material obliteration to which her desire has been pointing all along. Lucy has been left to hold an opacity, as if it contains the specular clue to the future owed to her.

Stuart Schneiderman reminds us that "the termination of a psychoanalysis involves a judgment on the part of the analysand that it is over":[5]

> As [Lacan] saw it, an analysis ends properly when the analysand has exhausted whatever purpose the analyst had served. At the end the analyst is discarded, like a worn and tattered garment. . . . The analysand *discards his analyst and buries his analysis* because . . . he has learned to negotiate with a desire that is elsewhere. . . . At the termination of a psychoanalysis an analysand knows that his desire is elsewhere.[6] (my emphasis)

Is it too much to claim that the analysand/narrator has exhausted her purpose, that she wants to discard and bury her reader? Lucy rapidly exits her narrative, once she has named the pause, the deferral, the material concealment that shapes her waiting. She will conclude and bid "farewell," her final word to us. Having made the journey of the backward glance, having transferred transference onto one who must remain conspicuously inaccessible, she is shown as now knowing her desire lies elsewhere. Fulfillment, as her spiritual plot has demanded, is infinitely deferred from her present standpoint, but visibly concealed within her spiritual vision as a potency. She must be a bourgeoise *dispossessed*. She, however, through the dispossession granted her by 'God', is finally privileged to a material concealment all her "own."

At this last gate, we can discover most directly the class limits Brontë's *Villette* writes, throughout, to Irigaray's celebrations. *Villette* makes clear that Lucy *rises* to bourgeois dispossession. This is a "dispossession" for pleasure that appears in *Villette* as a Christian privilege that privileged Christians can best afford—believers like Miss Marchmont and Lucy. Where do other bodies, differently classed, appear in these schemes, if they are not, like Lucy Snowe, "rising characters" in a plot written for them by 'God'?

Chapter 6

Recognizing George Eliot

~

Inserting Outwardness into Protestant Inwardness

As if at the seams of lovers and exchangers something is giving way, something causing slight rifts in their forms, an opaque trace of others intrudes upon the most inward moments in *Middlemarch*. Eliot, in fact, reveals the outwardness of Protestant inwardness, so that 'God' and others, or 'God' *as* others, appear at the brink of intensely private scenes. In *Middlemarch*, what we see straining at the novel's narrative joints is something that Irigaray only intimates: the material concealment of bodies that haunt the space of desire between those who love. For Eliot, by courtesy of Feuerbach's antitheological theology, 'God' is the set of opaque others who carve our identity and keep fresh the wound of our desire.

I initiate my reading of *Middlemarch* with this materialist blade. It cuts a line, I hope, through the Protestant value of inwardness, since I want to discover how *Middlemarch* resists and reconceives it, making material concealments seen and caught in their web of class relations. This issue requires us to examine how *reading* is related to opacities and to the forms of inwardness we think that we can see. Connecting the privacy of novel-reading to Protestant individuality, critics have perhaps too easily assumed that "classic realist" fiction forces inwardness and bourgeois individuality upon its reader. (Ian Watt is the obvious reference here.)* But do these relations necessarily hold? *Middlemarch*, given its long-acknowledged status

*Watt, *Rise of the Novel*. For versions of this argument, see Catherine Belsey, *Critical Practice*; and D. A. Miller, *The Novel and the Police*.

as the queen of realist fiction, offers possibilities for testing these queries.*
In fact, a look at the novel's narration reveals wide angles upon the Protestant inwardness the novel would have us view up close. The narrator's
gaze, specifically, I suggest, inserts otherness into inwardness. Far from
the transcendent observer, authorial representative, second self, or even
the collective, communal memory that some critics have noted, the *Middlemarch* narrator—that entity that provokes so much discussion in Eliot
criticism—is neither inside nor outside the text but implicated in a particular labor of desire.†

Desire leads us back, as always, to gender—and particularly, for *Middlemarch*, to the narrator's gender. This is the first dilemma to consider, one
which raises theoretical concerns for how we ever "fix" identities (along
with bodies) or discover them as finally opaque. Let me start by saying that
it is difficult not to read the narrator as masculine. 'His' implied access to
education, 'his' self-defined vocation as an "elegant historian," and 'his'
pointed investment in ideas-as-capital all seem to characterize a male
professional. There is also the question of 'his' identifications. Repeatedly
in *Middlemarch*, the narrator appears to identify directly with masculine
characters. A special sympathy is pleaded for, and then accorded to, Casaubon and Lydgate. The narrator identifies with the intellectual passions
and disappointments of these characters in a way that differs from 'his'
sympathy (though great) for Dorothea's restricted longings.‡

In Dorothea's case, the stress often falls on the obstacles 'we' (but who
are 'we'?) put in the way of women's material, intellectual advance ("But
we insignificant people with our daily words and acts are preparing the
lives of many Dorotheas").§ The connection with Lydgate's professional
sorrows seems, by contrast, a matter of immediate identification: "Only

---

*Indeed, Belsey uses *Middlemarch* as her prime example of a "classic realist" novel
in her discussion of "rounded character" and realism (*Critical Practice*, 50–51).

†For representatives of very different views on the narrator see Quentin Anderson,
"George Eliot in *Middlemarch*," in *From Dickens to Hardy*; Isobel Armstrong, "*Middlemarch*: A Note on George Eliot's Wisdom"; Edward Dowden, "George Eliot"; Elizabeth Ermarth, "Method and Moral in George Eliot's Narrative"; J. Hillis Miller, "The
Narrator as General Consciousness"; K. M. Newton, "The Role of the Narrator in
George Eliot's Novels"; and Dorothea Barrett, "Dialectic and Polyphony in *Middlemarch*," in *Vocation and Desire: George Eliot's Heroines*. For one of the most careful and
interesting discussions of Eliot's narrators, see Jacqueline Osherow, "'Within us as a
great yearning': George Eliot's Struggle Toward Female Self-Expression," Ph.D. diss.,
Princeton University, 1990.

‡One notes such phrases as, "For my part I am very sorry for him" and "The faults
will not, I hope, be a reason for the withdrawal of your interest in him."

§George Eliot, *Middlemarch*, 896. All references are to the Penguin edition.

those who know the supremacy of the intellectual life—the life which has a seed of ennobling thought and purpose within it—can understand the grief of one who falls from that serene activity into the absorbing soul-wasting struggle with worldly annoyances" (793). The narrator knows this supremacy and grief, or so the passage seems to suggest. And yet irony may adhere to this statement, which slants the narrator's identification in a slightly different direction than a simple reflection of a male professional's sorrow. The concluding phrase "worldly annoyances" carries with it an oblique judgment against the professional with whom the narrator appears to identify. For those who know Eliot's novels well, this phrase signals that Lydgate is to be held accountable, at least in some measure, for deeming matters of the world "annoyances"; such an estimation of everyday affairs could never characterize Dorothea's (or Eliot's own) investment in ordinary life. This complex identification, which entails subtle judgments along with sympathy, surfaces earlier and more obviously in the narrator's comic reference to a minor character, "whose standing had been fixed thirty years before by a treatise on Meningitis, of which at least one copy marked 'own' was bound in calf." "For my part," writes the narrator, emerging here as 'I', "I have some fellow-feeling with Dr. Sprague: one's self-satisfaction is an untaxed kind of property which it is very unpleasant to find depreciated" (186). This "self-satisfaction" in the "properties" of intellectual production proves a consistent theme in *Middlemarch*. Even if it is partly satirized, it signals masculine access to the capital privileged among professionals: ideas.

These recognitions (their ambivalence notwithstanding) lend a masculine edge to the "elegant historian," as if the authorial voice might belong to Lewes, not Eliot. Yet many complications attend a reading of "George Eliot"'s gender, as we will see shortly. What inhibits us, then, from reading the narrator as a woman (as Eliot)—a woman with social and moral concerns, critical of existing conditions for women, whose masculine intellect prompts her solidarity with male professionals? Surely in principle nothing stops us from reading the narrator as an intellectual woman. But the force of the text may work against this grain: it defines the professional exercise (not the urgency—which Dorothea consistently shows) of intellectual passions as a man's pursuit.

There is another complication, too. Jacqueline Rose has discussed how *Daniel Deronda*'s narrator begins the novel "by taking up the place of the man, miming perhaps, inflating certainly, the voyeurism which constitutes the woman as spectacle."[1] Rose thinks this gaze is unique to *Deronda*. I disagree. *Middlemarch* abounds with such glances at women—at the figures of *paired* women, for they and their (auto)erotic encounters are caught for us by the narrative gaze. The narrator fashions these women not only as the objects of a (masculine) look, but also as the potential objects of a (masculine) desire—a point that Rose does not address. For example, slipping from a report upon a character to a generalizing posture that solicits the reader, the narrator may seem to participate in Will's aestheticizing desire for Dorothea:

> Will, we know, could not bear the thought of any flaw appearing in his crystal: he was at once exasperated and delighted by the calm freedom with which Dorothea looked at him and spoke to him, and there was something so exquisite in thinking of her just as she was, that he could not long for a change which must somehow change her. Do we not shun the street version of a fine melody?—or shrink from the news that the rarity—some bit of chiselling or engraving perhaps—which we have dwelt on even with exultation in the trouble it has cost us to snatch glimpses of it, is really not an uncommon thing, and may be obtained as an everyday possession? (510)

Here, it seems, the narrator asks us to commiserate with Will, to lament a possible unhappy discovery that what we deemed a work of art—a "rarity"—has proved akin to a commodity (what "may be obtained as an everyday possession"). This opposition masks the realization that most "rarities," whether women or artworks, become commodities in their circulation, which is how they find their way to "men."* But, again, all of this supposed lament presumes that the narrator should be taken straight—that is, at face value. It is certainly possible to imagine that we should share with the narrator a small amusement at Will's (all too rarified) expense.

Even so, all irony aside, why should the narrator's desire for a woman necessarily mark the narrator as a man? This novel comes to climax, after all, in a scene between women. Their erotic dynamics—an orgasmic encounter between saint and supplicant—conveys the possibility that a

---

*Of course, at the end of chapter 19, book 2, Eliot shows Will seeing Dorothea as something beyond art. Even though this point, too, in its way, is tied to his worship of her as a woman, the passage touches on material opacity, perhaps suggesting how closely a concept of opacity sits next to woman-as-enigma: "Language gives a fuller image, which is all the better for being vague. After all, the true seeing is within; and painting stares at you with an insistent imperfection. I feel that especially about representations of women. As if a woman were a mere coloured superficies! You must wait for movement and tone. There is a difference in their very breathing: they change from moment to moment.—This woman whom you have just seen, for example: how would you paint her voice, pray? But her voice is much diviner than anything you have seen of her" (222).

woman might (unconsciously) desire another woman for the purpose of maintaining access to her 'own' opacity in marriage, which is to say her 'own' desire. In this way, the narrator's gaze upon women might represent a woman yearning after herself. The narrative could be read as *functioning autoerotically for a narrator* who, within the text and through the telling, takes the place of a desiring woman.

But if the narrator is neither fully a man nor a woman, it might be best to invoke a concept of gender borders—and of boundaries, in general— by which we can see them as pressured, not collapsed; as suspending bod- ies between various states: masculinity and femininity, desire and fulfill- ment, even marriage and virginity. If this description sounds like the lips—borders under pressure, not collapsed—it also sounds like Derrida's "hymen," on which Irigaray may well have modeled her deconstructive folds, but turned them obviously—a conceptual dazzle—toward women's pleasure. Though Derrida's folds may remove us from pleasure (if 'we' are women), the figure of the hymen proves crucial to *Middlemarch*. In "The Double Session," Derrida manipulates the hymen's doublings: hymen as "a membranous fold of tissue partly or completely occluding the vaginal external orifice" (*American Heritage Dictionary*) and hymen as marriage (in Greek mythology, the god of marriage). Derrida writes:

> The hymen, the confusion between the present and the nonpresent . . . pro- duces the effect of a medium (a medium as element enveloping both terms at once; a medium located between the two terms). It is an operation that *both* sows confusion *between* opposites *and* stands *between* the opposites "at once." What counts here is the *between*, the in-between-ness of the hymen. The hy- men "takes place" in the "inter-," in the spacing between desire and fulfill- ment, between perpetration and its recollection. . . . The hymen remains in the hymen. The one—the veil of virginity where nothing has yet taken place—remains in the other—consummation, release, and penetration of the antre.[2]

Once again, as with the lips, we are "in-between." The hymen is a border that creates and reveals a material conundrum: it is a boundary that ob- scures what it also divides. This puzzle is neatly figured by the formula, "The hymen remains in the hymen"; for example, hymen (in the sense of marriage) annihilates hymen (in the sense of virginity) so that hymen re- mains.* The hymen's implications (from the Latin *implicare*, "to fold") convey, in fact, the intimacies that are folded over concealed incrimina-

*For discussion on this point see Alice Jardine, *Gynesis: Configurations of Woman and Modernity*, 190.

tions in the *Middlemarch* web. My task, therefore, is to float this discussion somewhere between the hymen and the lips in order to elucidate Eliot's ambivalence (as opposed to Brontë's clear enthusiasm) over women's (auto)erotic possibilities. Eliot, it seems, can imagine only momentary breakouts of women's pleasure or sorrow amidst their confinement in marriage. This is why her novel hovers at a hymen—in spite of the lure, the promise, of lips.

We might additionally read the *narrative*'s folds as a hymen, recalling that hymen, in the Derridean sense, produces "the effect of a medium (a medium as element enveloping both terms at once; a medium located between two terms)." Following hymeneal logic, then, narrator and reader meet at this hymen to produce *Middlemarch*, which stands between the two as a medium. This "in-between–ness" raises, as always, the question of mirrors, and hymeneal boundaries, as by now we would imagine, involve us in reflections. Jacqueline Rose, in her work on the Imaginary, has cautioned against a theory of too-smooth return. She reminds us that the "apparent reciprocity [in the structure of the gaze] is grounded on the impossibility of complete return"; the subject is both seized and split by the object of its look, its position as all-perceiving, centered subject threatened, says Rose, by the fact that "the subject can never see its look from the point at which the other is looking at it."[3] This reminder (about incomplete return) shapes concerns for reading *Middlemarch*. For now it is enough to realize how imaginary—in the twin senses of mirroring and splitting—is our relation, as readers, to a narrator who asks us to mirror 'his' judgments. The splitting, of course, gets easily concealed, so that the narrator's persistent generalizations ("Will not a tiny speck very close to our vision blot out the glory of the world. . . ?") force our recognition in 'his' mirror. This is precisely that imaginary lure that Lacan and Rose both find so dangerous: the assumption of a complete return that fabricates binding fictions of smooth identities (the narrator's 'we').

One can even miss the cracks between *character* and narrator, for narrative slips occur quite slyly when, in the midst of quoting directly, the narrator shifts to report *indirectly* what a character was thinking. The narrator's seeing 'I' controls this conflation of identities, so that 'he' becomes one with the novel's characters to the point of domination. Here is the narrator, for example, that elegant historian who ostensibly merely reports what characters said and did, virtually concocting words for Fred and Farebrother: "Much of Fred's rumination might be summed up in the words. . . . Perhaps Mr. Farebrother's might be concentrated into a single shrug and one little speech" (728–29).* We find the same confident ability to deliver a character to the reader in this address: "At present I have to make the new settler Lydgate better known to any one interested in him than he could possibly be even to those who had seen the most of him since his arrival in Middlemarch" (170). The ubiquity of this emergent 'I', with 'his' claim to full knowledge of another's mind, suggests some grand assimilation of otherness.

Yet, if the narrator assumes too close a relation to these characters, there appears the suggestion, at points in the narrative, that characters and their scenes are delivered without a narrator's mediation: "No third person listening could have thoroughly understood the impetuosity of Will's repulse or the bitterness of his words. No one but himself then knew how everything connected with the sentiment of his own dignity had an immediate bearing for him on his relation to Dorothea and to Mr. Casaubon's treatment of him" (673). Since the narrator frequently emerges as a listening, seeing 'I', it is at once predictable and strange to find this "third-person" status disavowed. Predictable, because the narrator captures characters, to the point of merging with each individual consciousness. Strange, because the second sentence, "no one but himself then knew," is clearly contradicted by the report of Will's private feelings by a narrator who often shows up in the novel as 'I'. In contrast to those places where the narrator foregrounds 'his' observations ("the group I am moving toward is at Caleb Garth's breakfast-table in the large parlour" [434]), this passage on Will is slipped on our plates as if seeing could bypass mediation (which is also to say, bypass desire).

A similar but slightly different valence is attributed to the seeing 'I' in a scene between Rosamond, Dorothea, and Will:

> Dorothea put out her hand with her usual simple kindness, and looked admiringly at Lydgate's lovely bride—aware that there was a gentleman standing at a distance, but seeing him merely as a coated figure at a wide angle. The gentleman was too much occupied with the presence of the one woman to reflect on the contrast between the two—a contrast that would certainly have been striking to a calm observer. (470)

Dorothea looks upon Rosamond, hardly aware of the masculine gaze fixed upon her. The narrator's postulation of yet another, although here

*The full passage reads: "Much of Fred's rumination might be summed up in the words, 'It certainly would have been a fine thing for her to marry Farebrother—but if she loves me best and I am a good husband?' Perhaps Mr. Farebrother's might be concentrated into a single shrug and one little speech. 'To think of the part one little woman

only hypothetical, gaze—"a calm observer"'s look—creates an *almost* subjectless position for narrator and reader. Puzzles and hints such as these, however, remind us to read both the narrator *and ourselves* as always at the hymen in purportedly "private" encounters between characters. This mediation holds for the scene in which Dorothea, in spiritual inwardness, stares upon the portrait of Will's Aunt Julia; the scene in which Dorothea and Will meet "alone" to part; and—one of the novel's most inward scenes—Rosamond and Dorothea's erotic exchange around their sorrows. These intensely private scenes are always mediated by a narrative voice that, *by the very act of narration*, refashions inwardness as a more public scene, where even 'God' and others, or '*God*' *as others*, appear at the hymen of public/private boundaries. This host of others, between one and two, disturbs the standard depictions of privacy, domesticity, and spirituality that one finds common in Victorian writings.

If the narrator's position as a desiring subjectivity emerges in this text, though in largely hidden ways, the reader, who is asked to mirror the narrator, also gets entangled in the narrator's hidden work of desire. Although Rose, in her *Deronda* essay, does not talk in terms of desire, she does refer, interestingly enough, to the reader's "implication": "This question," she writes, addressing the question of whether *Deronda* resists or repeats dominant constructions of femininity, "is nothing less than the question of our own implication as readers in a structure and images which we challenge even as they bear down upon, and at moments seduce, us all."[4]

It is crucial to recognize our participation in the narrator's desire to fix on lives—as if these lives are property to which we have calculable access. And yet, we can resist the narrator's attributions and seductions. Refusing, in part, our interpellation as bourgeois men, we can resist by lining up, as *both* Lacan and Irigaray would say, on the side of 'woman'. To insert this concealment into the text, and thus to project it onto the mirror where we meet the narrator, would be to crack a (masculine) Imaginary with feminine fractures. Our own labor of desire would activate those scenes of desire between feminine characters, where the material concealments of other bodies become most resonant as concealed.

Before Irigarayan celebrations overwhelm, let me suggest that *Middlemarch*, like *Villette*, limits Irigaray's envisioned escapes. Hence, we can only partially assert 'our' difference from the narrator's (bourgeois) con-

---

can play in the life of a man, so that to renounce her may be a very good imitation of heroism, and to win her may be a discipline!' "

trol. My stance as an "independent" producer of *Middlemarch* is fraught with some of the problems that plague the novel's narrator, from whom I seek distance. Most obviously, there is the necessity of taking up a pronoun in relation to 'my' readers (addressing readers as 'you' or 'we'). Then, too, I find myself asking my readers to mirror my judgments. The "text itself" can never appear to render a definitive no to my claims.* At best, it remains an object of belief and respect, insofar as I accord it the status of a material concealment with which I engage. Indeed, this fiction may still prove necessary. It may guard me from assuming that no material text confronts me, as if "it" can be nothing apart from my reading. Belief in the text's material concealment may also keep me from assuming that I can fix or unlock it with some grand transparency. The whole attitude of this critical fix may be mediated by the narrator whose presumed omniscience poses such a problem.

> As the stone which has been kicked by generations of clowns may come by curious little links of effect under the eyes of a scholar, through whose labours it may at last fix the date of invasions and unlock religions, so a bit of ink and paper which has long been innocent wrapping or stop-gap may at last be laid open under the one pair of eyes which have knowledge enough to turn it into the opening of a catastrophe. (448)

Can a reading of *Middlemarch* resist these dichotomies—clown/scholar, kicked/fixed, innocent/knowledgeable—that structure familiar scenarios of reading? A saint at home with desire, and the sobs that must be returned to her, may have everything to do with such resistance.

The Saint at Home with Men at Work

If I proceed to recognize "George Eliot" before I produce an account of *Middlemarch*, it is to explore a text that is as much a work of desire and a testimony to material concealments as is "George Eliot"'s novel. Brontë's biography, I have argued, can be read as her ability to shape her vocation as a writer around her material losses, for which she sought to make a home by means of her faith. For Eliot, unlike Brontë, it is not a contact with loss that shapes her vocation as a writer; it is her effort to turn her invisible labors toward visibility and material compensation. Eliot's career as a desiring female "saint" (though often a fallen one) impeded but

*For a discussion of Eliot's novels that argues that the texts themselves often render such a no, see Osherow, "Within us as a great yearning."

also strangely engendered her career as a paid professional writer. I want, in this way, to respond to Daniel Cottom, who reads George Eliot as "a figure of patriarchy": a liberal intellectual and professional writer.* Reading any biography of Eliot quickly corrects Cottom's notion—not because "objective facts" urge us to read George Eliot as a woman, but because the biographical constructions themselves demonstrate how "the figure of patriarchy" was never simply read (or paid) as a liberal intellectual but always (also) as a woman.

This question of payment directly raises the issue of work. Clearly, George Eliot's work as an editor, and later as an author, does not constitute productive labor in orthodox Marxist terms. Nor does it constitute the kind of labor—directly or indirectly productive—that feminist Marxists, or even a feminist materialist like Delphy, would be likely to discuss. When Victorian women (Bodichon, in particular) argue for women's right to work, they seem to imagine the bourgeois professions that women would desire—not the factory jobs that were available and undesirable (if all too necessary) for working-class women.

But here, in the bourgeois terms of a woman's wish to work professionally, we find a class plot, nonetheless. Eliot's passage to professional work is plotted largely by her potential sexual labor for men. This plot writes her specific place in the circuits of a masculine economy that grants to men, bourgeois men explicitly, access to (sexual) desire and capital. Eliot's gendered slot in this economy grants her a woman's dichotomous opportunity: to perform a professional's work, overseeing production of journalistic commodities, while getting paid as a professional's mistress (or wife) who "helps" for free. This instance of surplus labor—where the *professional* woman sells her labor for free—Marx did not discuss (or fore-

*See Daniel Cottom, *Social Figures: George Eliot, Social History, and Literary Representation*, xx. Cottom attempts to elucidate how Eliot participated in the liberal intellectual focus on "feeling" and "human nature" that always, only, in Cottom's view, constituted bourgeois constructions. George Eliot, as an important instance of the modern professional intellectual, provides the opportunity, according to Cottom, to understand how intellectuals "could seem to be independent of class, party, and patronage" (15) while they wrote a "metaphysics of the individual" (xxii). Cottom produces a study that should happily obstruct critics' all too easy connections between Eliot's realism and her "humanity." Yet Cottom himself repeats a "bourgeois" masculine move. He treats all liberal intellectuals as men. In a study that asks us to demystify claims to neutrality and the intellectual posture of pluralism, it is difficult to accept straightforwardly his claim that "it is simply to say that [a feminist] approach differs from the present approach" (xxi). The critical decision to read George Eliot as "a figure of patriarchy," by reading the pseudonym as unproblematic, refuses to interrogate a crucial aspect of Eliot's production: the posture, "George Eliot."

see?). The story of making "George Eliot," therefore, is one that illuminates the hidden complications in the seemingly ordinary phrase that Barbara Bodichon champions: "Women want work."

For years, many readers and critics encountered Eliot's life through
Gordon S. Haight's "definitive" biography, entitled, simply enough,
*George Eliot.** The title's economy, nonetheless, masks a chronological re-
versal. It offers "George Eliot"—who was "born" much later than Mary
Anne Evans and who, therefore, must be read back into her life, if found
there at all. But Haight, it seems, does find "George Eliot" along the way.
He takes uncritically as his organizing principle John Cross's description
of Eliot's "absolute need of some one person who should be all in all to
her and to whom she should be all in all" (5). This comment is quoted by
Haight on page five of his text, carried back to her life's beginning, where
her relationship with her brother serves as "first example" of this need.
Haight thus begins presenting George Eliot, the woman who bore the
name of a man, on this stereotypically feminized note, later joined by the
similar phrase, "some one to lean upon."

The overt text of Haight's "recognition" is not hard to follow: George
Eliot was a needy, affectionate woman with a masculine intellect. Yet we
can produce what this story conceals, even working primarily with
Haight: the life of Mary Anne Evans, and, later, George Eliot, too,
evinces the skeins of sexual, spiritual, and professional concerns.† Amidst
these tangles, her desires and beliefs, not to mention her gendered identities, continually pull against and reform each other. Haight's presentation of her early Evangelicalism is a case in point, followed by his equally
revealing constructions of the episodes involving Dr. Brabant and John
Chapman.

He presents Mary Anne's Evangelical period ("seven dark years") as
initiated by (his version of) desire between women: the "affectionate relation" between Mary Anne and Miss Maria Lewis, an Evangelical governess at Mary Anne's boarding school. By Haight's description, this relationship would appear another example of "Eliot"'s "absolute need of
some one person." He depicts Mary Anne as "unprepossessing" and "impressible," while "more like an elder sister than a governess," Haight in-

*Gordon S. Haight, *George Eliot: A Biography*. All references to this work will appear
in the text.

†I am using Haight's biography against itself, rather than comparing Haight's version of George Eliot to other biographers' (Jennifer Uglow's, for example), because I
want to focus on the constructedness of Haight's account and the way in which even
this most conservative and long-standing version of Eliot tells another story.

forms us, "Miss Lewis gave the bright, eager little girl the sympathetic
support and affection that she needed" (10). Haight never implies any sexualized elements to this affair. He saves his observations on Mary Anne's
"indiscretions" and her "unfortunately balanced animal and moral regions" for her later relations with men. Even so, his repetition of "interest" ("immediate interest," "affectionate interest") as he presents this relationship has a curious resonance with a passage he later quotes, when
discussing the break-off of their relations. In this context, Haight quotes
Edith Simcox, who inquired of Sara Hennell about the relationship after
Eliot's death and recollects Hennell's opinion that

> Miss Lewis had been finding fault, governess fashion, with what was im-
> prudent or unusual in Marian's [Mary Anne's] manners and that Marian al-
> ways resented this and that it was some verbal *tu quoque* leading to a mis-
> understanding, as if Miss Lewis had reproached her with seeming to take too
> much interest in somebody—of the opposite sex: whereto she angrily: "It
> might as well be said that *you* have an 'interest' or are interested in your
> friendship for me." (61–62)

"Interest" clearly carries a sexual valence, especially as the sentence turns
the tables on "the opposite sex" after the colon: (the supposed quotation
of) Mary Anne's retort opposes Mary Anne's own ("normal") interest in
the opposite sex to Miss Lewis's perhaps more interesting interestedness.
Of course, as given here, it is Mary Anne who puts her finger on Miss
Lewis's calculations—a projection of her own? Her own sentence—but
whose is it? Mary Anne's? Edith's? Sara's?—begins as if to charge Miss
Lewis with the same interest in the opposite sex ("it might as well be said
that *you* have an 'interest' ") before it turns toward the opposite charge: a
different interest, in the same sex ("or are interested in your friendship for
me").

The sexual interest that may have been centrally a part of Mary Anne's
own Evangelicalism Haight does not discuss. He does remark that, after
her conversion at the hands of the Franklin sisters, daughters of the minister of the wonderfully named Cow Lane Baptist Chapel, Mary Anne
"began to neglect her personal appearance . . . and practised mild absti-
nences from innocent pleasures" (19). But this is simply to construct her
devotion in the familiar mode of renunciation. The negotiation between
her spirituality and sexuality appears more difficult. Both a fear of sensuality and a substitute sensuality emerge from her writings of this period,
many of which Haight does not present. It appears Mary Anne feared the
pain that might accompany sexual desire and sexual relations, writing to

her Evangelical teacher: "When I hear of the marrying and giving in marriage that is constantly being transacted I can only sigh for those who are multiplying earthly ties which though powerful enough to detach their heart and thoughts from heaven, are so brittle as to be liable to be snapped asunder at every breeze."[5] This passage recalls Brontë's concern with love's evanescence: "In the first place, it seldom or never meets with a requital; and, in the second place, if it did, the feeling would be only temporary: it would last the honeymoon, and then, perhaps, give place to disgust, or indifference worse, perhaps, than disgust." Probably Mary Anne feared what she saw, unmistakably, in herself: her own fiercely sensual tendencies. In a passage that might have been conceived by Lucy Snowe, who associates Catholicism with a threatening sensuality, Mary Ann (she has by this point dropped the "e") tells how "hysteria" befell her:

> When I had been there some time the conviction that I was not in a situation to maintain the *Protestant* character of the true Christian, together with the oppressive noise that formed the accompaniment to the dancing, the sole amusement, produced first headache and then that most wretched and unpitied of afflictions, hysteria, so that I regularly disgraced myself. Mrs. Bull [her hostess—another engaging name] was extremely kind. One good effect of a temporary annoyance and indisposition will be to render me more decided in rejecting all invitations of a dubious character. (28)

This is a curious passage, since one is never clear how this "hysteria" made itself seen, nor how its manifestation was related to her inability "to maintain the *Protestant* character of the true Christian."*

This incident suggests the difficult conjunction between Mary Ann's faith and her desire; it indicates how carefully her Evangelicalism was guarding, yet, in another sense, *acting out* her passions. Strongly sensuous, Mary Ann, in this period, renounced sexuality along with marriage, while shaping an alternate sensuality with God—a different strategy from the one Eliot constructs for Dorothea (her own St. Theresa), since Dorothea *marries* in order, seemingly, to *renounce* sensuality. In this respect, we may revisit a line from Mary Ann's letters (Haight quotes it, too), which betrays her fear of her sensuality, even after she moved out of Evangelical circles into her interest in Higher Criticism. Writing at the time of her father's death, Mary Ann recounts: "I had a horrid vision of myself last

---

*Haight does imply in a footnote to this passage that Mary Ann fell into scoffing at religion on this occasion. He makes this implication by quoting another Victorian woman: "In 1815 Jane Porter wrote: '(then a very young person) I burst into tears at a large table after dinner from horror and pity of some persons present, who were scoffing at religion without reprimand from any one'" (28n1). This is Haight's only comment to explain this extraordinary passage.

night becoming earthly sensual and devilish for want of that purifying, restraining influence" (67). It was no doubt due to this period that Eliot could write so insightfully in her novels about the displacement of desire onto spirituality; it is likely, too, that this worrisome (for her) clash between sexual and spiritual energies led Mary Ann to seek spiritual realms that would favor sensuality.

If Haight does not grasp the sexual implications of Mary Ann's Evangelical fervor, he seems more aware of how, even early on, her spirituality provided her with opportunities for intellectual work. He remarks, "If, as we are told, Mary Ann taught Sunday School near Griff before she was twelve years old, she was probably impelled as much by desire to exhibit her learning as by spiritual zeal" (19). In this way, Mary Ann's career as a "saint"—she copied in her notebook a poem entitled, "On Being Called a Saint," which Haight suspects she wrote herself—was engendering her career as a writer. Haight describes her letters from this period as "tissues of biblical quotation" (again, this recalls Brontë), influenced, no doubt, by the copious Evangelical letters, biographies, and missionary narratives she was then reading. Haight even reads Mary Ann through the lens of Maggie Tulliver or Dorothea Brooke, using tags from George Eliot's novels to describe Mary Ann's religious devotion, so that Haight's own description suddenly finds completion in a line from a novel ("We know that she [Mary Ann] relieved the poor and visited the sick, praying with them as if she were [and here the tag on Dorothea from *Middlemarch*] 'living in the time of the Apostles'" [22]). Nonetheless, he never thinks to construct her as Casaubon in her work of desire: even though, in 1839, Mary Ann planned an elaborate Chart of Ecclesiastical History at which she worked steadily "for some six months," Haight recounts, "before the publication of a similar chart brought her labour to an end" (24).

Strikingly, 1839 is the date Haight gives for the "cooling" of her Evangelicalism. Yet if her emotional commitment was lessening, her professional ties and material opportunities were being wed, ever more securely, to her interest in religion. Her new relationships with "freethinking" friends (the Brays and the Hennells), which drew her increasingly away from Evangelicalism, brought growing opportunities to work on theological writings. Her father and brother could see only the obvious and immediate change in her beliefs. Their unhappiness led to some remarkable sentiments on her brother's part, sentiments we encounter only through the expression they are given by Cara Bray to Sara Hennell:

> It seems that brother Isaac with real fraternal kindness thinks that his sister has no chance of getting the one thing needful—i.e. a husband and a settle-

ment—unless she mixes more in society, and complains that since she has
known us she has hardly been anywhere else; that Mr. Bray, being only a
leader of mobs, can only introduce her to Chartists and Radicals, and that
such only will ever fall in love with her if she does not belong to the church.
(48)

Here conservative religion is linked with materially successful love ("a
husband and a settlement") and is further proffered as a safeguard against
obviously disastrous love affairs with Chartists and Radicals. This conjunction of sexuality, religion, material advancement, and political alli-
ance gives evidence that, as much as she might have disdained such perspectives, Mary Ann's intellectual and theological interests were sexualized, and even politicized, by those around her.

The sexualization of Mary Ann's labors emerges when Haight reconstructs her relationship with Dr. Brabant, a 62-year-old pedant. Invited
into his home " 'to fill the place of his daughter' " (49), Mary Ann, together with Brabant, studied two theological languages (German and
Greek). To this opportunity for intellectual work Mary Ann gave a spiritual construction: "I am in a little heaven here, Dr. Brabant being its arch-
angel . . . time would fail me to tell of all his charming qualities. We read
and walk and talk together, and I am never weary of his company" (49).
The little narrative that arises from Haight makes clear what may happen
when a woman tries to work as a man (for we notice that she has construed
herself as Adam, Dr. Brabant as Raphael): her efforts, at least by others'
readings, become sexualized, and consequently, Adam becomes only Eve.
Indeed, as if to demonstrate Irigaray's slant on masculine economies,
Mary Ann was caught in rivalrous relationships among other women. Dr.
Brabant's sister-in-law fed the suspicions of Dr. Brabant's wife, and their
uneasiness was confirmed by Dr. Brabant's daughter, who visited the
house after her honeymoon. A large part of this story—and this becomes
more striking yet with the Chapman episode—Haight takes verbatim
from Chapman's diary, especially the account of the final blow-up. Haight
explains that Dr. Brabant's daughter told Chapman the story (which had
taken place in 1843) in 1851. The upshot of this episode, according to
Haight, quoting Chapman, was that "Miss Evans left," and "Mrs. B.
vowed she [Mary Ann] should never enter the house again, or that if she
did, she, Mrs. Brabant, would instantly leave it" (50).

Haight's construction of this material is significant, for he immedi-
ately follows this story with a passage from Charles Bray's autobiography.
Bray relates a phrenological reading of a plaster cast made from Mary
Ann's head:

Miss Evans's head is a very large one . . . 22¼ inches round; George Combe, on first seeing the cast, took it for a man's. In her brain-development the Intellect greatly predominates; it is very large, more in length than in its peripheral surface. In the Feelings, the Animal and Moral regions are about equal; the moral being quite sufficient to keep the animal in order and in due subservience, but would not be spontaneously active. The social feelings were very active, particularly the adhesiveness. She was of a most affectionate disposition, always requiring some one to lean upon, preferring what has hitherto been considered the stronger sex, to the other and more impressible. She was not fitted to stand alone. (51)

Bray's reading parallels not only her biographer's but also many critics' attempts to construct George Eliot at the poles: masculine in intellect (because intelligence, for these writers, is unquestionably masculine); feminine in her "affectionate disposition" (because women, for these writers, are "not fitted to stand alone"). Rather than interpreting the obvious interest behind Bray's reading—the division of Mary Ann into masculine and feminine—and rather than interrogating her fix as a woman anxious for intellectual labor, Haight uncritically adopts Bray's terms. Here, for example, one finds the phrase, "some one to lean upon," which Haight uses to title a chapter. More revealing still are the conclusions Haight draws about the Brabant affair in light of Bray's passage:

If the annoyance provoked by her behaviour with Dr. Brabant were unique, it might be attributed to provincial simplicity or ignorance, even at the age of twenty-four. But the same pattern—an intellectual friendship drawn by over-ready expansiveness into feelings misunderstood—reappears often enough to recall that phrenological cast with its moral regions sufficient to keep the animal in due subservience, but not spontaneously active. (52)

"Over-ready expansiveness" surely stands in for "desire." This charge constantly underlies Haight's rendition of Mary Ann's work with "her" men. He even follows his echo of Bray with another instance of the pattern he discerns. He implies that a misfire of Mary Ann's affections was involved in her relationship with the Rev. Francis Watts. On behalf of this minister, Haight remarks casually, Mary Ann had offered "to translate Vinet's *Mémoire* to be published as Watts's work." Her only compensation for this endeavor, Haight continues, was to be, as she put it, " 'the pleasure of being linked to your remembrance' " (52)—pleasure in (unpaid) work linked again to a man (of the cloth).

Repeating her contemporaries, Haight mistakes her desire to work for "over-ready expansiveness"—what he later describes as an "over-ready expansiveness betraying her into indiscretion." Yet her most significant pattern with men, even as reconstructed by Haight, is her attraction to men who provide her with work, labor that goes either unpaid or under-paid. For her translation of *Das Leben Jesu* (*The Life of Jesus*, David Fried-rich Strauss, 1846), a work on which her name did not appear, she was paid twenty pounds, even though, according to Haight, "few books of the nineteenth century have had a profounder influence on religious thought in England" (59). Mary Ann thought she could devote herself to what she termed "intellectual and religious loves," as opposed to sexual love with its potentially painful vicissitudes. These distinctions, however, were not so easily maintained for Mary Ann. Her work and spirituality were al-ways, in the last analysis, read by her culture as sexual affairs.

Haight's account of the Chapman episode provides an illustrative case in point. Marian (yet another spelling now) met Chapman when he asked her to do an article for his *Westminster Review*.* She was to write on a theo-logical book, which would give her an opportunity to turn her vast theo-logical knowledge, and former commitment to "sainthood," into the ca-reer of a professional writer. But if her past spirituality was tied directly to her work, her work was tied to men and sexuality. The men she worked for sexualized her labor: admiring as they were of her "masculine" intel-lect, they neglected to pay her as a man and, further, pursued her as a woman. Haight implies that Chapman sexually chased Marian when she moved in with him, his wife, and his mistress. Marian, for her part, took to teaching Chapman German—in her room. "To private lessons in Ger-man," Haight recounts, "Marian added readings of Latin and perhaps less abstruse subjects, sometimes at very curious hours" (82). Yet Chapman, as Marian stresses in a letter, spoke of her to the editor of the *Edinburgh Review* "as a man."†

This detail locates the operative principle of the fiction "George Eliot": a man at work (but not in pay), a woman at home. Haight aids this fabrication, especially by the way he structures his account of her relations with Chapman. Consider, for example, the way he fashions the following passage, offered when discussing visitors to Chapman's home on the Strand: "Dr. Brabant was there, too, obviously impressed with the de-velopment of his Deutera [his pet name for Marian, his second daughter], whom he took to the theatre. He kindly lent his telescope to Chapman, who, rising at 5:30, looked again at the crescent Venus, which he had seen

---

*It is interesting to note that Barbara Bodichon contemplated entering into "a per-manent extra-marital relationship with John Chapman" but married another man in-stead (Lacey, *Bodichon*, 21).

†A blessing was mixed with this emotionally complicated camouflage, since such a designation, which Marian hardly resented, enabled her to work.

for the first time on the day Marian arrived in the Strand" (83). Irigaray would not fail to note the specular sexualization of Marian in the men's exchange, as Haight has arranged it, of their viewing instrument—as if she had become a crescent to be spied on. Haight apparently intends to link the object of one of Marian's "indiscretions" (Dr. Brabant) to an object of an even greater indiscretion (Chapman, of course). He does not point out Marian's tendency, as I render it here, to get entangled with married men, at least in part, through her desire to work. This desire is clearly evident when she offers to write a review for Chapman of W. A. Greg's *The Creed of Christendom*, as she puts it, "not for money, but for love—of the subject as connected with the *Inquiry*." Work for love, not money, over the body of a theological text: who but a saint would make such an offer?

In Haight's reconstruction of her greater indiscretion, Marian is not a saint but a principal in "Chapman's relations with the three ladies." Again, Irigaray comes to mind in her insistence that, in a masculine sexual economy, women relate to one another as rivals. How fitting, from an Irigarayan point of view, that three women should be implicated in this little plot: a virgin (pure exchange value), a mother (private property, excluded from exchange), and a mistress (usage that is exchanged): "*These are the social roles imposed on women*," Irigaray writes, "[and] *neither as mother nor as virgin nor as prostitute has woman any right to her own pleasure*" (*TS*, 186–87). Most extraordinary, Haight reconstructs the situation by quoting from the diary—his only source. His slant is in evidence when he remarks with condescension that, since two entries are missing from Chapman's diary, "we can only guess at how he soothed the ruffled feelings" (84). It is further evident when he cites, without comment, Chapman's claim, "I am sure I have no [other] feeling on the subject than to obtain peace at any cost" (85).

I am not surprised at Haight's conclusions:

> There can be little doubt that Marian was guilty of some indiscretion, probably more serious than holding hands. Her over-ready expansiveness, her incapability of practising the required conventionalisms, her unfortunately balanced moral and animal regions—all come again to mind. John Chapman was a notorious philanderer. In youth his friends called him "Byron," surely not just for his noble profile or his literary bent. To his pervasive masculine attraction, which few women could resist, Marian's yearning for affection, the stronger for lying behind a plain exterior, made her doubly susceptible. When her father died she had had her vision of becoming earthly, sensual, devilish. Did John Chapman help her realize it? (86)

Here recur the familiar saws about "George Eliot" that Haight repeats throughout his narrative. Indeed, the passage serves as a particularly interesting pastiche of Haight's own chosen terms of analysis ("indiscretion," "over-ready expansiveness," "yearning for affection," and "plain exterior" are phrases of his making); Chapman's observation ("her incapability of practising the required conventionalisms" is a phrase from Chapman's account of the Dr. Brabant affair); and Marian's self-critiques (it is she who penned the phrase "my moral and animal regions are unfortunately balanced," in a letter written while she was staying with Dr. Brabant, a period that caused her to question her sensuality quite severely). Though Haight points out that Marian let Chapman pose as editor of the *Westminster Review*, while it was she who did the work, and though he acknowledges that she was never paid for her voluminous work as editor, still he insists on reading Marian's desire to work as her desire for Chapman. He reworks her statement, quoted earlier, that she would work "not for money, but for love—of the subject as connected with the *Inquiry*," into a play on her words: "She worked, not for money, but for love—of the nominal chief editor" (91). On a holier note, Haight brings to a close the Chapman episode. Again relying on Chapman's diary, he quotes Chapman's stated resolution: "We [Marian and Chapman] made a solemn and holy vow which henceforth will bind us to the right" (91). Perhaps even Haight smells an irony, for he ends his chapter with the solemn and holy pronouncement that "[Marian] would renounce the gratification of her own desires. . . . She returned to the Strand, a loyal 'helpmate' in editing the *Westminster Review*, but nothing more" (95). Despite her best efforts, it would seem, an Eve (a "helpmate") once again.

Haight, at last, turns to consider Marian with George Henry Lewes, presented in the chapters "The Need to Be Loved," "Some One to Lean Upon," and "Strong-Minded Woman" (Carlyle's epithet for Marian). Once again, though he comments that "the clearest evidence of her involvement with Lewes can be found in the way she helped him with his work" (135), and though he notes that she wrote some of the articles attributed to Lewes, Haight emphasizes that Marian, with her thirty-third birthday upon her, "needed desperately some one friend to be all in all to her" (125). Thus "one can easily imagine," says Haight, "how Marian's ready expansiveness would respond with sympathy and affection" to Lewes, embroiled as he was in his marital sorrow (134). What Marian found in Lewes, however, as much as anything else, was a man who enabled her career as a writer.* Lewes advanced her opportunities to work

---

*It is understandable in other ways why Eliot took Lewes as her companion: his domestic situation—in which he helped "for free" his wife's children by another man— put him in a position of feminized exchange.

as much, if not more, as he did his own, and eventually lobbied for "George Eliot" with publishers. We cannot discount the role Lewes played in encouraging Marian's material advancement: she earned 9,000 pounds for *Middlemarch*, compared with 20 pounds for her Strauss translation.

We may read, finally, a happy conjunction of Marian's sexuality, spirituality, and work in Haight's casual comment, "She was working hard at Feuerbach and pondering her future course with George Lewes" (141). It was in the writings of Ludwig Feuerbach, specifically in *The Essence of Christianity* (which Marian was translating for publication), that she found religious views to embrace. Feuerbach conceived his work as "a frankly sensuous philosophy."[6] He strove to unite spiritual existence with bodily existence. A happy coincidence: Marian eloped with Lewes to Germany one week after her Feuerbach translation was published in England. Of course, the decision whether or not to elope with a married man (a famous man, at that) was not to be taken lightly. Marian knew that to open herself to sexual desire was to risk great pain; but to share lodgings with the married Lewes was to bring certain scandal, for though Lewes and his wife were estranged, they could not obtain a legal divorce.* Significantly, Marian read her elopement through Brontë's *Villette*; to a friend, she wrote: "I am preparing to go to 'Labassecour' [Brontë's name for Belgium]" (147). Fully aware of the price she would pay—which she conveyed in biblical guise, "I have counted the cost"—Marian set off with Lewes for Germany.

Most interesting in the making of the figure "George Eliot": the author became both "Eve" and "Madonna" in relation to Lewes, and both at the same time—not to mention her role as Lewes's "clergyman" friend, while her authorship of "Amos Barton" and *Adam Bede* was still unknown. The immediate result of Marian's elopement was her status as a "fallen woman" (a "strong-minded woman," as Carlyle put it). This externally enforced identity marked Eliot even during her fame. Indeed, after many intense debates about the author of *Adam Bede*, in whom most readers discerned a clergyman, came the revelation: the clergyman author was a fallen woman. Marian's pleasure could now arise from paid work *as* a man of the cloth. But even as Eliot's critical acclaim, popularity, and income increased with each succeeding novel, so that now she was even paid as a man, her fallen status continued to make "respectable" women hesitant to visit. Lewes, of course, much as he was disliked by some, was busy dining out on the invitations that came with her renown.

*Lewes couldn't get a divorce, according to Haight, because "having once condoned [his wife's] adultery, [he] was forever precluded from appealing for divorce" (132).

Given this curious state of affairs, we may be struck by Eliot's return to "sainthood." Lewes and Eliot playfully regarded themselves as priests. Both men and women wrote to Eliot about religious experiences and marital troubles, the women especially apt to adopt her, Haight informs us, as their "spiritual mother." Significantly, however, the real turning point in Eliot's strange career as "a saint" came with the publication of *Middlemarch*. Along with accolades there emerged a new acceptance: "She was now often invited to dinner" (452). More significant still, Eliot's work, her accomplishments as a fallen woman writer (who as yet bore a masculine name), were best expressed in spiritual metaphors. Haight, for the last time:

> John Blackwood gave a letter of introduction to a Mrs. Chetwynd, who, he said, "is anxious to throw herself at your feet." Though he spoke jocosely, this devotional attitude was growing prevalent among the serious young worshippers of George Eliot's genius. Since the days of their Italian travels Lewes had sometimes called her "Madonna," and their friends were amused that two such staunch unbelievers should live in a house called the Priory. Dickens, for example, would write: "On Sunday I hope to attend service at the Priory." (453–54)

"George Eliot," it would seem, had written "his" plot while still Mary Anne, an Evangelical girl who copied into her notebook poems from *The Sabbath Harp*: "A Saint! Oh would that I could claim / The privileg'd, the honor'd name / And confidently take my stand / Though lowest in the saintly band!" (20).

Lowest and highest, feminine and masculine, animal and moral, Eve and Madonna, "George Eliot," we recognize, was fashioned at the poles.

Cooking Feuerbach

Dear Sara,

I have yet another service to beg of you—a very great one. It is to read as quickly as you can the portion of the appendix which I send you by today's post, and to tell me how far it will be necessary to modify it for the Eng[lish] public. I have written it very rapidly and have translated it quite literally so you have the *raw* Feuerbach—not any of my cooking. I am so far removed from the popular feeling on the subject of which it treats that I cannot trust my own judgment. With the ideas of Feuerbach I everywhere agree, but of course I should, of myself, alter the phraseology considerably. Before I do this however, I want you to tell me what I *must* leave out. Mind, I want to keep in as much as possible. Send it me back as soon as possible, and don't think of the *style* but only of the matter and the crudity of expressions. In great haste,

Your ever grateful,
Pollian*

We may recognize Eliot's spiritual discourse by recognizing how much it was constructed by writings that she herself constructed, or, as she puts it in her choice domestic metaphor, "cooked," for England. One senses from this metaphor, as well as from her letter, that Marian knew the extent to which, in translating Feuerbach, she was domesticating him for her English homeland. Clearly, she was making his discourse her own. In fact, this translation is her only text signed as "Marian Evans" (though current editions, to heighten recognition, read "George Eliot").

Examining Feuerbach at the hands of Marian, we encounter a number of dilemmas that center on spiritual materialism: chief among them, the difficulty, for Feuerbach, of keeping "materialism" separate from "idealism" (specifically, from spiritual conceptions) even when attempting to fashion a materialist philosophy. Marian, for her own part, in her intellectual pursuits following Evangelicalism, was drawn to spiritual conceptions that welcomed sensuality (if not quite materialism, at the start). Given this interest, one may note the obvious attraction of pantheism; in particular, Wordsworth's poetry and the writings of Carlyle. Yet, by Bernard Paris's account, Marian gradually grew away from pantheism and felt increasingly drawn to the more positivistic philosophies of Comte, Mill, Spencer, Feuerbach, and her future companion, George Henry Lewes.[7] This attraction to positivism may reflect her need to face, realistically, the pain and divisions of her life as a woman, without explaining them away through supernaturalism. As she wrote to a friend: "I have faith in the working-out of higher possibilities than the Catholic or any other church has presented. . . . The highest 'calling and election' is to *do without opium* and live through all our pain with conscious, clear-eyed endurance."[8]

As much as she moved toward objectivism and observation, Marian keenly realized that something resists scientific closure. In a letter, she confessed: "I feel every day a greater disinclination for theories and arguments about the origin of things in the presence of all this mystery and beauty and pain and ugliness, that floods one with conflicting emotions."[9] A. S.

*Eliot, *George Eliot Letters* 2: 153. "Pollian" is a name Marian used for herself among some of her friends. There is a play here on the name "Apollyon" (the angel of the bottomless pit in Revelation 9:2), made prominent by Bunyan's *Pilgrim's Progress* in which Apollyon is Christian's antagonist.

Byatt has suggested that Marian's views directly referred to a claim her friend Herbert Spencer had made: "The sincere man of science . . . truly sees that absolute knowledge is impossible. He alone knows that under all things there lies an impenetrable mystery."[10] It is precisely this impasse, this stopgap to closure, that continued to frame Marian's quest. Marian, like Irigaray, even sounds utopian when she hopes for "a breadth of ideal association which [would] inform every material object . . . with far-reaching memories and stored residues of passion, bringing into new light the less obvious relations of human existence."[11] We catch Marian here wishing to idealize materialities in order to make visible new or concealed relations.

There lies, importantly, a middle step in this production: the "frankly sensuous philosophy" she translated in Feuerbach's *The Essence of Christianity*, a spiritual discourse that helped her to shape her versions of desire, sensuality, sympathy, and mirroring in *Middlemarch*. Recall, first, that Feuerbach poses as an antitheologian, proclaiming boldly, "I . . . while reducing theology to anthropology, exalt anthropology into theology" (*EC*, xxxviii). He posits, in his famous dictum, that "Man and man—the unity of I and Thou—is God" (*EC*, xvi), or, in the words of another phrase, "God is the highest subjectivity of man abstracted from himself" (*EC*, 31). But even in these claims we see the validity of the theologian Karl Barth's remark: "[This] is an antithesis only to be established theologically," since Feuerbach's radical humanism radically depends upon, feeds upon, traditional "god-talk." And "who knows," Barth writes, "whether it should not be said that in inward reality he belonged, as legitimately as anyone, to the profession of modern Protestant theology?"[12]

Similar contradictions arise when we try to classify Feuerbach—too humanist for theologians, too utopian for Marxists—as idealist or materialist. Feuerbach clearly presents himself as both realist and materialist, being, he says, "in direct opposition to the Hegelian philosophy" and supporting the "Idea" only insofar as it is understood as "faith in the historical future" (*EC*, xxxiv). Even though he vehemently claims, "I hate that Idealism which tears man out of nature," Feuerbach's very idea of man, in which "man's essence" is "the most real being," itself appears abstract and ideal. Althusser implies as much when he criticizes Feuerbach as "an astonishing 'theoretician' of the mirror connexion, who unfortunately ends up in the ideology of the Human Essence."[13]

In a richly suggestive study—*Darwin's Plots: Evolutionary Narratives in Darwin, George Eliot and Nineteenth-Century Fiction*—Gillian Beer argues that a scientific discourse, informed by Eliot's in-depth knowledge of scientific controversies, shapes the themes and vocabulary of *Middlemarch*. Pointing to the novel's focus on species, even where it shades towards the transcendental, and to its concern with "infinite implications or infinite extension," Beer discovers Darwin's influence, as well as that of other scientists. I wish to suggest another source, equally important, for Eliot's pervasive discourse on species. This source agrees with Beer's observation that "the numinous must express itself in this book solely through the human"; and yet, on its way to confirm such a point, *The Essence of Christianity* makes "species" a sacred term.[14] Religion is consciousness of the species. And *God*, we learn, *is the species conceived of as an individual*, or "the unity of I and Thou."

If Eliot, then, as Beer suggests, was seeking communal insights and a way beyond single consciousness, Feuerbach's antitheological theology provided her with a discourse on community. Sympathy, for example, is much discussed in Feuerbach's text. It is a prime expression of a suffering held in common between I and Thou. The essence of the Christian Passion, therefore, is a love that proves itself by suffering, since "to suffer for others is divine" (*EC*, 60). Inasmuch as human feeling *is* God, sympathy touches upon the sensuousness that for Feuerbach "unites" spiritual and material, inner and outer. His gloss on Love as God makes this point:

> Love is *the middle term, the substantial bond*, the principle of reconciliation between the perfect and the imperfect, the sinless and sinful being, the universal and the individual, the divine and the human. Love is God himself, and apart from it there is no God. Love makes man God and God man. *Love . . . idealizes matter and materializes spirit.* . . . What the old mystics said of God, that he is the highest and yet the commonest being, applies in truth to love, and that not a visionary, imaginary love—no! a real love, a love which has flesh and blood, which vibrates as an almighty force through all living. (*EC*, 48; my emphasis)

This passage illustrates why reading Feuerbach is an exercise in spiritual materialism, such as we have seen in thinkers as diverse as Carlyle and Irigaray. Each of his concepts appears, initially, structured as a dyad, implicating opposites in one another to the point of a seemingly fused identity: "man God . . . God man." Yet there often emerges a third term that acts as a suture: "Love is the middle term, the substantial bond, the principle of reconciliation between . . . the divine and the human." Now a more complicated weave appears, for this third term has already been identified with one of the two terms that it supposedly bonds: "Love is God himself." Love is thus between God and man, and love is God is man. The third term, in this way, splits from itself in its roles as mediating and identical term.

This split asserts itself, again, in his discussion of desire. On the one hand, Feuerbach conceptualizes God as "the realized desire of the heart, lifted up to the certainty of its fulfillment and validity" (*EC*, xvii)—God as pleasure, one might say. On the other hand, Feuerbach also states (in the very same sentence) that God "is the sublime desire," so that God is not just *realized* desire or pleasure but God is what Feuerbach elsewhere states as "the yearning of man after himself, after his own nature" (*EC*, 45). Claiming that this is "the profoundest, truest expression of Christian mysticism," Feuerbach offers an aphorism from the mystic Sebastian Franck: "God is an unutterable sigh, lying in the depths of the heart" (*EC*, xvii). This conception accords well, of course, with Irigaray's focus on God as lack, as an elegant absence.

Though Feuerbach presents his views on God as unproblematic for human self-consciousness, we may note the contradiction that he veils: God is both what desire yearns toward, the autoerotic pleasure of "man [who yearns] after himself," and the gap, the lack, *the space of the yearning* between man and himself, and between man and man. Far from "the whole man" that Feuerbach's humanism claims to present, man is split from himself by desire, and 'God', as Irigaray presents 'Him' also, is (at) the gap. Indeed, Irigaray, too, in Feuerbachian fashion, makes 'God' both a destination (the divine lover the mystic yearns toward) and the desire that propels one toward that other just out of reach ('God' as the space of desire/pleasure between the mystic and 'Himself').*

This splitting is boldly manifested in the mirroring that takes place between God and man. God is not the simple unity of man and man but the self-division of subjectivity and the splintering implications between one and two. If, then, as Feuerbach proposes, "in the religious systole man propels his own nature from himself, he throws himself outward, [and] in the religious diastole he receives the rejected nature into his heart again," God is the difference between this projection and its return. Contrary to Feuerbach's seemingly complete identification between God and man, God *is that which escapes* between men, and between a man and his own self-consciousness. One could say that, for Feuerbach, God is Derrida's hymen or the space between Irigaray's lips: that which "*both* sows confusion *between* opposites *and* stands *between* the opposites 'at once.'"

At a crucial juncture, Feuerbach himself directly discusses the complications that trouble a presumed opposition or adherence between two

*For Irigaray's discussion of Feuerbach on different but related issues, see her essay "Divine Women" in *Sexes and Genealogies*, 57–72.

terms. Following his analysis of God's Son as the image of God, he turns to the related issue of "the self-distinguishing of God from himself" at the creation of the world:

> The world is not God; it is other than God, the opposite of God, or at least that which is different from God. But that which is different from God cannot have come immediately from God, but only from a distinction of God in God. The second Person is God distinguishing himself from himself in himself, setting himself opposite to himself, hence being an object to himself. . . . The idea of the production of the world, of another being who is *not* God, is attained through the idea of the production of another being who is *like* God. (*EC*, 81)

Even in this moment of supposed identity—"the idea of the production of another being who is *like* God"—the unavoidable suggestions of a difference appear, "God distinguishing himself from himself in himself." This is a common pattern in Feuerbach: a supposed identity, or adhesion between two, fractures into yearning, desire, even pleasure, between one and two. God thus becomes *not Feuerbach's intended unity*, but the range of infinite implications between God and man, and between man and man.

It is precisely this range of implications that Feuerbach is always in danger of ignoring, in favor of unities or precise opposition, in spite of his own obvious understanding of something like a fractured sameness. His tendency to suppress these rifts in his meditations on unity produces significant results for his thoughts on community and gender. For in spite of Karl Barth's claim that Feuerbach's theories bore an "unconscious but evident affinity to the ideology of the socialist workers' movement . . . where it is a matter of breaking down the abstraction of private property" (*EC*, xxv–xxvi), Feuerbach's communal emphasis spells the uncomplicated union of the self-assured I-Thou relation, where "self-consciousness" and "personality" function as forms of private property. Nowhere is this private ownership addressed more clearly than in Feuerbach's discussion of the body, which quickly shades into the "essential" distinctions between man and woman:

> Take away from thy personality its body, and thou takest away that which holds it together. The body is the basis, the subject of personality. . . . *Only by the exclusion of others* from the space it occupies does personality prove itself to be real. But a body does not exist without flesh and blood. Flesh and blood is life, and life alone is corporeal reality. But flesh and blood is nothing without the oxygen of sexual distinction. The distinction of sex is not superficial, or limited to certain parts of the body; it is an essential one: it penetrates bones and marrow. The substance of man is manhood; that of woman, woman-

hood. . . . Hence personality is nothing without distinction of sex; personality is essentially distinguished into masculine and feminine. Where there is no *thou*, there is no *I*; but the distinction between *I* and *thou*, the fundamental condition of all personality, of all consciousness, is only real, living, ardent, when felt as the distinction between man and woman. . . . Man exists only as man and woman. The strength, the healthiness of man consists therefore in this: that as a woman, he be truly woman; as man, truly man. (*EC*, 91–92; partly my emphasis)

Here assured gender assignments uphold and support assured individuality ("only by the exclusion of others"). Body-image boundaries are clearly set off in "space." Yet for all of the supposed clarity Feuerbach offers, confusions subtly but indelibly surface as he crosses from "man," as masculine gender, to "man," as (supposedly generic) humanity. In the wonderfully suggestive slippage of this logic, the healthiness of (generic) man consists in "his" being "truly woman."

The construct "George Eliot," like the construct of Eliot's own *Middlemarch* narrator, offers an instance of trespass in writing "individual" identity. We have seen the way in which Haight's biography draws its boundaries as Haight fashions the manly author and the womanly woman. He does not see, in the story he tells, the tangled relations between a woman's work and her desire. Yet the potential of these relations to trespass against assured and fully accountable identities comes clear in the muddled readings of 'her' as clergyman, fallen woman, and saint. If Eliot's *Middlemarch* insists on the intimations, incriminations, and indirections of mirrors, we should not be surprised. In translating Feuerbach, she took to herself a discourse on species, sensuality, desire, and the image. In *Middlemarch*, however, Feuerbach's thoroughly masculine Imaginary, which posits unity between individuals, finds itself "cooked," yet again, into a domestic but less stable mix.

Chapter 7

At Home with Desire:
The Domestication of St. Theresa
in Eliot's *Middlemarch*

~

St. Theresa at the Hymen

For Lacan, St. Theresa, as figured by Bernini, evokes the *jouissance* that "goes beyond." For Irigaray, St. Theresa, or, more accurately, her writings, tell a tale of ecstatic escape. *Middlemarch*, too, begins with St. Theresa and proceeds to examine the divide between St. Theresa of Avila and the many unknown "later-born Theresas" who mirror her desire for "some illimitable satisfaction." The figure of St. Theresa even galvanizes women's vocational and sexual sorrows, while gesturing toward an incalculable pulse: the beat that, in the heat of sorrows, liquefies a woman's strict constraints.

Eliot's text calls us forth with a heartbeat:

> Who that cares much to know the history of man, and how the mysterious mixture behaves under the varying experiments of Time, has not dwelt, at least briefly, on the life of Saint Theresa, has not smiled with some gentleness at the thought of the little girl walking forth one morning hand-in-hand with her still smaller brother, to go and seek martyrdom in the country of the Moors? Out they toddled from rugged Avila . . . with human hearts, already beating to a national idea; until domestic reality met them in the shape of uncles, and turned them back from their great resolve. (25)

From the start, we are seduced by a female saint into something to know about "the history of man" (does the "healthiness of [generic] man" depend on his being "truly woman"?). In particular, we are led to dwell upon limits set to spiritual searches—something that, in turn, can aptly illustrate what Eliot is most anxious to convey, after all: the limitations set upon women's vocations. For St. Theresa's obstacle even then, at least as the narrator renders it, was "domestic reality." And just as "spiritual grandeur" still holds sway for modern-day Theresas, this religious "ardour" still hits the wall of "domestic reality," now in the shape of bourgeois marriage. In fact, support for a woman's vocation as an unmarried saint cannot be easily found in England—unless in "sisterhoods"; thus Anna Jameson is convinced that a Protestant Sisters of Charity could improve the lot of English women, offering them meanings other than marriage.

The particular fix of the *Middlemarch* bourgeoise shows at the hymen, where she is caught between virginity and marriage. Oddly, marriage *preserves* virginity, as we shall see, and yet virginity, for saints who can remain undomesticated, enables public work, and even pleasure.* The narrator details the matted path to these pleasurable occupations in terms that evoke the image of a tangle:

> With dim lights and tangled circumstance they tried to shape their thought and deed in noble agreement; but after all, to common eyes their struggles seemed mere inconsistency and formlessness; for these later-born Theresas were helped by no coherent social faith and order which could perform the function of knowledge for the ardently willing soul. Their ardour alternated between a vague ideal and the common yearning of womanhood: so that the one was disapproved as extravagance, and the other condemned as a lapse. (25)

Women are caught in a web by their struggles that remain opaque to "common eyes." In their "inconsistency" and "formlessness" they are left to oscillate between the poles of spirituality—"a vague ideal . . . disapproved as extravagance"—and some form of less lofty longings that may include commercialism and surely include some form of sexuality—"the common yearning of womanhood . . . condemned as a lapse." As *Middlemarch* reveals, however, spirituality, contrary to its familiar associations with Victorian mores, cannot so blithely be counted a partner in the Victorian penchant for renunciations. In *Middlemarch*, in fact, for the community at large, spirituality and sexuality constitute twin dangerous extremes between which Victorian Theresas might vibrate. And yet, for all her promised dangers, the modern Theresa, as the narrator testifies, is "a foundress of nothing"—her potentially significant power (in the eyes of Eliot) frustrated by unpropitious circumstance. For what hope for mate-

---

*Vicinus reminds us: "Unmarried women often portrayed themselves either as asexual saints, a role the religious found particularly attractive, or as strong women whose sexuality was sublimated into a wider sphere of action" (*Independent Women*, 17). In Dorothea Brooke, I will argue, we have the figure of a *sexual* saint.

rial change can result from dispersing saintly ardor among the hindrances of domestic reality?*

From this bleak beginning, the text proceeds to its own St. Theresa: Dorothea Brooke is framed by the narrator as a present-day conundrum. Dorothea, we are told, possessed "the impressiveness of a fine quotation

Middlemarch, like *Villette*, was charged with a pervading sense of melancholy. (A review in *The Spectator* titled its address, "The Melancholy of *Middlemarch*.") As with *Villette*, this seemingly hopeless melancholy troubled Victorian readers who deemed *Middlemarch* a religious novel. Wrote one reviewer: "The most remarkable thread of spiritual melancholy in the book constitutes the real end for which it is written—the picture of Dorothea's beautiful and noble, but utterly unsatisfied and unresting character, and the illustration of the wreck of happiness which results from her unguided spiritual cravings" (*The Spectator*, June 1, 1872). Wrote another: "If *Middlemarch* is melancholy, it is due perhaps to its religion being all duty, without a sufficient admixture of hope" (*Saturday Review*, Dec. 7, 1872). Still another remarked that the novel's "remarkable tinge of melancholy" is tied to the fact that "we are allowed to gather that for the most part ideals are unattainable, and the highest aspirations only serve to give a grandeur to the failure in which they inevitably end" (*Blackwood's Magazine*, Dec. 1872). Characteristically, none of these reviewers connects the melancholy they notice with women's sexual and economic complaints. In fact, the *Times* reviewer (Mar. 7, 1873) undercuts any possible feminist reading: "There is a certain school which will find satisfaction in thinking that Dorothea's story involves some impeachment of the fitness of the present female lot. We do not think this is at all intended, and if it be intended it is certainly not justified. . . . [Dorothea's] failures and mistakes are not due to the fact of her being a woman, but are simply those which belong to the common lot of human life. . . . Unsatisfied ambitions are masculine rather than female ills."

The narrative's fashionings of spirituality, sexuality, and work have continued to receive separate inquiry as unrelated issues. Gillian Beer has advanced the level of discussion on *Middlemarch* by considering issues of work and class, particularly exploring "how fully this work was in touch with the issues being debated in the women's movement of the 1850s and 1860s, and how thoroughly it entered the debates" (*George Eliot*, 148). Dorothea Barrett's study on Eliot's heroines, *Vocation and Desire: George Eliot's Heroines*, would seem from its title also to promise some relation to my examinations—especially given Barrett's desire to counter George Eliot's "reputation as reactionary" with her own view that Eliot's fiction was "dangerously erotic and iconoclastic" (1–2). Barrett's study, however, treats its title terms in extremely broad ways that are quite divergent from my interests in desire between women as a form of labor. As Barrett informs her reader: "The two terms of my title, vocation and desire, are intended to embrace, between them, all human need"; "they are therefore meant in their widest possible senses, and they form a dichotomy that is implicit in all George Eliot's work" (17).

Aside from Mary Wilson Carpenter's fine study on apocalyptic history in Eliot (*George Eliot and the Landscape of Time*), three critics have given sustained attention to Eliot's religious constructions, but none has given a reading that links the questions of women and religion, or religion and sexuality. See, for example, U. C. Knoepflmacher, *Religious Humanism and the Victorian Novel: George Eliot, Walter Pater, and Samuel Butler*; Thomas Vargish, *The Providential Aesthetic in Victorian Fiction*; and Alan Mintz, *George Eliot and the Novel of Vocation*. See also T. R. Wright, "*Middlemarch* as a Religious Novel,

from the Bible," as if she were, in her person, an exemplary instance of
spiritual discourse. By word and image, Dorothea is set apart, and the narrator continues as if anxious to stake her at the spiritual pole. For this reason, her sister Celia is introduced and, around this arrangement of paired
women, the outlines of a narrative gaze take their shape. On the one hand,
the narrator downplays their differences in order to construct them as together set apart from more "common" women by ancestry and taste.
Their connections, we are told, "were unquestionably 'good' " and they
"naturally regarded frippery as the ambition of a huckster's daughter."
This delineation of class position forms a major feature of the narrator's
gaze, although there is a certain attempt to displace class onto a question
of taste, as will become increasingly evident. Here, in fact, in these initial
distinctions established between the Brookes and common women lies the
preparatory move to make Rosamond's self-commodification (her taste
for "frippery") a sign of her character, when it is more likely a sign of her
class (as a manufacturer's daughter). On the other hand, if the narrator associates the sisters in common taste, the narrator clearly cuts between
them by the "shade of coquetry" in Celia's dress (which places her more
towards the sexual pole) and by Dorothea's religious, theoretic mind
(which splits Dorothea from sensuality).

Along this edge, the initial problem of Dorothea is posed. If we might
assume that Dorothea's religious devotion, combined with her resemblance to Madonnas, would fashion her as a domestic saint, we begin to
realize that *Middlemarch* is fraught with contradictions. For a single woman's religious devotion, when vigorously pursued, too easily becomes a
masculine call, so that she loses femininity and her interest in marriage.
This religious vocation further inculcates the kind of ardor (or extravagance) that, even in marriage, spills over carefully marked borders, so that
life's once neatly segregated domains become dangerously enmeshed. The
narrator is sharply aware of these dangers. When describing Dorothea's
"strange whims of fasting like a Papist, and of sitting up at night to read
old theological books," the narrator suddenly shifts to a warning, only
partly comical: "Such a wife might awaken you some fine morning with
a new scheme for the application of her income which would interfere

---

or Life without God"; and Katherine M. Sorensen, "Evangelical Doctrine and George
Eliot's Narrator in *Middlemarch*." That we are not yet done with Eliot as moral master
and her novels as moral casebooks is evident from Bert G. Hornback's recent study,
Middlemarch: A Novel of Reform. As we have already seen with Cottom, critics' concern
with Eliot's humanistic posture has returned in a different guise: the novelist as bourgeois intellectual who dispenses humanist ideology.

with political economy and the keeping of saddle-horses" (31).* More dangerous than Butler's passion for a project—by means of which Butler had envisioned incorporating "harmless" lunatics into families—Dorothea's religious ardor might seek to implicate neighbors in a web not susceptible of maintaining social distinctions, for "the great safeguard of society and of domestic life was that opinions were not acted on. Sane people did what their neighbours did, so that if any lunatics were at large, one might know and avoid them" (31).

From the beginning, Dorothea threatens conventional economies with her passionate vocation as an unmarried saint. (Celia thinks her "too religious for family comfort.") When Dorothea, however, is read by men as sexually alluring, she, like Celia, is perfectly assimilable into society; we are told that "most men thought her bewitching when she was on horseback" (32). For her own part, Dorothea manifests an intriguing attraction to the sensational pleasure that men might read as allure: "Riding was an indulgence which she allowed herself in spite of conscientious qualms; she felt that she enjoyed it in a pagan sensuous way, and always looked forward to renouncing it" (32). To be sure, Dorothea challenges religious injunctions when she "merges" sensuality with "her mystic religious joy" (36). Here is a clue that she doesn't affirm the Protestant ethic that Weber views as a friend to capitalism, for this is an ethic, Weber says, that suppresses mystical and emotional yearnings (*PE*, 241). Neither does her passion for building cottages—an aid to poor people—complement Calvin's concern with an afterlife. The mystical elsewhere that captures her attention has pointed sensual and economic slants.

The scene with Dorothea, Celia, and their mother's jewels imbues these contradictions with a subtle heat. This is the text's first feminine mirroring, the first of many mirrorings later tinged with the class implications that Irigaray cannot see. As we have been led by the narrator to expect, Dorothea and Celia at first react oppositely to the jewels that figure feminine sexuality. Dorothea, initially consistent with her views, subtly disdains her dead mother's gems, which, significantly, until this time, have remained locked in a cabinet. Celia, by contrast, inspires the inspec-

---

*Vicinus unwittingly supplies an insight into Eliot's characterizations when she informs us: "The 1850's and 1860's saw a spate of advice books for [spinsters], all recommending religion and restraint. The married author of *The Afternoon of Unmarried Life* (1858) . . . recommended gardening as an innocuous antidote to 'that state of unbalanced religious excitement' to which many older spinsters were prone" (*Independent Women*, 13). Elsewhere she states: "[One's] married state ensured that [one] was not a dangerous enthusiast" (68).

tion and argues with Dorothea that "surely there are women in heaven now who wore jewels" (34).

This encounter, for all of its possibility of underscoring distinctions, takes place around a mirror; we are told that Celia, when Dorothea fastened a necklace round her neck, could see herself "in the pier-glass opposite." In fact, both women, by the descriptions we are given, would appear in this mirror. Their resemblance gains radiance when Dorothea, through this opening onto gems, is pierced by sudden gleams:

> [Celia] was opening some ring-boxes, which disclosed a fine emerald with diamonds, and just then the sun passing beyond a cloud sent a bright gleam over the table.
>
> "How very beautiful these gems are!" said Dorothea, under a new current of feeling, as sudden as the gleam. "It is strange how deeply colours seem to penetrate one, like scent. I suppose that is the reason why gems are used as spiritual emblems in the Revelation of St. John. They look like fragments of heaven." (35)

Dorothea, "under a new current of feeling," is held by her sudden sensual confusion. She refers herself, as did Lucy Snowe, to heaven's sensuality, as rendered with force in the Book of Revelation (the colored gems that "penetrate" her, Dorothea likens to "fragments of heaven"). Her attempts to justify her pleasure, however, along with Celia's belief that "her sister was going to renounce the ornaments, as in consistency she ought to do" (36), indicates a Protestant hesitation that, finally, Dorothea will crush: the belief that sensuality is incompatible with religious commitment.* Even here, at this early juncture—since it happens before either character marries—this scene could depict the self-sexual pleasure of women together that *Middlemarch* hints takes place after marriage in only hidden ways. As proof of the woman-to-woman nature of this seemingly private penetration by gems, the novel implies that Dorothea and Celia are conducting themselves to their mother's sexuality. Dorothea's inspection of "the casket" containing her dead mother's jewels figures, moreover, a remaining contact (even a surprisingly material contact) with her mother's body, rendered almost as an image of nursing at the mother's breast (or even her own?): "[Dorothea] thought of often having them by her, to feed her eye at these little fountains of pure colour" (36).

The scene ends with Celia's returning to her tapestry and Dorothea's recommencing plans for building cottages. In this division of labor, we

---

*One could also read Dorothea's confused feelings as the commingling influences of Evangelicalism and the Oxford Movement in Victorian culture.

discover yet another reading of Dorothea's ambivalence towards her mother's jewels. In relation to her religious vocation, Dorothea has not been constructed as feminine. She pursues her plans more like a man, so that in response to Sir James's obvious flirtations we are told that she spoke "very much with the air of a handsome boy" (44). To be linked unambiguously to the gems, however, would unambiguously feminize Dorothea, and it is one of the crucial aspects of *Middlemarch* that before her marriage Dorothea is not fully scripted as feminine. For this reason, she is portrayed as believing that she, a woman, can intervene in the political economy.

Dorothea mistakenly believes she can participate in professional and even political endeavors by making her religious vocation her marriage and her marriage her education. In an earlier novel, *Adam Bede*, the female Methodist preacher Dinah Morris refuses marriage to give herself to God. In *Middlemarch*, Dorothea marries Casaubon to do the same, for marriage is precisely how a good bourgeoise is supposed to find God. By the contradictory logic of Victorian domesticity, Dorothea's *marriage* is her *religious act of sexual renunciation* (hymen remains in hymen), for she believes that "a really delightful marriage must be that where your husband was a sort of father." By seeking marriage to this fatherly scholar, Dorothea, "not satisfied by a girlish instruction," seeks entry into the realms of culture—what Lacan has theorized as the subject's substitutions for lost contact with the mother's body (in *Middlemarch*, the mother's gems). She seeks an academic expansion that will eradicate lack (or so she imagines); she seeks "a guide who would take her along the grandest path. . . . It would be like marrying Pascal." Appropriately, Dorothea finds herself wooed by pamphlets on the early church instead of by bouquets.

In her enthusiasm for a religious vocation, as a wife who will receive an in-depth education, Dorothea matches Anna Jameson's proposals for *married* Sisters of Charity. Dorothea even *trades herself* on the market, going against the advice of her bachelor uncle, whose own sexuality remains conspicuously ambivalent. She markets herself in masculine fashion, pursuing Casaubon as he pursues her. She ends up, however, unavoidably feminized, and the text increasingly binds Dorothea into a passive role with her suitor. The narrator, in a passage that changes her construction from "boy" to "mistress," gauges Dorothea's disappointing transition: "Mr. Casaubon consented to listen and teach for an hour together [with Dorothea], like a schoolmaster of little boys, or rather like a lover, to whom a mistress's elementary ignorance and difficulties have a touching fitness" (88–89).

Anna Jameson had urged that married women, too, might join the ranks of a Protestant Sisters of Charity, working alongside their unmarried counterparts in the charitable reform of prisons, schools, and hospitals. Anticipating this "communion of labor" with her educated husband, Dorothea foresees the time and opportunity, in her wifely leisure, to occupy herself with her plans to build cottages. These plans form the chief expression of her ardor, and she represents them in biblical terms, making reference to the famous biblical poor man, "Lazarus at the gate," and energetically proposing that "we deserve to be beaten out of our beautiful houses with a scourge of small cords" (54; see John 2). Casaubon, however, whom we may easily read as representing Church of England orthodoxy, shows no interest in Dorothea's religiously motivated plans. This lack of interest puzzles Dorothea; she hopes through her educational marriage that she will learn why great men "who knew the classics appeared to conciliate indifference to the cottages with zeal for the glory [of God]" (88). She is shown, then, as not yet understanding how church, marriage, and the education of women are bound up together in producing "followers" who maintain a system of gentry and cottagers. At this juncture of her betrothal, early on, Dorothea only feels disappointment that, as the narrator puts it, "no looms no Dissent" characterizes Lowick. This seemingly placid state of affairs, in her future husband's parish, threatens to short-circuit her religious vocation.

Between Images: Women's Work

We last see Dorothea, "under her maiden name," at a party. Now Dorothea is compared, by a group of men, not to her sister, but to Rosamond Vincy. Dorothea is about to be dismissed from the novel until she reappears in her honeymoon chapter, while Rosamond is being introduced. The text thus shifts from the soon-to-be-married Sister of Charity to two other types of women and their "domestic reality": Rosamond Vincy and Mary Garth.

By this arrangement, St. Theresa's domestication takes place alongside women's work relations, so that Dorothea's religious vocation cannot be seen in isolation. For as much as the text, on one level, suggests that Dorothea, Rosamond, and Mary inhabit discrete, unrelated social positions (Dorothea as a married Sister of Charity who seeks the social good, Rosamond as an "accomplished female" who appears as both commodity and consumer, Mary as an honest, working domestic who pursues modest aims), the novel's examination of women's work is, on another level, forged by means of mirrors, suggesting the difficulty of fixing, with precision, women's class positions.

The Dorothea/Rosamond pairing returns late in *Middlemarch* to form a flood of sorrows that binds sex to sobs. At this earlier moment, Lydgate projects his fantasies of Rosamond onto the screen of Dorothea's body, as if women wear each other on their skins. As with Dorothea, we hear about Rosamond through men's assessments before we "see" her—although what we hear itself constructs a gaze. The description of her body that we first receive—"blond, with a certain gait, and a swan neck" (115)—the next chapter supplements with Lydgate's assessments (for he, too, is introduced to the reader at the prenuptial party). This is the beginning of the textual fashioning of Tertius Lydgate. Though initially the quintessential bachelor, Lydgate, increasingly, is rendered as a Victorian family spokesperson, for he, more than any other fictional subject, gives voice to what women and men should be:

> Lydgate, in fact, was already conscious of being fascinated by a woman strikingly different from Miss Brooke: he did not in the least suppose that he had lost his balance and fallen in love but he had said of that particular woman, "[Rosamond] is grace itself; she is perfectly lovely and accomplished. That is what a woman ought to be: she ought to produce the effect of exquisite music.". . . To his taste, guided by a single conversation, here was the point on which Miss Brooke would be found wanting, notwithstanding her undeniable beauty. She did not look at things from the proper feminine angle. The society of such women was about as relaxing as going from your work to teach the second form, instead of reclining in a paradise with sweet laughs for bird-notes, and blue eyes for a heaven. (121–22)

Here is the attribution of masculinity to Dorothea's educational ambitions. Yet, once again, the bourgeois woman who seeks to join in masculine passions ends up feminized. Lydgate—note how the narrator seems seated within his mind—reflects that conversing with such a "woman" as Dorothea would be like "teach[ing] the second form" (Dorothea as a womanly boy, perhaps, but not a man). The passage, of course, makes another comparison. Before Rosamond appears center stage, we have her fashioned as "accomplished female," whose vocation is femininity, not religion. Rosamond exemplifies the feminine vocation that Dorothea, by society's dictates, should take upon herself as a married saint.

When the curtain is drawn up and we do first see her, Rosamond is working over her embroidery. If as a bourgeois woman of leisure, she is the novel's consummate consumer, she is also frequently shown at her tasks of embroidery, sewing, or chainwork. Yet even if we lean on Delphy's definition of domestic production, it is difficult to define Rosamond's "work" as productive labor for household consumption: she mainly fashions luxury items that she herself wears. Much of what Rosamond "produces," therefore, goes toward producing *herself* as a luxury, one that will gain fair price on the market. These narrative touches demonstrate how women are positioned to fortify their commodification, while strengthening ties between luxury and capitalism.* On the surface,

*For a version of cultural and economic history that makes women co-conspirators with men in the movement toward capitalism, see Werner Sombart, *Luxury and Capitalism*. Against Weber's stress on frugality and asceticism, Sombart makes luxury his focus and directly addresses women's role in its development. In so doing, he (unknowingly) hits upon a contradiction of major proportions: women not only appear the premier commodities in Euro-American societies, they also are positioned as the premier consumers. This desire for "conspicuous consumption," Sombart argues, dramatically influenced the growth of capitalism. Sombart's thesis rests on his account of how religious views were supplanted by a secularized conception of "love" that ties women to luxury. Bourgeois wives, Sombart theorizes, particularly from the beginning of the seventeenth century, gradually adopted the tastes and styles fostered by court mistresses, so that "after the 17th century, luxury became an affair of the home; women began to draw it within the confines of the domestic sphere" (95). When analyzing this sexual exchange, Sombart emphasizes the exorbitant expenditures undertaken by court dignitaries and men of commerce in keeping their women. What these men exacted from their mistresses is mystified under Sombart's term "free love," even though Sombart handily proves that "love" at the court was anything but free! To be sure, in his nightmare version of the female consumer, Sombart remains unable to theorize women's commodification at court and in the bourgeois home, where women are bought for their capacities to produce themselves as luxury items. Yet Sombart ends by paying odd tribute to the female consumer (at least she's good for business), a tribute that calls pointed attention to women's economic status as commodities: "As a fitting conclusion to this treatise, I wish to quote the dedication appearing in Godard d'Aucourt's *Memoires turcs* (dedicated to Madame Duthe, the great actress and courtesan), which sums up the situation admirably: 'Indeed, my dear ladies, *you are the true luxury*, indispensable to every nation; *you are the alluring bait* by means of which strangers and their guineas are attracted: twenty modest maidens are of less value to the royal treasury than a single one among you" (111–12; my emphasis).

More recently, though not in response to Sombart, Mary Ann Doane has addressed the "only apparently" double character of "Irigaray's theory of woman as commodity and the historical analysis of woman's positioning as a consumer" (*Desire to Desire*, 23). Discussing the rise of consumerism—a development that, according to Doane, begins with overproduction toward the end of the nineteenth century—Doane explains that, though commodities lure women into taking jobs to increase their earning and spending power, they also lure women back into luxurified domestic spaces. Consumerism, insofar as it is linked to self-image, also strengthens women's attention to their bodies as sets of parts to be improved (made feminine) by the purchase of commodities (cosmetics, clothing, accessories, etc.). The bottom line, for Doane, is a fix that bears "the aspect of a trap": "[Woman] is the subject of a transaction in which her own commodi-

of course, Rosamond's self-production as a luxury, which results in Lydgate's investment in her (since he has an eye for luxurious women), appears distinct from Dorothea's privileged escape from being exchanged by either a father or her uncle, Mr. Brooke. What both women elaborately share, nonetheless, is the extent to which their different class positions are precariously determined by their marriages (hence Dorothea's decline in class standing through her marriage to Will). For this reason, Dorothea's labor of desire as domestic saint, and its potential to produce pleasurable loss, can be seen only in light of a position that traps them both, not just Rosamond.

Rosamond reflects how Dorothea is caught on the hook of femininity in another way as well: she dramatizes a woman's intended place in the dominant Symbolic, especially with regard to education—an issue that figures so prominently in Dorothea's contemplation of marriage in the earlier chapters. In her introductory scene, in fact, Rosamond and Fred argue over language. Against her plea for "correct English . . . that is not slang," her brother counters that "all choice of words is slang . . . [that] marks a class." Fred's obvious point is that language use is class-bound—"correct English is the slang of prigs who write history and essays." Fred's set-to with Rosamond indicates his mastery of his own class slang, and, priggishly, Fred concludes their debate: "Aha, Miss Rosy, you don't know Homer from slang. I shall invent a new game; I shall write bits of slang and poetry on slips, and give them to you to separate" (126). Delineations belong to the bourgeois man's intellectual position, not to women's more prosaic accomplishments—and besides, women cannot properly separate, even from each other. This is a point—women's troubled separation from each other—that surfaces next, when the conversation after this quarrel turns to Fred's love interest, Mary Garth, from whom Rosamond tries to separate by appearing superior. Like Dorothea and Rosamond, however, Mary gets introduced before she takes the novel's stage, and Mary, too, is defined by her work: "'Mary Garth can bear being at Stone Court, because she likes that better than being a governess,' said Rosamond, folding up her work. 'I would rather not have anything left to me if I must earn it by enduring much of my uncle's cough and his ugly relations'" (129). The novel's next chapter expands upon Rosamond's contempt for Mary by standing these women together at the mirror: the idle woman (or luxury item, as I have suggested) appears in the mirror with the woman who must

---

fication is ultimately the object" (33, 30). Something of this trap, I would argue, is already beginning to surface in Eliot's portrayal of Rosamond's self-manufacture as a good marriageable prospect.

work outside the home. Mary Garth is first seen, then, in the context of her work for her dying uncle Featherstone—a man whose eventual sex-ualization of her labor may perhaps be signaled by the way he rubs "his stick between his knees." Mary is even introduced mid-sentence, as a do-mestic suspended in service to an impotent masculine body: "Mrs. Waule had to defer her answer till [Featherstone] was quiet again [from cough-ing], till Mary Garth had supplied him with fresh syrup, and he had begun to rub the gold knob of his stick, looking bitterly at the fire" (132)—a scene that is quite distant in tone from Lucy's care of the dying Miss Marchmont. When Rosamond arrives on the scene, the narrator amplifies this portrait of Mary as a worker in a relative's home. Though we are told of their "many memories [held] in common" since they were girls, this scene between women (in Mary's chamber) underscores their differences:

> They did not think of sitting down, but stood at the toilette-table near the window while Rosamond took off her hat, adjusted her veil, and applied lit-tle touches of her fingertips to her hair—hair of infantile fairness, neither flaxen nor yellow. Mary Garth seemed all the plainer standing at an angle be-tween the two nymphs—the one in the glass, and the one out of it, who looked at each other with eyes of heavenly blue. (139)

Fair, slim angel of feminine ease versus the plain, stouter working-woman of low-statured build: we are meant to read these women as di-vergent. Yet here Mary Garth stands "between the two nymphs," Rosa-mond and Rosamond's reflection in the glass. Mary Garth stands angled, wedged, between Rosamond's projection and return, so that Rosamond's image returns to her as if passed through Mary, her pleasure in receiving herself thus dependent upon this detour.* More poignantly, perhaps, since marriage binds the Garths to the Vincys, making both women nieces to Featherstone, Rosamond, if not for their different class positions, might have held Mary's job nursing their uncle. Rosamond, to this extent, stands incriminated in Mary's labor; she stands between Mary's domestic work and its paltry return. This incrimination, through hints of marriage, is suggested in their final exchange, before they both descend the stairs:

> "If your mamma is afraid that Fred will make me an offer, tell her that I would not marry him if he asked me. But he is not going to do so, that I am aware. He certainly never has asked me."

*We discover another striking example of this self-alienation in a passage that makes Rosamond's talents for acting a form of self-splitting: "(Every nerve and muscle in Ro-samond was adjusted to the consciousness that she was being looked at. She was by nature an actress of parts that entered into her own *physique*: she even acted her own character, and so well, that she did not know it to be precisely her own)" (144).

"Mary, you are always so violent."

"And you are always so exasperating."

"I? What can you blame me for?"

"Oh, blameless people are always the most exasperating. There is the bell—I think we must go down." (143)

Mary resists the mystification of "blameless people," as if anyone could remain fully outside the hymen's tangled class discriminations, which always become incriminations in *Middlemarch*. Mary even smudges Rosamond with servanthood, when to the bell that summons her ("'Ring the bell,' said Mr. Featherstone; 'I want Missy to come down'") Mary responds, "There is the bell—I think *we* must go down" (my emphasis).

Mary's fix, as Delphy would put it, arises from her role as the domestic servant/relative who is never fully taken into account. Mary, in fact, in her capacity as a servant, operates as a material opacity that the text makes visible as a shadow (a point I will amplify). Lydgate speaks to her without really seeing her; Featherstone introduces Lydgate to Rosamond but not to Mary. Yet Mary's labor is clearly required for the smooth operation of the social machinery. On the one hand, Mary obliges the system by committing herself to "duty" and "work"—the unquestionable values she preaches to Fred. On the other hand, her "satiric bitterness" files the edges of her discontent. When Mary refuses to help her uncle burn his will, we learn not only how much depends upon dutiful service, but also how drastically disobedience might threaten established social borders. Remarkably, after the narrator comments that Mary is not a saint, Mary's rebellion rises up as her refusal of a (sexual) "favor," requested by a demon. Featherstone exits the novel as a kind of masturbatory devil who, without cooperation from his female servant, cannot consummate his last transaction:

"I cannot help that, sir. I will not let the close of your life soil the beginning of mine. I will not touch your iron chest or your will." She moved to a little distance from the bedside.

The old man paused with a blank stare for a little while, holding the one key erect on the ring; then with an agitated jerk he began to work with his bony left hand at emptying the tin box before him. . . .

Mary, standing by the fire, saw its red light falling on the old man, propped up on his pillows and bed-rest, with his bony hand holding out the key, and the money lying on the quilt before him. . . .

He lifted the stick, in spite of her being beyond his reach, and threw it with a hard effort which was but impotence. (351–53)

This passage is rich in metaphorical possibilities: the question of soiling, the refusal to touch, the key held erect, the agitated jerk, the hard effort, and the resulting impotence. Suggestive of the brotherhood between men's capital and seminal productions is the image of Featherstone's "bony hand holding out the key, and the money lying on the quilt before him." This line calls up the story of Onan, who displeased God by spilling his seed—here his capital—on the ground.* In this matrix, Mary's duty and honesty have collided with her disobedience in such a way that, whatever her intention, she is implicated—inextricably so—in producing a will that could reorganize economic relations (369).

In a very different way, Garth family values underwrite the social formation that oppresses them. The Garths' class position is, indeed, a vexed question. Although they appear the "lowest" social rank of characters constructed for our consistent contemplation—they are failed bourgeois—their values of duty, honesty, and work, coupled with obedience and subordination with few complaints, are elevated as *the* values that readers should adopt. We can even read Mrs. Garth as a strong representative of what Althusser would specify as the Educational ISA, which in Victorian England constructs and separates genders and classes.

In contrast to Mrs. Vincy, Mrs. Garth had worked as a teacher before she married. After marriage, in "the passage from governess into housewife," she took on several students, who followed her about her kitchen while she performed a veritable maze of household duties:

> She thought it good for them to see that she could make an excellent lather while she corrected their blunders "without looking,"—that a woman with her sleeves tucked up above her elbows might know all about the Subjunctive Mood or the Torrid Zone—that, in short, she might possess "education" and other good things ending in "tion," and worthy to be pronounced emphatically, without being a useless doll. . . .
>
> Mrs. Garth at certain hours was always in the kitchen, and this morning she was carrying on several occupations at once there—making her pies at the well-scoured deal table on one side of that airy room, observing Sally's movements at the oven and dough-tub through an open door, and giving lessons to her youngest boy and girl, who were standing opposite to her at the table with their books and slates before them. A tub and a clothes-horse at the other end of the kitchen indicated an intermittent wash of small things also going on. (275–76)

In Mrs. Garth a wealth of contradictions appear: she is a woman whose unpaid domestic duties absurdly consume her and yet a woman

---

*"And Onan knew that the seed should not be his; and it came to pass, when he went in unto his brother's wife, that he spilled *it* on the ground, lest that he should give seed to his brother. And the thing which he did displeased the Lord: wherefore he slew him also" (Genesis 38:9, 10).

whose ethic is complete obedience beneath the yoke: "She had that rare sense which discerns what is unalterable, and submits to it without murmuring" (274). She is so anxious to set herself apart from the likes of Mrs. Vincy ("a useless doll"—a luxury item?) that the narrator tells us she was "apt to be a little severe towards her own sex, which in her opinion was framed to be entirely subordinate" (275). Unable as she is to discern her entanglement with the "useless doll[s]" of bourgeois luxury, Mrs. Garth upholds the Symbolic—a system that sustains, like a long low note, clear distinctions between men and women and clear separations between social classes, along with their variable command of "the slang," as Fred would have it, "of the prigs who write history and essays." Thus she explains to her son why he must learn his grammar: "To teach you to speak and write correctly, so that you can be understood. . . . Should you like to speak as old Job does?" (276–77). "In a general wreck of society," we are told, "Mrs. Garth would have tried to hold her 'Lindley Murray' above the waves."

Mrs. Garth illustrates how the domestic sphere's stability reproduces the public sphere's relations of production. The novel, in fact, stitches together Mrs. Garth's domestic work with what her daughter, Mary, performs in other homes. Central to *Middlemarch*, the suturing of one woman's circumstances to another's is rendered through women's mirrored relations, as if to "glass" them in a crystal knit. Indeed, the narrator observes the extent to which mother and daughter look alike, then supplements their twinning with a wish for their continued conjunction: "Looking at the mother, you might hope that the daughter would become like her, which is a prospective advantage equal to a dowry. . . . 'Such as I am, she will shortly be'" (276). Women's only guaranteed link to capital may be their dowries, which quantify their worth in masculine measures. And, as this rather Althusserian line suggests ("Such as I am, she will shortly be"), interpellation of her daughter constitutes the mother's capital investment in an otherwise seminal affair.

Finally, in a scene in which the Garths discuss Caleb's work, Mrs. Garth ends by praising her husband as "a father whose good work remains though his name may be forgotten" (438). If the reader wonders what of women's work remains to testify to future ages, since Mrs. Garth's or Mary's work is never discussed in these lofty terms, the novel shifts to a scene that shows (and by means of which Eliot intends us to see) how women's work is recorded, only to be forgotten: "Caleb, rather tired with his day's work, was seated in silence with his pocket-book open on his knee, while Mrs. Garth and Mary were at their sewing, and Letty in a cor-

ner was whispering a dialogue with her doll" (438). The opacity of
women and their work is suggested here. Whereas Caleb can mark the end
of his day by his work's completion and can calculate, further, in his pock-
etbook ledger, what his work has brought him, the women silently continue their labor: tasks that neither mark a project's conclusion nor, for
women, yield calculable returns. Women's work is as insignificant and yet
as all-determining for the social formation as a girl in a corner, whispering
a dialogue with her doll ("Such as I am, she will shortly be"). And yet, as
we shall see, the incalculable potential of feminine mirroring to fashion
women's work as desire, stands, sits, as a hidden threat to the dominant
economy that works to contain it.

Capital and Seminal

   If Dorothea, as the portrait of a domesticated saint, is hung high
against a background of women—their commodifications and domestic
labors—she must also be viewed against the backdrop of Christianity's
contract with capitalism. This contract carries anxieties in *Middlemarch*, especially since it foregrounds the further meshing of capital gains with
masculinity. Four of the novel's male characters suggest signal bonds between capital (in the form of money or ideas) and masculine sexuality. The
novel forges this brotherhood, moreover, by registering Victorian shifts
from religious to secular vocations, whereby "vocation" comes to con-
note a profession, as well as a "call from God."*

   Business is the God that calls Bulstrode and Garth, whereas Casaubon
and Lydgate heed the call of scholarship. Each pair of characters, grouped
in this way, would seem to be contraries: Bulstrode, the quintessential religious hypocrite, Garth, the model of humane faith and duty; Casaubon,
the intellectual impostor, Lydgate, the true intellectual adventurer. Yet all
of these characters are held close together by associative rings: *Middle-*

---

   *Alan Mintz offers an entire study on the question of vocation in George Eliot's nov-
els (and *Middlemarch* receives the bulk of his attention). Mintz, however, does not interrogate what I am calling the text's anxiety over the conjunction of capitalism and
Christianity; nor does he make gender a significant focus of his investigations. Although Dorothea Barrett, too, does not address the relationship between capitalism and
Christianity in the novel's portrayal of vocational opportunities, she does consistently
address gender issues. The bulk of her chapter on *Middlemarch* is devoted to discussions
of the appropriateness (or inappropriateness) of Will Ladislaw and Lydgate as mates
(and vocational matches) for Dorothea. The various forms of women's work in the
novel (particularly vocational links between the class-differentiated characters of Dorothea, Rosamond, and Mary) she does not discuss.

march examines an explicitly masculine access to capital and suggests that "vocations" imagine a 'God' who calls only men.

No character registers the threat of capitalism's conjunction with Christianity more than Bulstrode. Nor could Weber have drawn a more Weberian portrait: this Evangelical banker of strong ascetic tendencies is described as having Franciscan tints and half starving himself. Other traits, too, recall Weber's theory: his moral accounting and spiritual book-keeping, rendered in his righteous pronouncements on Fred; his obvious division of Middlemarchers into regenerate and unregenerate ranks, stim-ulating a clergyman's comment that Bulstrode is among those who "look on the rest of mankind as a doomed carcase which is to nourish them for heaven" (206); his interpretation of business ventures according to Cal-vin's doctrine of Providence, so that any transaction might theoretically be "sanctified by the right application of profits in the hands of God's ser-vant"; his rise, first to bourgeois preeminence in his role as banker/churchman/public benefactor, and then to landed gentry in his purchase of Stone Court; finally, his strict attempt to separate the public sphere of financial transactions from the private sphere of domestic security, a sep-aration Raffles puts at risk, so that Bulstrode dreads that "the black spot might reappear and become inseparable even from the vision of his hearth" (575).

Weber suggests that new accounting methods, such as bookkeeping, were essential developments in capitalism's evolution. Here the real inter-est of Bulstrode emerges, for Eliot's anxiety about capitalism poses as anx-iety about "accounting" and "calculation." The most blatant evidence of this textual worry involves Bulstrode's secret career as a Calvinist "con-fidential accountant" in a West End, money-laundering scheme. As the retrospective narrative of his career unfolds, the text implicates, which is to say incriminates, Bulstrode in money-changing ambitions with Feath-erstone's illegitimate son, Joshua Rigg, and Rigg's stepfather, John Raffles.

The narrator must overcome 'his' uneasiness "in calling attention to the existence of low people [such as Rigg and Raffles] by whose interfer-ence, however little we may like it, the course of the world is very much determined" (448). And though "it would be well, certainly, if we could help to reduce their number," as the narrator expresses it, these clerk/ac-countant types in search of "a little capital" must be represented. Just as the novel most frequently uses "desire" to typify Bulstrode's drive, whereas "longing" and "yearning" name Dorothea's, so Rigg's ambi-tions, like those of Featherstone, are rendered as "a passion":

> The one joy after which his soul thirsted was to have a money-changer's shop
> on a much-frequented quay, to have locks all round him of which he held the
> keys, and to look sublimely cool as he handled the breeding coins of all na-
> tions, while helpless Cupidity looked at him enviously from the other side of
> an iron lattice. The strength of that passion had been a power enabling him
> to master all the knowledge necessary to gratify it. (564)

Unmasking the sexual dynamic of capitalism, Rigg's "soul-thirst" to handle "breeding coins" and "to have locks all round him of which he held
the keys" reveals that what is capital becomes seminal as well. Rigg's fantasized compact among passion, power, and knowledge (a conjunction
Foucault would relish) even inverts the threat of the masculine gaze upon
women: capital that is seminal produces pleasure by being *the object of* Cu-
pidity's envious (and helpless!) stare. The mention of locks and keys,
however, reconjures not only Featherstone's passion but also his impotence, for capital that "breeds" cannot always be controlled.

   Raffles differently figures the dynamic of capitalist desire: he figures
its restlessness. Bearing "a stale odour of traveller's rooms in the commercial hotels of that period" (450), Raffles, in his peregrinations ("I've
no particular attachment to any spot" [571]) and in his quest for "independence," suggests the threat of capitalism to rural stability when no domestic rootedness checks pursuits of profit. This threat informs the report
that in comparison to "the labourers who were loading the last shocks of
corn . . . [Raffles] looked as incongruous amid this moist rural quiet and
industry as if he had been a baboon escaped from a menagerie" (452). Interestingly, Raffles stands in direct contrast to Bulstrode's aim at becoming
"landed"—as though Raffles figures some intrinsic drive of capitalism
that is stronger than the nostalgic urge to mime the old aristocracy.

   Amidst these portraits of "calculating" "low people," Bulstrode's
character is fitted to its place, although here worries about calculations importantly receive a religious twist. Along with the decidedly economic
ring to his "spiritual interests" and "sacred accountableness," the narrator
describes him as having been in his youth "as clever in figures as he was
fluent in speech and fond of theological definition" (663). All of Eliot's
novels jest at the niceties of theological definition. In *Middlemarch*, ironically, it is Mr. Vincy, the manufacturer, who expresses religion's incom-
patibility with precise measurement, when he objects to Bulstrode's moral
accounting: "If you come to religion, it seems to me a man shouldn't want
to carve out his meat to an ounce beforehand:—one must trust a little to
Providence and be generous" (156). There even lies another complaint in
Vincy's statement: calculation cannot have any truck with sympathy.

It is a central feature of *Middlemarch* that as references to "calculation" and "capital" proliferate in the novel's last third, so do various references to "sympathy." Here the spiritual construction of sympathy, much as it relies, ostensibly, upon humanist individuality, becomes sharply antithetical to precise discriminations. Along with burgeoning references to sympathy, references to incriminating implications accumulate. Bulstrode becomes enmeshed with Rigg and Raffles in dirty capital; Lydgate, Rosamond, and Mrs. Bulstrode all become tainted by Bulstrode's fall from grace. Bulstrode's meeting with Will further illustrates how intimacy turns toward incrimination: to atone for injustice he has done to Will's mother, Bulstrode offers Will annual income plus "a proportional capital at my death" (671). Will's outrage is paradigmatic: "My unblemished honour is important to me. . . . now I find there is a stain which I can't help" (672). *Middlemarch* depicts supposedly "blameless people" as incriminated in wrongs performed by others—hence, Will's connection to Bulstrode's shady past. The narrator even implicates the reader in rather unflattering ways. For example, when discussing Bulstrode's tendency to justify his profits by believing God has chosen him, the narrator instructs us: "This implicit reasoning is essentially no more peculiar to evangelical belief than the use of wide phrases for narrow motives is peculiar to Englishmen. There is no general doctrine which is not capable of eating out our morality if unchecked by the deep-seated habit of direct fellow-feeling with individual fellow-men" (668).

The irony here is that individuality, in the sense relevant to "individual fellow-men," is itself undercut by the narrative's depictions of "direct fellow-feeling" and incriminations. There is an important sense in which acts of sympathy, because they show the lie of fully separable lives, reveal the incriminations of so-called "blameless people" in the class inequities the Reform Bill was created to address. This incrimination of the sympathetic relation reveals the power of the novel's historical retrospection, back to "the national struggle" for Reform; this incrimination is largely worked out through feminine mirroring, which, in *Middlemarch*, locates an infinity of others between one and two. The feminine fracture of Dorothea and Rosamond's erotic foray into sympathy provides a retrospect on the many incriminations that precede it. It throws into question the rational, assured calculations on which the political economy proceeds—even the liberal politics of Reform ("put the figures and deduce the misery," Mr. Brooke instructs Will, as Brooke prepares for his political speech [500]). Feminine mirroring, with its splittings at the moments of its identifications, also strikes against Brooke's liberal mystification of "all one family . . . [in] all one cupboard" (543). This is a simplification unmasked by Mr. Mawmsey's retort: "But as to one family, there's debtor and creditor, I hope; they're not going to reform that away" (544).

Another character relates to Bulstrode and to textual worries over calculations. Caleb Garth, posed in nearly every way as Bulstrode's obverse, stands as Eliot's attempt to redeem "accounting" and "valuing" from the taint of "capital." Robert Scholes reads this split between accounting and capital as the text's repression of contradictions between Protestantism and capitalism: Garth's love of "business" is supposedly redeemed because "he knew values well, but he had no keenness of imagination for monetary results in the shape of profit and loss" (284); he "gave himself up entirely to the many kinds of work which he could do without handling capital" (284).[1] (This stress on not "handling" capital poises Garth against Featherstone's masturbatory attempts to handle coins.) Even so, it would not be fully accurate to speak of Garth as a capitalist without capital. Eliot's representation of Garth is one of her loving portraits of a yeoman—a portrait rendered fascinating, to be sure, by Eliot's distrust of capitalism in its more contemporary manifestations. If anything, Garth is a failed capitalist. The narrative alludes to a time when he went into business for himself but could not meet its necessary demands. The novel's obvious investment in Garth finds telling expression when the narrator parenthetically addresses the reader at the end of a loving description of his mannerisms: "(pardon these details for once—you would have learned to love them if you had known Caleb Garth)" (265). We are clearly being asked to admire Caleb Garth as a surveyor/valuer/agent who, though he will teach Fred Vincy the "accounts" and "values" that go along with "business," most of all inculcates love of hard work for its own "religious" sake. In fact, the narrator renders Garth's gospel of work in a passage reminiscent of Carlyle:

> Caleb Garth often shook his head in meditation on the value, the indispensable might of that myriad-headed, myriad-handed labour by which the social body is fed, clothed, and housed. It had laid hold of his imagination in boyhood. The echoes of the great hammer where roof or keel were a-making, the signal-shouts of the workmen, the roar of the furnace, the thunder and plash of the engine, were a sublime music to him; the felling and lading of timber, and the huge trunk vibrating star-like in the distance along the highway, the crane at work on the wharf, the piled-up produce in warehouses, the precision and variety of muscular effort wherever exact work had to be turned out,—all these sights of his youth had acted on him as poetry without the aid of the poets, had made a philosophy for him without the aid of phi-

losophers, a religion without the aid of theology. His early ambition had been to have as effective a share as possible in this sublime labour . . . .

Though he had never regarded himself as other than an orthodox Christian, and would argue on prevenient grace if the subject were proposed to him, I think his virtual divinities were good practical schemes, accurate work, and the faithful completion of undertakings: his prince of darkness was a slack workman. (283–84)*

We recall Carlyle's *Past and Present*, where the masculine work force is paraded by the reader: "Ploughers, Spinners, Builders; Prophets, Poets, Kings; Brindleys and Goethes, Odins and Arkwrights; all martyrs, and noble men, and gods are one grand Host. . . . noble every soldier in it; sacred and alone noble." Women's labor, as in Carlyle's passage, is noticeably absent from Garth's meditation, remaining a truly "imprisoned god," as Carlyle would have it. Along with "the felling and lading of timber," we do not find that dishwashing, laundering, and nursing "had laid hold of [Garth's] imagination in boyhood." Unlike Carlyle's passage, however, Garth's meditation enshrines the work without the workers, as if the wheels of "sublime labour" were divinely set in motion and divinely maintained. The struggles and stratifications of the work force, along with the gender divisions of labor, are fully mystified by this gospel of work, in which business *is* God. But business as God and God as business is Bulstrode's trademark, so that Garth is tellingly entangled with Bulstrode by the text's admiring portrayal of him.

So much for capital becoming seminal. What is "seminal" in *Middlemarch* ("germinal; originative [a seminal book]") also becomes its own kind of capital. The novel's uneasiness about calculation and capital gains finds expression in a twin worry over knowledge acquisition and professional development. In her sociological analysis *The Rise of Professionalism*, Magali Sarfatti Larson relates the problem of professions to the general problem of intellectuals in class societies. Larson notes that "the ethics of disinterestedness claimed by professionals appear to acquit them of the capitalist profit motive" so that, as Gramsci warned, "the class context in which authority is delegated and privileges are granted to the particular occupations tends to be neglected." Relating intellectual producers to economic markets and stressing "skills" as a " 'modern' form of property," Larson defines professionalization as "an attempt to translate one order of

---

*We have seen Featherstone as a masturbatory devil who, bathed in red light, works his key at the box of his capital. Here is another take on God's nemesis, a construction that capitalists particularly impressed upon their workers: the devil as "a slack workman."

scarce resources—special knowledge and skills—into another—social and economic rewards," since the often unacknowledged goal is to increase " 'marketability' of . . . specific cognitive resources."[2]

In *Middlemarch*, intellectual training, and the ideas it produces, ties professionals to capitalist markets and masculine sexuality. The narrator's casual comment that one's "self-satisfaction is an untaxed kind of property" (186) associates Casaubon with Lydgate in their complacencies that function as forms of capital. Their views on women further associate these diverse professionals in seminal pursuits. Both, for example, are defined against the manly aristocrat, Chettam. In *Middlemarch*, the proverbial emasculation of the professional classes, their distance from the manly hunting and sporting portrait of the aristocracy, receives redefinition. Chettam is not the sexually potent center of the novel; he is dismissed early on, when Dorothea prefers Casaubon, and returns to the narrative only in cameos. Conversely, Lydgate plays romantic lead. His professional appetite to compete in the realm of scientific discovery is coded as sexual energy and desire.

Casaubon, by contrast, portrays the impotent-though-not-emasculated academic man. Along with Featherstone, he shares the honors of the "dead hand" of patriarchy. And since he supremely represents the privilege of patriarchal language (he responds to Dorothea with quotations, woos her with pamphlets, and courts her through letters), the masculine Symbolic is tinged with a kind of sexual impotence, for the novel relentlessly ridicules Casaubon's lack of "bloom," fulfilling an observer's prediction: "This marriage is as good as going to a nunnery." His inability to provide, or to feel, sexual stimulation is depicted as expressing his lack of spiritual sympathy—another indication that sympathy is coded as desire in *Middlemarch*. More damning still, an analogy to baptism fashions the clearest figure for Casaubon's sexual impotence:

> He determined to abandon himself to the stream of feeling, and perhaps was surprised to find what an exceedingly shallow rill it was. As in droughty regions baptism by immersion could only be performed symbolically, so Mr. Casaubon found that sprinkling was the utmost approach to a plunge which his stream would afford him; and he concluded that the poets had much exaggerated the force of masculine passion. (87)

The "stream of feeling" and "immersion" return, forcefully, in Dorothea's later scene with Rosamond. There we encounter the unmistakable sexual valence of the "warm stream" and "waves" that "rush over" the women with a "conquering force," so that baptismal immersion becomes the passion of orgasmic "shipwreck."

Joining the "seminal" to "capital," the novel connects Casaubon's waning passion to a decrease in the capital of his self-satisfaction. Though the narrator describes him as "longing to get the nearest possible calculation" of his remaining years, Casaubon assesses his life "on all collateral accounts insignificant" (459). The "Synoptical Tabulation," "The Key to All Mythologies," that Casaubon would have Dorothea complete (he would "demand much interest and labour from her" [517]), constitutes, again, the employer's attempt to make the servant take the "key" and perform a particularly incriminating duty. Featherstone tries to make Mary take his key in order to burn one of his wills; Bulstrode's wine-cooler key "was thrust through the inch of doorway" (763) to his housekeeper, who unknowingly becomes Raffles' killer. In all of these versions, the forcing of the key upon a woman subservient to a man—Dorothea here associated with Mary Garth and with Bulstrode's housekeeper—carries sexually exploitative connotations. For Casaubon, passing his "Key to All Mythologies" to Dorothea assures transmission of his seminal production, tellingly described as "an elfin child" "withered in birth" (519). This act of academic transmission, moreover, would consummate their marriage. For this reason, Dorothea, after much struggle, offers herself to her husband, sexually and intellectually, with the rich dedication: "I am come, Edward; I am ready" (523)—phrasing that alludes to the Bride and the Bridegroom from the Book of Revelation (see 22:17, 20). As it happens, she is stranded in the undecidable hymen of marriage, left a *virginal wife* by all accounts, since Casaubon has died before her announcement.

Lydgate is the novel's other avatar of seminal studies. In shifting from Casaubon to Lydgate, we might seem to shift from a religious calling to a secular scientific profession.* Weber, once again, attentuates these distinctions—this time in his essay "Science as a Vocation." Even though he argues that science, first conceived by Protestantism as a way "to show the path to God," must now in a more secular age be considered an "irreligious power," Weber conceives the scientist's devotion as "passion" and "calling." He writes:

> And whoever lacks the capacity to put on blinders, so to speak, and come up
> to the idea that the fate of his soul depends upon whether or not he makes the

---

*I offer a different reading here from that of Thomas Vargish, who, though he notes parallels between Casaubon and Lydgate, argues that "Lydgate does stand higher than Casaubon in the values that *Middlemarch* supports. . . . His ambition does not derive from an arcane and anachronistic mythography but belongs instead to the heroic saga of modern scientific advance" (*Providential Aesthetic*, 222–23). Barrett also views Lydgate in this more positive light. See also Mintz's discussion of this secular vocation for comparison with my reading (*George Eliot*, 78–96).

correct conjecture at this passage of this manuscript may as well stay away
from science. He will never have what one may call the "personal experience" of science. Without this strange intoxication, ridiculed by every out-
sider; without this passion . . . without this, you have *no* calling for science
and you should do something else. For nothing is worthy of man as man unless he can pursue it with passionate devotion.[3]

This stress upon intellectual passion, upon intoxication and calling, all of
which conveys an Evangelical "enthusiasm," finds expression in *Middlemarch*. Consider how the narrator renders "the moment of vocation,"
when Lydgate, as a young man, felt called to scientific pursuits:

But he opened the volume which he first took from the shelf: somehow, one
is apt to read in a makeshift attitude, just where it might seem inconvenient
to do so. The page he opened was under the heading of Anatomy, and the
first passage that drew his eyes was on the valves of the heart. He was not
much acquainted with valves of any sort, but he knew that *valvae* were folding doors, and through this crevice came a sudden light startling him with
his first vivid notion of finely adjusted mechanism in the human frame. A
liberal education had of course left him free to read the indecent passages in
the school classics, but beyond a general sense of secrecy and obscenity in
connection with his internal structure, had left his imagination quite un-
biased, so that for anything he knew his brains lay in small bags at his temples, and he had no more thought of representing to himself how his blood
circulated than how paper served instead of gold. But the moment of vocation had come, and before he got down from his chair, the world was made
new to him by a presentiment of endless processes filling the vast spaces
planked out of his sight by that wordy ignorance which he had supposed to
be knowledge. From that hour Lydgate felt the growth of an intellectual passion. (173)

This overwrought passage begins with a play on the Puritan's practice
of randomly opening the Scriptures for a word: Lydgate opened to a
page on anatomy. Next, apropos of seminal studies, the neutral focus
on "the valves of the heart" begins to shade associatively toward the
genital lips and a sudden gleam (from God?) between them: the "valvae"
are described as "folding doors . . . through [which] crevice came a
sudden light" (173), a description made more suggestive by the line
that follows. Now we are told of Lydgate's previous encounters with
"indecent passages in the school classics" and of his earlier "sense of secrecy and obscenity in connection with his internal structure." There even
emerges a subtle association between "seminal" (semen) and "seminal"
(originative intellectual power) in the suggestion of his brains lying "in
small bags at his temples"—an image that relocates his testicles to his

head. Adding to our sense that seminal studies bind their fortunes to capital concerns, the narrator asserts that prescientific Lydgate "had no more thought of representing to himself how his blood circulated than how paper served instead of gold." This assertion, if reversed, concludes that the pursuit of scientific knowledge promises both pleasure (a "first vivid notion of finely adjusted mechanism in the human frame") and power, akin to the capitalist's knowledge of how money circulates—all this at a time when scientific discovery was opening bold new capitalist markets.

Weber himself joins science to business, making "ideas" a form of capital and a sign of calling:

> Does an "idea" occur or does it not? [The scientific worker] may be an excellent worker and yet never have had any valuable idea of his own. It is a grave error to believe that this is so only in science, and that things for instance in a business office are different from a laboratory. A merchant or a big industrialist without "business imagination," that is, without ideas or ideal intuitions, will for all his life remain a man who would better have remained a clerk or a technical official.[4]

Weber perpetrates, with this remark, more than a little mystification—as if the "big industrialist" were set apart from the clerk primarily by ideas, rather than by other forms of capital that presumably divide them. Are we to consider the big industrialist as "called" to his empire by his capital ideas? And yet ideas, as Larson shows in line with Weber, can function as resource, commodity, and capital. Weber links the scientist to the capitalist in another sense: the increasing rationalization that is "created by science and by scientifically oriented technology" means that "no mysterious incalculable forces come into play, but rather that one can, in principle, master all things by calculation."[5] How fitting, in light of this tie to mastery, that *Middlemarch* offers a colonial analogy to capture Lydgate's professional ambitions:

> We are apt to think it the finest era of the world when America was beginning to be discovered, when a bold sailor, even if he were wrecked, might alight on a new kingdom; and about 1829 the dark territories of Pathology were a fine America for a spirited young adventurer. Lydgate was ambitious above all to contribute towards enlarging the scientific, rational basis of his profession. (176–77)

Again, the reader learns how capital and seminal investments conjoin, even for this scientist: the narrator remarks that "the primitive tissue was still [Lydgate's] fair unknown" (305). In Lydgate the "scientific view of woman" bends round to the romantic.* This implication of romantic passion in his professional scientific devotion surfaces unmistakably following the report on his discovery of vocation. The narrator meditates on how we should be as interested to tell and listen to stories of intellectual passions as we now "are not afraid of telling over and over again how a man comes to fall in love with a woman and be wedded to her" (173). (This Victorian passion for stories about professionalism meets Freud's later theories on work as the sublimation of sexual desire.) A connection is forged between Lydgate and Casaubon in the narrator's maxim on how intellectual ardor may dissipate: "For perhaps their ardour in generous unpaid toil cooled as imperceptibly as the ardour of other youthful loves, till one day their earlier self walked like a ghost in its old home and made the new furniture ghastly" (174). The allusion is seemingly directed at Lydgate, but, as the reader soon learns, Casaubon is the ghost that haunts Lowick Manor (even when alive), and it is Casaubon we think of later when we are told that "the stag" in Dorothea's bedroom tapestry "looked more like a ghost" (306).

Lest we consider ourselves exempt from seminal passions, whether these passions be rising or falling, the narrator counts "us" in on this tragedy: "Nothing in the world more subtle than the process of their gradual change! In the beginning they inhaled it unknowingly; you and I may have sent some of our breath towards infecting them, when we uttered our conforming falsities or drew our silly conclusions: or perhaps it came with the vibrations from a woman's glance" (174). Here is the theme of the gaze once again: a designing woman looking at a man. In this case, a woman's disturbing "vibrations"—with the male professional the object of her glance—are charged with disrupting men's passion for knowledge.† This is one of those narrative junctures that seems to fashion readers as men or, at least, as masculine. That is to say, the reader, who is drawn into the professional's cooling ardor, is presumably not to feel reproached as the source of such "a woman's glance"—for such a glance belongs not to the public realm of actions, but to the private sphere of domestic (fallen or unfallen) bliss.‡

*See Jacqueline Rose's discussion on Lydgate and Laure in her essay "George Eliot and the Spectacle of Woman" (*Sexuality in the Field of Vision*, 109–14).

†In a crucial way, the parallelism of "our conforming falsities" and "the vibrations from a woman's glance"—both of which "infect" the male professional—is undermined by the shift from first- and second-person pronouns to the seemingly distant "vibrations from a woman's glance" that do not seem to include "us."

‡Again, we need to keep Eliot's irony in view as a subtle tension in passages such as this. For it could be argued that it is Lydgate's crude attitude toward women as luxury

Hymeneal Men

Membrane men, characterized not by their accumulations but by their permeability and their fluid states: There is something about religious calling that does not fully lift men out of domestic spheres but, rather, installs them at the hymeneal membrane between public and private domains. We have seen how consistently capital, represented as money or ideas, is fastened by the novel to masculinity. Access to professional callings has likewise been designated masculine. By contrast, the pursuit of religious vocations (even in the form of Romantic pursuits), as opposed to vocations in science, business, or academic theology, appears more ambiguous. Will's Romantic piety, Farebrother's compromised position as a clergyman, and Fred's potential pursuit of the ministry put them at risk of perpetual virginity, on the level of plot, and of femininity, on the level of character. Since they hover at these borders, and since their associations with capital and seminal concerns rest uncertain, we might construe them as hymeneal men.

Will Ladislaw, "unworthy" lover to Dorothea (in the eyes of Middlemarchers and critics alike), is one of these border-runners. Several touches feminize Will. Dorothea, for a start, sees in Will's face the portrait of his grandmother; she finds the faces remarkably alike, except that, tellingly, "[Will's] mouth and chin [had] a more prominent, threatening aspect than belonged to the type of the grandmother's miniature" (104). Casaubon calls attention to Will's Romantic position outside the capital and seminal spheres of public action and the systematic pursuit of knowledge. He informs Dorothea that Will "wants to go abroad again, without any special object. . . . He declines to choose a profession" (106). Casaubon considers Will's nonprofessionalization in terms of a missing taste for exploration, where exploration, as we've seen with Lydgate, carries hints of colonization:

"He has a thirst for travelling; perhaps he may turn out a Bruce or a Mungo Park," said Mr. Brooke. "I had a notion of that myself at one time."

"No, he has no bent towards exploration, or the enlargement of our geognosis: that would be a special purpose which I could recognize with

objects that makes him susceptible to Rosamond's glance; Dorothea's glance, on the contrary, which is the one to which he should respond, would presumably sustain him in professional projects. Of course, the force of this caveat is still based upon a division between women who distract male professionals and those who would assist men in their vocations, even at the expense of their own (which is how some critics interpret Dorothea at the novel's end).

some approbation. . . . But so far is he from having any desire for a more accurate knowledge of the earth's surface, that he said he should prefer not to know the sources of the Nile, and that there should be some unknown regions preserved as hunting-grounds for the poetic imagination." (106–7)

Here Will seems to affirm material concealments as concealments because they make possible appropriately impossible Romantic quests. In this, he appears Lydgate's opposite—Lydgate, a scientific Bruce or Mungo Park, whose intellectual pursuits resemble the "adventuring" that colonized America (and whose passion for anatomy may resemble "desire for a more accurate knowledge of the earth's surface"). Will diverges, too, from that other seminal adventurer, Casaubon, who, again linked to Lydgate, deems exploration "a special purpose which I could recognize with some approbation." Though his nonprofessional, noncolonizing stance emerges from his stance as Romantic devotee of "the poetic imagination," which would seem to connect him to great male writers, Will's location outside public circuits makes him feminine. And though he could pursue a masculine vocation in the public sector, his refusal to do so, his attention instead to "attitudes of receptivity," places him close to Dorothea—so much so, in fact, that Dorothea may be speaking for herself as well as Will when she says that "people may really have in them some vocation which is not quite plain to themselves, may they not?" (107–8). Will's aimlessness, along with his experiments in "ecstasy" and his incubation of the "dubious eggs called possibilities" (an appropriate feminine image) may constitute Romantic tropes for one who waits for genius to beckon; but these Romantic tropes suit Dorothea, too.* Will's educational journey to the Continent—standard Romantic fare that the novel partly satirizes—is mirrored by Dorothea's feminized version of this educational plan: her honeymoon to Rome.

It would be too simple to argue that Will is unquestionably feminized. His many feminine characteristics, we have seen, emerge from Romantic tropes that cannot be read, straightforwardly, as feminine. More to the point, the character who starts out as Romantic artist at the text's beginning, later in the novel shapes a vocation as a politician. The clue to this

---

*At the beginning of chapter 10, the narrator satirizes Will's aspirations to Genius: "The attitudes of receptivity are various, and Will had sincerely tried many of them. He was not excessively fond of wine, but he had several times taken too much, simply as an experiment in that form of ecstasy; he had fasted till he was faint, and then supped on lobster; had made himself ill with doses of opium. Nothing greatly original had resulted from these measures; and the effects of the opium had convinced him that there was an entire dissimilarity between his constitution and De Quincey's" (109).

development comes with the narrator's comment that Will was "[return-ing] to England [from the Continent] to try his fortune, as many other young men were obliged to do whose only capital was in their brains" (325) (money-"bags at his temples"?). This phrase recalls us to Weber's suggestion of ideas as capital—a necessary endowment, in Weber's think-ing, for men who pursue business or science. The phrase, to this extent, associates Will with the pursuits of other masculine characters, and the de-piction of his thoughts as capital certainly splits him off from Dorothea, for a woman's ideas in this period of time do not count professionally.

When Will moves into the political mainstream, his character seems to become more masculine. Even so, Eliot seems concerned to keep him at the hymen between separate spheres of influence. The constant re-minder of his "foreign extraction," along with his status as "a sort of gypsy," is presumably meant to mark him as not subsumed by his (mas-culine) bourgeois vocation. Eliot, in fact, invests herself in a classless Lad-islaw. We are told that Will was "enjoying the sense of belonging to no class; he had a feeling of romance in his position" (502). At a meeting for Reform, he speaks with "the violence of an energumen"—a fanatical de-votee, French Revolution style. The narrator even offers a particularly gypsylike portrait of Will with little children:

> This dangerous aspect of Ladislaw was strangely contrasted with other habits which became matter of remark. He had a fondness, half artistic, half affec-tionate, for little children. . . . We know that in Rome he was given to ramble about among the poor people, and the taste did not quit him in Middlemarch.
> He had somehow picked up a troop of droll children, little hatless boys with their galligaskins much worn and scant shirting to hang out, little girls who tossed their hair out of their eyes to look at him. . . . This troop he had led out on gypsy excursions to Halsell Wood at nutting-time, and since the cold weather had set in he had taken them on a clear day to gather sticks for a bonfire in the hollow of a hillside, where he drew out a small feast of gin-gerbread for them, and improvised a Punch-and-Judy drama with some pri-vate home-made puppets. (503)

This portrayal, which places Will somewhere between the pied piper and Jesus, blends political commitment to "poor people" with domestic ten-derness; the only other character we could picture making a gingerbread feast along with a puppet-show is Mrs. Garth (though Fred offers possi-bilities, too).

If these portrayals of "classlessness" and revolutionary passion are meant to mitigate Will's increasing political professionalism, Weber would not buy this implicit argument. In "Politics as a Vocation," Weber reads lack of social fixity (not the same as classlessness, to be sure) as a prime characteristic of the journalist—the career that prepares for Will's political vocation. Remarks Weber:

> In common with all demagogues and, by the way, with the lawyer (and the artist), the journalist shares the fate of lacking a fixed social classifica-tion. . . . The journalist belongs to a sort of pariah caste, which is always estimated by 'society' in terms of its ethically lowest representative. Hence, the strangest notions about journalists and their work are abroad. Not every-body realizes that a really good journalistic accomplishment requires at least as much 'genius' as any scholarly accomplishment.[6]

Weber's assessment of the political journalist fits Will Ladislaw remark-ably well. It helps us to relate his Romantic aspects—his gypsy aimless-ness—to his ultimate vocation. It should not surprise us, then, given Will's progressive masculinization and professionalization, to find him impli-cated in a prototypical capital pursuit: toward the novel's end, we learn of "a letter from Will Ladislaw to Lydgate, which turned chiefly on his new interest in plans of colonization" (811). Perhaps a Bruce or a Mungo Park, after all.

Finally, if Will seems masculine in any pursuit, it is in his stance before his object of desire. The point, on the surface, is too obvious to belabor; phrases such as "Will . . . could not bear the thought of any flaw appear-ing in his crystal" and "Dorothea, he said to himself, was ever enthroned in his soul" make the case clear. Yet just as Will's feminization at the start must not be overstated, neither should his masculinization at the end.

Farebrother's calling, far more directly than Will's Romantic piety, dramatizes the dilemma of men's religious vocations—especially for es-tablishing secure masculinity and for placing one with confidence in cap-italist domains. Larson emphasizes that professions like the clergy cannot be thought of in terms of the " 'marketability' of their specific cognitive resources," since they "do not transact their services on the market."[7]* And though the clergy would seem constructed masculine by its nonad-mittance of women, Farebrother figures a domesticated clergyman, as rooted to his home as he is tied to his public occupation as vicar (then as rector). Chapter 17, in which we meet him through Lydgate's eyes, takes place in his domestic niche. In fact, his three-woman household subsumes the narrative focus: "Lydgate had not expected to see so quaint a group:

*Actually, in Victorian England "livings" became a transactable commodity, even a form of speculative investment. See Owen Chadwick, *The Victorian Church, Part II*, 207–14.

knowing simply that Mr. Farebrother was a bachelor, he had thought of being ushered into a snuggery where the chief furniture would probably be books and collections of natural objects" (198). Three women need his financial support and all are stalled at the hymen of marriage, like the rector himself: his widowed mother; his maiden aunt; and his spinster sister, who is "well-looking like himself, but nipped and subdued as single women are apt to be who spend their lives in uninterrupted subjection to their elders." This sister doubles Farebrother, in the sense that she, like him, finds restricted opportunities for marriage. Unlike her, Farebrother holds a vocation—though not his chosen one—and occupies "a den" apart from the women where he pursues his hobby, natural history.

The novel hints that this hobby might have formed his preferred profession if his domestic responsibilities had not proved so pressing. Farebrother, then, is domesticated by his compromise calling. No wonder the narrative joins him to Lydgate around the interests of his den and around the question of vocation. As one who would share Lydgate's dedication, Farebrother is shown both as warning Lydgate to keep "independence" and as looking to Lydgate for masculine inspiration. In their discussion of "making your value felt"—a phrase that recalls "self-satisfaction [as] an untaxed kind of property"—"independence" takes on a masculine ring when Farebrother comments that "a good wife—a good unworldly woman—may really help a man, and keep him more independent" (205). How women, if they do not take wives, might find this independence is not discussed, though this is the central problem of *Middlemarch* insofar as Dorothea is its central character. In this specific context, we are left to read Farebrother as feminized by his own account, since he does not succeed in pursuing marriage. Perhaps his feminization explains his desire "to make an exchange" of scientific specimens with Lydgate. Such an interpretation—the feminized character seeks masculinizing gestures—makes sense of his closing remarks to Lydgate, in which the text reconnects Lydgate to exploration. Says Farebrother: "I can't spare you. You are a sort of circumnavigator come to settle among us, and will keep up my belief in the antipodes. Now tell me all about them in Paris" (206).

Along with Ladislaw and Farebrother, Fred is a hymeneal man. For most of the novel, he stands at the crossroads of marriage and ministry, uncertain as to both. Although Fred finds his place in the Symbolic regarding education and expectations, he is feminized by his precarious potential role as clergyman and his precarious grasp of capital. When first we meet him, we are shown his stance at the borders between public and domestic domains, between masculine and feminine character traits. Fred is introduced as "the family laggard"—a designation that, along with his lounging, paints him as a kind of leisured lady. (Like Rosamond, he hungers for luxury items.) Immediately, we learn that Fred is slated not for life as a capitalist (where masculinity and capital cohere) but for life as a gentleman. Fred is associated with a masculine command of language, to be sure. His discussion with Rosamond on slang and prigs makes evident his gentlemanly education. And yet his orientation towards ministry places him, like Farebrother, outside the circuits of professional pursuit that would put him in touch with production and exchange. Not surprisingly, the text's small details reveal Fred as feminized. We are told, for instance, that Rosamond disapproves his flute playing on the grounds that "a man looks very silly playing the flute."

Chapter 23 could be titled "Why Fred Cannot Be a Capitalist." Here the reader follows his speculations on the horse-trading market. From the first paragraph, where the narrator intimates that Fred is among those "addicted to pleasure," we realize that Fred ill fits Weber's paradigm of the frugal capitalist, whose asceticism aids accumulation of profits. Even his father, Mr. Vincy, is a less frugal capitalist than those that Weber discusses—with the predictable result that his business suffers. Interestingly, we discover yet another version of ideas as capital, when the narrator informs us that " 'judgment' [is] always equivalent to an unspecified sum in hard cash" (262) (later in the chapter, Bambridge "gives forth his ideas without economy"). But "judgment," along with money, constitutes capital that Fred does not possess. Fred woefully lacks experience with the accounts in which Caleb Garth will instruct him.

It is important for recognizing the way that spiritual talk communicates economies that Fred's bad judgment in financial affairs is rendered through a play on a well-known parable. The gospels' sower parable conveys the different fates of the seeds of God's Word, sown along the path of life. Some fall on good soil, some among thorns, some on rocky ground, and some along the roadside, each seed multiplying in accordance with the place upon which it falls. In the novel's version, Fred's seed falls unpropitiously—whether by Providential design or the unpredictability of capital investments, we are not told. Says the narrator:

> But he meant to make the sum complete with another sixty, and with a view to this, he had kept twenty pounds in his own pocket as a sort of seed-corn, which, planted by judgment, and watered by luck, might yield more than threefold—a very poor rate of multiplication when the field is a young gentleman's infinite soul, with all the numerals at command. . . .

> But the twenty pounds' worth of seed-corn had been planted in vain in
> the seductive green plot [of billiards gambling]—all of it at least which had
> not been dispersed by the roadside—and Fred found himself close upon the
> term of payment [of his debt] with no money at command. (267)

Here is another link between "seminal" ("of or containing seed or semen") and "capital" (seed-corn worth twenty pounds in Fred's pants-
pocket). The phrase "all the numerals at command" is ironic, and beto-
kens not Fred's ability to handle accounts but the opposite: the purely fan-
tasmatic accumulation of ciphers in daydream, with no connection to the
realities to which the numbers should refer. Fred clearly lacks (in the realm
of finance) what this novel deems essential capital: good judgment.* We
may note, as well, the "seductive" role of Lady Luck ("the vibrations
from a woman's glance"?) that causes Fred, like Featherstone, to spill
(here, "disperse") his seed upon the ground.

The general instability of capitalist desire is further made evident
when the horse Fred gained through his slick trading "without the slightest warning exhibited in the stable a most vicious energy in kicking"
(273). The result is a lame horse that must be destroyed and a debt that
cannot be paid. If gems in this novel consistently figure feminine sexuality, as they did in *Villette*, it is fitting that the name of the horse lost to Fred
turns out to be Diamond. As if to strengthen this connection, the novel
next informs us that "there was no more redress for this [Diamond's vi-
ciousness] than for the discovery of bad temper after marriage." Simultaneously lost to Fred are capital investments and seminal possibilities.

If we follow Christine Delphy's theory that the domestic mode of
production is a system (a separate system) of production, consumption,
and transmission of goods, where transmission takes the form of inheritance, then Fred is securely found within this mode—not as a producer,
but as one who consumes and who stands expectant of receiving an inheritance. Yet, like many women, Fred is passed over by the Featherstone
will that Mary does not burn. Like women, again, Fred remains unsettled
vis-à-vis the question of vocation. As with many other *Middlemarch* characters, Fred's discovery of a calling—and the question of religious vocation is particularly pointed in Fred Vincy's case—is tied to his relation to
a woman. (Mary will not marry Fred if he's a clergyman.) By solving his
vocation, he can solve the difficulties surrounding his masculinity and his
marriage. It is not without import, then, that Caleb Garth determines "to

*Fred's judgment is somewhat redeemed by his eventual choice of Mary as a wife
and Caleb Garth as his model for work.

make a man . . . of Fred" by leading him in the ways of "accounts." But if Fred forsakes the ministry to pursue this new vocation, his entry into Caleb's business indoctrinates him into Garth's own gospel of work. His implication in the worship of Bulstrode's business god even seems to follow, since Fred, with Garth's help, inhabits Stone Court after Bulstrode vacates.

"Hymeneal men" describes those characters that hover about or cross back and forth over the borders of public and domestic scenes, masculine and feminine identifications, and the sexual states of virginity and marriage. There is something peculiar about religious vocation that is not fully seminal—at least not like the intellectual passions that drive business and science. Now we must return to that aspect of *Middlemarch* that most involves these contradictions. As we have come to expect from *Middlemarch*, as well as from "theory," the question of shifting boundaries returns us to 'woman' and 'God'.

St. Theresa at the Lips

Religious vocations, in Eliot's novel, seem to feminize masculine characters. Yet, as if it is pulled through a tapestry, drawn through a cloth (and through men of the cloth) to its opposite side, inverting the pattern, this thread of a calling masculinizes the novel's female saint. At least in this sense: an unmarried woman's religious vocation may foster her masculine passage to work, not her readiness for marriage. The novel hints that, in numerous ways, Dorothea's religious yearning bears potential for disturbing conventions. Even so, as we have seen, it is Dorothea's trust that marriage can augment religious vocation that domesticates her as aspiring saint—to the point that her education and reforms seem to her unattainable.

And yet, her "ardour" finds its channels. In Romantic teleologies, as M. H. Abrams famously explained, men's educational journeys lead them from home into circuits of adventure, desire, and self-alienation, before they return, enlightened, to embrace "the feminine other."* Most unexpectedly, Dorothea makes such a journey as a *wife*, when she takes her

*Abrams writes: "The beginning and end of the journey is man's ancestral home, which is often linked with a female contrary from whom he has, upon setting out, been disparted. The goal of this long inner quest is to be reached by a gradual ascent, or else by a sudden breakthrough of imagination or cognition; in either case, however, the achievement of the goal is pictured as a scene of recognition and reconciliation, and is often signalized by a loving union with the feminine other, upon which man finds himself thoroughly at home with himself, his milieu, and his family of fellow men" (*Natural Supernaturalism*, 255).

honeymoon trip to Rome. In fact, an Irigarayan slant on teleology summons a curious feature of Dorothea's exile into marriage—an exile that, for Irigaray, marks a woman's passage into alien sexual economies. The curious feature I refer to is this: the novel's references to autoeroticism increase in Dorothea's marital phase, as if her self-touching grows especially insistent during her "exile."

Our first view of Dorothea, since she was exiled in chapter 10, announces this turn, stilled as it's caught in the narrator's lens. As if Lacan were training our sights on Bernini's St. Theresa, the narrative arrests us with Naumann's plea to Will: "Come here, quick! else she will have changed her pose" (219). Here commence several narrative clips that recall scenes from Brontë's *Villette*—transpositions, almost, of *Villette* into *Middlemarch*. The chapters that render the honeymoon journey could even be read as Eliot's reading of Brontë's novel, for Eliot, we have seen, read her own elopement by means of *Villette*. Dorothea's pose, for a start, introduces a Brontëan echo: reminiscent of Lucy, Dorothea is "clad in Quakerish grey drapery" as she "dreamily" looks past "the reclining Ariadne, then called the Cleopatra, [who] lies in the marble voluptuousness of her beauty." The reader of *Villette* may recall Lucy's troubled relation to the sensuous Cleopatra (who "lay half-reclined on a couch"), from whom Lucy disclaims all affinity (herself garbed in Quaker gray, looking like a nun) but whom she begins oddly to desire and to resemble when she tells how she "sank supine into a luxury of calm before ninety-nine out of a hundred of the exhibited frames" in the gallery.*

Villette and *Middlemarch* ostensibly oppose the voluptuous statue of Cleopatra to the devout and sexless Christian woman. Consistently, however, both novels' heroines linger over a double (re)pose. Dorothea, in particular, wavers at the hymen between the pull of virginity and the pull of marriage, stalling conventional visions of a honeymoon maiden being inducted into sensual ecstasy. Will's friend, Naumann, renders this antithesis which quickly dissolves its own distinctions:

> What do you think of that for a fine bit of antithesis? . . . There lies antique beauty, not corpse-like even in death, but arrested in the complete contentment of its sensuous perfection: and here stands beauty in its breathing life, with the consciousness of Christian centuries in its bosom. But she should be dressed as a nun; I think she looks almost what you call a Quaker; I would dress her as a nun in my picture. However, she is married! I saw her wedding-ring on that wonderful left hand, otherwise I should have thought the sallow *Geistlicher* was her father. (220)

*See Brontë's chapter entitled "Cleopatra" in *Villette*, 270–82, especially 274–75.

Naumann's surprise that this "nun" is married indirectly questions—as, indeed, the book questions—the viability of Anna Jameson's plan for a married Sisters of Charity. Could marriage, with its call to femininity and "domestic reality," cohabit with unrestrained religious ardor? And, if so, could this religious ardor keep itself "pure" from sensuality? Naumann's further assessment that Dorothea is "sensuous force controlled by spiritual passion" attributes this fix to the married nun. And though spirituality here seems ascendant, one might have expected sensuous "passion" held in rein by spiritual "force."

Sensuality's encroachment upon spiritual vows spreads further now, to stronger echoing vibrations from *Villette*. As if she were writing a day-time version of Lucy's drugged wandering, Eliot renders the "dreamlike strangeness of [Dorothea's] bridal life" (224). Whereas Lucy formed delusions around what she suspected was her loss of marriage plans, marriage itself forms the nightmare in *Middlemarch*. Dorothea's haunting takes the form of the sensual desires she avoids through her virginal marriage and, yet, increasingly seeks outside of it. Brontë used Catholic Belgium as a setting for assaults of sensuality upon Lucy's English Protestant calm. In a similar way, Eliot makes Rome assault Dorothea with its "vast wreck of ambitious ideals, sensuous and spiritual, mixed confusedly with the signs of breathing forgetfulness and degradation, [which] at first jarred her as with an electric shock, and then urged themselves on her with that ache belonging to a glut of confused ideas which check the flow of emotion" (225).

The density of this prose, its thick extravagance, strikingly recalls the peculiar density of Lucy's dream sequence. Even Lucy's paranoia at the festival, arising as she wanders among an array of costumed burghers and pasteboard scenes, has been recaptured here, conveying Dorothea's sexual and religious discomfort with "the weight of unintelligible Rome":

> She had ended oftenest by choosing to drive out to the Campagna where she could feel alone with the earth and sky, away from the oppressive masquerade of ages, in which her own life too seemed to become a masque with enigmatical costumes. . . . Ruins and basilicas, palaces and colossi, set in the midst of a sordid present, where all that was living and warm-blooded seemed sunk in the deep degeneracy of a superstition divorced from reverence; the dimmer but yet eager Titanic life gazing and struggling on walls and ceilings; the long vistas of white forms whose marble eyes seemed to hold the monotonous light of an alien world. (225)

Every image weights this scene with strivings that have strangely, disturbingly, congealed, yielding marble eyes and, again, arrested forms.

The yearnings of her marriage are dimmed by this "monotonous light of an alien world," as if the adage "See Rome and die" promises Dorothea no dying of ecstasy. Indeed, Casaubon pointedly informs her that "in your case I would propose an emendation and say, See Rome as a bride, and live thenceforth as a happy wife" (231). Her husband's substitution of wifehood for ecstasy strikes the right chord for rendering Dorothea's domestic fix as a virginal wife.

I have argued that Dorothea meets desire on her journey to Rome. Countering her congealed relations, the spur to her more electric alienation is Will, who is studying art in Rome (on his own educational journey, as it happens). When Dorothea first met Will, she had been struck by the fact that his mouth and chin were "of a more prominent, threatening aspect" than his grandmother's—a hint of his sexual threat. Nonetheless, when she meets him in Rome, Dorothea sits between the fire and the window as if poised between heat and light. Emblematic of this change, Dorothea, we are told, "felt that she was getting quite new notions as to the significance of [the] Madonnas" (246) she sees in Rome. We are told as well that "some things which had seemed monstrous to her were gathering intelligibility and even a natural meaning." Yet while Dorothea crosses into desire, Will's chivalric worship indicates that women wear the face of God for men. The insistence on his courtly love ("the inclination to fall at the Saint's feet and kiss her robe" [249]) shows that he misses her in just the way that Lacan describes: "The whole of his realisation in the sexual relation comes down to fantasy." (Even Will fashions Dorothea as a saintly wife: "It was beautiful to see how Dorothea's eyes turned with wifely anxiety and beseeching to Mr. Casaubon: she would have lost some of her halo if she had been without that duteous preoccupation" [250].)

Against the grain of masculine worship, the narrative gathers women together, collects them around its depictions of pleasure. Eliot, though always in hesitant shades, places her premium on autoeroticism. Some of the novel's most sexual scenes do not involve women with men, but women with women, or women with gems. Even a scene that would seem to offer "women with men" gets turned, slyly, toward a split focus: the man intent on worshiping his saint; the saint, unconsciously, intent on handling gems. In the honeymoon chapters, this suggestive episode takes place around the cameos that Dorothea is buying for her sister. Recalling the novel's earlier scene in which she and Celia inspect their mother's jewels, this encounter, once again, sexualizes women's gems. Will and Dorothea, in a ritual of desire, falter around the cameos they discuss: she declines interest, while "having a cameo bracelet in her hand" ("No, frankly,

I don't think them a great object in life"); he would convince her that she should care ("I fear you are a heretic about art generally" [251]). Yet even if he challenges Dorothea's asceticism, telling her "the best piety is to enjoy," his aestheticism, by which he worships her ("You *are* a poem" [256]), still precludes an account of her pleasure. When Dorothea returns from her honeymoon journey to Casaubon's Lowick (a sexual pun?), her home appears sterile, while she emerges as ever more sensuous. A "uniform whiteness" hangs outside her window; the furniture seems to her to have shrunk; and "the stag in the tapestry looked more like a ghost." Dorothea, by contrast, is "glowing" from her morning toilette, exposing "warm red life in her lips." A "gem-like brightness" adorns "her coiled hair," as if her body were becoming jeweled. And, as if to prepare for evocations of pleasure soon to follow, the narrator tells us that Dorothea laid down the cameo cases and "unconsciously kept her hands on them" (307).

It is remarkable how in Eliot, too, not just in Brontë, spirituality encourages autoeroticism, for this growing sensuality, just described, is succeeded by a spiritual experience that sustains it. We are told that "[Dorothea's] sense of connection with a manifold pregnant existence had to be kept up painfully as an inward vision" (307). Outwardness, in *Middlemarch*, is reached through the avenues of Protestant inwardness. This inward vision of outward connections—Eliot's version of material concealment—cups these connections in ears and eyes, and catches their intensities, which seem to expand on "the lips and chin." For Dorothea gazes upon Will's grandmother, a portrait that functions as icon and mirror. Again, we are centered on St. Theresa's pulse and on the material relations that beat, concealed, behind their "formulas":

> All existence seemed to beat with a lower pulse than her own, and her religious faith was a solitary cry, the struggle out of a nightmare in which every object was withering and shrinking away from her. . . . Dorothea could fancy that it was alive now—the delicate woman's face which yet had a headstrong look, a peculiarity difficult to interpret. . . . She felt a new companionship with it, *as if it had an ear for her and could see how she was looking at it.* Here was a woman who had known some difficulty about marriage. Nay, the colours deepened, the lips and chin seemed to get larger, the hair and eyes seemed to be sending out light, *the face was masculine and beamed on her with that full gaze* that tells her on whom it falls that she is too interesting for the slightest movement of her eyelid to pass unnoticed and uninterpreted. The vivid presentation came like a pleasant glow to Dorothea. (308; my emphasis)

Protestant inwardness, to which both narrator and reader are privy, hands Dorothea, in Feuerbachian sympathy, to the elsewhere of a human species that looks on her with "full gaze"; and yet, it sees and recognizes Dorothea as herself a gazer ("could see how she was looking at it"). This gaze upon a gaze, a complication between Dorothea's projections and returns, causes Dorothea to graze an other who seems to be almost, strangely, within her, suffusing Dorothea with "deepened" "colours"—perhaps a trace of her mother's gems, whose colors seemed to "penetrate" her. Deftly, it seems, this passage is redeeming "the vibrations from a woman's glance"—that potential to disturb professional focus—assuring us that "the vivid presentation came like a pleasant glow to Dorothea." This "pleasant glow," subtly sexualized, even becomes a feminine embrace, as if a face could cradle a face, hold and rock with lips and eyes. And yet the text, as if demure in the face of sexuality, shifts this spiritual experience toward something that is sexual and spiritual in a mottled way.

In fact, the cunning confusion here of sexual identities—the miniature suddenly beams on her with a masculine visage—supports an Irigarayan reading: autoeroticism (in the sense of a woman's touching a woman by means of mirroring) can at least secure for women some shade of "their" pleasure apart from men, even as they proceed to seemingly more conventional relations. The carefully planted phrase "the lips and chin seemed to get larger," along with the assertion "the face was masculine," surely calls up Will, even as it refuses to name him, relying, then, on the reader's remembrance that "[Will's] mouth and chin [had] a more prominent, threatening aspect than belonged to the type of the grandmother's miniature" (104). Just as the earlier "mouth and chin" changes slightly in the rendering here to "lips and chin" (nice from an Irigarayan point of view), so, too, another modulation appears: the icon's gaze "that tells her on whom it falls that she is too interesting for the slightest movement of her eyelid to pass unnoticed and uninterpreted" makes Dorothea an object of attention without fashioning her, as Will so often does, as an object of art. The purifying, but no less sensual, mediation of a woman's visage burns off that disturbing aura, opening the way for new (and safer?) possibilities with men. Indeed, later on, when Dorothea discovers new dimensions of desire with Will, we are informed that "the presence of that delicate miniature, so like a living face that she knew, helped to concentrate her feelings." Or, as the narrator implicates the reader in affirming Dorothea's concentration of her feelings: "Can any one who has rejoiced in woman's tenderness think it a reproach to her that she took the little oval picture in her palm and made a bed for it there . . . ?" (591–92), as if the clue to her sexual pleasure will rest, recline, in the bed of her hand.

Although these depictions may be, overtly, ones of "sympathy," Eliot's novel clearly suggests that spiritual experience can nurture (and intensify) sexual desire. How fitting, then, to this sense of mirroring, repetition, intensification, and desire is Casaubon's suspicion that "in religion [Will] could be, as long as it suited him, the facile echo of Dorothea's vagaries." The notion that Will, in religion, "echoes" Dorothea's "vagaries" begins to uncover the intricacies of Dorothea's religious ardor that spells desire. We have seen how Will echoes the iconographic miniature of a woman's face, or how it echoes him. This echoing effect suggests the causally ambiguous part Will plays for Dorothea: does he cause or reflect her desire? For surely it is possible that the feminine aspect of Will mediates to Dorothea her perception and enjoyment of the erotic gaze of women.

I began by discussing Dorothea's honeymoon—her exile from Middlemarch to Rome, which drops her into desire—and have ended by discussing her return home to Lowick. The rest of the novel seeks to define what "home" might mean in "the home epic" (as the narrator puts it) of St. Theresa. More significant still, this final phase fashions her work as desire in domestic spheres. Before we can examine this conclusion, however, we must first consider whose story does not receive a telling—rests opaque—in the novel's home epic, and which characters, consequently, cannot embrace their material concealment for themselves.

A Rhetoric of Spacing and the Unexamined Hole

There are other border-runners. There are hymeneal men and hymeneal women who are themselves the hymeneal membranes between desiring bodies. There are bodies in the hole—indeed, who make the hole—between the "two" who revel in their lack (a lack that, also, to the point of pleasure pains them). If pleasure depends upon self-alienations (what I have called self-partings for pleasure), but pleasure needing others leads to social dangers, the question becomes: how can one achieve the self-separations needed for pleasure without also feeding familiar exploitations? Or, to put the question in the realm of home epics: how can one be at home with lack without relations of stable domination? Here the material concealment of women's work of desire intersects the unseen labors of servants, for servants open the space of desire without any access to lack for themselves.

To begin, we must grasp that *Middlemarch* oscillates between different images of lack, conveyed *spatially*. That is to say, like *Villette*, *Middlemarch* oscillates between those spaces depicted as vistas, which make expansions of relations possible, and spaces represented as blanks, which limit relational possibilities. Presumably, the way we can distinguish between various spaces is to fathom how a character is positioned towards them. A space is a vista, if a character appropriately nurtures lack. A space is a blank, if a character denies lack or tries to fill it so as to close spacing. Either way, *Middlemarch* oddly values lacking as the only means of ultimately not lacking.

In the novel, intricate renderings emerge in which relationships are depicted as spacing, and sex is conveyed as fracture and loss. Chapter 62 offers one of the many scenes between Will and Dorothea in which their sexual nearness revolves around liquids and solids, proximity and distance, open windows and angles of walls. On first reading, this scene appears to trace a standard Victorian line: characters morally and spiritually renouncing sexual possibility. Will has come to take leave of Dorothea, renouncing his claim for what he regards as her financial well-being; Dorothea stands ready to sacrifice her own claims for what she regards as Will's love for Rosamond. The approach and deferral, expansion and nearness the text will eventually write for Dorothea (first with Rosamond, only later with Will) is adumbrated through spatial images. The pain of lack— represented as making these relationships possible—finds figuration in the open window. Around this architectural "hole" in domestic space, Eliot arranges her characters' movements.

The scene is one of parting and, also, preparation, on the level of plot. The spacing that is rhetorically rendered here returns with a vengeance (and with greater sexual tension) in the later scene between Dorothea and Rosamond. As in that encounter, a servant prepares for this sexual contact by conducting these characters into proximity—also by opening the requisite "hole": when Dorothea requests her servant to "open the shutters for me," the servant replies, "The shutters are open, madam" (678). The servant next plays the role of go-between ("Mrs. Kell close to his elbow said—'Mrs. Casaubon is coming in, sir' "), the effect of which is the building of suspense (and desire) for the reader. Then the account is off and running, with the play of desire rendered through the characters' careful arrangement around the open window:

> Will turned round quickly, and the next moment Dorothea was entering. As Mrs. Kell closed the door behind her they met: each was looking at the other, and consciousness was overflowed by something that suppressed utterance. It was not confusion that kept them silent, for they both felt that parting was near, and there is no shamefacedness in a sad parting. (679)

> Will rose from his chair with the last word and went—he hardly knew where; but it was to the projecting window nearest him, which had been open as now about the same season a year ago, when he and Dorothea had stood within

it and talked together. . . . He seemed to have turned away from her as if she too had been part of the unfriendly world. . . . Then in her ardent way, wanting to plead with him, she moved from her chair and went in front of him to her old place in the window. . . . When Will saw her there, he gave a start and moved backward out of the window, without meeting her glance. Dorothea was hurt by this movement. (680)

But Will at last turned away from his portfolio and approached the window again. . . . "I have not spoken too strongly now," said Will, leaning back against the angle of the wall. . . . "What I care more for than I can ever care for anything else is absolutely forbidden to me. . . . Of course I shall go on living as a man might do who had seen heaven in a trance." . . . It could not be fairly called wooing a woman to tell her that he would never woo her. It must be admitted to be a ghostly kind of wooing. (681)

They were parted all the same, but—Dorothea drew a deep breath and felt her strength return—she could think of him unrestrainedly. . . . It was as if some hard icy pressure had melted, and her consciousness had room to expand. . . . The joy was not the less—perhaps it was the more complete just then—because of the irrevocable parting. (683)

As in *Middlemarch* generally, spiritual renunciation, which takes on lack and intensifies it through this acceptance, *creates* sexual tension in the scene. This renunciatory jockeying about the open window registers desire in the strongest terms. And this desire is kept alive by Will's religious ardor: to "go on living as a man might do who had seen heaven in a trance" (a phrase close to Brontë's for Lucy's euphoric wooing of Ginevra). In fact, this particular erotics of fracture—parting as the fracture that makes relations possible but union forbidden—does not subside when Dorothea and Will reunite at the end. This "ghostly kind of wooing" gives way only to the more intense spacing between the women, Dorothea and Rosamond. And there, in later scenes, Dorothea, not Will, sees "heaven in a trance," when her spiritual mission turns (auto)erotic.

It is the servant, I have said, who initiates contact between parting lovers by ushering Dorothea (and the reader) into the room with Will. We can now see that the novel's least canny grip on relational boundaries involves the *Middlemarch* domestics. The novel's rhetoric of spacing does not stress, or even account for, the work they perform in initiating and mediating the novel's major dramas.* We may miss, for instance, the way a servant's body finds itself positioned in the space between characters or

---

*W. R. Greg, in his 1862 treatise, "Why Are Women Redundant?" does not include domestic servants in his calculations of redundant women because "they fulfill both essentials of women's being; *they are supported by and they minister to men*" (436).

is represented (almost in absentia) as producing the meal or opening the shutters around which characters play out important scenes. For example, a servant emerges in parentheses to take the baby when Celia confronts Dorothea in discussion: "You are not to go [says Celia] till Mr. Lydgate says you may go. And he has not said so yet (here you are, nurse; take baby and walk up and down the gallery). Besides, you have got a wrong notion in your head as usual, Dodo—I can see that: it vexes me" (531). In the scene where Fred asserts that "all choice of words is slang [that] marks a class," the servant becomes a ghostly presence who performs domestic labors as brother and sister carry on their argument. Commands in this scene are addressed to the servant, to which there is no reply ("Knock at Mr. Fred's door again, Pritchard, and tell him it has struck half-past ten"); the servant's movements are used to mark the resumption of dialogue ("when the servant left the room," "when the servant had cleared the table"); and signs of the servant's labor appear without any mention of the servant himself ("Ah, here comes my grilled bone"). Significantly, this chapter, which contains so many hints of the servant's ghostly labor, also, for the first time, mentions Mary Garth—an introduction that marks her as a domestic.

At the level of plot, the novel's servant-characters perform essential work. They advance the plot by participating in stratagems or by delivering messages that move one character into important encounters with another ("[Lydgate] had been stopped by a servant on horseback with a message calling him in to a house of some importance. . . . The servant was Sir James Chettam's, and the house was Lowick Manor" [305]). One can sense the difficulty of deeming these servant-characters "characters," for they are not "well-rounded" in the usual novelistic sense: they are not shown as pained, desiring, or conflicted in the realms of love, marriage, or vocation.* Often, they are not given names. Servants, in multiple senses, function as boundary lines, then; they mark class position *as well as sanity*. Bourgeois characters talk about servants as necessary companions for young ladies abroad or as necessary class markers or signs of propriety for young widows at home. Relating concern over Dorothea's companions, the narrator remarks, "It was not credible that Dorothea as a young widow would think of living alone in the house at Lowick. . . . Mrs. Cadwallader said, privately, 'You will certainly go mad in that house alone, my dear. You will see visions'" (581).

If servants function as boundaries, however, these borders are perme-

---

*It is the case, of course, that they often register their employer's emotions (shades of Lucy Snowe with Miss Marchmont).

able, for representations of the women characters touch upon the depictions of servants. Mrs. Garth, for instance, performs the same domestic
chores we see or hear about being performed by the more ghostly servants. Her household routines—making pies, washing clothes, minding
children, giving lessons—mark her as a domestic servant in her own
home, thus conveying that other servants' labor is anything but effortless.
Even Dorothea, the novel's premier lady, substitutes for hired labor: "And
when [Casaubon] had seen Dorothea he believed that he had found even
more than he demanded: she might really be such a helpmate to him as
would enable him to dispense with a hired secretary" (313). In a less direct
association, the text juxtaposes Lydgate's fantastic meditation on Rosamond as one "who would create order in the home and accounts with still
magic" with his intention to "hire servants who will not break things"
(387). Later, when Rosamond appears to Lydgate as one who creates domestic disorder, Lydgate displaces her reckless management onto the servants: "It is wonderful [he says] what an amount of money slips away in
our housekeeping. I suppose the servants are careless" (699). Borders,
then, between women and servants crosscut their lines, even though Dorothea as gentry is most removed from this connection, Mrs. Garth as (the
wife of a) failed bourgeois, least removed.

Another character tests domestic borders. As we have seen, Mary
Garth performs domestic labor as a special instance of the domestic servant: the relative who is paid to nurse a sick uncle. This duty puts her at
the brink of a hymen—a family hymen—where Mary not only forms the
border between the family and the family's outsides (Mary *as* a hymeneal
membrane), but where she threatens to break it open to outside influence
(Mary as a break in the border).* The text, as we have seen, writes her into
family dramas of sexual and economic desire. In her roles as messenger to
Featherstone and "manager of [Featherstone's] household," she is clearly
poised at the family borders she is paid to maintain. The novel even
suggestively slides from a depiction of Mary as nurse to a portrait of Mary
as wife, when Trumbull, the doctor, notes her as "sensible": "She minds

---

*I am evoking Clément and Cixous's famous theorization of the maid/governess/
nurse as "the hole in the social cell" (*Newly Born Woman*), made famous, in part, by
Gallop's discussion of it in her essay "Keys to Dora" (*Daughter's Seduction*). There Gallop elucidates the hysteric's (and, later, the governess's) ambiguous role as one who
breaks the family circle ("the cell walls burst" [135]) but who is also contained by it
("the family assimilates her otherness, and like an amoeba, finds its single cell revital-
ized, stronger than before" [133]). I purposely slide from "cell" to "hymen" because
Derrida's figure of the hymen, which simultaneously signifies virginity and marriage,
aptly applies to the borders of the family itself.

what she is doing, sir. That is a great point in a woman, and a great point for our friend upstairs, poor dear old soul. A man whose life is of any value should think of his wife as a nurse: that is what I should do if I married" (347). And yet, the relatives' suspicions of her as one who might receive Featherstone's patrimony ("all eyes were turned on her as a possible legatee, or one who might get access to iron chests") marks her as poised to break open the boundary, wielding the key that might open onto capital. Mary indeed is drawn into Featherstone's capital/seminal wish to consummate a final transaction. As is true with Dorothea, Mary's *refusal* of the offered key breaks the family hymen, opening it to the likes of Rigg and Raffles. In relation to the Vincy family, moreover, Mary both sutures established borders (she sews handkerchiefs for Rosamond's wedding) and pressures the strict recognitions that exclude her. The novel records this contested boundary in its humorous depiction of Mrs. Vincy, who "smiled towards her three little girls, aged from seven to eleven": "But in that smiling glance she was obliged to include Mary Garth, whom the three girls had got into a corner to make her tell them stories" (693).

By such a move, by placing Mary's body in the way of Mrs. Vincy, by making Mary a forced inclusion that we are made to feel as forced, Eliot makes us see a concealment: Mary as a covered-over "hole" in the family's "social cell." It is this Symbolic hole—the unrepresented body that rises up opaque—that we are further made to feel in the space of desire between women, as *Middlemarch* makes its turn toward home.

St. Theresa Feels the Hole Between Them

Irigaray wants women, at the very least, to feel for themselves the Symbolic hole that they represent, to embrace this hole and feel it between them—a clue to their material opacity. It is time now to see how *Middlemarch*, as it draws to its close, speaks to this urge, and how, as I have consistently promised, Eliot (like Brontë) reveals the limits we must consider to Irigaray's hopes.

Indeed, as *Middlemarch* approaches its climax, numerous representations collide: nightmares in marriage; mirrorings between women; passions of sainthood; and discomforts with money. Bodies' borders become confused as the narrative demonstrates class complications of projection and return in mirroring relations. Most significant, in this regard, and indicative of intimacy's strong ties to concealed incriminations, we now discover a great chain of feminine mirrorings. Dorothea's marriage is mir-

rored by Rosamond's; Rosamond's mirror image is passed through her
poor relation, Mary Garth; and Mary's domestic labor is mirrored by the
novel's many servants, so that even if Dorothea never meets Mary Garth
in *Middlemarch*, and even if Dorothea is most removed from the domestic
servant class, her image becomes entangled in theirs, and their images—
Mary's and the servants'—are projected on the mirrors that confuse the
seemingly opposite identities of Rosamond and Dorothea. This is a chain
of material relations, of class relations, that becomes visible as concealed
relations when Dorothea and Rosamond turn their longings toward each
other—and exchange loss.

There is another aspect to this spiritual framework and its rendering
of unseen material relations. According to M. H. Abrams, in the final
movement of Romantic teleologies, which generally appear as educational journeys, the masculine protagonist discovers a "higher unity" after
passing through desire and self-alienation. The drive toward closure is figured by rediscovery of a home and by "reunion with a feminine other"
(the very fantasy Lacan sought to challenge). In *Middlemarch*, the protagonist is a feminized saint, not a masculine artist; and reunion with the feminine other, stunning climax though it is, prepares for heterosexual marriage. The novel shifts the desire for home to at-home-ness with desire
that, in turn, keeps the feminine saint not-at-home. If Dorothea, more
importantly, seeks the unity of saintly identity, she ends up embroiled in
the multiple "hints of [the] imprints of identities." And 'God', or divinity,
figures the difference between a woman's projection and return. Dorothea's (auto)eroticism even issues from odd, though spiritual, partings
from herself. This pleasure in parting entangles Dorothea with the bodies
who underwrite but also threaten her established identity.

Indeed, the novel's approach to climax—women who exchange in the
heat of their sorrows—grows out of the construction of women as rivals.
This representation of rivalry, furthermore, as Irigaray would predict,
emerges from mirrors. Early in the novel, the narrator shows how Rosamond gazed upon "the Miss Brookes"—the sisters, here, a mirroring
pair. In the context of explaining that marriage to Lydgate stood for Rosamond as the "prospect of rising in rank and getting a little nearer to that
celestial condition on earth in which she would have nothing to do with
vulgar people," the narrator muses:

> It was part of Rosamond's cleverness to discern very subtly the faintest aroma
> of rank, and once when she had seen the Miss Brookes accompanying their
> uncle at the county assizes, and seated among the aristocracy, she had envied

them, notwithstanding their plain dress. . . . For Rosamond, though she would never do anything that was disagreeable to her, was industrious; and now more than ever she was active in sketching her landscapes and market-carts and portraits of friends, in practising her music, and in being from morning till night her own standard of a perfect lady. . . . But Mrs. Plymdale thought that Rosamond had been educated to a ridiculous pitch, for what was the use of accomplishments which would be all laid aside as soon as she was married? (195–97)

Rosamond's gaze upon the "Miss Brookes" situates Irigaray's and Feuerbach's issues of projection/return in relation to class. By comparing herself to the sisters' "rank," Rosamond envisions herself as a lady—a particularly "celestial," if not exactly saintly, perch. And yet the narrator splits a seam between Rosamond's projection of aristocratic promise and its too enthusiastic, newly monied return: The passage admits the "industry" required to transform the manufacturer's daughter into a lady of rank. This class crack alludes, for instance, to the plainness of the sisters' dress, over and against what Eliot fashions as Rosamond's eager self-commodification as a luxury item. Her observer, Mrs. Plymdale, hints that Rosamond may have to forsake her celestial heights and her garments—her "accomplishments" themselves a class masquerade—when she gets married.

In a later passage, the novel more pointedly draws our attention to the women's class distinctions: "When the drawing-room door opened and Dorothea entered, there was a sort of contrast not infrequent in country life when the habits of the different ranks were less blent than now" (470). Subtly, however, this class fracture gets reconceived as the contrast between Dorothea's effortless taste and Rosamond's studied presentation of herself. Following a long description of Dorothea's classical dress ("if she had entered before a still audience as Imogene or Cato's daughter, the dress might have seemed right enough"), we, as readers, are focused on a gaze that takes place between women, and we ourselves are constructed as that "calm observer" who, along with the narrator, would note Rosamond's excessive display:

To Rosamond [Dorothea] was one of those county divinities not mixing with Middlemarch mortality, whose slightest marks of manner or appearance were worthy of her study; moreover, Rosamond was not without satisfaction that Mrs. Casaubon should have an opportunity of studying *her*. What is the use of being exquisite if you are not seen by the best judges? . . . Dorothea put out her hand with her usual simple kindness, and looked admiringly at Lydgate's lovely bride—aware that there was a gentleman standing at a dis-

tance, but seeing him merely as a coated figure at a wide angle. The gentleman was too much occupied with the presence of the one woman to reflect
on the contrast between the two—a contrast that would certainly have been
striking to a calm observer. They were both tall, and their eyes were on a
level; but imagine Rosamond's infantine blondness and wondrous crown of
hair-plaits, with her pale-blue dress of a fit and fashion so perfect that no
dressmaker could look at it without emotion, a large embroidered collar
which it was to be hoped all beholders would know the price of, her small
hands duly set off with rings, and that controlled self-conscious manner
which is the expensive substitute for simplicity. (470–71)

The effect here is twofold. By emphasizing Dorothea's "simplicity,"
the text turns a class distinction into a character trait, and good character
here is gauged as a matter of superior taste. It is not understood as her
own class dress—ease and timelessness as the privileged garments of those
who need not work at display. Additionally, Rosamond's commodification, complete with "the expensive substitute" of her "controlled self-
consciousness of manner," appears to be more of a character flaw than a
class rite of passage for an aspiring bourgeoise. By drawing this contrast
(here I would point to a second effect), the novel *obscures* its own construction of the women's mirrored "looks." For their mirroring reveals their
common obligation to dress as women whose class position is determined by
men ("[Dorothea] looked admiringly at Lydgate's lovely bride"). *Middlemarch* has convinced us, after all, that Dorothea's choice between Casaubon's will and Will Ladislaw will determine her class; just as Rosamond's
ability to project herself onto Dorothea is predicated upon Rosamond's
class rise through marriage. This mutual desire, then, to study one another, to the point of Dorothea's seeing Will "merely as a coated figure at
a wide angle," stresses their conjunction as objects of the gaze. For even
in a moment of being gazers, each absorbed by what she sees at her other's
surface ("their eyes were on a level"), their gazes are turned back onto
themselves, as brides who are the objects of study by men. This last point
is made abundantly clear when the passage shifts from Dorothea's gaze, to
Will's gaze, to the "calm observer's" gaze. Once again, the reader is positioned as a man who, unlike a woman, can distance "himself" from the
self-reflexive "looks" that entrap women of diverse class positions.

A chapter epigraph, which imagines "full souls," captures the complications of a woman-turned-on-woman gaze: "Full souls are double
mirrors, making still / An endless vista of fair things before, / Repeating
things behind" (789). This canny sense of mirror turned on mirror, repeating and confusing reflections to infinity, recalls Irigaray's attempts to

fracture the imaginary dyad, to produce what I have called a "fractured sameness." When women who are fashioned as mirrors to men turn their gazes toward each other, they are then returned upon themselves with complications. Difference is not erased in such a vista (an "endless vista"). Rather, the likeness each mirror produces repeats identification so as to shatter singularity; the observing "I" registers each image as *infinitely implicated* in its other. Infinite imprints fill the space between the mirrors, between one and two.

Preparatory to a climax of mirror turned on mirror and the concealed incriminations it crucially reveals, we are given Dorothea's dark night of the soul. Cooked up by Feuerbach's spiritual materialism, this scene depicts Dorothea's connection to "the species"—hence, the renewal of her sacred vocation. Her saintly mission to "save Rosamond" will end up portrayed as a work of desire, although Eliot cites Wordsworth's "Ode to Duty" in the chapter's epigraph, as if to signal that renunciation returns her to sympathy. Granted, references to "the vacant room" where she holds her vigil, "the waves of suffering" that engulf her, and "the spiritual struggles of man" which overtake her, all contribute to this scene's ascetic tinge. But Dorothea's suffering, typical of *Middlemarch*, shifts towards a lacking that represents desire. Thus are we told that "[Will and Dorothea's] nearness was a parting vision: she discovered her passion to herself in the unshrinking utterance of despair" (844).

This portrait of despair returns, moreover, to the question of exchange. Dorothea fears that Will has withdrawn his capital/seminal investment in her, failing to offer fair price for her goods: "Why had he brought his cheap regard and his lip-born words to her who had nothing paltry to give in exchange? . . . to make her believe that he gave her the whole price of her heart, [when he] knew that he had spent it half before" (845). Dorothea is shown, now, as confronting something that she registers as her own commodification, even as a lady; here she imagines that "her heart" has been translated into monetary terms—whereas, presumably, it is only her body that a masculine economy can commodify. In light of this inner confrontation, Dorothea "force[s] herself to think of [her grief] as bound up with another woman's life" (845). Dorothea's Feuerbachian I-Thou relation is thus more complex than a simple discovery of fellow-feeling.* It is shown bound up with her status as "exchanged," a

---

*This segment, nonetheless, fashions her sympathy as the humanistic religious projection of the self, outward to others, that Feuerbach discusses. The spiritual construction of this awakening to species is unmistakable: "And what sort of crisis might not this be in three lives whose contact with hers laid an obligation on her as if they had

status she shares with her rival, Rosamond. As much as Dorothea has been setting herself apart as sacred rescuer, compelling pain to silence, the text now makes her "clutch" pain, to the point of cutting her at her surface, where another woman stands at her brink. Significant for Eliot's web of desire and domestic relations, this climactic encounter between two women occurs "at home," as if to fix (on) the family hymen.

We should note the different readings we could give to this scene. On the level of plot, Dorothea's ministry cements both herself and Rosamond into domesticity, by cementing them both back into marriage. This domestic securement suggests, at its worst, that the family can still contain the woman (in the sense of controlling her), even when she is opened by desire. Read as Martin and Mohanty might read, this climax could demonstrate what a bourgeois woman must deny—the loss that opens onto pleasurable longing—if she would "clutch" her bourgeois privilege. Seen in this way, a woman's self-sexual pleasure is the sacrificial lamb to her marriage. Seen differently, however, this scene could be read as asserting what the novel as a whole may assert: women need autoerotic relations that caress "their" desire in the midst of their marriage. Consistently, *Middlemarch* shapes women's sexual longings in the context of relations with women (or even with themselves), as if to plead for the maintenance of pleasure—a trace of the lips that might loom larger and redder than the hymen. This plea for the lips would explain why the novel's climax, in length and intensity of depiction, is a scene between women—not the scene between Will and Dorothea, which follows as an echo.*

However it may function, this scene assures that whatever might be 'spiritual' doubles back upon whatever might be 'sexual':

> Dorothea's face had become animated, and as it beamed on Rosamond very close to her, she felt something like bashful timidity before a superior, in the presence of this self-forgetful ardour. . . . Rosamond, with an overmastering pang, as if a wound within her had been probed, burst into hysterical

---

been suppliants bearing the sacred branch? The objects of her rescue were not to be sought out by her fancy: they were chosen for her. She yearned towards the perfect Right, that it might make a throne within her, and rule her errant will. 'What should I do—how should I act now, this very day if I could clutch my own pain, and compel it to silence, and think of those three!' . . . Far off in the bending sky was the pearly light; and she felt the largeness of the world and the manifold wakings of men to labour and endurance. She was a part of that involuntary, palpitating life, and could neither look out on it from her luxurious shelter as a mere spectator, nor hide her eyes in selfish complaining" (846).

*That is to say, I am referring to the structural weight of the scene, where form speaks louder than theme or even narrator's voice.

crying. . . . [Dorothea] was beginning to fear that she should not be able to suppress herself enough to the end of this meeting, and while her hand was still resting on Rosamond's lap, though the hand underneath it was withdrawn, she was struggling against her own rising sobs. (853–54)

"Marriage is so unlike everything else [said Dorothea to Rosamond]. There is something even awful in the nearness it brings.". . . The waves of her own sorrow, from out of which she was struggling to save another, rushed over Dorothea with conquering force. She stopped in speechless agitation, not crying, but feeling as if she were being inwardly grappled. Her face had become of a deathlier paleness, her lips trembled, and she pressed her hands helplessly on the hands that lay under them.

Rosamond, taken hold of by an emotion stronger than her own—hurried along in a new movement which gave all things some new, awful, undefined aspect—could find no words, but involuntarily she put her lips to Dorothea's forehead which was very near her, and then for a minute the two women clasped each other as if they had been in a shipwreck. (855–56)

The revulsion of feeling in Dorothea was too strong to be called joy. It was a tumult in which the terrible strain of the night and morning made a resistant pain:—she could only perceive that this would be joy when she had recovered her power of feeling it. (856–57)

This encounter around a woman's wound, being "probed" by another, puts the reader at the brink between seemingly separate moments of Protestant inwardness. Each woman is shown as engulfed by her own private apocalypse, yet crucially, each woman's sobs rush over her from outside. By situating in the embrace *between women* what might read like St. Theresa's ecstasy, the text displays the wound and the jewel of a feminine fracture. This clasping allows a woman to feel herself as a hole in the dominant Symbolic by allowing her to feel another woman's hole. This clasping further allows both women to touch the opacity of their sexual pleasure: "a new movement which gave all things some new, awful, undefined aspect." This shipwreck, that is to say, proves orgasmic (waves, rush, conquering force, inward grappling, deathlier paleness, new movement, lips, revulsion, tumult). Compared with the language of Irigaray's forays, the discourse that renders this movement proves mystical:

Everything is so relentlessly immediate in this marriage of the unknowable, which can never be evaded once it has been experienced. . . . the heart of the crypt to which "God" alone descends when he has renounced modes and attributes. For this most secret virginity of the "soul" surrenders only to one who also freely offers the self in all its nakedness. This most private chamber opens only to one who is indebted to no possession for potency. (*S*, 196)

If 'God', for Irigaray, is not a centered subject but a lover who is and who loves by spacing, then 'God' hangs between Dorothea and Rosamond, probing and soothing them into implications. Figured here in the account from *Middlemarch* is a surrender between women (at the family hymen) of the "most secret virginity of the 'soul.'" The breaking open of Dorothea and Rosamond could even be described by Irigaray's mystical, imaginary formula, borrowed, it appears, from the Gospel of John: "Thus, I am to you as you are to me, mine is to yours and yours mine, I know you as you know me, you take pleasure with me as I take pleasure with you." Dorothea and Rosamond are captured by sensations that are not their own, but that still may be counted as "reflex[es] of [their] own energy." Dorothea's projections do not return in any simple way, passed, as they are, through another woman's body. One even finds here the mystic conversion of pain to desire, which Irigaray celebrates when she cunningly converts castration into autoerotic *jouissance*:

> Could it be true that not every wound need remain secret, that not every laceration was shameful? Could a sore be *holy*? . . . She is closed over this mystery where the love placed within her is hidden, revealing itself in this secret of desire. . . . Finally I see myself seeing you in this fathomless wound which is the source of our wondering comprehension and exhilaration. (*S*, 200)

> Rosamond, with an overmastering pang, as if a wound within her had been probed, burst into hysterical crying. . . . The waves of her own sorrow . . . rushed over Dorothea with conquering force. She stopped in speechless agitation, not crying, but feeling as if she were being inwardly grappled. . . . It was a tumult in which the terrible strain of the night and morning made a resistant pain:—she could only perceive that this would be joy when she had recovered her power of feeling it. (853, 855–57)

One wonders how much of this chapter's force could be traced back to Eliot's domesticated Feuerbach. Feuerbach, in Eliot's words, fashions 'God' as "the sublime desire," the yearning of "man after himself"—an autoerotic formulation, after all. 'God' thus figures the difference between projection and return, being that which escapes between men, and between a man and his own self-consciousness. Eliot, taking her cue from Feuerbach, domesticates "god-talk": divinity, along with redemption, inheres in desire's sublimity held between women, a gaping between "saint" and "supplicant" that opens onto pleasure—and guilt.

I have said that *Middlemarch* insists on presenting Dorothea as the saint, Rosamond as the supplicant. By the novel's end, however, we may realize just how much Dorothea's saintliness ("to Rosamond she was one of those county divinities not mixing with Middlemarch mortality") depends upon her struggle with her money and the privileges that this same struggle grants to her. Her mercy mission involves, for example, a class condescension, insofar as she, a lady, deigns to visit and make herself vulnerable to a manufacturer's daughter. Dorothea's saintly struggles to give away her money (she views it as a burden) are further class-privileged, since no such dissonance would occur for a woman who worked as a domestic (which may explain why Eliot does not portray Mary Garth as a saint but only as a dedicated worker). Dorothea's religious ardor is thus depicted as fed by her vast financial resource, which makes her seek to disperse it through charity.

So saint and supplicant are religious constructions that cannot be read free of class distinctions. Yet, as persistently occurs in *Middlemarch*, the moment of class positioning is also the moment of bodies bleeding into one another at the mirror. The projection of Dorothea's emotion and energy onto Rosamond, I have said, does not return in simple ways. It is passed back through Rosamond, the would-be lady whose commodification as a luxury item reflects back upon Dorothea as the domesticated saint. The mirroring is even more complex, since Rosamond's own image is returned to her through Mary Garth—who "seemed all the plainer [in that earlier scene] standing at an angle between the two nymphs—the one in the glass, and the one out of it, who looked at each other with eyes of heavenly blue" (139). Since Mary is the woman whose domestic service to their uncle makes possible Rosamond's self-manufacture as a leisured lady, Mary, in turn, mirrors for the reader the domestic servants whose stories do not receive a telling in *Middlemarch*, even though, as characters, they perform what I have called "ghostly labor" in the *Middlemarch* narrative.

Between Dorothea and Rosamond, then, a host of "others" appears opaquely. The *reader*, by virtue of mirroring chains, may feel Mary Garth as a hole between women. The self-divisions of subjectivity and the yearning of "man after himself," both of which Feuerbach discusses as 'God', make their appearance in Eliot's novel as the infinite wound in relations that subsists in the spaces between and within "individuals." This particular wound in relations parallels, but in a more political manner, Irigaray's theorizing on autoeroticism: "Woman always remains several, but she is kept from dispersion because the other is already within her and is autoerotically familiar to her. . . . Nearness so pronounced that it makes all discrimination of identity, and thus all forms of property, impossible. Woman derives pleasure from what is *so near that she cannot have it, nor have* *herself"* (*TS*, 31). "Self-satisfaction as an untaxed kind of property" proves to be a masculine venture in *Middlemarch*, for the novel defines all forms of capital in relation to men. Yet Eliot, too, like Irigaray, ponders women's exchanges, taking place at least partially outside of women's relations with men (although their class positions are based on their men). There is no way fully to measure such exchanges, especially when women are exchanging their loss. One would have to refer to the economy that does not even measure women's sexual and domestic labors performed for men. Women's work of desire produces anticapital, nonetheless. This is a hoarding of loss that, released in a rush of sobs, yields strains and "inward grappling[s]" that convert to "awful, undefined" joy. This domestic collectivity, shaped around a hole, questions the domestic axioms of individuality, family stability, and homes free from the vicissitudes of desire. A woman who is "opened" by another woman, therefore, threatens to break the family hymen, unless such an opening can be redomesticated. Lydgate's return home closes the chapter ("I was haunted by two pale faces . . . I thought that I had not done my duty in leaving you together" [857]), and signals a move to contain their displays and the spread of their wounds.*

When the scene next moves to Will and Dorothea, the denouement of this long-deferred romance is anticlimactic. The chapter's epigraph, taken from Donne, at first seems the height of sentimental subterfuge: "Love . . . makes one little room, an everywhere." But in a sense *Middlemarch* earns this sentiment. Written onto intimate relations, especially between two private "individuals," is the web of identities, self-divisions, class-divisions, and constructions of desire that make them who they are. How fitting, then, that Dorothea, before Will enters the room, is sitting down "in the library before her particular little heap of books on political economy and kindred matters, out of which she was trying to get light as to the best way of spending money so as not to injure one's neighbors" (863). Dorothea's growing discomfort with her money, though in one sense a mystified impulse toward philanthropy, can also be read as Eliot's acknowledgment that privilege oppresses by repressing the pleasures of collectivities.

Dorothea began with religious aspirations to intervene in political economy, though *Middlemarch* was quick to show her as blocked by her

---

*Indeed, the chapter ends by affirming Lydgate, in a passage that many critics cite as proof of his nobility in the face of his wife's egoism: "He had chosen this fragile creature, and had taken the burthen of her life upon his arms. He must walk as he could, carrying that burthen pitifully" (858).

"domestic reality" as a married bourgeoise. Now the text has come full circle, to an unmarried saint, who once again stands on the threshold of marriage and seeks to redistribute her former husband's capital. The novel's plot at this point reveals a cultural plot against even *bourgeois* women's roles in "handling" capital. Dorothea is still an object of exchange, even though, as she did before, she brings herself to market, and even though she must now "choose" between her husband's will and Will Ladislaw. Dorothea is going to be redomesticated; as one cut out of Casaubon's patrimony, married next to a bourgeois professional, Dorothea, in terms of Delphy's analysis, will find her place in the domestic mode of production. ("I never could do anything that I liked," she says to Celia. "I have never carried out any plan yet.") Her only outlet for religious vocation will continue to be her at-homeness-with-desire—a guerrilla position at the family hymen that wins her designation from Celia as "the dangerous part of the family machinery." Her scene with Will appropriately concludes on a note that is biblical and economic: "I shall learn what everything costs" (Luke 14).

Middlemarch ends in a curious fashion, with a class leveling among its three women—Mary, Rosamond, and Dorothea (though distinctions are not wholly lost even here). All three women are clearly domesticated. They all produce offspring (Mary blessed with boys; Rosamond narratively punished with girls). And they all inhabit the bourgeoisie vis-à-vis their husbands. Mary has risen toward the level of the others, since Fred has proved a successful Mr. Garth ("owner of the stock and furniture at Stone Court"), and Mary has proved a version of her mother ("Such as I am, you will shortly be"), securing Fred's hearth by redeeming his occasional looseness with capital. And if their community suspects the signatures that grace their respective books—since a former aspiring gentleman would surely write on the classics, an aspiring bourgeoise on the economy of cattle-feeding—the attributed signatures may actually suit Fred as a rising capitalist-farmer (*Cultivation of Green Crops and the Economy of Cattle-Feeding*) and Mary as heir to her mother's role as educational representative (*Stories of Great Men, taken from Plutarch*).* Rosamond still

*In the chapter before the finale, Mary sounds the keynote of deferral that characterizes desire, even in her comic ending with Fred ("Not so fast sir; how do you know that I would not rather defer our marriage for some years? That would leave you time to misbehave"). The point is lighthearted, yet this sexual deferral is matched in this chapter by the kind of deferral that Weber outlines in *The Protestant Ethic*. Says Mary to Fred: "Should you call it bad news to be told that you were to live at Stone Court, and manage the farm, and be remarkably prudent, and save money every year till all the stock and furniture were your own, and you were a distinguished agricultural char-

appears the would-be lady, married now to a wealthier professional; and she still appears the novel's scapegoat as a luxury item (now herself a "bird of paradise" in a gilded cage) which drains a man's capital in its triple sense of money, ideas, and self-satisfaction. (Lydgate can only write a treatise on gout and die prematurely.) Dorothea has "come down" in rank to join her "sisters," rendered by Eliot as a bourgeois woman whose vocation now consists of giving "wifely help." The attribution to Dorothea of a kind of sexual impropriety demonstrates the way in which society's constructions of sainthood shift with sexual and economic alignments:

> She was spoken of to a younger generation as a fine girl who married a sickly clergyman, old enough to be her father, and in little more than a year after his death gave up her estate to marry his cousin—young enough to have been his son, with no property and not well-born. Those who had not seen anything of Dorothea usually observed that she could not have been "a nice woman," else she would not have married either the one or the other. (896)

This melancholic end to the novel's saint provides yet another shift. Dorothea's status as a saint to the end, albeit a domesticated St. Theresa, returns her to desire, when the narrator alludes, one last time, to her religious ardor:

> Her finely-touched spirit had still its fine issues, *though they were not widely visible*. Her full nature, like that river of which Cyrus broke the strength, spent itself in channels which had no great name on the earth. But the effect of her being on those around her was *incalculably* diffusive. (896; my emphasis)

Significant for its fashioning of the bourgeois domestic, *Middlemarch* can only diffuse its own closure. The novel fails to close upon its saint. What has been the narrator's desire to tell this story to the point of completion at last falls feminine; becomes a desire to have an ending by lacking one. And yet one might wonder, at this final juncture, to what extent the system of valuation by which Eliot, through her narrator, is judging Dorothea's tragedy is itself questionable. Is this a system according to which the consummation of the desire to do a great work is *fame*? How much is Eliot, and Dorothea through her, touched with this most classical and masculine of desires (to have one's life recounted by Plutarch)? I cannot say. I can only stress that working underneath all of this desire and yearning is indeed a desire for cultural visibility (one of St. Theresa's goals, after

---

acter . . . ?" (888). Here is the deferral, tied to accumulation and material increase, that writes a Weberian plot for Fred and Mary. The chapter even ends with a textual deferral, since Fred and Mary are called to supper just as they are about to kiss.

all)—yet one that would have to create forms of vision that can see opacities. In any event, we as readers are asked to confess our implication in two directions: as those who harmfully aid the "sacrifice" of women's religious ardor that might otherwise "reform a conventional life"; as those who benefit from women's spiritual work of desire, which pressures set boundaries (for "that things are not so ill with you and me as they might have been, is half owing to the number who lived faithfully a hidden life").

This domesticated St. Theresa, at home with desire, does reform the religious order, being as she is, "a foundress of nothing," a foundress of fracture. With the imprisoned 'God' of women's labor (still a labor/lacking) folded into her hidden channels, she remains for the reader a visible sign of concealed relations that have yet to meet with the future owed to them.

Postlude

_✒_

For Bodies and 'God' in the Age of AIDS

In the night, 'God' between us, 'God' between my lips, in my most private chamber, I touch my lover's arm, and at the surface of her skin, where our burning takes place, I touch many bodies. Each time that I move in closer, as if to wring that space between us of its last wetness, its last tear, more bodies arise around us. I had pulled apart an armful of flowers, torn them petal by petal from their stems, and flung them first at your face and neck. Such an attempt I made to get to you—just you and by myself—but every petal, especially the roses, became a body. The chamber seemed full and the bed thickly settled with everyone we have known or met or loved, or not known but met, or should have loved and known: the man who said he would "hijack" me but who just needed money—I found him on your wrist; your mother lay by your elbow, my father at your ear; I touched your cheek and saw a secretary there with a man, a lover of yours, now dead, that I had never met ("inside you there are sobs you can't explain"). So many bodies upon and around you, I can never touch you without them. Folded between and into our love they are 'God' between our lips. They split us from ourselves and from each other, for 'God' is always the wound between projection and return. Look for me there, at the brink of you: I am touching all of those bodies and gathering up all of the sobs that must be returned to you and wept.

251

Reference Matter

Notes

Chapter 1

1. Rose, *Sexuality in the Field of Vision*, 90–91.
2. Doane, "Post-Utopian Difference," 209. See also Weed, "A Man's Place," 74.
3. See Schor, "This Essentialism"; Fuss, *Essentially Speaking*; Whitford, "Luce Irigaray and the Female Imaginary."
4. Barthes, *Mythologies*, 158–59.
5. Poovey, *Uneven Developments*, 18.
6. Lacan, "God and the *Jouissance* of The Woman," 147.
7. Altick, "Introduction," xii.   8. Carlyle, *Sartor Resartus*, 195.
9. Ibid., 57.   10. Ibid., 219.
11. Lacan, "Desire," 28.
12. Silverman, *Subject of Semiotics*, 185, 186, 188.
13. Derrida, *Spurs*, 61.

Chapter 2

1. Mitchell, "Introduction-I," 25.
2. Carlyle, *Sartor Resartus*, 104.
3. Rose, *Sexuality in the Field of Vision*, 15.
4. Ibid., 102.
5. Martin and Mohanty, "Feminist Politics," 193.
6. Ibid., 208.
7. Ibid., 198, 208.

Chapter 3

1. Smith, "Domestic Labour," 210–11.
2. Delphy, *Close to Home*, 158.   3. Ibid., 19.
4. Ibid., 23–27, 210nn3, 4.   5. Ibid., 166.
6. Houghton, *Victorian Frame of Mind*, 242.
7. Newman, *Sermons* 2:153.
8. Martin and Mohanty, "Feminist Politics," 206, 196.

Chapter 4

1. Quoted in Allott, *The Brontës: The Critical Heritage*, 172, 174, 183, 205.
2. Schneiderman, *Jacques Lacan*, 52.   3. Ibid., 52–53.
4. Ibid., 113–14.   5. Ibid., 6.
6. Shorter, *Brontës*, 1:141.   7. Burkhart, *Charlotte Brontë*, 20.
8. Shorter, *Brontës* 1:186.
9. Shorter, *Charlotte Brontë and Her Circle*, 216.
10. Moglen, *Charlotte Brontë*, 49.
11. Quoted in Blackburn, *Brontë Sisters*, 37.
12. Ibid., 39.   13. Ibid., 40.
14. Shorter, *Letters* 1:453.   15. Shorter, *Letters* 2:15.
16. Quoted in Blackburn, *Brontë Sisters*, 61.
17. Quoted in Lloyd Evans and Lloyd Evans, *Everyman's Companion to the Brontës*, 85.
18. Quoted in Blackburn, *Brontë Sisters*, 90.
19. Jay, *Religion of the Heart*, 31.
20. Lloyd Evans and Lloyd Evans, *Everyman's Companion to the Brontës*, 72.
21. J. H. Miller, *Disappearance of God*, 181.
22. Hopkins, *Father of the Brontës*, 55.
23. Baillie, "Religion and the Brontës," 60.
24. See George, "Evangelical Revival," 2141A; and Hudson, "Religious Temper," 4006A.
25. Merrett, "Conduct of Spiritual Autobiography," 9.
26. Gaskell, *Life of Charlotte Brontë*, 507–8.
27. Baillie, "Religion and the Brontës," 65.
28. Langbridge, *Charlotte Brontë*, 153.
29. Quoted in Lloyd Evans and Lloyd Evans, *Everyman's Companion to the Brontës*, 99.
30. Gilbert and Gubar, *Madwoman*, 415.
31. J. H. Miller, *Disappearance of God*, 7.
32. Ibid., 1–2.   33. Ibid., 6.
34. Ibid., 13.   35. Qualls, *Secular Pilgrims*, 4.
36. Ibid., ix–x.   37. Ibid., 76.

Chapter 5

1. Brontë, "Mort de Moïse," 368, 370, 372, 374.
2. Gallop, *Daughter's Seduction*, 36–38.
3. Schneiderman, *Jacques Lacan*, 10, 11, 12, 14.
4. Maynard, *Charlotte Brontë and Sexuality*, 179.
5. Schneiderman, *Jacques Lacan*, 98.
6. Ibid., 83–85.

Chapter 6

1. Rose, *Sexuality in the Field of Vision*, 116.
2. Derrida, *Dissemination*, 212, 215.
3. Rose, *Sexuality in the Field of Vision*, 194.
4. Ibid., 121.
5. *George Eliot Letters* 1: 6.
6. Quoted in Barth, "Introductory Essay," xii.
7. Paris, *Experiments*. 8. *George Eliot Letters* 3: 366.
9. *George Eliot Letters* 2: 341. 10. Byatt, "Introduction," 23.
11. Quoted in Paris, *Experiments*, 35. 12. Barth, "Introductory Essay," xi.
13. Althusser, *Lenin and Philosophy*, 181n22.
14. G. Beer, *Darwin's Plots*, 156, 174.

Chapter 7

1. See Scholes, "Novel as Ethical Paradigm?" 188–96.
2. Larson, *Rise of Professionalism*, xiii, xvi–xvii.
3. *From Max Weber*, 135. 4. Ibid., 136.
5. Ibid., 139. 6. Ibid., 96.
7. Larson, *Rise of Professionalism*, xvii.

Works Cited

Abrams, M. H. *Natural Supernaturalism: Tradition and Revolution in Romantic Literature*. New York: Norton, 1971.

Acton, William. *Prostitution*. New York: Praeger Press, 1969.

Allott, Farris Miriam. *The Brontës: The Critical Heritage*. London: Routledge & Kegan Paul, 1974.

Althusser, Louis. *Lenin and Philosophy and other Essays*. Trans. Ben Brewster. New York: Monthly Review Press, 1971.

Altick, Richard D. "Introduction." In Thomas Carlyle, *Past and Present*. Boston: Houghton Mifflin, 1965.

Anderson, Quentin. *From Dickens to Hardy*. Harmondsworth, Eng.: Penguin, 1958.

Armstrong, Isobel. "*Middlemarch*: A Note on George Eliot's Wisdom." In Barbara Hardy, ed., *Critical Essays on George Eliot*. New York: Barnes & Noble, 1970.

Armstrong, Nancy. *Desire and Domestic Fiction: A Political History of the Novel*. New York: Oxford University Press, 1987.

Auerbach, Nina. *Communities of Women: An Idea in Fiction*. Cambridge, Mass.: Harvard University Press, 1978.

Baillie, J. B. "Religion and the Brontës." *Brontë Society Transactions* 7 (1931): 59–69.

Baker, Houston A., Jr. *Blues, Ideology, and Afro-American Literature: A Vernacular Theory*. Chicago: University of Chicago Press, 1984.

Bal, Mieke. "Sexuality, Sin, and Sorrow: The Emergence of Female Character (Reading of Genesis 1–3)." In Susan Rubin Suleiman, ed., *The Female Body in Western Culture: Contemporary Perspectives*. Cambridge, Mass.: Harvard University Press, 1985, 1986.

Barrett, Dorothea. *Vocation and Desire: George Eliot's Heroines*. London: Routledge, 1989.

Barth, Karl. "Introductory Essay." In Ludwig Feuerbach, *The Essence of Christianity*, trans. George Eliot. New York: Harper & Row, 1957.

Barthes, Roland. *Mythologies*. Trans. Annette Lavers. New York: Hill and Wang, 1957.

———. *The Pleasure of the Text*. Trans. Richard Miller. New York: Hill and Wang, 1975.

Bataille, Georges. "The Notion of Expenditure." In Mark C. Taylor, ed. *Deconstruction in Context: Literature and Philosophy*. Chicago: University of Chicago Press, 1986.

Beer, Gillian. *Darwin's Plots: Evolutionary Narrative in Darwin, George Eliot and Nineteenth-Century Fiction*. London: Routledge & Kegan Paul, 1983.

———. *George Eliot*. Bloomington: Indiana University Press, 1986.

Beer, Patricia. *Reader, I Married Him*. New York: Barnes & Noble, 1974.

Belsey, Catherine. *Critical Practice*. London: Methuen, 1980.

Benston, Margaret. "The Political Economy of Women's Liberation." *Monthly Review* 21, no. 4 (Sept. 1969): 13–27.

Blackburn, Ruth H., ed. *The Brontë Sisters*. Boston: D. C. Heath, 1964.

Blake, Kathleen. *Love and the Woman Question in Victorian Literature: The Art of Self-Postponement*. Totowa, N.J.: Barnes & Noble, 1983.

Blom, M. A. "Charlotte Brontë, Feminist Manquée." *Bucknell Review* 21 (1973): 87–102.

Bodichon, Barbara Leigh Smith. *Women and Work*. New York: C. S. Francis, 1859.

Brontë, Charlotte. *Jane Eyre*. Ed. Margaret Smith. Oxford: Oxford University Press, 1975.

———. "La Mort de Moïse" ("The Death of Moses"). 1843. Trans. Phyllis Bentley. *Brontë Society Transactions* 12, pt. 65.

———. *Villette*. Ed. Mark Lilly. New York: Penguin, 1979.

———. *Villette*. Ed. Herbert Rosengarten and Margaret Smith. Oxford: Clarendon Press, 1984.

Brown, Gillian. *Domestic Individualism: Imagining Self in Nineteenth-Century America*. Berkeley: University of California Press, 1990.

Brownmiller, Susan. *Against Our Will: Men, Women, and Rape*. New York: Simon and Schuster, 1975.

Burkhart, Charles. *Charlotte Brontë: A Psychosexual Study of Her Novels*. London: Victor Gollancz, 1973.

Burton, Hester. *Barbara Bodichon, 1827–1891*. London: John Murray, 1949.

Butler, A. S. G. *Portrait of Josephine Butler*. London, 1954.

Butler, Josephine, ed. *Women's Work and Women's Culture*. London: Macmillan, 1869.

Butler, Judith. "Imitation and Gender Insubordination." In Diana Fuss, ed., *Inside/Out: Lesbian Theories, Gay Theories*. New York: Routledge, 1989.

Byatt, A. S. "Introduction." In George Eliot, *The Mill on the Floss*, ed. A. S. Byatt. New York: Penguin, 1979.

Caine, Barbara. *Victorian Feminists*. New York: Oxford University Press, 1992.

Callinicos, Alex. *Althusser's Marxism*. London: Pluto Press, 1976.

Carlisle, Janice. "The Face in the Mirror: *Villette* and the Conventions of Auto-biography." *Journal of English Literary History* 46 (Summer 1979): 262–89.

Carlyle, Thomas. *Past and Present.* Ed. Richard D. Altick. Boston: Houghton Mifflin, 1965.

———. *Sartor Resartus.* Ed. Kerry McSweeney and Peter Sabor. New York: Oxford University Press, 1987.

Carpenter, Mary Wilson. *George Eliot and the Landscape of Time: Narrative Form and Apocalyptic History.* Chapel Hill: University of North Carolina Press, 1986.

Chadwick, Owen. *The Victorian Church, Part II.* New York: Oxford, 1970.

Chase, Karen. *Eros and Psyche: The Representation of Personality in Charlotte Brontë, Charles Dickens, and George Eliot.* New York: Methuen, 1984.

Clément, Catherine, and Hélène Cixous. *The Newly Born Woman.* Trans. Betsy Wing. Minneapolis: University of Minnesota Press, 1986.

Cottom, Daniel. *Social Figures: George Eliot, Social History, and Literary Representation.* Minneapolis: University of Minnesota Press, 1987.

Coward, Rosalind. *Female Desires.* New York: Grove Press, 1985.

Crosby, Christina. "Charlotte Brontë's Haunted Text." *Studies in English Literature* 24, no. 4 (Autumn 1984): 701–15.

———. *The Ends of History: Victorians and "The Woman Question."* New York: Routledge, 1991.

Davies, Emily. *Thoughts on Some Questions Relating to Women, 1860–1908.* Cambridge, Eng.: Bowes and Bowes, 1910.

Davis, Angela Y. "The Approaching Obsolescence of Housework." In *Women, Race, and Class.* New York: Vintage Books, 1981.

Delphy, Christine. *Close to Home: A Materialist Analysis of Women's Oppression.* Trans. Diana Leonard. Amherst: University of Massachusetts Press, 1984.

Derrida, Jacques. *Dissemination.* Trans. Barbara Johnson. Chicago: University of Chicago Press, 1981.

———. *Spurs: Nietzsche's Styles/Eperons: Les Styles de Nietzsche.* Trans. Barbara Harlow. Chicago: University of Chicago Press, 1979.

Derrida, Jacques, and Christie V. McDonald. "Choreographies." *Diacritics* 12 (1982): 66–76.

Doane, Mary Ann. *The Desire to Desire: The Woman's Film of the 1940's.* Bloomington: Indiana University Press, 1987.

———. "Post-Utopian Difference." In Elizabeth Weed, ed., *Coming to Terms: Feminism, Theory, Politics.* New York: Routledge, 1989.

Donovan, Josephine. *Feminist Theory: The Intellectual Traditions of American Feminism.* New York: F. Ungar, 1985.

Dowden, Edward. "George Eliot." In Gordon S. Haight, ed., *Century of George Eliot Criticism.* Boston: Houghton Mifflin, 1965.

Eagleton, Terry. *Myths of Power: A Marxist Study of the Brontës.* London: Macmillan, 1975.

Eliot, George. *The George Eliot Letters.* Ed. Gordon S. Haight. 9 vols. New Haven, Conn.: Yale University Press, 1954–78.

———. *Middlemarch.* Ed. W. J. Harvey. New York: Penguin, 1965.

Engels, Frederick. "Review of Thomas Carlyle's *Past and Present*." In Howard Selsam & Harry Martel, eds., *Reader in Marxist Philosophy*. New York: International Publishers, 1963.

Ermarth, Elizabeth. "Method and Moral in George Eliot's Narrative." *Victorian Newsletter*, no. 47 (Spring 1975): 4–8.

Felski, Rita. *Beyond Feminist Aesthetics: Feminist Literature and Social Change*. Cambridge, Mass.: Harvard University Press, 1989.

Feuerbach, Ludwig. *The Essence of Christianity*. Trans. George Eliot. New York: Harper and Row, 1957.

Fletcher, J. S. *The Making of Modern Yorkshire (1750–1914)*. London: George Allen and Unwin, 1918.

Fuss, Diana. *Essentially Speaking: Feminism, Nature, and Difference*. New York: Routledge, 1989.

Gallop, Jane. *The Daughter's Seduction: Feminism and Psychoanalysis*. Ithaca, N.Y.: Cornell University Press, 1982.

———. *Intersections: A Reading of Sade with Bataille, Blanchot, and Klossowski*. Lincoln: University of Nebraska Press, 1981.

———. *Reading Lacan*. Ithaca, N.Y.: Cornell University Press, 1985.

———. "Annie Leclerc Writing a Letter, with Vermeer." In Nancy K. Miller, ed., *The Poetics of Gender*. New York: Columbia University Press, 1986.

———. *Thinking Through the Body*. New York: Columbia University Press, 1988.

Gaskell, Mrs. E. C. *The Life of Charlotte Brontë*. Edinburgh: John Grant, 1907.

George, Robert Francis. "The Evangelical Revival and Charlotte Brontë's *Jane Eyre*." *DAI* 42, no. 5. (Nov. 1981): 2141A.

Gilbert, Sandra M., and Susan Gubar. *The Madwoman in the Attic: The Woman Writer and the Nineteenth-Century Literary Imagination*. New Haven, Conn.: Yale University Press, 1979.

Gilman, Charlotte Perkins. *Herland*. New York: Pantheon Books, 1979.

Greg, W. R. "Why Are Women Redundant?" *National Review* 15 (1862): 62–87.

Grosz, Elizabeth. *Sexual Subversions: Three French Feminists*. Sydney: Allen & Unwin, 1989.

———. *Jacques Lacan: A Feminist Introduction*. New York: Routledge, 1990.

Haight, Gordon S. *George Eliot: A Biography*. Oxford: Oxford University Press, 1968.

———, ed. *The George Eliot Letters*. 9 vols. New Haven, Conn.: Yale University Press, 1954–78.

Haraway, Donna. "A Manifesto for Cyborgs: Science, Technology, and Socialist Feminism in the 1980's." *Socialist Review* 80, no. 2 (Mar.–Apr. 1985): 65–107.

———. *Primate Visions: Gender, Race, and Nature in the World of Modern Science*. New York: Routledge, 1989.

———. "Situated Knowledges: The Science Question in Feminism and the Privilege of Partial Perspective." In *Simians, Cyborgs, and Women: The Reinvention of Nature*. New York: Routledge, 1991.

Hartmann, Heidi. "The Unhappy Marriage of Marxism and Feminism: Towards a More Progressive Union." In Lydia Sargent, ed., *Women and Revolution.* Boston: South End Press, 1981.

Hawkins, Peter S. *Getting Nowhere: Christian Hope and Utopian Dream.* Cambridge, Mass.: Cowley, 1985.

Heath, Stephen. "Difference." *Screen* 19, no. 3 (1978): 51–112.

Heilman, Robert B. "Charlotte Brontë's 'New' Gothic." In Robert C. Rathburn and Martin Steinmann, Jr., eds., *From Jane Austen to Joseph Conrad.* Minneapolis: University of Minnesota Press, 1958.

Herstein, Sheila R. *A Mid-Victorian Feminist: Barbara Leigh Smith Bodichon.* New Haven, Conn.: Yale University Press, 1985.

Hollis, Patricia, ed. *Women in Public, 1850–1900: Documents of the Victorian Women's Movement.* Boston: Allen & Unwin, 1979.

Holmlund, Christine. "The Lesbian, the Mother, the Heterosexual Lover: Irigaray's Recodings of Difference." In *Feminist Studies* 17, no. 2 (Summer 1991), 283–308.

Hopkins, Annette Brown. *The Father of the Brontës.* New York: Greenwood Press, 1968.

Hornback, Bert G. *Middlemarch: A Novel of Reform.* Boston: Twayne, 1988.

Houghton, Walter E. *The Victorian Frame of Mind, 1830–1870.* New Haven, Conn.: Yale University Press, 1957.

Hudson, Aida Regina. "The Religious Temper of Charlotte Brontë's Novels." *DAI* 42, no. 9 (Mar. 1982): 4006A.

Irigaray, Luce. *Speculum of the Other Woman.* Trans. Gillian C. Gill. Ithaca, N.Y.: Cornell University Press, 1985.

———. *This Sex Which Is Not One.* Trans. Catherine Porter with Carolyn Burke. Ithaca, N.Y.: Cornell University Press, 1985.

———. *Sexes and Genealogies.* Trans. Gillian C. Gill. New York: Columbia University Press, 1993.

Jacobus, Mary. "The Buried Letter: Feminism and Romanticism in *Villette.*" In Mary Jacobus, ed., *Women Writing and Writing About Women.* New York: Barnes & Noble, 1979.

Jacobus, Mary, Evelyn Fox Keller, and Sally Shuttleworth, eds. *Body/Politics: Women and the Discourses of Science.* New York: Routledge, 1990.

Jameson, Mrs. Anna. *Sisters of Charity, Catholic and Protestant, and the Communion of Labor.* 1856. Reprinted. Westport, Conn.: Hyperion Press, 1976.

Jameson, Fredric. *The Political Unconscious: Narrative as a Socially Symbolic Act.* Ithaca, N.Y.: Cornell University Press, 1981.

Jardine, Alice A. *Gynesis: Configurations of Woman and Modernity.* Ithaca, N.Y.: Cornell University Press, 1985.

Jay, Elizabeth. *The Religion of the Heart: Anglican Evangelicalism and the Nineteenth-Century Novel.* Oxford: Clarendon Press, 1979.

Kavanagh, James H. *Emily Brontë.* New York: Basil Blackwell, 1985.

Keefe, Robert. *Charlotte Brontë's World of Death.* Austin: University of Texas Press, 1979.

Kent, Susan. *Sex and Suffrage in Britain, 1860–1914.* Princeton N.J.: Princeton University Press, 1987.

Knoepflmacher, U. C. *Religious Humanism and the Victorian Novel: George Eliot, Walter Pater, and Samuel Butler.* Princeton, N.J.: Princeton University Press, 1965.

Kucich, John. *Repression in Victorian Fiction: Charlotte Brontë, George Eliot, and Charles Dickens.* Berkeley: University of California Press, 1987.

Kuhn, Annette, and AnnMarie Wolpe, eds. *Feminism and Materialism: Women and Modes of Production.* London: Routledge & Kegan Paul, 1978.

Lacan, Jacques. "Desire and the Interpretation of Desire in *Hamlet.*" Trans. James Hulbert. *Yale French Studies* 55/56 (1977): 28.

———. *Ecrits: A Selection.* Trans. Alan Sheridan. New York: Norton, 1977.

———. *Feminine Sexuality: Jacques Lacan and the École Freudienne.* Ed. Juliet Mitchell and Jacqueline Rose. Trans. Rose. New York: Norton, 1985.

———. *The Four Fundamental Concepts of Psycho-Analysis.* Ed. Jacques-Alain Miller. Trans. Alan Sheridan. New York: Norton, 1981.

Lacey, Candida Ann, ed. *Barbara Leigh Smith Bodichon and the Langham Place Group.* New York: Routledge & Kegan Paul in association with Methuen, 1987.

Langbridge, Rosamond. *Charlotte Brontë: A Psychological Study.* Garden City, N.Y.: Doubleday, Doran, 1929.

Larson, Magali Sarfatti. *The Rise of Professionalism: A Sociological Analysis.* Berkeley: University of California Press, 1977.

Lawrence, Karen. "The Cypher: Disclosure and Reticence in *Villette.*" *Nineteenth-Century Literature* 42, no. 4 (March 1988): 466–88.

Lerner, Laurence, and John Holmstrom, eds. *George Eliot and Her Readers: A Selection of Contemporary Reviews.* New York: Barnes & Noble, 1966.

Levine, Philippa. *Victorian Feminism, 1850–1900.* Tallahassee: Florida State University Press, 1987.

Lewis, C. S. *The Weight of Glory and Other Addresses.* Grand Rapids, Mich.: William B. Eerdmans, 1965.

Lim, Linda Y. C. "Capitalism, Imperialism, and Patriarchy: The Dilemma of Third-World Women Workers in Multinational Factories." In June Nash and María Patricia Fernandez-Kelly, eds., *Women, Men, and the International Division of Labor.* Albany: SUNY Press, 1983.

Lloyd Evans, Barbara, and Gareth Lloyd Evans. *Everyman's Companion to the Brontës.* London: J. M. Dent & Sons, 1982.

MacKinnon, Catharine A. "Feminism, Marxism, Method, and the State: An Agenda for Theory." *Signs* 7, no. 3 (Spring 1982): 515–44.

Martin, Biddy, and Chandra Talpade Mohanty. "Feminist Politics: What's Home Got to Do with It?" In Teresa de Lauretis, ed., *Feminist Studies/Critical Studies.* Bloomington: Indiana University Press, 1986.

Marx, Karl. *Capital: A Critique of Political Economy.* Trans. Ben Fowkes. Harmondsworth, Eng.: Penguin, 1976.

———. *The Economic and Philosophic Manuscripts of 1844.* New York: International Publishers, 1964.

Maynard, John. *Charlotte Brontë and Sexuality*. Cambridge, Eng.: Cambridge University Press, 1984.

Melville, Stephen. "Psychoanalysis and the Place of *Jouissance*." In Françoise Meltzer, ed., *The Trial(s) of Psychoanalysis*. Chicago: University of Chicago Press, 1987.

Merrett, Robert James. "The Conduct of Spiritual Autobiography in *Jane Eyre*." *Renascence* 37, no. 1 (Autumn 1984): 2–15.

Michie, Helena. *Sororophobia: Differences Among Women in Literature and Culture*. New York: Oxford University Press, 1992.

Miller, D. A. *The Novel and the Police*. Berkeley: University of California Press, 1988.

Miller, J.Hillis. *The Disappearance of God: Five Nineteenth-Century Writers*. Cambridge, Mass.: Harvard University Press, 1963.

———. "The Narrator as General Consciousness." In *The Form of Victorian Fiction*. Notre Dame: University of Notre Dame Press, 1968.

Millett, Kate. *Sexual Politics*. Garden City, N.Y.: Doubleday, 1970.

Mintz, Alan. *George Eliot and the Novel of Vocation*. Cambridge, Mass.: Harvard University Press, 1978.

Mitchell, Juliet. "Introduction-I." In Jacques Lacan, *Feminine Sexuality: Jacques Lacan and the École Freudienne*, ed. Juliet Mitchell and Jacqueline Rose, trans. Rose. New York: Norton, 1985.

Moglen, Helene. *Charlotte Brontë: The Self Conceived*. New York: Norton, 1976.

Moi, Toril. *Sexual/Textual Politics: Feminist Literary Theory*. New York: Methuen, 1985.

Morris, Richard. *The Edges of Science: Crossing the Boundary from Physics to Metaphysics*. New York: Prentice Hall Press, 1990.

Mulvey, Laura. *Visual and Other Pleasures*. Bloomington: Indiana University Press, 1989.

Nash, June, and María Patricia Fernandez-Kelly, eds. *Women, Men, and the International Division of Labor*. Albany: SUNY Press, 1983.

Nestle, Joan, ed. *The Persistent Desire: A Femme-Butch Reader*. Boston: Alyson, 1992.

Newman, John Henry. *Sermons and Discourses*. Ed. C. F. Harrold. 2 vols. New York: Longmans, Green, 1949.

Newton, Judith, and Deborah Rosenfelt, eds. *Feminist Criticism and Social Change: Sex, Class, and Race in Literature and Culture*. New York: Methuen, 1985.

Newton, K. M. "The Role of the Narrator in George Eliot's Novels." *Journal of Narrative Technique* 3, no. 2 (May 1973): 97–107.

Osherow, Jacqueline. " 'Within us as a great yearning': George Eliot's Struggle Toward Female Self-Expression." Ph.D. diss., Princeton University, 1990.

Paris, Bernard J. *Experiments in Life: George Eliot's Quest for Values*. Detroit: Wayne State University Press, 1965.

Platt, Carolyn V. "How Feminist Is *Villette*?" *Women & Literature* 3 (1975): 16–27.

Plaza, Monique. " 'Phallomorphic Power' and the Psychology of 'Woman'." *Ideology and Consciousness* (Autumn 1978): 57–76.

Poovey, Mary. "Speaking of the Body: Mid-Victorian Constructions of Female Desire." In Mary Jacobus, Evelyn Fox Keller, and Sally Shuttleworth, eds., *Body/Politics: Women and the Discourses of Science*. New York: Routledge, 1990.

———. *Uneven Developments: The Ideological Work of Gender in Mid-Victorian England*. Chicago: University of Chicago Press, 1988.

Putzell-Korab, Sara M. "Passion Between Women in the Victorian Novel." In Don Richard Cox, ed., *Sexuality and Victorian Literature*. Knoxville: University of Tennessee Press, 1984.

Qualls, Barry V. *The Secular Pilgrims of Victorian Fiction: The Novel as Book of Life*. Cambridge, Eng.: Cambridge University Press, 1982.

Ragland-Sullivan, Ellie. *Jacques Lacan and the Philosophy of Psychoanalysis*. Urbana: University of Illinois Press, 1986.

Rooney, Ellen. "Commentary: What Is to Be Done?" In Elizabeth Weed, ed., *Coming to Terms: Feminism, Theory, Politics*. New York: Routledge, 1989.

Rose, Jacqueline. "Introduction-II." In Jacques Lacan, *Feminine Sexuality: Jacques Lacan and the École Freudienne*, ed. Juliet Mitchell and Jacqueline Rose, trans. Rose. New York: Norton, 1985.

———. *Sexuality in the Field of Vision*. London: Verso Press, 1986.

Rubin, Gayle. "The Traffic in Women: Notes on the 'Political Economy' of Sex." In Rayna R. Reiter, ed., *Toward an Anthropology of Women*. New York: Monthly Review Press, 1975.

Ruskin, John. "Of Queens' Gardens." In *Sesame and Lilies*. Chicago: McClurg, 1892.

Schneiderman, Stuart. *Jacques Lacan: The Death of an Intellectual Hero*. Cambridge, Mass.: Harvard University Press, 1983.

Scholes, Robert. "The Novel as Ethical Paradigm?" *Novel: A Forum on Fiction* 21 (Winter/Spring 1988): 188–96.

Schor, Naomi. "Dreaming Dissymmetry: Barthes, Foucault, and Sexual Difference." In Elizabeth Weed, ed., *Coming to Terms: Feminism, Theory, Politics*. New York: Routledge, 1989.

———. "This Essentialism Which Is Not One: Coming to Grips with Irigaray." *Differences* 1, no. 2 (Summer 1989): 38–58.

Sedgwick, Eve Kosofsky. *Between Men: English Literature and Male Homosocial Desire*. New York: Columbia University Press, 1985.

———. "Jane Austen and the Masturbating Girl." *Critical Inquiry* 17 (Summer 1991): 818–37.

Shaw, David W. *Victorians and Mystery: Crises of Representation*. Ithaca, N.Y.: Cornell University Press, 1990.

Shorter, Clement K. *The Brontës: Life and Letters*. 2 vols. 1908. New York: Haskell House, 1969.

———. *Charlotte Brontë and Her Circle*. London: Hodder and Stoughton, 1896.

Silver, Brenda R. "The Reflecting Reader in *Villette*." In Barbara Timm Gates, ed., *Critical Essays on Charlotte Brontë*. Boston: G. K. Hall, 1990.

Silverman, Kaja. "Histoire d'O: The Construction of a Female Subject." In Carole

S. Vance, ed., *Pleasure and Danger: Exploring Female Sexuality*. Boston: Routledge, 1984.

──────. *The Subject of Semiotics*. New York: Oxford University Press, 1983.

Smith, Paul. "Domestic Labour and Marx's Theory of Value." In Annette Kuhn and AnnMarie Wolpe, eds., *Feminism and Materialism: Women and Modes of Production*. London: Routledge & Kegan Paul, 1978.

Smith-Rosenberg, Carroll. "The Female World of Love and Ritual: Relations Between Women in Nineteenth Century America." In *Signs* 1, no. 1 (Autumn 1975): 1–29.

Sombart, Werner. *Luxury and Capitalism*. Introduction by Philip Siegelman. Trans. W. R. Dittmar. Ann Arbor: University of Michigan Press, 1967.

Sorensen, Katherine M. "Evangelical Doctrine and George Eliot's Narrator in *Middlemarch*." *Victorian Newsletter* 74 (Fall 1988): 18–26.

Spivak, Gayatri Chakravorty. *In Other Worlds: Essays In Cultural Politics*. New York: Methuen, 1987.

──────. "The Political Economy of Women as Seen by a Literary Critic." In Elizabeth Weed, ed., *Coming to Terms: Feminism/Theory/Difference*. New York: Routledge, 1989.

Spretnak, Charlene, ed. *The Politics of Women's Spirituality: Essays on the Rise of Spiritual Power Within the Feminist Movement*. Garden City, N.Y.: Anchor Books, 1982.

Stallybrass, Peter, and Allon White. "Below Stairs: The Maid and the Family Romance." In *The Politics and Poetics of Transgression*. Ithaca, N.Y.: Cornell University Press, 1986.

Stockton, Kathryn Bond. "Spiritual Discourse and the Work of Desire: Feminine Sexual Economies in Theory and the Victorian Novel." Ph.D. diss., Brown University, 1989.

Strachey, Ray. *The Cause; A Short History of the Women's Movement in Great Britain*. Port Washington, N.Y.: Kennikat Press, 1969.

Tayler, Irene. *Holy Ghosts: The Male Muses of Emily and Charlotte Brontë*. New York: Columbia University Press, 1990.

Taylor, Mark C. *Altarity*. Chicago: University of Chicago Press, 1987.

Tillich, Paul. "Critique and Justification of Utopia." In Frank Manuel, ed., *Utopias and Utopian Thought*. Boston: Houghton Mifflin, 1965.

Todd, Margaret. *The Life of Sophia Jex-Blake*. London: Macmillan, 1918.

Trungpa Chögyam. *Cutting Through Spiritual Materialism*. Berkeley: Shambhala, 1973.

Uglow, Jennifer. *George Eliot*. New York: Pantheon, 1987.

Umansky, Ellen M., and Dianne Ashton, eds. *Four Centuries of Jewish Women's Spirituality: A Sourcebook*. Boston: Beacon Press, 1992.

Underhill, Evelyn. *Mysticism: A Study in the Nature and Development of Man's Spiritual Consciousness*. New York: New American Library, 1974.

Vargish, Thomas. *The Providential Aesthetic in Victorian Fiction*. Charlottesville: University Press of Virginia, 1985.

Vicinus, Martha. *Independent Women: Work and Community for Single Women, 1850–1920.* Chicago: University of Chicago Press, 1985.

Vogel, Lise. "The Earthly Family." *Radical America* 7, nos. 4 and 5 (July–Oct. 1973).

Walkowitz, Judith. *Prostitution and Victorian Society: Women, Class, and the State.* Cambridge, Eng.: Cambridge University Press, 1980.

Wallace, Michele. *Invisibility Blues: From Pop to Theory.* London: Verso, 1990.

Watt, Ian. *The Rise of the Novel: Studies in Defoe, Richardson, and Fielding.* Berkeley: University of California Press, 1957.

Weber, Max. *The Protestant Ethic and the Spirit of Capitalism.* New York: Scribner's, 1958.

———. *From Max Weber: Essays in Sociology.* Trans. H. H. Gerth and C. Wright Mills. New York: Oxford University Press, 1946.

Weed, Elizabeth. "A Man's Place." In Alice Jardine and Paul Smith, eds., *Men in Feminism.* New York: Methuen, 1987.

———, ed. *Coming to Terms: Feminism, Theory, Politics.* New York: Routledge, 1989.

Whitford, Margaret. "Luce Irigaray and the Female Imaginary: Speaking as a Woman." *Radical Philosophy* 43 (Summer 1986): 2–9.

———. *Luce Irigaray: Philosophy in the Feminine.* New York: Routledge, 1991.

Williams, Merryn. *Women in the English Novel, 1800–1900.* London: Macmillan, 1984.

Wright, Robert. "Science, God and Man." *Time,* 28 December 1992, pp. 39–44.

Wright, T. R. "*Middlemarch* as a Religious Novel, or Life Without God." In David Jaspar, ed., *Images of Belief in Literature.* New York: St. Martin's Press, 1984.

Zaretsky, Eli. *Capitalism, the Family and Personal Life.* New York: Harper & Row, 1976.

Index

In this index an "f" after a number indicates a separate reference on the next page, and an "ff" indicates separate references on the next two pages. A continuous discussion over two or more pages is indicated by a span of page numbers, e.g., "57–59." *Passim* is used for a cluster of references in close but not consecutive sequence.

Abrams, M. H., 8n, 35n, 124n, 226, 238
Acton, William, 88n
AIDS, xiii, xxii
Alienation, 9, 14, 28, 35ff, 39, 41
Althusser, Louis, 4, 25, 69, 188, 207
Angels, 52n
Aristotle, 4n
Armstrong, Nancy, xvii, 74n
Asceticism, 70–71
Augustine, 34n, 132
Autoeroticism, *see* Irigaray; *Middlemarch*; *Villette*

Baillie, J. M., 116f
Baker, Houston, xviii, 9n
Bal, Mieke, 124n
Barrett, Dorothea, 195n, 208n, 215n
Barth, Karl, 188, 191
Barthes, Roland, 6, 14–15, 46n, 51n
Bataille, Georges, 62n
Baudrillard, Jean, 3n
Beer, Gillian, 83, 150n, 188f, 195n
Belsey, Catherine, 166n
Biology, 3f, 6, 14f, 17, 48n, 50n

Blake, Kathleen, 101n, 107n, 118n
Blom, M. A., 150n
Bodichon, Barbara, 65n, 78–79, 83–87, 175f, 182n
Body, the, xv, xvi, 3, 5–6, 15, 18–23
Brontë, Charlotte, 99–121; and Irigaray, xiii–xxiii, 110, 122, 152, 156f, 161f; and Eliot, xiii–xxiii, 174, 178, 185; and Evangelicalism, xx, xxi, 101, 103, 115–16, 119; and death, 100, 102, 108f, 111, 113ff; and Lacan, 100–106 *passim*, 137–38, 143, 156, 160, 164; and Constantin Heger, 108–17 *passim*, 134, 147, 155; and Catholicism, 116, 119, 135–41 *passim*, 145, 152, 158f, 163. *See also Villette*
Brown, Gillian, xvii
Browning, Elizabeth Barrett, 84
Browning, Robert, 18n
Brownmiller, Susan, 9n
Burkhart, Charles, 109, 123n
Burton, Hester, 83n
Butler, Josephine, 78–79, 87–92
Butler, Judith, xviii, 95n, 197
Byatt, A. S., 187

269

Library of Congress
Cataloging-in-Publication Data

Stockton, Kathryn Bond, 1958–
God between their lips : desire between women in Irigaray,
Brontë, and Eliot / Kathryn Bond Stockton.
p.   cm.
Includes bibliographical references (p.   ) and index.
ISBN 0-8047-2312-5 (cl.)   ISBN 0-8047-2344-3 (pbk.)
1. English fiction—Women authors—History and criticism.
2. Feminism and literature—England—History—19th century.
3. English fiction—19th century—History and criticism.
4. Brontë, Charlotte, 1816–1855—Characters—Women.
5. Eliot, George, 1819–1880—Characters—Women.   6. Erotic stories—
History and criticism.   7. Irigaray, Luce—Characters—Women.
8. Lesbians in literature.   9. Desire in literature.   I. Title.
PR878.F45S76   1994
823'.809352042—dc20   94-1597   CIP